A Naturalist's Guide to the Great Plains

Sites, Species, and Spectacles

Paul A. Johnsgard

School of Biological Sciences
University of Nebraska–Lincoln

Zea Books,
Lincoln, Nebraska: 2018

Abstract

This book documents nearly 500 US and Canadian locations where wildlife refuges, nature preserves, and similar properties protect natural sites that lie within the North American Great Plains, from Canada's Prairie Provinces to the Texas-Mexico border. Information on site location, size, biological diversity, and the presence of especially rare or interesting flora and fauna are mentioned, as well as driving directions, mailing addresses, and phone numbers or internet addresses, as available. US federal sites include 11 national grasslands, 13 national parks, 16 national monuments, and more than 70 national wildlife refuges. State properties include nearly 100 state parks and wildlife management areas. Also included are about 60 national and provincial parks, national wildlife areas, and migratory bird sanctuaries in Canada's Prairie Provinces. Numerous public-access properties owned by counties, towns, and private organizations, such as the Nature Conservancy, National Audubon Society, and other conservation and preservation groups, are also described.

Introductory essays describe the geological and recent histories of each of the five multistate and multiprovince regions recognized, along with some of the author's personal memories of them. The 92,000-word text is supplemented with 7 maps and 31 drawings by the author and more than 700 references.

Title page illustration: *Greater sage-grouse*

ISBN: 978-1-60962-126-1

doi: 10.13014/K2CF9N8T

Composed in Segoe types.

Zea Books are published by the University of Nebraska–Lincoln Libraries.

Electronic (pdf) edition published online at
https://digitalcommons.unl.edu/zeabook/

Print edition sold at
ttp://www.lulu.com/spotlight/unllib

UNL does not discriminate based upon any protected status.
Please go to unl.edu/nondiscrimination

Nebraska
UNIVERSITY OF
Lincoln

Dedicated to the memories of those who historically had
the foresight to preserve these natural treasures for posterity,
and to those with the present-day courage and will
to prevent them from being destroyed
by thoughtless politicians.

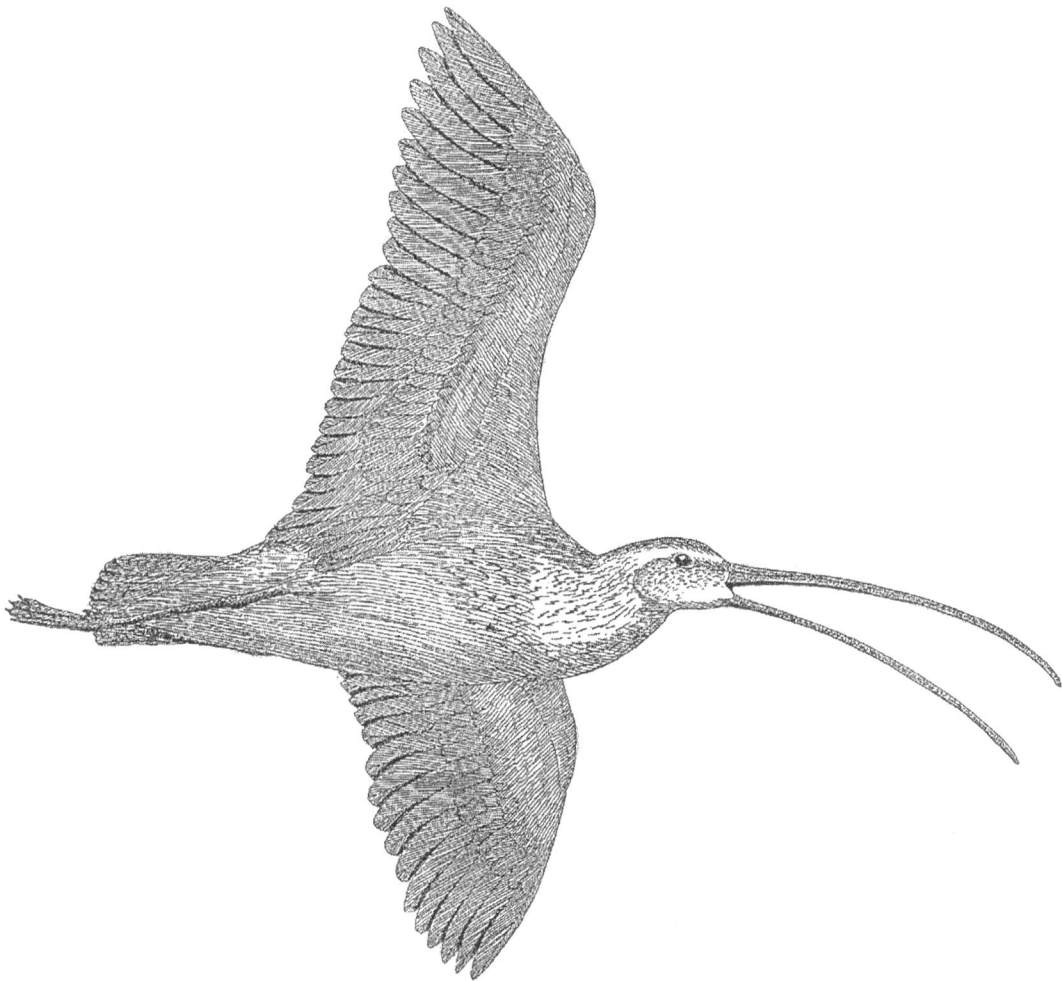

Long-billed curlew

Contents

Maps

Figures

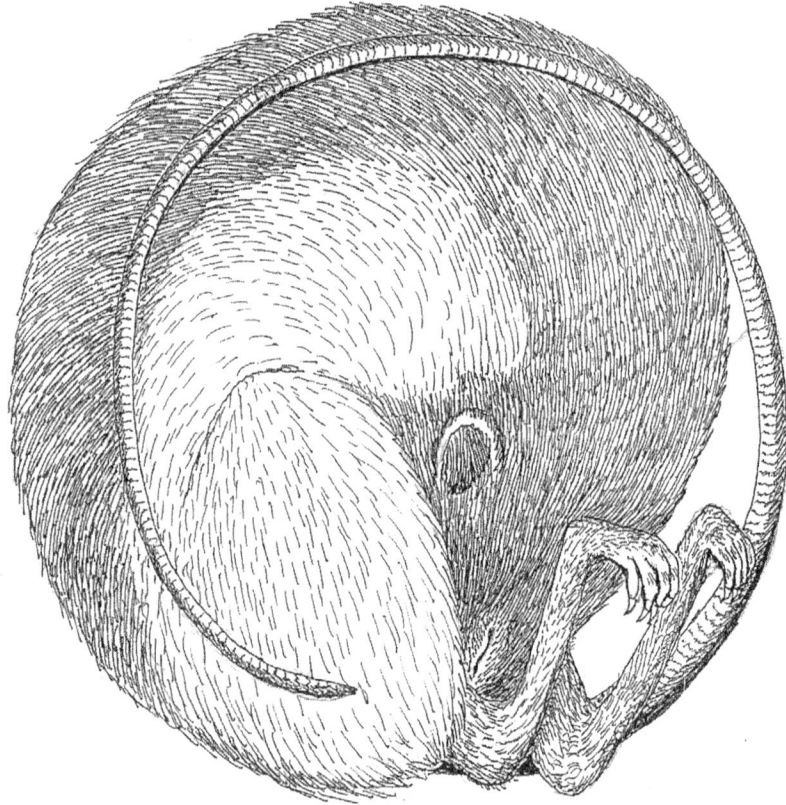

Harvest mouse, adult hibernating.

Acknowledgments

The idea for this book came about as I have toured throughout the Great Plains, visiting natural areas such as state and federal parks and other areas that have preserved native regional habitats. In particular I have sought out biologically important places, such as wildlife refuges and sanctuaries, and those sites that have preserved unique Great Plains habitats, such as native grasslands and wetlands. A typical tourist guide devotes very little information to these locations, as they tend to attract few tourists, the very feature that a naturalist is likely to value most.

My criteria for selecting about 350 such locations were broad and eclectic, and although those chosen primarily represent biological sites, they also include some sites of geological, paleontological, and anthropological interest. My personal special interests in such charismatic Great Plains animals as cranes, waterfowl, bison, and prairie dogs are also obviously reflected in my choices for inclusion. The sites additionally reflect my interests in Native American history in the Great Plains and especially the related important biological and historical significance of the Lewis and Clark expedition of 1804–6.

As a nearly lifelong resident of the Great Plains region, which lacks most topographic landmarks and boundaries such as coastlines and mountains, I have always thought that the Great Plains' most significant geographic boundaries are its natural ones, such as geological or biological units, rather than those that are politically defined. Thus, I drew the maps in this book to emphasize biological attributes and ecological boundaries, reflecting historic climatic influences, vegetational histories, current landforms, and drainage patterns, rather than the locations of towns or political boundaries. Most of these maps have already been published in my earlier books on the Great Plains, and they are more fully discussed there.

Some parts of this book's text that relate to descriptions of specific sites have also been extracted from earlier writings of mine. Three of these consist of essays I wrote for the monthly environmentally oriented newspaper *Prairie Fire*, which was published in Lincoln for nearly nine years, from 2007 to 2015. The following essays from *Prairie Fire* were used in whole or in part: "Nature Notes: The Wings of March" (March 2009, pp. 1, 17, 18, 19), "The Drums of April" (April 2010, pp. 12–13), and "Aransas National Wildlife Refuge: The Whooping Crane's Vulnerable Winter Retreat" (May 2014, pp. 12–13). I wish to thank the *Prairie Fire* editor, Cris Trautner, for permission to reprint them.

I also sincerely thank retired University of Nebraska–Lincoln art department professor David Routon for his very kind permission to let me use his wonderful drawing of me on this book's back cover. He described himself to me as an "old professor," but I have him beat on that measure by a few months. I consider it a real honor to have been included in his series of marvelous drawings of Nebraska's most famous authors.

The essay on the burrowing owl and prairie dog, "The Howdy Owl and the Prairie Dog," was first published in the American Birding Association's *Birding* magazine (January/ February 2006, pp. 40–44). My description of North Dakota wetlands and the American bittern display, titled "Bittern Surprise," first appeared in *BirdWatching* magazine (30 (2): 36–39, 2016). The introductory and terminal italicized quotations that appear in each chapter were extracted from various of my books but have been converted from normal text to free verse and were mostly published earlier in this form (Johnsgard, 2006).

My descriptions of individual sites are to a large extent based on and variably derived from several of my earlier Great Plains books, although many of the descriptions have been updated or otherwise modified. The source books include *Birds of the Great Plains: Breeding Species and Their Distribution*; *Wings over the Great Plains: Bird Migrations in the Central Flyway*; *Wetland Birds of the Central Plains: South Dakota, Nebraska, and Kansas*; *Prairie Dog Empire: A Saga of the Shortgrass Prairie*; *Great Wildlife of the Great Plains*; *Sandhill and Whooping Cranes: Ancient Voices over America's Wetlands*; and *Lewis and Clark on the Great Plains: A Natural History*.

Locational information details such as zip codes, telephone area codes and numbers, and postal addresses are relatively labile. Therefore, the reader should double-check on such information in this book when planning to visit the site, using current internet sources.

Several friends kindly read parts of this book, and others contributed valuable suggestions and corrections, for which I am most grateful. As usual, I must sincerely thank Paul Royster, coordinator of Scholarly Communications for the University of Nebraska–Lincoln Libraries, for taking on yet another of my writing projects, and also once again thank Linnea Fredrickson for her invariably sharp-eyed editing efforts.

Paul A. Johnsgard
Lincoln, Nebraska

Adult male bighorn sheep.

Preface

As a child, my mother lived on a farm in southeastern North Dakota, situated along the Sheyenne River in northern Richland County. Near her home, the winding, slow-flowing Sheyenne encounters the sandy soils deposited in late Pleistocene times. There the river once flowed into glacial Lake Agassiz and, depositing its water-carried sand, formed a mostly flat delta but with scattered sand dunes. This is the largest of the more than 30 such relict deltas in the Red River valley that are the present-day legacy of the now vanished Lake Agassiz. Because the resulting sandy soils were impractical to cultivate, homesteaders spared their tall prairie grasses for grazing. As a result, that small region of southeastern North Dakota supports the last major remnants of native prairie in the entire state, which now, a century later, is preserved as the Sheyenne National Grassland.

As a further result of this obscure geologic event that occurred 10,000 to 15,000 years ago, my mother came to know the prairie grasses and prairie birds intimately when as a child she walked or rode her horse through the region's lush big bluestem and Indiangrass meadows. She passed her knowledge of prairie plants and grassland birds on to me when I was a child; it was perhaps the greatest of all the many gifts she gave me. On the warm summer day of her funeral nearly two decades ago, I left the cemetery as soon as possible and drove 30 miles to a place near where her parent's home had been, and spent the afternoon alone, amid the sounds and sights of western meadowlarks, upland sandpipers, bobolinks, and our other beloved prairie birds and grasses. I believe that is how my mother would have wanted me to respond to her death, by being surrounded by vibrant life.

Today the relict prairies that remain across the Great Plains must also have been responsible for many similar memories of homesteaders, families, and individuals lucky enough to learn the quiet beauty of prairies. The family names that are often associated with these prairies are a testimony to the pride with which these persons cared for and protected tiny remnants of an earlier time, and of a richly diverse, wonderful landscape.

Someone once wrote, and it could only have been Aldo Leopold, that in its biomass a ruffed grouse makes up only a minuscule part of the forest, but to remove it is to remove much of the life from the forest. Similarly, a horned lark or Sprague's pipit represents an almost immeasurably tiny part of the prairie ecosystem, but a prairie without the song of a horned lark or a Sprague's pipit overhead is no prairie at all. And a place with no prairies at all is not a place that will stir the heart.

Prairie Birds: Fragile Splendor in the Great Plains (Johnsgard, 2001)

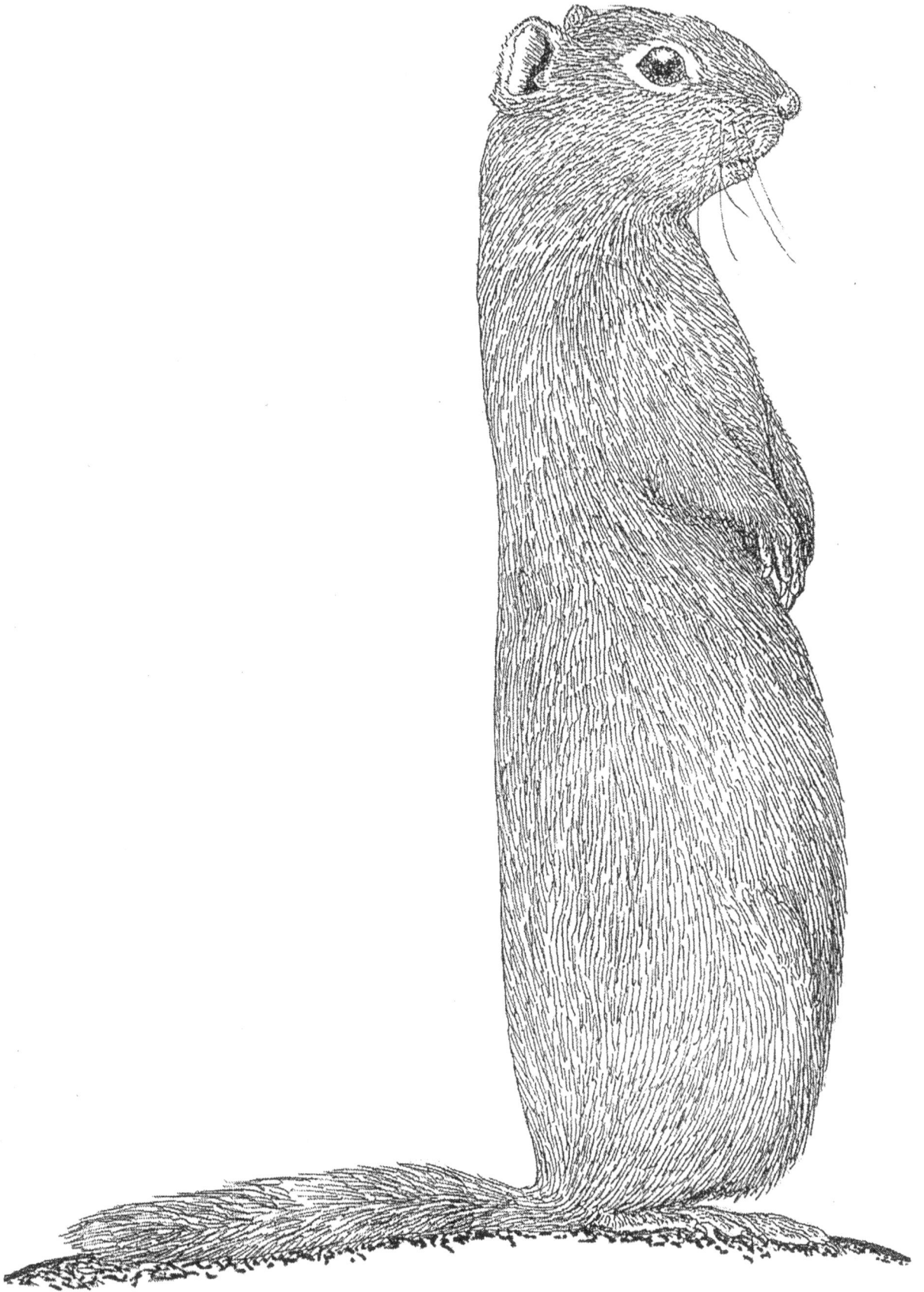

Richardson's ground squirrel

Introduction

In this book, the chosen sites, states, and provinces are sequenced alphabetically within the five larger (north to south) geographic groupings. Collectively they include descriptions of about 350 preserved natural sites, which were primarily selected for being public-access locations having important biological, geological, or scenic characteristics. Another group of more than 150 locations (shown in italics) are briefly mentioned but considered to be of more limited importance or for which little information was available. Instructions as to driving access vary in detail. National and state sites that are well known and appear on standard highway maps are given little or no such attention, whereas the locations of privately owned or relatively obscure places are usually much more fully explained.

I have put strong emphasis on mentioning some of the typical or unusual birds of the more fully described sites, partly because the available information on birds is always more extensive than that for other animal or plant groups and partly because they are important prairie indicator species. The presence of especially characteristic High Plains biota, such as prairie dogs, bison, pronghorns, and burrowing owls, is also mentioned wherever possible.

As a reflection of the great role that federal lands play in preserving our contemporary natural treasures, more than 70 of the sites described in this book are national refuges, the largest single category of included sites. There are also nearly 60 state parks, 40 state or provincial wildlife management areas, 19 national parks and/or monuments, and 16 provincial parks.

Because of my own interests in prairies and prairie biology, more than 40 of the described sites are prairie preserves or national grasslands. I have earlier (2005) described the locations and characteristics of more than 200 High Plains grasslands, and (2008,

A Guide to the Tallgrass Prairies) of more than 70 tallgrass prairies of eastern Nebraska and adjacent states.

A comprehensive survey and splendid discussion of the ecology of more than 160 North American prairie preserves can also be found in Jones and Cushman's superb 2004 guide *The North American Prairie*. Another valuable survey of North American prairies is the *Prairie Directory of North America* (Adelman and Schwartz, 2001).

Additionally, although the subject may be of less general interest to naturalists, I often refer to the Lewis and Clark 1804–6 expedition's experiences on encountering the wildlife and Native Americans of the then-pristine Great Plains. The reader is referred to Burroughs (1961), *Moulton (1993–99)*, Phillips (2003), and Johnsgard (2003, *Lewis and Clark*) for details of their monumental contributions to America's history.

Although space does not allow for descriptions of all the birds and birding opportunities one can encounter within the Great Plains, many of the locations included in this book are outstanding birding locations. Numerous recent state and local guides identifying bird- or wildlife-finding localities within the Great Plains are also available and are included in this book's references. For example, the Watchable Wildlife series of state-based books published by Falcon Press covers many of the Great Plains states. Nebraska's volume (Knue, 1992) describes 68 sites, Iowa's 77 (Dinsmore et al., 1995), North Dakota's 81 (Knue, 1992), Montana's 109 (Fisher and Fisher, 1995), Colorado's 110 (Gray, 1992), and Texas's 142 (Graham, 1992). Zimmerman and Patti (1988) documented 74 Kansas localities along with some in western Missouri, and a wildlife-watching guide by Gress and Potts (1993) describes 101 Kansas sites. The guides to Texas birding by Wauer and Elwonger (1998) and Kutac (1998) respectively describe

200 and 290 sites. I published a bird-finding guide for Nebraska with more than 300 localities (Johnsgard, 2011, *Nebraska Bird-Finding Guide*) as well as one for Nebraska's central Platte River valley and adjacent Rainwater Basin with 155 sites (Johnsgard, 2015, *Birding Nebraska's Central Platte Valley*).

Understanding the importance of and preserving these fragile and increasingly threatened sites, and other remnants of the natural Great Plains, is not only a truly moral and uniquely human act but in doing so we are also preserving countless other plants and animals that evolved within the grassland ecosystem and are historically connected with it, linking us to the grasslands in ways we cannot fully comprehend. The information in this book should help readers learn where they might find areas of preserved nature, and it might help them better appreciate some of the biota they encounter there. These pages also offer a hint of the biological diversity and aesthetic values that these places hold as unique repositories of the endless enchantments offered by the natural world.

Adult horned lark.

I

The Great Plains

Landforms, Landscapes, and Loess

Few geographic regions of North America possess a greater capacity for the imagination to run free than the simple words "Great Plains": visions of bison covering the landscape from horizon to horizon, endless blue skies painted over limitless fields of grass waving hypnotically in the breeze, the smell of newly wetted black soil and fresh ozone in the air after a sky-shattering thunderstorm, and the bronzy color of bluestem and Indiangrass in late fall. There is also the confident feeling that one might hike in any direction for an entire day without making detours or ever losing sight of the place you have left or the one you are headed toward. Compasses are a needless luxury in the plains.

Great Wildlife of the Great Plains (Johnsgard, 2003)

For most Americans, especially those living along the Atlantic or Pacific coasts, the Great Plains are not so much a destination as they are a nuisance to be avoided. This avoidance can be comfortably achieved by flying over them at an altitude of at least 30,000 feet, preferably while reading a book or sipping a drink. If the occupant makes the mistake of looking out the airplane window, he is likely to be disappointed—no mountains, coastlines, or great metropolis are to be seen, and the only green reminders of the forests of home are often neatly spaced rows of perfectly round vegetation circles.

These alien-appearing landmarks identify the places where center-pivot irrigation systems are busily sucking up fossil water from the vast Oglala aquifer far below the land surface and transforming it into corn. There, gravels and sands deposited during preglacial and glacial times have produced a sponge-like

repository for the rainfall and snowmelt accumulated during hundreds or thousands of millennia of deep time. Probably much of this underground ocean has been transported eastward from distant Rocky Mountain origins since late Pleistocene times and is still slowly inching its way east between layers of sedimentary rocks that greatly predate the water that they are passively transporting.

Much earlier in geological time, from about 570 million to 70 million years ago, the region that is now called the Great Plains was covered by a vast shallow sea, the Western Interior Seaway (Map 1), the western limits of which merged with a swampy plain. Farther west was a dry piedmont region (the Colorado Piedmont), beyond which were newly forming mountain ranges. These mountains, destined to become the Rocky Mountains, rose gradually, lifting the lowlands to the east, and gradually forcing the inland sea to drain southward.

Erosion from the rising mountains added sediments eastwardly, and periodic volcanic activity provided supplemental ashy materials to the mix. By 20 million to 30 million years ago, water-carried sands and gravels had spread over the entire Great Plains from Canada to Texas, producing a gently eastward-sloping plain that was interrupted only by a few ancient mountain masses such as the Black Hills.

Southward, an uplift (the Central Texas Uplift) of similarly ancient rocks and volcanic lava flows produced many lava-capped mesas across the southern parts of the Great Plains. In the central Great Plains, unimaginable amounts of wind-blown sand and silt (loess) and water-carried sands produced an unstable mantle of varied thickness (Map 2). The largest and deepest of these deposits consists of the Nebraska Sandhills, which range up to more than 600 feet in thickness, and have southern and eastern margins of loess that are up to about 65 feet deep.

Down-cutting of streams coming out of the western

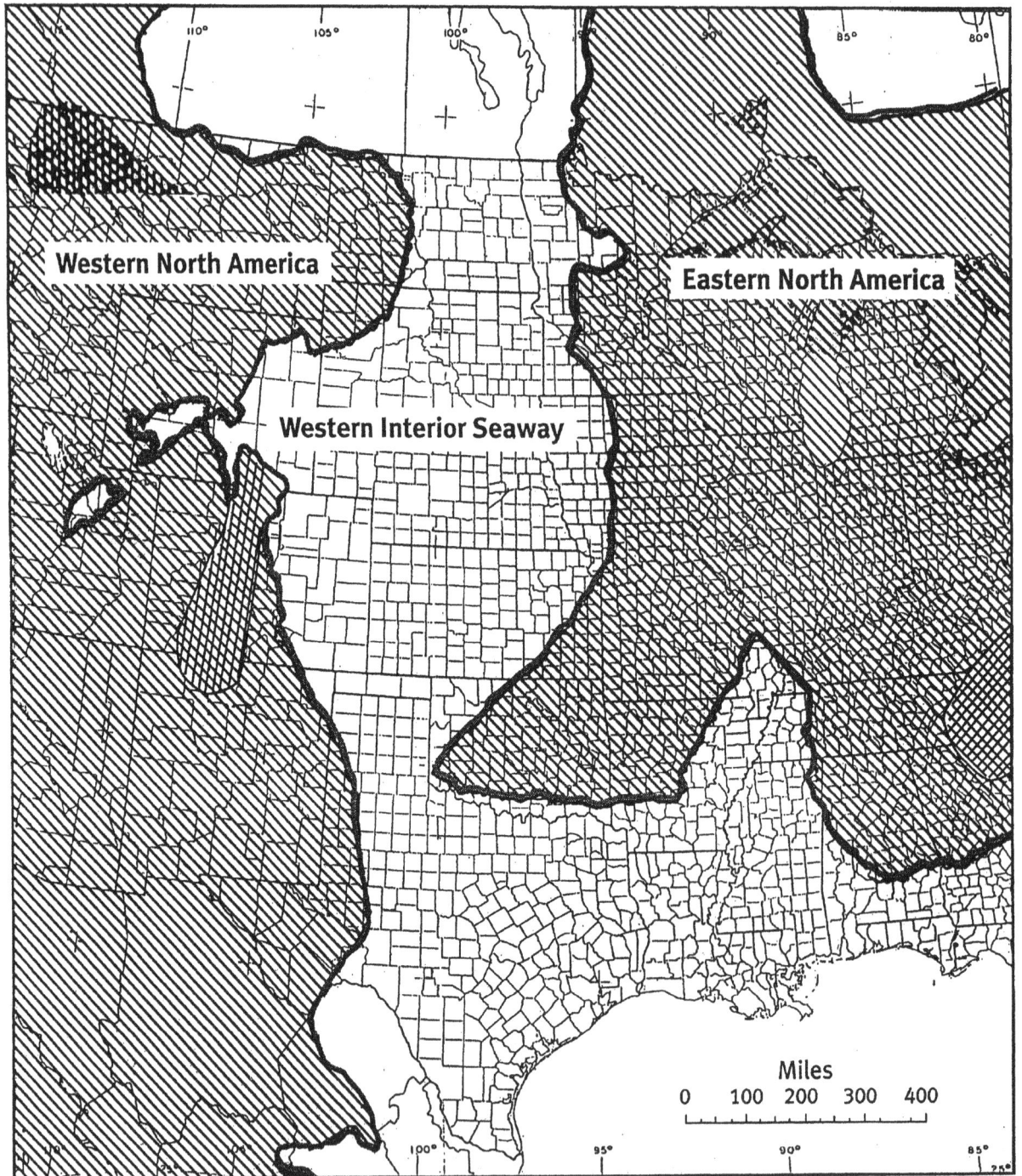

Map 1. Presumptive geography of North America during the late Mesozoic era (ca. 74 million years ago). Cross-hatched areas indicate ancient mountain ranges. Adapted from a map ("North America in the Age of Dinosaurs") published by the National Geographic Society, January 1993.

mountains and regional uplifts produced local erosion effects that resulted in deeper river valleys and scattered buttes, bluffs, and ridges, such as Nebraska's Scotts Bluff, Pine Ridge, and Wildcat Hills. Farther north, those erosive features associated with the Missouri River, formed the highly dissected Missouri Plateau. In eastern Wyoming an ancient igneous pillar of basalt was gradually exposed as its surroundings were progressively eroded away, gradually exposing the iconic Devils Tower.

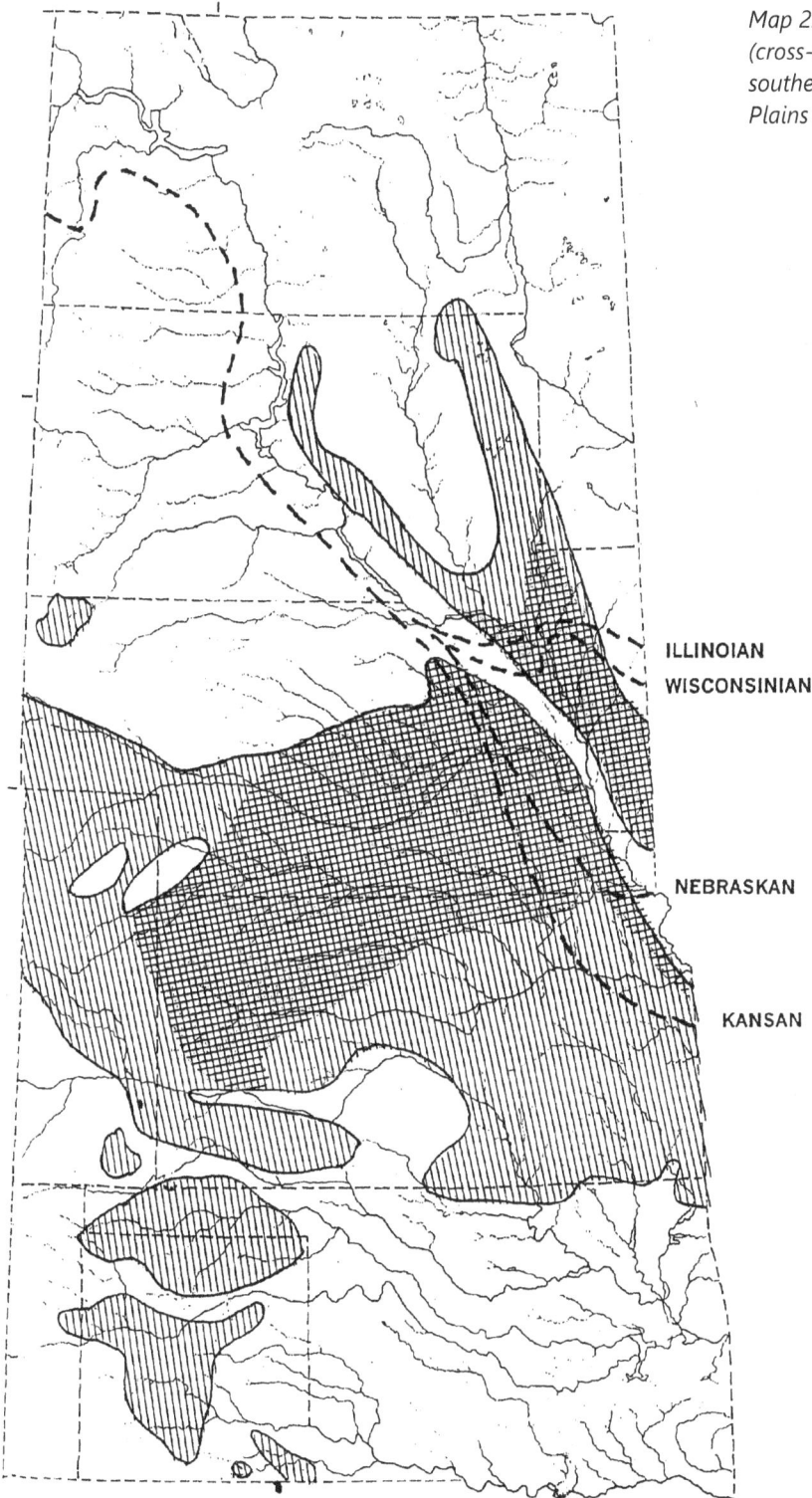

Map 2. Regions of lighter (hatching) and heavier (cross-hatching) loess deposition and the southern limits of major glaciations in the Great Plains states (after various sources).

ILLINOIAN
WISCONSINIAN

NEBRASKAN

KANSAN

During the past 2 million years several periods of continental glaciation occurred, of which the southern edges of four extended south as far as the northern and central and central Great Plains (Map 2). Although the ancient Missouri River had once flowed northeast from what is now North Dakota north into Hudson Bay, it was forced by the ice barriers to flow southeast along the glacial margins, eventually finding and flowing into the Mississippi valley.

To the north and east of the redirected Missouri

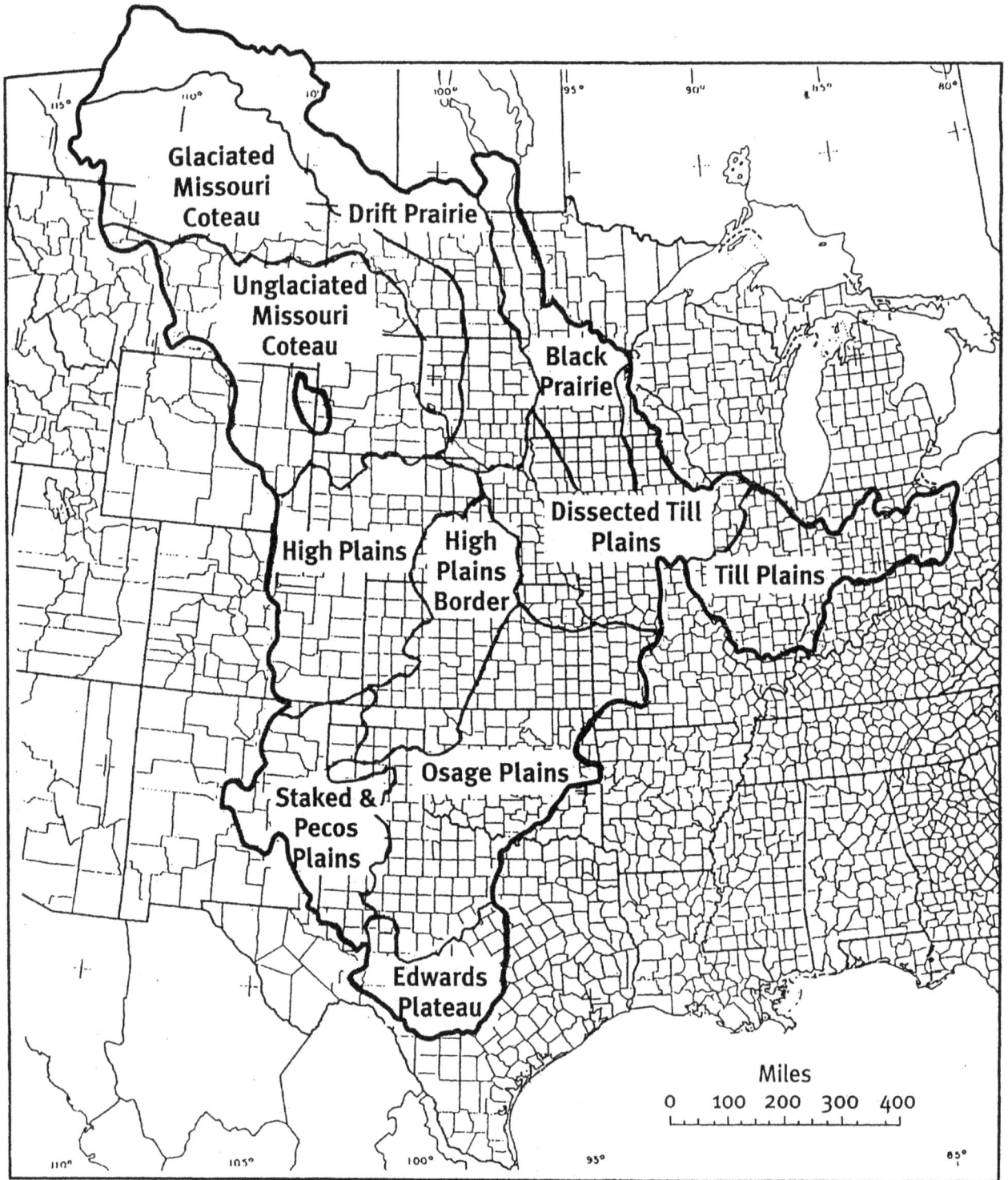

Map 3. Physiographic regions of the Great Plains and Central Lowlands (after Johnsgard, 2001, The Nature of Nebraska).

valley is the Glaciated Missouri Plateau of eastern Montana, the Dakotas, and the southern parts of the Prairie Provinces (Map 3). There, dead-ice moraines late in the Pleistocene epoch produced a region of hilly to rolling topography that resulted in the thousands of present-day marshes and shallow "potholes" that are scattered across the Dakotas and northern Montana, transforming the region into a wetland paradise,

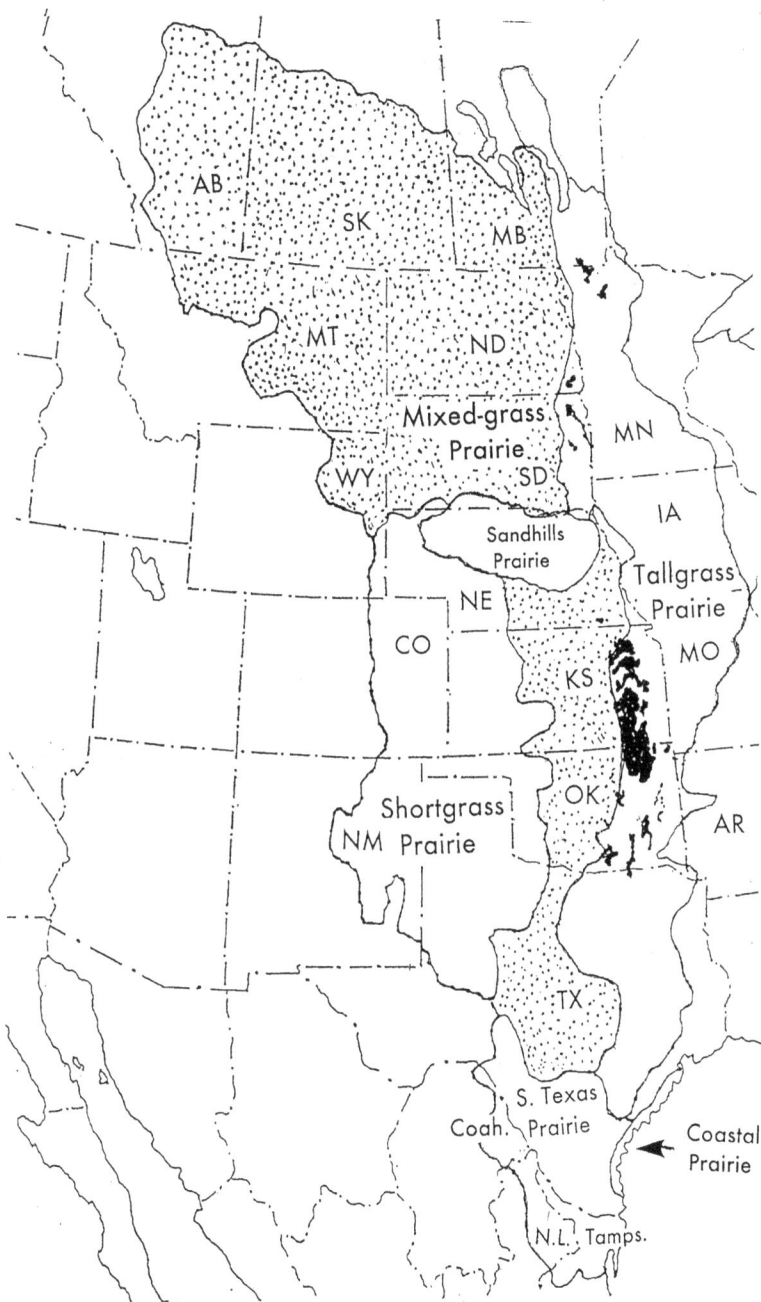

Map 4. Historic distribution of major vegetation communities in the Great Plains, showing tallgrass prairie (with relict areas of tallgrass shown by inking), mixed-grass prairie (stippled), short-grass prairie, Nebraska Sandhills prairie, South Texas prairie, and coastal tallgrass prairie. Limits of Great Plains after various sources, including Johnsgard (2003, Great Wildlife) and Forsberg et al. (2009).

or "duck factory." The Unglaciated Missouri Plateau to the south and west of the glaciated region is a more arid region that is marked by a variety of generally low and small mountain ranges having diverse volcanic, sedimentary, and igneous origins.

Surprisingly few estimates of the area of the entire Great Plains region are available, which is not surprising considering the great diversity of opinion as to their exact geographic limits. Wishart (2004) produced a map, based on a computer-generated and geographically composed estimate derived from about 30 sources, and which totaled about 500,000 square miles (https://en.wikipedia.org/wiki/Great_Plains). A generally similar map, reproduced by Forsberg et al. (2009), illustrates a region covering about 1 million square miles, with a total north-south distance of 1,800 miles, north to the vicinity of Edmonton, Alberta, and south to Nuevo León and Tamaulipas, Mexico. This corresponds closely with my map (Map 4), which is partly based on that of Forsberg et al. My own areal estimate of this region is approximately 750,000 square miles. However, Robinson and Dietz (2017) estimated the total area of the Great Plains, based on landform geology, to be approximately 1,125,000 square miles (2.9 million square kilometers). This larger estimate assumed the limits to be the Mackenzie River delta at the Arctic Ocean coast to the north, the Rio Grande at the south, the Canadian Shield and Interior Lowlands to the east, and the Rocky Mountains to the west.

Current Vegetation and Major Plant Communities

The present climate and vegetation of the Great Plains are largely products of the just-described regional variations in geology and topography. Probably the single most important component of these are the Rocky Mountains, which effectively block most of the precipitation that would otherwise be arriving on moisture-rich air from the Pacific coast. Instead, this moisture is mostly squeezed out and dropped on the western slope of the mountains, where the rising air currents are cooled as they pass over the high peaks, reducing their capacity to retain moisture.

The result is a "rain shadow" drying effect that extends eastward and influences precipitation patterns along the eastern slope of the Rocky Mountains as well as the plains beyond for hundreds of miles. For example, Denver, Colorado, receives only 8 to 15 inches of annual precipitation, whereas Vail, only about 60 miles to the west on the mountains' windward slope, averages 28 inches.

Much of the Great Plains would thus be similarly doomed to enduring a permanent semidesert climate were it not for the Gulf of Mexico. Gulf-based precipitation, carried north mostly by spring and summer flows of moist warm fronts, causes a gradual increase in local annual Great Plains precipitation in direct proportion to the locality's distance east from the Rocky Mountains and north from the Gulf.

For example, in northwestern Texas, Amarillo receives about 20 inches of precipitation per year, whereas Oklahoma City, 260 miles to the east, receives 36.5 inches, an average increase of about 6 inches annually per 100 miles eastwardly.

In Nebraska, Scottsbluff receives 16.7 inches annually, but Omaha, 450 miles east of Scottsbluff, receives 30.6 inches, indicating an average overall increase of

about 3 inches of annual precipitation per 100 miles eastwardly.

In North Dakota, Dickinson receives 15.75 inches annually, whereas Fargo, 290 miles to the east, receives 22.6 inches, representing an average eastward increase in precipitation of about 2.5 inches per 100 miles, a rate of increase about one-third as large as that mentioned for Texas.

Thus, the influence of Gulf Coast moisture diminishes inversely with increasing distance northward from the Gulf as well as increasing directly with relative distance eastward from the Rocky Mountains. Only by understanding the complex relationships existing among regional geography, topography, atmospheric movements, and precipitation patterns is it possible to also understand the general Great Plains' distributions of native vegetation.

In the southwestern Great Plains, low-stature grasslands (also often called "steppes" or "sage-steppes") are widespread (Map 4). Important grasses of this community type include buffalo grass and various grama grasses. These arid-adapted plant communities have low collective species diversity, including plants that have leaves or stems that may be poisonous, distasteful, or covered with spines and are unlikely to be grazed. As in true deserts, succulent water-storing plants such as cacti are also common, and some shrubby plants drop their leaves during the driest past of the year.

Other desert-adapted plants have evolved annual rather than perennial life cycles, in which only a brief rainy period and small amounts of precipitation might be needed to allow for seed germination, growth, flowering, and setting of seeds, all within the span of a few months. As precipitation increases eastwardly, the shortgrass prairies merge with and are progressively replaced by mixed-grass prairies of greater average vegetation height, increased moisture requirements, and higher species diversity (Map 5).

Few if any unique plants or vertebrate species are endemic to the mixed-grass prairie region, but it is an economically important region for grazing and dryland agriculture. Little bluestem (*Schizachyrum scoparium*) is the grass species that is most prevalent, with an associated array of grama grasses (*Bouteloua*, especially *B. gracilis* and *B. curtipendula*), needlegrasses (*Stipa*), wheatgrasses (*Agropyron*), and fescues (*Festuca*). I (2005) estimated that, of an overall historic geographic acreage of about 140 million acres of mixed-grass

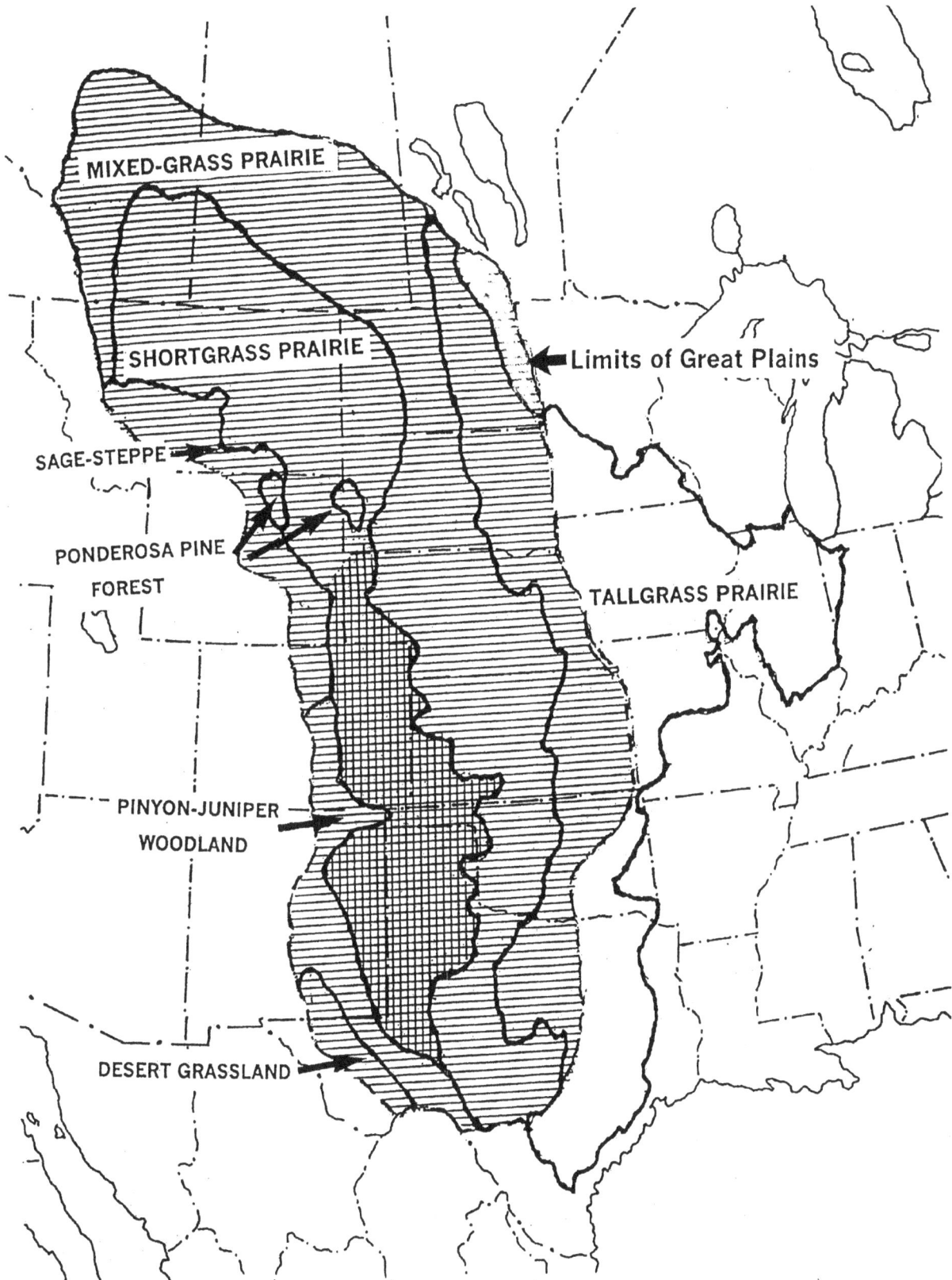

Map 5. Major native vegetation types of the Great Plains and their historic distribution (various sources). The hatched area encompasses the Great Plains region (Wishart, 2004); cross-hatching indicates the southern shortgrass region. Adapted from Johnsgard (2003, Great Wildlife).

prairies in North America (compared with about 152 million original acres of shortgrass), the largest components were in North Dakota (35 million acres), Saskatchewan (33 million), Kansas (24.5 million), Nebraska (19 million), and Texas (17.4 million).

Estimated recent percentage declines in those historic acreages differ greatly among the states and provinces but, based on available data, about 18 percent of the original mixed-grass prairie probably still remained in variably degraded states as of 2000, as compared with about 30 percent of the shortgrass prairie (Johnsgard, 2005).

Tallgrass prairies are the easternmost and most water-dependent of all the Great Plains grassland types. They are notable for their very high species diversity and high biological productivity. In the eastern Great Plains, big bluestem (*Andropogon gerardi*), Indiangrass (*Sorghastrum nutans*), and switchgrass (*Panicum virgatum*) usually dominate in the moister sites such as at the bottom of hills, whereas lower-stature grasses, especially little bluestem, side-oats and blue grama, and needlegrass are among the many species typical of sunny hillside slopes. These same species are important components of the mixed-grass prairies in regions of lower precipitation.

Because of the high fertility of their associated soils, nearly all of the tallgrass prairies were rapidly plowed up for agricultural use during settlement. Those that weren't plowed underwent gradual ecological succession, becoming deciduous forests after the once-frequent prairie fires had been gradually brought under control by homesteaders and villagers. Thus the "prairie peninsula," which historically extended east from Iowa into Illinois and western Indiana, eventually became the heart of the corn-growing economy in the American Midwest. Only about 1 percent of the historic North American tallgrass prairie east of the Mississippi River still existed, and possibly about 4 percent of the continental total still existed, at the start of the twenty-first century (Johnsgard, 2001, *Prairie Birds*).

To the south and southwest of these three primary Great Plains grasslands are the desert grasslands of the American Southwest, which grade northwardly into small-stature pinyon-juniper woodlands ("pygmy forests"). At higher elevations these woodlands transition into taller and denser Rocky Mountain coniferous forests. At lower elevations ponderosa pines form an important, relatively drought-tolerant component. Other isolated, often savanna-like, ponderosa pine forests occur in the Black Hills of South Dakota and adjacent Wyoming and form fringing connections with mixed-grass prairies.

In Canada the northern ("boreal") trans-Canadian closed-canopy coniferous forests are mostly dominated by cold-tolerant spruces and firs. Along the Canada-US border, these forests transition into mixed-grass and tallgrass prairies through areas of "aspen-oak savannas" and "aspen parklands" that are a varied mixture of taller grasslands, brushy thickets, and isolated aspen groves, the last of which are locally called "islands" or "bluffs." This mixed mosaic of grasses, shrubs, and deciduous trees, especially aspens, in the northern Red River valley is now generally called the Tallgrass Prairie Parkland, and it covers more than 12 million acres (Chapman, Fischer, and Ziegenhagen, 1998). Although aspens are very fire sensitive, they can quickly recover from recurrent burns through rapid stem regrowth, eventually resulting in groves of genetically identical aspen clones.

One minor divergence from these simple geographic-climatic patterns occurs in north-central Nebraska, where Nebraska's Sandhills prairie (Map 4) is an arid-tolerant grassland community mostly dominated by mid-height sand-adapted grasses such as sand dropseed (*Sporobolus cryptandrus*), sand reed grass (*Calamovilfa longifolia*), and blowout grass (*Muhlenbergia pungens*). There, the absence of an effective water-holding organic soil mantle favors the survival of highly arid-adapted grasses and forbs, the latter including yuccas (*Yucca* spp.) and several species of cacti (*Opuntia* spp.) as well as an endemic species of "blowout" penstemon (*Penstemon haydenii*) that is ecologically restricted to recently exposed bare sand slopes (Bleed and Flowerday, 1998). However, even here the high water table of the Oglala aquifer often reaches the bases of the sand dunes, producing thousands of small, shallow wetlands that transform the Sandhills into one of the Great Plains' most important waterfowl and shorebird breeding areas (Keech and Bentall, 1971; Bleed and Flowerday, 1998).

Although the historic tallgrass prairie is now only a memory, it once extended eastward into the Central Lowlands to the vicinity of Lake Michigan, where it was rapidly converted into farmland during the 1800s and became the center of the Corn Belt (Map 5).

As precipitation patterns increase toward the eastern edge of the Great Plains, tree-lined rivers become more numerous, and deciduous forest communities

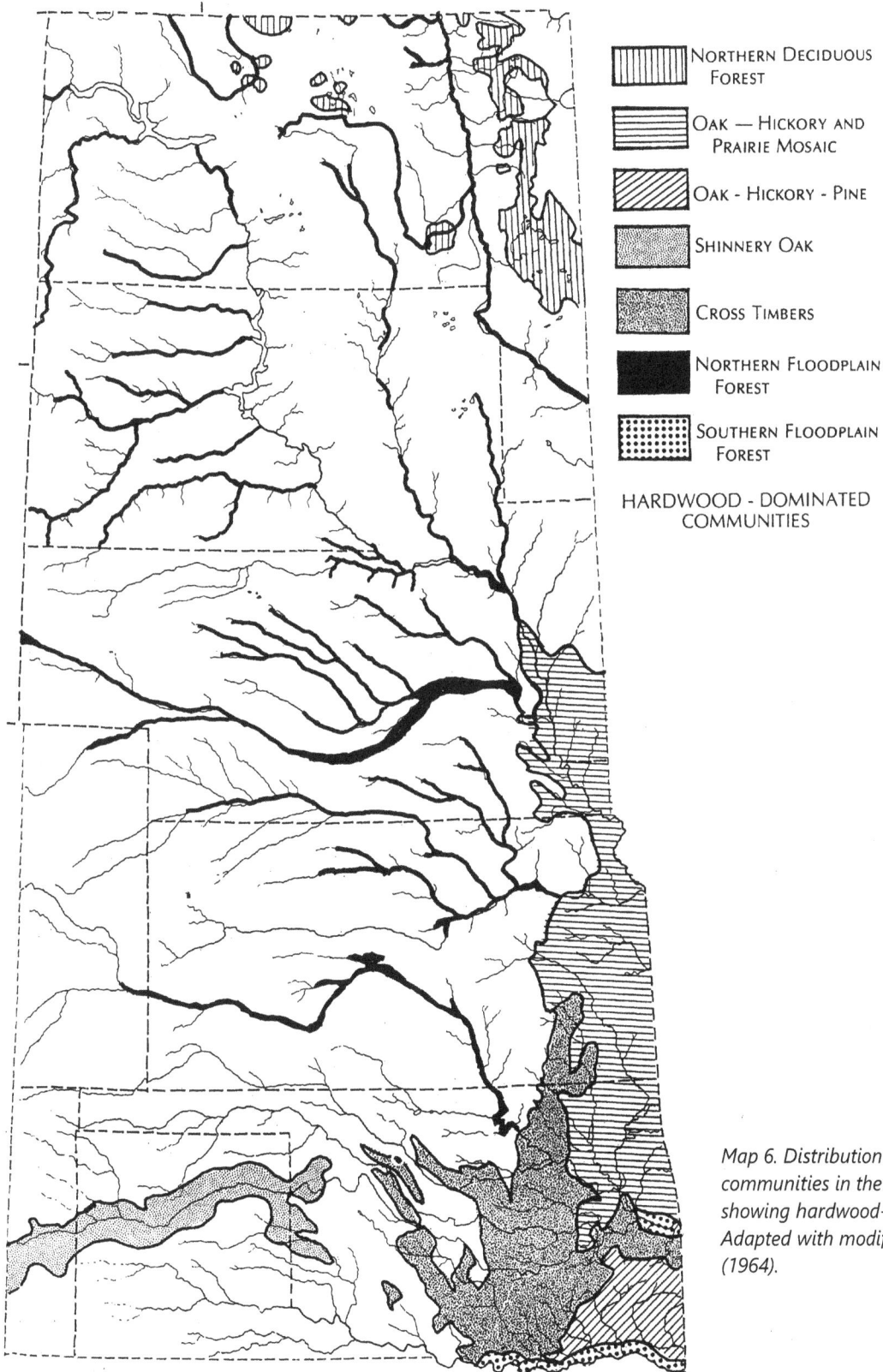

Map 6. Distribution of natural plant communities in the Great Plains states, showing hardwood-dominated types. Adapted with modifications from Küchler (1964).

increasingly merge into, or alternate with, the grasslands. Finally, toward the Great Plains' eastern limits, forests replace the grasslands, with cold-hardy coniferous trees dominating in the northern plains and deciduous hardwoods dominating southwardly. The southernmost forests in the region take on a

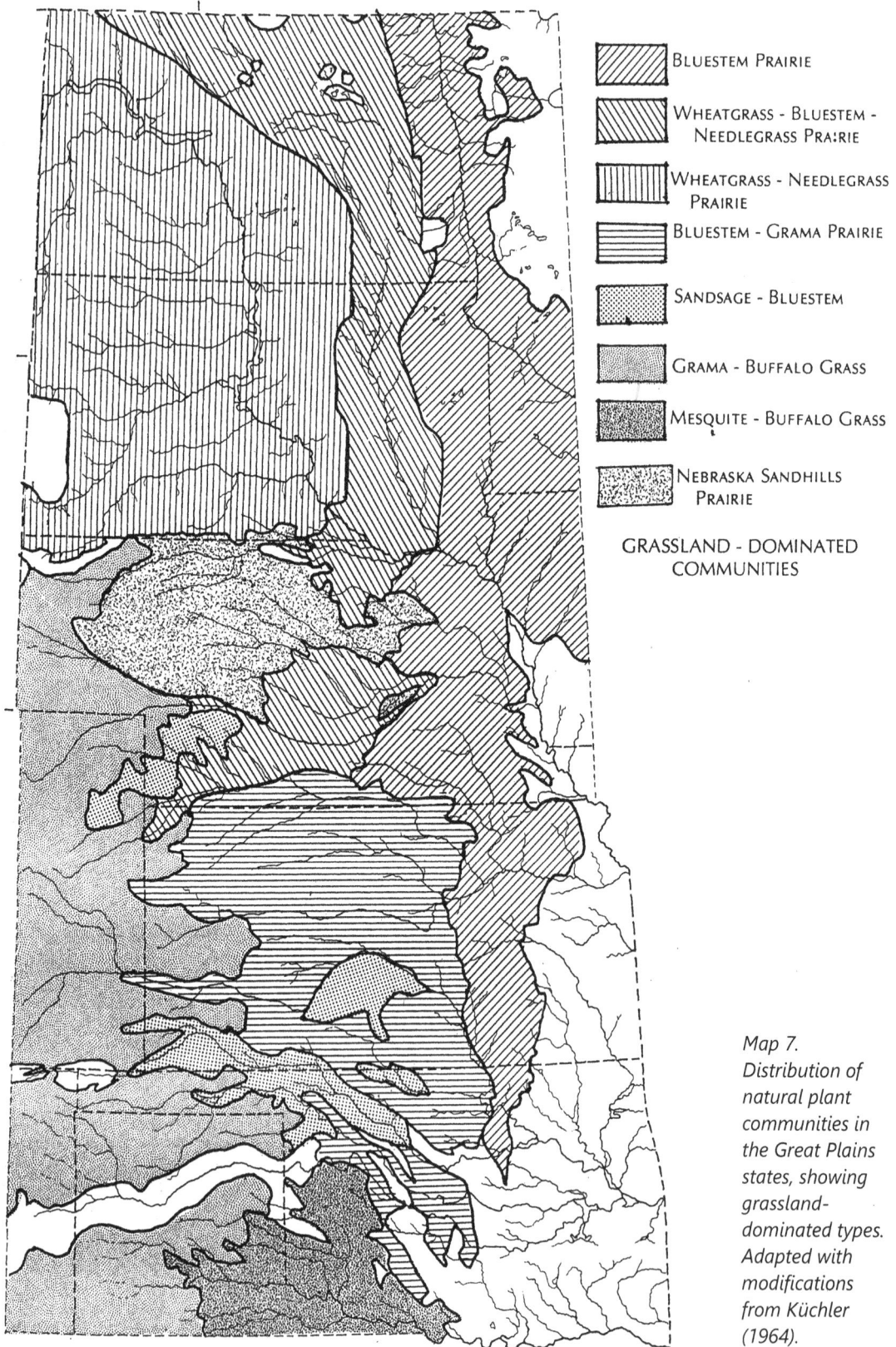

Legend:
- Bluestem Prairie
- Wheatgrass - Bluestem - Needlegrass Prairie
- Wheatgrass - Needlegrass Prairie
- Bluestem - Grama Prairie
- Sandsage - Bluestem
- Grama - Buffalo Grass
- Mesquite - Buffalo Grass
- Nebraska Sandhills Prairie

GRASSLAND - DOMINATED COMMUNITIES

Map 7. Distribution of natural plant communities in the Great Plains states, showing grassland-dominated types. Adapted with modifications from Küchler (1964).

subtropical aspect, with many of the broad-leaved species of the southern floodplain forest retaining their leaves throughout the mild winters and able to tolerate long periods of flooding (Maps 6 and 7).

Tallgrass Prairie Musings and Memories

When I was a youngster in the Red River valley of eastern North Dakota, I sometimes hiked in summer along the railroad track right-of-way from our family house in Christine to a friend's house about a mile north of town. I didn't know then that the "turkey-foot grass" that grew higher than my head was something special, and that under its more formal name of big bluestem it is a charter member of the tallgrass prairie that once covered much of eastern North Dakota, and in locales extends all the way to the Atlantic coast.

A few years later my mother began to teach me some of the native prairie grasses and flowers that grew in low meadows near her family's homesteaded farm. The farm was located about 20 miles northwest of Christine, near Kindred in northern Richland County. There I learned to identify such beautiful plants as tall blazing star and Canada goldenrod, and acquired at least a nodding acquaintance with the many similar species of sunflowers, plus some of the other more common and colorful wildflowers. I also learned to associate patches of native prairie with such glorious birds as western meadowlarks, marbled godwits, and bobolinks.

Today this area has been preserved as part of the Sheyenne National Grassland, the largest federally owned area of tallgrass prairie in America, including 70,180 acres of public land, and situated among more than 64,000 additional acres of privately owned land (Chapman, Fischer, and Ziegenhagen, 1998; Moul, 2006).

Most of the native plants and birds of that region were confined to hilly areas too steep or rocky to plow (on glacial moraines). Others were limited to the gravelly and sandy edges of what were once the shorelines of glacial Lake Agassiz, which drained and gave rise to the present-day Red River valley when the Pleistocene ended 10,000 to 20,000 years ago. As Lake Agassiz slowly drained, it formed a steplike series of low benches, each representing a temporary beach, comprising mostly mixtures of gravel, sand, and silt. Probably because of their relatively low fertility and suitability for growing corn, many of these beaches remained intact long after the nearby flat, black-soil bottomlands of Lake Agassiz had been put under the plow.

During the years my parents had a lake cottage in Ottertail County in western Minnesota, I always looked forward to our family drives east over the prairie-covered areas representing relict Lake Agassiz beaches, west of Fergus Falls and Rothsay, because it was in those rather narrow north-south belts of prairie that I was most likely to see marbled godwits, upland sandpipers, and stands of blazing stars and pasque flowers. At times I would plead with my parents to stop the car long enough to pick a handful of flowers to take on out to the cottage.

I eventually learned that many of these relatively rare and highly localized prairie plants and animals are "indicator species" of undisturbed tallgrass prairie, and that if one wishes to find and protect them, it is necessary to protect the entire prairie community. Very luckily, several relict stands of these ancient beach prairies that I cherished as a youngster have been preserved (five in Wilkin County and three in Clay County, while others exist farther north in Minnesota's Becker, Norman, and Polk Counties) (Chapman, Fischer, and Ziegenhagen, 1998).

When I came to Lincoln, Nebraska, in 1961, there were still dozens of relict prairies near town, where I saw some of the prairie birds and plants of my childhood. But, as the years passed, these prairies disappeared one by one to agriculture or suburban developments, like Lewis Carroll's vanishing Cheshire cat. However, these disappearing cats usually didn't leave so much as a smile but instead offered a legacy of highly fertile land, destined to be turned into endless cornfields and eroding soil.

Of the original prairie vegetation, a few scattered relict stands were often all that remained near Lincoln in the early 1960s, in ditches and at the edges of fields. There the deep roots of perennial grasses like big bluestems allowed them to continue for a time their losing battles against plows and herbicides. Even the fairly new house we bought at the then-edge of Lincoln in 1963 still had a few shoots of big bluestem that fought valiantly for a few years against the socially acceptable bluegrass. After being warned by the city authorities about tolerating such "weeds" in my yard, I too accepted defeat and, refusing to use herbicides, let natural selection determine the plant composition of our yard.

One of the few remaining public-access prairies persisting near Lincoln into the 2000s is Nine-Mile Prairie, so named for the fact that it was a nine-mile buggy ride out to it from central Lincoln. The area was once a privately owned pasture of some 800 acres, situated on a hilly glacial moraine. The site had been studied intensively during the 1930s by Professor John Weaver and his students and became known as one of the best-studied tallgrass prairies in North America.

During World War II, part of the prairie was taken over by the military for use as an ammunition storage site, and the prairie gradually shrank to somewhat more than 200 acres. Nine-Mile Prairie was acquired by the University of Nebraska in 1983 and is now protected and managed both for research and as an example of a historic prairie. It is now available to the public for nonconsumptive purposes, such as nature study, birding, and hiking.

By a stroke of good fortune, and some ambitious money-raising on the part of the state office and local chapters of the National Audubon Society, a 626-acre prairie was acquired in 1998 that is just 18 miles south of Lincoln, in southwestern Lancaster County. This prairie is also located on unplowed glacial moraine, and is almost as botanically diverse as Nine-Mile Prairie. Spring Creek Prairie Audubon Center is now the jewel in Nebraska's tallgrass prairie crown, with an interpretive center and a staff including several trained biologists. Wachiska Audubon Society, the local Audubon chapter, later purchased and donated an additional 14-acre adjacent woodland.

More recently, two adjoining parcels of prairie were purchased to add to Spring Creek Prairie, bringing the prairie's total acreage to about 850 acres, of which about 650 acres are native prairie. The new additions are in the process of prairie renovation by controlled burning, mowing, and other techniques, which allows a visitor to see how overgrazed prairies can gradually be restored to near-pristine condition.

The animal list for Spring Creek Prairie includes more than 220 bird species and about 30 mammals, 50 butterflies, and countless other invertebrates. The flora of Spring Creek has now been well inventoried and includes over 370 plant species. Excluding trees, aquatic plants, and woods-adapted plants, these include more than 200 prairie species. Although the majority of the individual plants are perennial grasses, grasses actually make up only about 20 percent of the native prairie flora. Broad-leaved herbs, collectively called forbs, compose about 70 percent of all the species, while shrubs and a few woody vines add the remaining 8 percent.

So, it is the forbs that give the greatest structural complexity to prairies, and these includes a large number of plants in the sunflower (aster) family, fewer in the legume family, and very few in such families as the orchids, only one of which is known to occur at Spring Creek. Although the grasses are wind-pollinated, many of the forbs are pollinated by insects, and it is this latter adaptation that has produced the displays of multicolored and scented flowers throughout spring and summer that at times turns the tallgrass prairie into a garden. At Spring Creek Prairie, the flowering of the purple coneflower in late June and July is a summer highlight, while several asters such as New England aster and other blue to purple asters vie with downy gentians to be the final fall hosts to honeybees and bumblebees during late October.

Spring is my favorite time to visit Spring Creek, when the migratory birds are returning and the first spring flowers, such as violets and pucoons, rush into bloom to complete their flowering before being shaded out by the cool-season grasses and taller forbs. But each season has its attractions. The tall prairie grasses are nearly all "warm-season" species, waiting for the oppressive heat of midsummer to put on their most rapid growth. By September, the Indiangrass and big bluestem may easily exceed seven or eight feet in a wet year, and to lie down in a stand of these grasses and look to the sky above is to know how an ant's view of its world might appear.

The tall moraine hills of Spring Creek Prairie are among the highest points in Lancaster County, affording a spectacular unobstructed view in all directions. Sitting on one of these hilltops, one can close one's eyes and listen to the sounds of near-solitude, sometimes marked only by the songs of a distant meadowlark, the scream of a soaring red-tailed hawk, or, in spring, the soft kettledrum sounds of courting greater prairie-chickens.

A few years ago, the autumnal equinox happened to fall almost exactly on the night of the September full moon, so I decided to watch the simultaneous sunset and moonrise from the top of one of Spring Creek's highest hills. I sat on a large, rounded Sioux quartzite boulder that protruded a few feet above the ground, a souvenir of a melting glacier that had shaped these hills toward the end of the last ice age. The simultaneous sunset and moonrise was like watching one beautiful curtain fall in the west as another equally stunning curtain was rising in the east.

By November, the prairie becomes quiet, with the starches, sugars, and other carbohydrates that were manufactured by perennial plants during summer now safely stored in root systems many feet below ground, well out of reach of grazing animals. What is left are the rusty brown skeletons of leaves and stems that make for spectacular fall panoramas, especially when contrasted with the red leaves of shrubby sumacs and the ethereal blues of cloudless fall skies.

Winter is a time for hardy souls to walk the prairie trails in search of snowy tracks marking the passage of cottontail rabbits, white-tailed deer, raccoons, white-footed and deer mice, and other mammals such as bobcats and coyotes that otherwise are likely to remain hidden.

Much of the winter activity of small rodents occurs under deep snow; its insulating quality allows the temperature at ground level to remain only a few degrees below freezing, even if the air temperature above the snow should approach zero. Foxes, coyotes, and some owls can hear the sounds made by unseen mice and voles scurrying about unseen below the snow and will suddenly pounce on them from above. By December, the long blue shadows of grass cast on the snow by the pallid winter sun provide only cold comfort, but they do offer the promise of a sun that by January will be gradually rising earlier each day, slowly increasing in strength and providing both life-giving light and heat to the waiting plants and animals.

The Great Plains are thus a biological meeting place for northern, southern, eastern, and western elements, acquiring a kind of collective uniqueness simply by virtue of their central position, thereby becoming a sort of biological melting pot into which plants and animals have seeped from around all their edges. Like America itself, the Great Plains region represents a kind of composite or self-assembled land, whose strength lies in diversity, and whose remnants must be treasured and protected, if only in fragmentary remnants and locations.

Great Wildlife of the Great Plains
(Johnsgard, 2003)

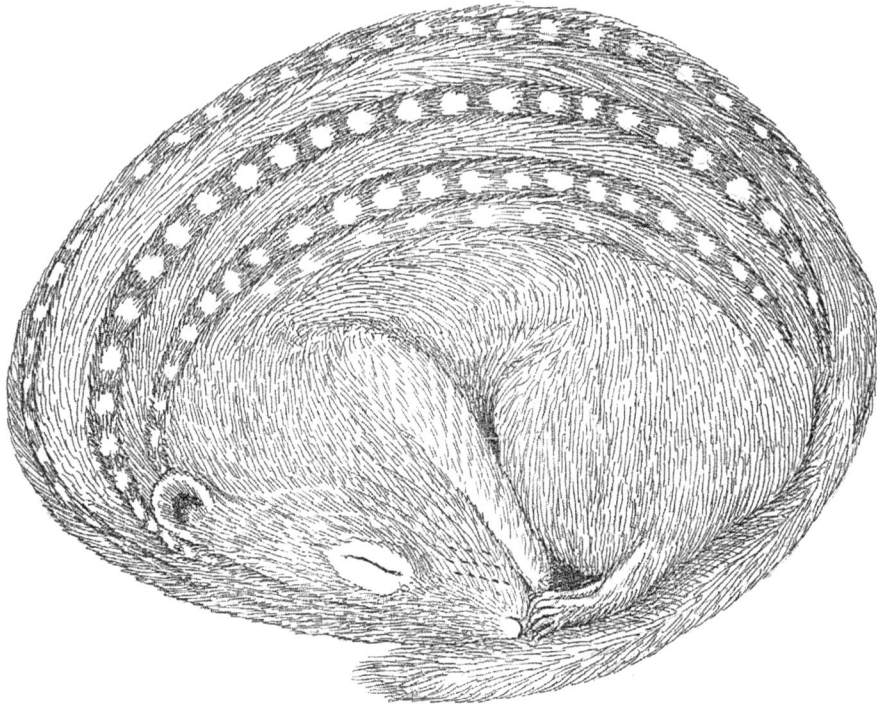

Thirteen-lined ground squirrel, adult hibernating.

II

The Canadian Prairie Provinces

Cherished Memories of the Canadian Plains

Three books from my early years played vitally important roles in my later life. One of them, a popular edition of Audubon's *The Birds of North America,* was a 1940 Christmas gift to me from my "city" aunt, Beatrice, given to me when I was just ten years old. It became a kind of field guide for me at a time when I had never heard of field guides, and it allowed me to identify many species of both plants and birds that I had seen but had been unable to identify.

Another still-treasured gift was a 1943 Christmas present from my parents of *The Ducks, Geese and Swans of North America.* It was written by a Toronto industrialist, F. H. Kortright, and contained the best waterfowl painting I had ever seen, by Terry Short, an artist at the Royal Ontario Museum. This book had a profound and lifelong effect on me by shaping my primary biological interests toward waterfowl. In 1955 F. H. Kortright gave me a copy of his personally funded English translation of Konrad Lorenz's seminal work on the comparative social behavior of ducks. This work provided me with a sort of Rosetta stone insight into an understanding of waterfowl pair-forming behavior, which five years later became the primary focus of my post-doctoral research.

A year later I was similarly given a Christmas gift of H. A. Hochbaum's classic book on waterfowl ecology, *The Canvasback on a Prairie Marsh.* Hochbaum's ink drawings entranced me, and I was greatly influenced by his ability to describe the complex aspects of a species' biology in nontechnical language and an engaging manner. It set me to hoping that I might eventually write a similar book on some species of waterfowl that I hoped to likewise study. It also made me decide

that I must one day visit the Delta Waterfowl Research Station near Portage la Prairie, Manitoba, where Hochbaum had done his research and was its scientific director. The enormous Delta marsh is located at the south end of Lake Manitoba and was only some 400 miles from my hometown of Wahpeton, North Dakota.

It was not until I was attending North Dakota Agricultural College (now North Dakota State University) at Fargo that I was able to make my first trip to Delta. "Al" Hochbaum spent many hours visiting with me, and I listened at length and with fascination to his stories about the marsh, the local waterfowl, and his undergraduate days at Cornell University. I also learned about his graduate work under Aldo Leopold, another of my literary heroes as the author of *A Sand County Almanac.* Al also talked about writing for publication ("everything you write should be washed seven times before you submit it for publication") and making the memorable pen-and-ink artwork that I later tried to emulate in my own publications. It was then that I began to hope I might follow in his footsteps and also attend Cornell University, a dream that finally materialized about five years later.

To add to the story of Al's later life, in 1978 he received Canada's esteemed Order of Canada medal, which is given periodically to selected scientists, artists, and celebrities. He also received a host of other awards from organizations such as the Manitoba government, the American Ornithologists' Union, and the National Wildlife Federation. Like F. H. Kortright, Terry Shortt, George Archibald, Tom Barry, Graham Cooch, Fred Cooke, Paul Geraghty, and other dear Canadian friends, Al Hochbaum influenced my life as few others have and instilled in me a special fondness for both Canada and Canadians.

I stopped at Delta again much later in May of 1973, when I was on my way north to study the birds of the

Arctic tundra around Churchill, Manitoba. I then had with me two young sons, who were eager to see the tundra and especially to do some fishing along the way. Al Hochbaum had been retired from the scientific directorship of Delta Waterfowl Research Station since 1970 and was replaced by a much younger waterfowl biologist. Seeing Al no longer having any professional duties or responsibilities, I thought of him as being something of a lonely figure. However, in his later years he produced two more major books on waterfowl movements and migrations, liberally illustrated with his drawings and paintings.

After leaving Delta, my boys and I headed north into Manitoba's dense spruce-fir forest, where we stopped in a few promising spots so the boys could try out the fishing. I left my car at the last place we could easily drive to by car (The Pas), and from there we caught a train, which was the only existing land transportation to Churchill. The railroad track had been built through the boreal forest and over a muskeg and permafrost substrate during the 1930s to carry grain to Churchill for export through Hudson Bay. The train was very slow; a person could flag it down and get on or off anywhere along its entire route (very handy for fishermen). However, it was (and perhaps still is) the only track in North America on which one could ride a train all the way from tallgrass prairie (Winnipeg) to Arctic tundra!

Before getting on the train, I removed a small Honda motorbike from my Volkswagen minivan and stored it in the baggage car of the train. On arrival at Churchill I unloaded the bike, and within ten minutes I was watching red phalaropes foraging in a tundra pool at the edge of town! The bike also allowed me rapid access to the many shorebirds nesting well beyond the limits of the few roads that radiated out from Churchill. Being able to sit three feet away from golden plovers and stilt sandpipers as they brooded their young was a once-in-a-lifetime experience.

My later observations at the snow goose colony at La Perouse Bay provided me with firsthand observations of snow goose broods and the breeding-season ecology of snow geese, and allowed me to finish writing my first popular book, *Song of the North Wind: A Story of the Snow Goose*. That book, which gifted Toronto artist Paul Geraghty beautifully illustrated for me, started me on a pathway to writing occasional books for general naturalists and bird-lovers rather than only for professional biologists.

Nearly a decade later, celebrating my son Scott's high school graduation, we traveled through the grasslands, forests, and mountains of Alberta, Saskatchewan, and Manitoba during an auto trip across western Canada, After driving to Vancouver and taking a ferry north along the coast of British Columbia, we drove from Prince Rupert east through the major Rocky Mountain parks. We then drove across the mixed-grass fescue prairies, via Edmonton, Saskatoon, Regina, and Winnipeg, and finally turned south toward Nebraska.

Along the route through southern Alberta, we passed through some beautiful meadows with clumps of tall (rough) fescue (*Festuca halli*), one of the most conspicuous perennial grasses of the Canadian mixed-grass prairie. The summer prairie and marshland-edge shorebirds there include such wonderful birds as the long-billed curlew, upland sandpiper, marbled godwit, Wilson's phalarope, and Franklin's gull. Typical prairie songbirds of that region that we also looked for included the horned lark, Sprague's pipit, chestnut-collared longspur, western meadowlark, lark bunting, and several regional sparrows, including Baird's and Le Conte's.

In contrast to the United States, which has no federal parks dedicated to the preservation and protection of prairies and prairie biota, Canada's first prairie park, Grasslands National Park, was established in 1981 in south-central Saskatchewan near the Montana border. It covers 340 square miles and is divided into two blocks that are separated by about 25 air miles, or about an hour's drive by road. It is the best place for seeing what remains of central Canada's once vast mixed-grass and short-grass prairies, and their associated larger grassland mammals, including pronghorns, bison, elk, and coyotes. A few other great rarities, such as swift fox, grizzly bears, and wolverines, have also been reported in Grasslands National Park. In 2005 a group of 71 plains bison was transferred from Alberta's Elk Island National Park, and in the spring of 2006 they were released into a fenced section of about 45,000 acres in Grassland National Park's western block. By 2015 the group had expanded to more than 300 adults.

The park's drier areas of short-grass vegetation also support the ferruginous hawk, common nighthawk, and loggerhead shrike, while the Sprague's pipit and chestnut-collared longspur are found in somewhat taller mixed-grass stands. The long-billed curlew, short-eared owl, and McCown's longspur are

Upland sandpiper

present and classified as species of special concern. The extremely rare (Canada-endangered) greater sage-grouse is limited to a few areas of sagebrush in southern Saskatchewan and Alberta. Prairie-adapted reptiles and amphibians of Grasslands National Park are the greater short-horned lizard (Canada-endangered), northern leopard frog (species of special concern), prairie rattlesnake, yellow-bellied racer, and Plains spadefoot toad.

Frenchman River valley in the park's western block may be the only place left in Canada where a person may be able to wild see black-tailed prairie dogs and, with great good luck, the nationally endangered burrowing owl. In 2009 a captive-raised group of 34 black-footed ferrets, a species extirpated regionally some 70 years ago, were introduced into the park's prairie dog towns, and others were added later A survey in 2012 revealed 12 ferrets in the park, three of which were survivors of the initial release. Other third-generation animals born since the release were also found. Additional ferrets have been periodically released since 2009, but the project's long-term success remains uncertain, since prairie dogs are highly vulnerable to diseases that might quickly eliminate an entire local population.

*We have far too few sacred natural sites in
    the Great Plains;*
*Most of the holy sites of the Native Ameri-
    cans that once ruled the plains*
*Have since been cleared and "developed,"
    or their exact locations have been long
    forgotten.*
*But we must not forget the locations of
    prairie-chicken leks;*
*They whisper to us of secret places where
    grama-grasses and bluestems grow
    thick on the ground,*
*And where flint arrowheads are likely to lie
    buried beneath the thatch and loess.*
*They tell us of meadowlark and dickcissel
    song-perches,*
And of traditional coyote hunting grounds.
*They are as much a connection to our past
    as are the ruts left in the soil by Cones-
    toga wagons,*
*Or the preserved costumes of Native
    American cultures carefully stored in
    museums.*

Grassland Grouse and Their Conservation
(Johnsgard, 2002)

The Sites: Glacial Relicts, Godwits, and Grebes

Canada has 52 national wildlife areas and 92 migratory bird sanctuaries that total 46,000 square miles. The Canadian Wildlife Service's website provides maps and detailed information on national wildlife areas and migratory bird sanctuaries throughout western Canada. Most national wildlife areas and migratory bird sanctuaries do not allow unrestricted public access. Wildlife management areas are free and open to the public for multiple use. Visiting some migratory bird sanctuaries requires advance permission from the Canadian Wildlife Service. Ramsar Sites are wetlands that have been designated as being of international importance, and Important Bird Areas are sites officially recognized by BirdLife International as areas of special significance to certain species or groups of species. For additional information on wildlife preserves and bird sanctuaries, contact Environment and Climate Change Canada, Prairie and Northern Region, Canadian Wildlife Service, Twin Atria Bldg., 2nd floor, 4999 98th Ave., Edmonton, AB, Canada T6B 2X3 (401-468-8075), or Canadian Wildlife Service Protected Areas and Stewardship Unit, 115 Perimeter Road, Saskatoon, SK, Canada S7N 0X4 (1-800-668-6767, in Canada only).

ALBERTA

Alberta (AB) has 5 national parks, 76 provincial parks, 32 wildland provincial parks, 203 provincial recreation areas, 139 natural areas, 15 ecological reserves, 3 wilderness areas, and 2 heritage rangelands. Of these, 13 are classified as World Heritage Sites. The total protected area throughout Alberta including both federal and provincial protected areas is approximately 35,000 square miles.

In addition to Canada's Grasslands National Park, many other important mixed-native prairies have been established. In southeastern Alberta they include (1) the Suffield National Wildlife Area (northwest of Medicine Hat), within a much larger military base, with 165 square miles (106,000 acres) of mixed-grass prairie, sand hills, and riparian habitat; (2) the Prairie Coulees-South Ecological Reserve, along the South Saskatchewan River near Medicine Hat, with 5.5 square miles (3,500 acres) of grasslands; and (3) the Kennedy Coulee Ecological Reserve, south of Foremost, with 4.1 square miles (2,600 acres) of grasslands.

For specific information on Alberta's provincial natural areas, contact the Alberta Fish and Wildlife Division, Department of Energy and Natural Resources, Main Floor, North Tower, Petroleum Plaza, 9945 108th St., Edmonton, AB, Canada T5K 2C9 (403-442-2605). For tourism information, contact Travel Alberta, 400–410 9th Ave. SE, Calgary, AB, Canada T2G 0H4 (403-648-1000), email info@travelalberta.com.

Beaverhall Lake Provincial Ramsar Site. 71,781 acres (112 square miles). This site is located near Tofield, about 40 miles southeast of Edmonton. It is an important waterfowl staging area (spring and fall) with more than 200,000 birds regularly using the site each year. During spring migration, more than 150,000 geese stage here, including daily numbers of 50,000–75,000 snow geese and 50,000–100,000 greater white-fronted geese. In fall, 40,000–70,000 dabbling ducks (mostly mallards and northern pintails) are also present. The lake is also an important waterfowl molting area, with up to 25,000 molting ducks. Sandhill cranes also stage here during spring migration, with up to 8,000 recorded in late April.

Cypress Hills Interprovincial Park. (See section in Saskatchewan.)

Dinosaur Provincial Park. 18,000 acres. This park, 30 miles north of Brooks, is known primarily for its famous dinosaur fossils, of which 58 late Cretaceous species have been found. The park's bird list includes 185 bird species, about half of which are breeders. There are also many fish and other reptile species but few mammals and birds. The nearby *Royal Tyrrell Museum* northwest of Drumheller (1-888-440-4240) has a world-class exhibit of dinosaurs. The *Hand Hills Ecological Reserve*, 55,007 acres, is about 18 miles southeast of Drumheller, west of Little Fish Lake Provincial Park. It is mostly upland grasslands, with breeding ferruginous hawks, and with piping plovers nesting on the shore of Little Fish Lake. *Hand Hills Reserve address:* Box 1918, Provincial Bldg., Drumheller, AB, Canada T0J 0Y0 (403-528-5228 or 403-742-7510). *Dinosaur Park address:* Box 60, Patricia, AB, Canada T0T 2K0 (402-378-4342, ext. 235).

Dry Island Buffalo Jump Provincial Park. 8,500 acres. This park is located in south central Alberta, about 64 miles southeast of Red Deer, and along the Red Deer River. Vegetation includes mixed-grass prairie, badlands, aspen parkland, and spruce forest. Its badlands topography include a tall plateau, where Cree Native Americans drove bison off the edge of the cliffs 3,000 years ago. There are also Mesozoic dinosaur remains, including the tyrannosaurus-like Albertosaurus. At least 150 bird species have been documented here. *Address:* Hwy. 21, Elnora, AB, Canada TOM OYO (403-823-1749).

Elk Island National Park. 48,000 acres. This national park in central Alberta is located about 20 miles from Edmonton in the Beavershills area. It is famous for its ungulate populations, which include elk (about 600 in 2007), moose (about 300), white-tailed deer (about 500), plains bison (about 450), and wood bison (315 in 2007). Coyotes, beavers, black bears, and timber wolves have also been reported. More than 250 bird species have been recorded, including breeding by the trumpeter swan, red-necked grebe, American white pelican, American bittern, and double-crested cormorant. *Address:* 54401 Range Rd. 293, Fort Saskatchewan, AB TBL DV3 (780-822-5790).

Hay-Zama Lakes Wildland Provincial Park. 198,840 acres (226 square miles). This wetland complex attracts large populations of migratory birds during spring and fall migrations. Over 250,000 ducks and 177,000 geese have been observed during a single migration. It lies on the path of three waterfowl flyways—the Pacific, Central, and Mississippi—making it an important molting and staging area for numerous waterfowl species, the primary factor leading to its Ramsar designation as a Wetland of International Importance.

Head-Smashed-In Buffalo Jump Area. 3,000 acres. This site is located ten miles west of Fort Macleod on Hwy. 785. The site was used as a buffalo jump for 5,500 years, and the bone deposits are 39 feet deep. An estimated 150,000 bison were killed there. Mammals found there include reintroduced bison, pronghorns, mule deer, bobcats, and coyotes. Some local birds include golden eagle, Swainson's and red-tailed hawks, ruffed grouse, and northern saw-whet owl (Jones and Cushman, 2008). No bird list is available. The site includes an interpretive center that illustrates traditional

Adult male elk.

Blackfoot culture and is a UNESCO World Heritage Site. *Address:* Fort Macleod, Fort Macleod, AB, Canada TOL OZO (403-553-2731).

Inglewood Migratory Bird Sanctuary. 636 acres. This MBS is located in central Calgary at 2425 9th Ave. SE. The sanctuary is being expanded into a regional park, *Bend in the Bow*, and is open to visitors. A total of 270 bird species, 21 mammal species, and 347 plant species have been reported there. *Address:* Canadian Wildlife Service, Protected Areas and Stewardship Unit, Eastgate Offices, 9250 49th St., Edmonton, AB, Canada T6B 1K5 (1-800-668-6767, in Canada only).

Peace-Athabasca Delta. 1,277,746 acres (1,996 square miles). Located at the western end of Lake Athabasca, its marshes, lakes, and mud flats are an important habitat for waterfowl nesting and provide a staging area for migration. As many as 1 million ducks, geese, and swans pass through this area in the fall. Designated as a Ramsar Wetland of International Importance.

Spears Lake National Wildlife Area. 160 acres. Spears Lake is about 100 miles southeast of Edmonton, near Endiang. It mostly consists of rough fescue grassland, with associated grassland birds such as western meadowlark, Savannah and vesper sparrows, American avocet, Wilson's phalarope, marbled godwit, and willet. The threatened piping plover also nests along the alkaline wetlands. Limited public access is allowed. *Address:* Endiang, AB, Canada TOJ 1GO. Contact Environment and Climate Change Canada, Prairie and Northern Region Canadian Wildlife Service, Protected Areas and Stewardship Unit, Eastgate Offices, 9250 49th St. NW, Edmonton, AB, Canada T6B 1K5 (1-800-668-6767, in Canada only).

Writing-on-Stone Provincial Park (Áisínai'pi National Historic Site of Canada). 4,500 acres. Near the town of Milk River, this park contains one of the largest areas of native prairie in any of Alberta's parks, as well as the largest concentration of Native American petroglyphs and pictographs ever found in the Great Plains. The carved drawings and other artwork are thought to be 500 to 5,000 years old. Larger mammals include white-tailed deer, pronghorn, coyotes, badger, white-tailed jackrabbit, and beaver (Jones and Cushman, 2004). About 60 bird species are known nesters. These include such prairie species as sharp-tailed grouse, long-billed curlew, marbled godwit, short-eared owl, Sprague's pipit, chestnut-collared , and Baird's sparrow. *Address:* Box 297, Milk River, AB, Canada TOK IMP (403-647-2364).

MANITOBA

Manitoba (MB) has 94 provincial parks, 51 recreation parks, 30 ecological reserves, 18 natural parks, 8 heritage parks, and 4 wilderness parks. In total these sites occupy 7.4 percent of Manitoba's land area, or 18,374 square miles. Manitoba has recently established a *Pine to Prairie International Birding Trail* that is an extension of Minnesota's birding trail, and extends from the end of the Minnesota trail at Warroad north to southeastern Lake Winnipeg. Sites described include (1) Hecla Grindstone Provincial Park, (2) Grand Beach Provincial Park, (3) Birds Hill Provincial Park, (4) Lockport Provincial Park, (5) Oak Hammock Marsh Wildlife Management Area (WMA), (6) Narcisse WMA, (7) Sandy Bar, (8) Spur Woods WMA, (9) Tall Grass Prairie Preserve, (10) Rat River WMA, (11) St. Malo WMA and Provincial Park, (12) The Living Prairie Museum (Winnipeg), (13) Assiniboine Park and Forest, (14) Hwy. 26 (St. François Xavier to Portage la Prairie), (14) St. Ambroise Provincial Park, and (15) Delta Marsh WMA. A free PDF file can be downloaded at https://www.gov. mb.ca/watchablewildlife/pdf/pine_to_prairie_birding_ trail.pdf.

Important protected tallgrass prairies in Manitoba include (1) the Manitoba Tallgrass Prairie Preserve, with about 6,000 acres of tallgrass prairie, aspens, and wetlands near Tolstoi; (2) the Lake Francis Wildlife Area, about 20 miles northwest of Winnipeg, with about 2,000 acres of wet-mesic tallgrass prairie plus marshes and aspen groves; and (3) the *Oak Hammock Wildlife Management Area*, about 20 miles northeast of Winnipeg, with 280 acres of tallgrass prairie and an interpretive center (Chapman Fischer and Ziegenhagen, 1998).

For additional information on Manitoba's natural areas, contact the Manitoba Department of Natural Resources, Box 24, 1495 St. James St., Winnipeg, MB, Canada R3H OW9 (204-945-6784). For tourism information contact Travel Manitoba, Business Development and Tourism, Winnipeg, MB, Canada R3C 3H8 (204-845-3777 or 1-800-665-9949).

Asessippi Provincial Park. 5,700 acres. This park is located about 21 miles south of Roblin in southwestern Manitoba. Geologically situated in the glaciated Souris Till Plain natural region, Asessippi Provincial Park is in the mixed-grass aspen parkland transition zone along the shoreline of the Shell River. The grasslands are rich in rough fescue, June grass, and blue grama grasses, and the forests mostly comprise aspen, balsam poplar, bur oak, birch, Manitoba maple, and willow. The impounded Lake of the Prairies is an important staging area for migrating western grebes, ducks, and geese. Prairie birds include such grassland species as the horned lark, while the forests support eastern species such as the rose-breasted grosbeak as well as several warblers and vireos. Its large mammals include moose, white-tailed deer, elk, coyotes, and raccoons. *Address:* Dropmore, MB, Canada ROJ OLO (1-888-482-2267).

Beaudry Provincial Park. 2,356 acres. This park is located six miles west of Winnipeg on Hwy. 241 along the Assiniboine River. Tallgrass prairie is being restored here, and the riparian woods have notably large basswoods, cottonwoods, and maples. Six nature trails along the river range in length from about one to three miles. No bird or wildlife species lists are available. *Address:* MB241, Springstein, MB, Canada R0G 2N0 (1-800-214-6497).

Birds Hill Provincial Park. Located 15 miles northeast of Winnipeg off Hwy. 89, this 8,600-acre park includes glacial relicts such as esker ridges, wet meadows, bogs, aspen–bur oak groves, and mixed boreal forest communities. More than 200 species of birds have been recorded, including both ruffed and sharp-tailed grouse as well as pileated woodpecker and (in winter) great gray owl. Mammals include white-tailed deer, lynx, mountain lion, black bear, coyote, and white-tailed jackrabbit (Jones and Cushman, 2004). There are trails for bikers, hikers, and horseback riders. *Mailing address:* Manitoba Conservation, Birds Hill District Office, Box 183 RR 2, Dugald, MB, Canada R0E 0K0 (204-223-9151).

Delta Marsh Wildlife Management Area. Delta Marsh WMA is a 44,000-acre wetland located along the south shore of Lake Manitoba, approximately 15 miles north of Portage la Prairie. The marsh is perhaps the largest freshwater marsh in Manitoba and a waterfowl breeding and staging area of major importance, especially for snow and Canada geese and a variety of ducks. Waterfowl and songbirds are especially abundant in the marsh, both as breeding residents and seasonal migrants. Warblers migrate through in waves of thousands. The site is a Ramsar Wetland of International Importance. The marsh was evocatively described in *The Canvasback on a Prairie Marsh*, a book by H. A. Hochbaum, first director of the *Delta Waterfowl Research Station*, now *Delta Waterfowl and Wetlands Research Station* (15,800 acres), where waterfowl and other bird research has been conducted since the 1950s. *Delta Marsh Bird Observatory*, operated by the University of Manitoba, is the most active bird-banding station in Canada, banding an average of about 1,500 passerine birds every year. *Address:* Unit 22–62 Scurfield Blvd., Winnipeg, MB, Canada R3Y 1M5 (204-956-7766).

Duck Mountain Provincial Park. 352,000 acres. This park is located about 60 miles southeast of Swan River, and within Duck Mountain Provincial Forest, in the aspen parkland–boreal forest transition zone. It consists of glaciated moraine, with thick beds of till deposited over Cretaceous shales. The coniferous trees consist of white and black spruce, tamarack, balsam fir, and jack pine, with aspen, poplar, and birch hardwoods also present. *Address:* Manitoba Conservation, Box 640, Swan River, MB, Canada R0L 1Z0 (204-734-3429).

Hecla-Grindstone Provincial Park. 267,000 acres. This park consists of a group of islands (including Hecla Island) and a peninsula jutting into the western side of Lake Winnipeg. It consists of cliffs and sandy beaches, forests, and wetlands Many boreal species occur here, such as spruce grouse, great gray owl, northern hawk-owl, American three-toed and black-backed woodpeckers, and boreal chickadee. The park is about 150 miles north of Winnipeg via Hwy. 8. For information, contact Manitoba Conservation and Water Stewardship in Winnipeg (204-945-6784).

Lake Francis Wildlife Management Area. 16,000 acres. This WMA encompasses about 2,000 acres (3.1 square miles) of wet-mesic tallgrass prairie, plus marshes and aspen groves ("bluffs"). The area includes Lake Francis and part of the Lake Manitoba shoreline. From Provincial Trunk Hwy. 101 in Winnipeg, drive northwest 19 miles on Hwy. 8. At Provincial Road 411, proceed west 10 miles to the site. The site is considered a critical stopover point for migrating warblers and is owned by the Rural Municipality of Woodlands (Chapman, Fischer, and Ziegenhagen, 1998). *Contact:* Travel Manitoba, 21 Forks Market Rd., Winnipeg, MB, Canada R3C 47T (1-800-665-0040).

Living Prairie Museum. This urban Winnipeg site contains 26 acres of tallgrass prairie and an interpretive center, with more than 160 species of native plants. Commonly seen birds include great crested flycatcher, warbling vireo, gray catbird, clay-colored sparrow, LeConte's sparrow, yellow warbler, and western meadowlark (Chapman, Fischer, and Ziegenhagen,1998). *Address:* 2795 Ness Ave., Winnipeg, MB, Canada R3J 3S4 (204-832-0167).

Manitoba Museum. Previously known as the Museum of Man and Nature, this is the largest museum in Winnipeg. Its galleries include Earth History, Arctic/Sub-Arctic, Boreal Forest, Parklands/Mixed Woods, and Grasslands. *Address:* 190 Rupert Ave., Winnipeg, MB, Canada R3B ON2 (204-956-2830.)

Manitoba Tallgrass Prairie Preserve. 6,000 acres (in three units). To experience tallgrass prairie, aspen groves, and wetlands, drive 5 miles north of the US-Canada border to Tolstoi and turn east on Provincial Road 209 toward Gardenton; the prairie land begins at 1.5 miles east of Tolstoi (Chapman, Fischer, and Ziegenhagen, 1998). It includes the world's largest known population of western prairie fringed orchids as well as ten other orchid species. Local mammals include moose, elk, white-tailed deer, coyote, gray wolf, badger, and white-tailed jackrabbit. Probable or known breeding birds include the sandhill crane, sharp-tailed grouse, marbled godwit, upland sandpiper, yellow rail, bobolink, and clay-colored and LeConte's sparrows (Jones and Cushman, 2004). Owned by the Rural Municipality of Stuartburn and the Nature Conservancy of Canada. Information is available from the Critical Wildlife Habitat Program, Box 24, 200 Saultaux Crescent, Winnipeg, MB, Canada R3J 3W3 (204-945-7775).

Narcisse Wildlife Management Area. 29,343 acres. Located north of Narcisse, south of Poplarfield, and adjoining Chatfield, this aspen-oak parkland contains what may be the world's largest red-sided garter snake communal wintering site, or hibernaculum. Thousands of snakes emerging from winter dens are best seen from late April to the end of May. There are four dens, connected by a trail. This WMA is about 100 miles north of Birds Hill Provincial Park. For information contact Manitoba Conservation and Water Stewardship, Winnipeg (204-945-6784).

Sasndhill cranes

Oak Hammock Marsh. 5,000 acres. This marsh is located a few miles north of Winnipeg and has reported 300 species of birds; 193 of these are present on a regular basis. The wetland, a restored prairie marsh, is a staging area for waterfowl and shorebirds during migration, when up to 400,000 birds might be seen in a day. It also hosts a wide variety of songbirds, including some Manitoba rarities such as yellow rail, Nelson's sparrow, and LeConte's sparrow. Oak Hammock Marsh was designated a Ramsar Wetland of International Importance in 1987, and also has been named an Important Bird Area by BirdLife International. The associated *Oak Hammock Wildlife Management Area* is owned by the Rural Municipality of Rockwood and includes 280 acres of tallgrass prairie and an interpretive center. From Winnipeg, drive north 11 miles on Provincial Trunk Hwy. 7 to Provincial Trunk Hwy. 67. Then drive 5 miles east to Provincial Rd. 220, turn north, and proceed 2 miles to the *Oak Hammock Interpretive Center* (Chapman, Fischer, and Ziegenhagen, 1998). *Address:* Oak Hammock Interpretive Center, Stonewall Box 1160, Oak Hammock Marsh, MB, Canada R0C 2Z0 (204-467-3300).

Pope National Wildlife Area. 77 acres. Located about 65 miles northwest of Brandon. This wetland was formed behind an earthen dam, providing nesting habitat for marsh species such as the horned grebe, great blue heron, several ducks, and a variety of grassland and shoreline songbirds such as Savannah and song sparrows. Limited public access allowed. *Address:* Canadian Wildlife Service, Suite 150, 123 Main St., Winnipeg, MB, Canada R3C 4W2 (1-800-668-6767, in Canada only).

Riding Mountain National Park. 1,146 square miles. This park rests on the Manitoba Escarpment, 60 miles north of Brandon, and is a varied mixture of grasslands, upland boreal forest, and eastern deciduous forest. It is best reached via Manitoba Hwy. 10 from Brandon. This road bisects the park, which has a southern entrance at Wasagaming. A total of 233 bird species have been seen in the park. It also has one of the highest populations of black bears in North America, along with about 60 other mammal species that include moose, wolf, mountain lion, lynx, white-tailed deer, and a captive herd of about 40 bison. At least 669 species of plants have been recorded in the park. The park is classified as a UNESCO Biosphere Reserve. *Address:* 135 Wasagaming Dr., Wasagaming, MB, Canada R0J 2H0, (204-848-7275).

Rockwood National Wildlife Area. 79 acres. Located 19 miles north of Winnipeg, off 87 Rd. N, this site is an artificial wetland surrounded by dikes and is located within a parcel of planted grassland in the aspen parkland zone. Key grassland breeding species using the area include the bobolink, Savannah sparrow, and possibly the northern harrier and short-eared owl. Limited public access allowed. *Address:* Canadian Wildlife Service, Suite 150, 123 Main St., Winnipeg, MB, Canada R3C 4W2 (1-800-668-6767, in Canada only).

Spruce Woods Provincial Park. 104 square miles. Located in south-central Manitoba, south of Carberry, and along a glacial-age delta of the Assiniboine River formed where the river, carrying vast amounts of sediments from melting glaciers about 12,000 years ago, flowed into glacial Lake Agassiz. The park is a mixture of mixed-grass prairie, upland deciduous forest, spruce parkland, sand dune vegetation, and riverine forests. Elk and white-tailed deer are common, and some rather rare typical prairie reptiles, such as the western hog-nosed snake and northern prairie skink, also occur. *Address:* Manitoba Conservation, Box 900, Carberry, MB, Canada R0K 0H0 (204-834-8800).

St. Ambroise Beach Provincial Park. This small park, located west of St. Ambroise on the southern shore of Lake Manitoba, attracts great numbers of migrating geese, pelicans, and other waterbirds during spring migration in April. Many migrating songbirds pass through as well. A boardwalk (Sioux Pass boardwalk) offers access out into a wetland. The nationally endangered piping plover nests on the bare sandy shoreline. From Winnipeg, drive Hwy. 1 west 8.1 miles to Hwy. 26, and then travel northwest 26.1 miles to Provincial Rd. 430. Turn right and drive 16.8 miles to the park. *Address:* Saint Ambroise, MB, Canada R0H 1G0 (1-866-626-4862).

Turtle Mountain Provincial Park. 72 square miles. This park lies along the North Dakota border and is about 25 miles south of Boissevain. It is nearly adjacent to the Turtle Mountain Provincial Forest and the International Peace Garden. The park is mostly covered by deciduous trees, especially quaking aspen, but the forests also include balsam poplar, green ash, white birch,

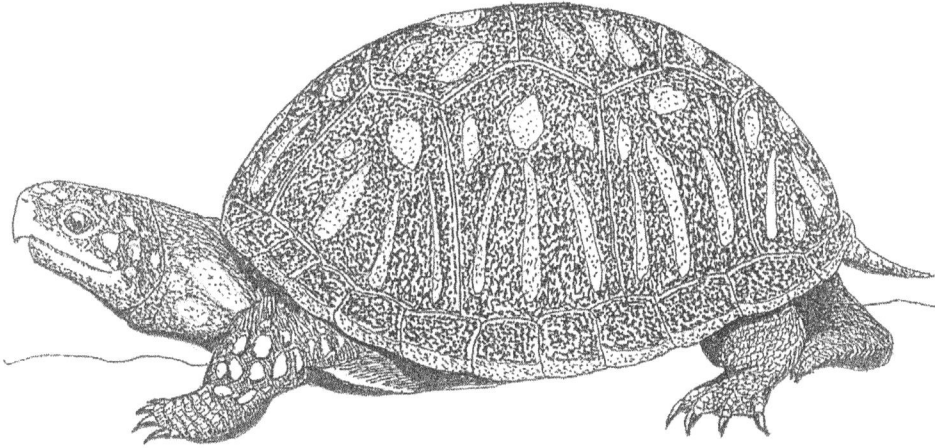

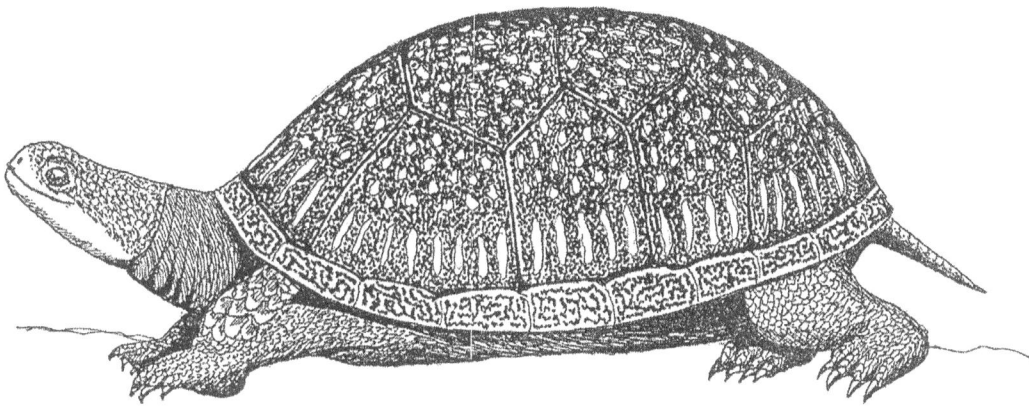

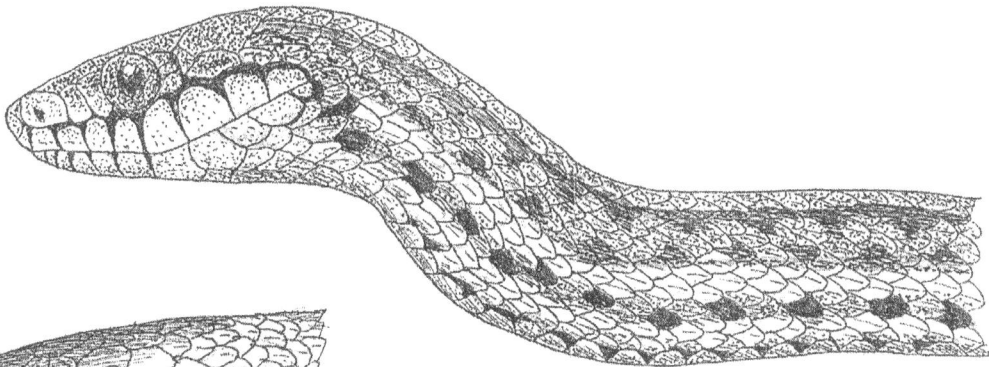

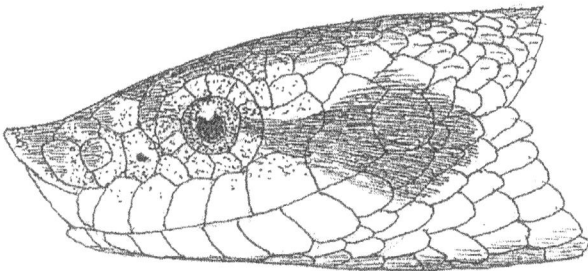

Typical turtles and snakes of the Great Plains, including (top to bottom) ornate box turtle, Blanding's turtle, Plains garter snake, and eastern hognose snake.

Manitoba maple, and bur oak. No bird or other species lists are available. *Address:* Manitoba Conservation, Box 820, Boissevain, MB, Canada R0K 0E0 (204-534-2028).

Yellow Quill Prairie. 2,080 acres. This Nature Conservancy of Canada site is a mixture of mixed-grass prairie and aspen parkland, and requires advance permission before visiting. Drive from Douglas south about 15 miles, and turn east on the country road before crossing the Assiniboine River. Then drive a mile east to a dirt road that is the southwest corner of the property. Access points are along the southern boundary at about 2.5 and 3 miles from this corner (Jones and Cushman, 2008). *Address:* Manitoba Nature Conservancy of Canada, 200-611 Corydon Ave., Winnipeg, MB, Canada R3L OP3 (204-942-4845).

SASKATCHEWAN

Saskatchewan (SK) has 1 national park, 35 provincial parks, and 4 regional parks. Several important and large areas of variably protected native grasslands exist in southwestern Saskatchewan. They include (1) the Nature Conservancy's Butala (Old Man on His Back) Ranch, near Frontier, with 13,135 acres of grasslands; (2) Saskatchewan Landing Provincial Park, north of the South Saskatchewan River and east of Saskatchewan Landing, with 14,300 grassland acres; and (3) Matador Grasslands Protected Area, near Swift Current, with 1,900 acres of grasslands. Additionally, the Great Sand Hills region, south of the South Saskatchewan River near the Alberta border, covers 733 square miles (470,000 acres) and is a mixture of sand dunes and sand-adapted grasslands.

For general information on Saskatchewan's protected natural areas, contact the Department of Parks, Recreation, and Culture, 3211 Albert Street, Regina, SK, Canada S4S 5W6 (306-787-2700). For tourism information, contact Tourism Saskatchewan, 2103 11th Ave., Regina, SK, Canada S4P 3V7 (306-565-2300). Saskatchewan park information is available from the Saskatchewan Parks, Recreation, and Culture, 3211 Albert St., Regina, SK, Canada S4S 5W6 (306-787-2700) or Tourism Saskatchewan (above) or the Canadian Wildlife Service, PO Box 280, Simpson, SK, Canada S0G 4M0 (306-836-2010).

Basin and Middle Lake Migratory Bird Sanctuary. 34,578 acres. This site about five miles east of St. Benedict is important for waterfowl and shorebirds. During surveys completed in 1988 and 1989, an average of 9,578 shorebirds were recorded during three one-day surveys. In addition to shorebirds, up to 20,000 ducks on Basin Lake, and 10,000 ducks on Middle Lake have been recorded at this site during the summer molting period. See also the following Lenore Lake account. Limited public access is allowed at landowner discretion. *Contact:* Canadian Wildlife Service Protected Areas and Stewardship Unit, PO Box 280, Simpson, SK, Canada S0G 4M0 (306-836-2010).

Bradwell National Wildlife Area. 310 acres. This NWA is located about 25 miles southeast of Saskatoon. It consists of native grasslands and wetlands connected by a system of ditches and dikes. Bradwell NWA provides nesting habitats for ducks such as redheads and canvasbacks, as well as hawks, shorebirds, and songbirds. Limited public access is allowed at landowner discretion. *Contact:* Canadian Wildlife Service Protected Areas and Stewardship Unit, PO Box 280, Simpson, SK, Canada S0G 4M0 (306-836-2010).

Buffalo Pound Provincial Park. 2,700 acres. Located 20 miles northeast of Moose Jaw via Hwy. 2 and 202. This is mostly prairie grassland, but sandhills prairie vegetation is also present. The site was once used by Plains Native Americans to corral bison. Bison have recently been reintroduced here. *Nicolle Flats Nature Area* is within the park and offers hiking and wildlife viewing. No bird or wildlife lists are available. *Address:* 110 Ominica St. W., Moose Jaw, SK, Canada S6H 6V2 (306-694-3229).

Cypress Hills Interprovincial Park. With a collective total area of about 133 square miles, this huge park straddles the Saskatchewan-Alberta border and is a transitional region of aspens, conifers, mixed-grass prairie, and fescue prairie, a mixed-grass variant. Notable local mammals include elk, moose, pronghorn, coyote, lynx, snowshoe hare, and white-tailed jackrabbit. Probable or known breeding birds include trumpeter swan, red-necked grebe, ruffed grouse, sharptailed grouse, black tern, common poorwill, and Sprague's pipit (Jones and Cushman, 2008). Its bird list includes more than 200 species (Godfrey, 1950).

Address: Cypress Hills Park, Box 850, Maple Creek, SK, Canada S0N 1N0 (306-662-4471).

Douglas Provincial Park. 11,000 acres. This provincial park is located nine miles southeast of Elbow at the southwest end of Lake Diefenbaker. There are extensive sandy beaches, sand dunes with hiking trails, and wooded areas. No wildlife lists are available. *Address:* Box 59, Elbow, SK, Canada S0H 1JO (306-787-8676).

Duncairn Reservoir Migratory Bird Sanctuary. 6,164 acres. This sanctuary is located southwest of Swift Current, near the village of Duncairn, and is a reservoir on Swift Current Creek. It serves mainly as a molting and staging area for waterfowl, especially for tundra swans, geese, and mallards. Limited public access is allowed at landowner discretion. *Contact:* Canadian Wildlife Service Protected Areas and Stewardship Unit, PO Box 280, Simpson, SK, Canada S0G 4M0 (306-836-2010).

Grasslands National Park. 233,000 acres (364 square miles). Canada's largest area of protected tallgrass prairie is preserved in two blocks. Grasslands National Park is located southeast of Val Marie and north (75 miles) of Malta, Montana. The West Block can be reached only from Wood Mountain. The grasslands are mostly of intermediate height, and the East Block also contains badlands topography and short-grass prairie. Notable mammals include mule and white-tailed deer, pronghorn, bobcat, badger, swift fox, coyote, and white-tailed jackrabbit. A bird list of 177 species is available (although the number of nesting species is unreported). Known or probable breeding birds include Swainson's and ferruginous hawks, prairie falcon, sharp-tailed grouse, upland sandpiper, marbled godwit, long-billed curlew, burrowing owl, short-eared owl, loggerhead shrike, Sprague's pipit, lark bunting, and Baird's sparrow (Jones and Cushman, 2008). *Address:* PO Box 150, Val Marie, SK, Canada S0N 2T0 (306-298-2257).

Last Mountain Lake National Wildlife Area. 18,850 acres (29.5 square miles). This wildlife area is located about 50 miles northwest of Regina. Drive Hwy. 2 to Hwy. 15, then go east on Hwy. 15 for 8.3 miles. Turn south at the wildlife area sign and go 2 miles to the headquarters. The north end of Last Mountain Lake is one of Canada's most important waterfowl staging

Adult burrowing owl.

areas and is a crucial stopover for migratory waterfowl and other water and land birds. During the fall, up to 50,000 sandhill cranes, 450,000 geese, and several hundred thousand ducks may be present seasonally. More than 280 species of birds have been recorded here, and over 100 of these species have been documented to breed in the area, including ducks (13 nesting species), shorebirds (9 nesting), and songbirds (43 nesting). The area offers important habitat for 9 of Canada's 36 rarest birds: the piping plover, Caspian tern, whooping crane, burrowing owl, ferruginous hawk, Cooper's hawk, peregrine falcon, loggerhead shrike, and Baird's sparrow. Colonial nesters such as the American white pelican, double-crested cormorant, and a variety of gulls, terns, and grebes are also present. It is a designated Important Bird Area and a Ramsar Wetland of International Importance. Nearby is Stalwart National Wildlife Area (2,700 acres, see account). *Contact:* Canadian Wildlife Service Protected Areas and Stewardship Unit, PO Box 280, Simpson, SK, Canada S0G 4M0 (306-836-2010).

Lenore Lake Migratory Bird Sanctuary. 35,115 acres (56 square miles). Lenore Lake is a partly saline lake near the town of Lake Lenore. It is part of the Lenore Lake Basin, which includes several saline lakes (including Basin and Middle Lake—see earlier section). Lake Lenore is a globally significant site for staging waterbirds. Tremendous concentrations of birds are present during fall migration, notably 80,000 ducks (mostly mallards) and 40,000 geese. In the summer, about 4,000 ducks (mainly mallard, canvasback, and lesser scaup) use the lake as a molting area. During periods when good habitat is available, the numbers of shorebirds can be as high as 25,000 individuals. Large numbers of double-crested cormorants breed at the lake, as do American white pelicans. The nationally endangered piping plover has been recorded nesting in small numbers. Various grebes, terns, ducks, gulls, and great blue herons also nest on the island. The site has been designated a provincial Important Bird Area. Public access is limited to the discretion of the local landowner, while various public roads also provide some access. *Raven Island National Wildlife Area* (240 acres) is a large island at the southern end of the lake. Public access is not allowed, but observations from the mainland shore or boats is allowed. *Contact:* Canadian Wildlife Service, Protected Areas and Stewardship Unit, PO Box 280, Simpson, SK, Canada S0G 4M0 (306-836-2010).

Moose Mountain Provincial Park. 154 square miles. Located 15 miles north of Carlyle in southeastern Saskatchewan, this park has hilly topography with woodlands of aspen, white birch, poplar, and ash, plus some shallow lakes. There are about 400 moose in the park, similar numbers of elk, and uncountable white-tailed deer. No species lists are available. *Address:* Box 220, Kenosee Lake, SK, Canada S0C 2S0 (306-577-2600).

Murray Lake Migratory Bird Sanctuary. 4,653 acres. This sanctuary is situated about 18 miles north of North Battleford and includes the entirety of Murray Lake. It is mainly used as a staging area for waterfowl in spring and fall, with more limited use by breeding waterfowl. Limited public access is allowed at landowner discretion. *Contact:* Canadian Wildlife Service, Protected Areas and Stewardship Unit, PO Box 280, Simpson, SK, Canada S0G 4M0 (306-836-2010).

Neely Lake Migratory Bird Sanctuary. 3,100 acres. This sanctuary is located 30 miles southwest of the town of Hudson Bay and consists of a shallow lake in bog and peatland habitat. It is used mainly for fall staging by Canada geese, but breeding ducks include mallard, blue-winged teal, canvasback, lesser scaup, bufflehead, and common goldeneye. Limited public access is allowed at landowner discretion. *Contact:* Canada Wildlife Service, Protected Areas and Stewardship Unit, PO Box 280, Simpson, SK, Canada S0G 4M0 (306-836-2010).

Old Wives Lake Migratory Bird Sanctuary. 102,635 acres (160 square miles). Old Wives Lake is a shallow saline lake less than 20 miles southwest of Moose Jaw. This lake, in conjunction with Reed Lake and Chaplin Lake, is considered a site of hemispheric importance in the Western Hemisphere Shorebird Reserve Network. The sanctuary is an important breeding, molting, and staging area that attracts large concentrations of ducks, Canada and snow geese, and tundra swans. An estimated 500,000 shorebirds use Old Wives Lake as a stopping point while on migration from their Central or South American wintering grounds to their Arctic breeding grounds. A considerable percentage of this site comprises mixed-grass prairie. Native prairies in the aspen parkland zone are typically dominated by fescues. These prairies are richer in plant species than are most mixed-grass prairies, but their avifaunas are very similar. Other parks in this same aspen transition zone include Duck Mountain Provincial Park (see earlier in Manitoba section) and Moose Mountain Provincial Park (see earlier), both of which are mostly wooded. Limited public access is allowed in the sanctuary at landowner discretion. *Contact:* Canadian Wildlife Service, Protected Areas and Stewardship Unit, PO Box 280, Simpson, SK, Canada S0G 4M0 (306-836-2010).

Opuntia Lake Migratory Bird Sanctuary. 5,567 acres. Opuntia Lake MBS is located 36 miles southwest of Biggar in southwestern Saskatchewan. It is a shallow, saline lake with rushes, sedges, and other aquatic vegetation that is heavily used by migrating waterfowl, hosting up to 20,000 geese, 30,000 ducks, 2,000 sandhill cranes, and 500 tundra swans. Limited public access is allowed at landowner discretion. *Contact:* Canadian Wildlife Service, Protected Areas and Stewardship Unit, PO Box 280, Simpson, SK, Canada S0G 4M0 (306-836-2010).

Prairie National Wildlife Area. This NWA is actually a scattered group of 28 wetland units that total 7,247 acres. The largest of these is Stalwart National Wildlife Area (see in separate section), and others range from 158 to 950 acres in area. Many are in the general vicinities of Saskatoon and Swift Current. These prairie wetlands are managed for waterfowl, with limited public access at landowner discretion. *Contact:* Canadian Wildlife Service, Protected Areas and Stewardship Unit, PO Box 280, Simpson, SK, Canada S0G 4M0 (306-836-2010).

Quill Lakes. 252,527 acres (395 square miles). The Quill Lakes are located immediately north of the town of Wynard in east-central Saskatchewan. During fall migration, the globally threatened whooping crane is regularly observed at this site. The Quill Lakes are also significant as a shorebird staging area, with a one-day peak count of 197,155 shorebirds recorded during the spring of 1993. During a 1989–92 study, several species were recorded in numbers that exceeded 1 percent of their total estimated world populations, including Hudsonian godwit, least sandpiper, Baird's sandpiper, American avocet, and the two dowitchers. Especially large numbers of white-rumped sandpipers and stilt sandpipers have been noted. The lakes also support an exceptional number of breeding piping plovers. The lakes are also known as an important waterfowl breeding and staging area, with hundreds of thousands of sandhill cranes, Canada geese, snow geese, and ducks using the area each fall. For information, contact Canadian Wildlife Service, Protected Areas and Stewardship Unit, PO Box 280, Simpson, SK, Canada S0G 4M0 (306-836-2010).

Redberry Lake Migratory Bird Sanctuary. 25,452 acres (40 square miles). This MBS is located six miles east of Hafford in central Saskatchewan. Redberry Lake is a medium-sized saltwater lake near Hafford and is notable in an area characterized by mostly freshwater aquatic environments. More than 188 species of birds have been reported here. The lake is an important spring and fall staging ground for ducks and other waterfowl. Its islands serve as the nesting grounds for several hundred American white pelicans, more than a thousand California and ring-billed gulls, black and common terns, great blue heron, black-crowned night heron, double-crested cormorant, and white-winged scoter. There is also breeding by piping plovers (20

pairs), and rare migrants include the area's regular use by whooping cranes. The site is classified as an Important Bird Area and a UNESCO Biosphere Reserve, with a small research center at the northern end of the lake. Limited public access is allowed at landowner discretion. For information, contact Canadian Wildlife Service, Protected Areas and Stewardship Unit, PO Box 280, Simpson, SK, Canada S0G 4M0 (306-836-2010).

Rowan's Ravine Provincial Park. 667 acres. Located 14 miles west of Bulyea, on the east side of Last Mountain Lake, this park consists of sand beaches, mixed-grass prairie, and marshes. No wildlife lists are available, but see the Last Mountain Lake account earlier. *Address:* Box 370, Strasbourg, SK, Canada S0G 4V0 (306-295-5200).

Saint-Denis National Wildlife Area. 890 acres. This NWA is located about 25 miles east of Saskatoon and consists of grasslands and prairie potholes, with bird populations similar to those of Stalwart NWA (see section). It is also important for graduate research activities on waterfowl for students at the nearby University of Saskatchewan. For information, contact Canadian Wildlife Service, Protected Areas and Stewardship Unit, PO Box 280, Simpson, SK, Canada S0G 4M0 (306-836-2010).

Saskatchewan Landing Provincial Park. 13,800 acres. Located in the South Saskatchewan River valley at the west end of Lake Diefenbaker, about 30 miles north of Swift Current on Hwy. 4. Located in a predominantly grassland region, the park includes hiking trails, historic sites, and an interpretive center. Although the park is a popular recreational area, there are many natural habitats in the nearly 14,000 acres for wildlife viewing. No bird or other species lists are yet available. *Address:* Box 419, Kyle, SK, Canada S0L 1T0 (306-375-5525).

Scent Grass Lake Migratory Bird Sanctuary. 2,505 acres. This MBS is located in the aspen parkland region, 15 miles northeast of North Battleford in west-central Saskatchewan. The lake is spring-fed and densely vegetated with aquatic and shoreline plants. It is used by both migrating birds (up to 20,000 ducks and 7,000 geese), and a wide variety of breeding marsh and waterbirds. These include sora, willet, marbled godwit, Wilson's phalarope, Franklin's gull, and yellow-headed blackbird. Limited public access is allowed at landowner discretion. For information, contact Canadian Wildlife Service, Protected Areas and Stewardship Unit, PO Box 280, Simpson, SK, Canada S0G 4M0 (306-836-2010).

St. Victor Petroglyphs Provincial Historic Park. 9 acres. Located one mile south of Victor (and about 25 miles southeast of Assiniboia), this park has more than 300 petroglyphs of unknown origin but probably made between 500 and 1700 AD that have been carved on the horizontal surface of a cliff. Guides are provided by the Friends of St. Victor Petroglyphs, Monarch Lodge Interpretive Center, Main St., Victor. *Address:* Saint Victor Petroglyphs, Box 1993, Assiniboia, SK, Canada S0H 0B0 (306-642-5386).

Stalwart National Wildlife Area. 3,090 acres. Located immediately east of Stalwart and west of Last Mountain Lake. Consists of grasslands and marshes managed for waterfowl breeding and as a staging area for migrant waterfowl. Breeders include redheads, canvasbacks, terns, rails, grebes, coots, and marshnesting songbirds. Limited public access is allowed at landowner discretion. For information, contact Canadian Wildlife Service, Protected Areas and Stewardship Unit, PO Box 280, Simpson, SK, Canada S0G 4M0 (306-836-2010).

Tway National Wildlife Area. 640 acres. This NWA is located at Tway Lake, at the headwaters of the Carrot River, between Prince Albert and the village of Tway. Consisting of wetlands surrounded by hayfields and aspen forests, it is an important waterfowl staging area and a breeding areas for Canada geese, ducks, coots, and grebes. Limited public access is allowed at landowner discretion. For information, contact Canadian Wildlife Service, Protected Areas and Stewardship Unit, PO Box 280, Simpson, SK, Canada S0G 4M0 (306-836-2010).

Upper Rousay Lake Migratory Bird Sanctuary. 900 acres. This MBS is located three miles southeast of Yorkton, in southeastern Saskatchewan. The lake is shallow and part of a much larger wetland complex that has been managed to provide breeding and molting habitat for waterfowl. Breeding birds include a variety of ducks, Canada geese, four species of grebes, sora, and marsh wren. Nine species of shorebirds are known or suspected breeders, along with American bittern, great blue heron, and black-crowned night-heron. Limited public access is allowed at landowner discretion. For information, contact Canadian Wildlife Service, Protected Areas and Stewardship Unit, PO Box 280, Simpson, SK, Canada S0G 4M0 (306-836-2010).

Val Marie Reservoir Migratory Bird Sanctuary. 1,065 acres. This MBS is located six miles northwest of Val Marie on the Frenchman River in southwestern Saskatchewan. It is a spring and fall staging area for migrant Canada geese and ducks, and several hundred pairs of Canada geese breed here. Other nesting species include double-crested cormorant, great blue heron, black-crowned night-heron, ring-billed and California gulls, and common tern. Limited public access is allowed at landowner discretion. For information, contact Canadian Wildlife Service, Protected Areas and Stewardship Unit, PO Box 280, Simpson, SK, Canada S0G 4M0 (306-836-2010).

Wascana Lake Migratory Bird Sanctuary. 300 acres. This urban MBS lies within a larger city park complex, the *Wascana Centre,* just west of University Park, Regina. More than 115 species of migrant birds have been reported here, and nesting waterfowl include Canada geese, mallards, northern pintails, and blue-winged teal.

Webb National Wildlife Area. 1,065 acres. This NWA is located about 16 miles west of Swift Current along the Trans-Canada Highway. It includes a *Prairie Wildlife Interpretive Center* that is also a wildlife rehabilitation facility (204-510-1855). The wetlands consist of a shallow saline lake, Goose Lake, plus backwater wetlands and seasonal streams. At least 115 bird species, 20 mammals, and 6 amphibians have been reported here. Limited public access is allowed. *Contact:* Canadian Wildlife Service, Protected Areas and Stewardship Unit, PO Box 280, Simpson, SK, Canada S0G 4M0 (306-836-2010).

III

The Northern Plains

North Dakota Nostalgia

Snow geese, like pasque flowers, have always been my personal symbol of spring. North Dakota winters are so long and dreary that as a teenager I literally began counting the days in March until the first snow geese arrived in the just-melting marshes near my hometown at the south end of the Red River valley. Hearing their wild, excited voices overhead was enough to make me forget everything else and plead with my father to let me borrow the family car long enough to experience the arrival of the incoming flocks. Then, standing knee deep in the near-freezing water of glacial-age marshes and hidden by head-high phragmites, I would exult in the sheer joy of the moment, imagining that I was alone with uncountable wild geese and headed with them for unknowable lands still much farther to the north. It was another twenty years before I finally traveled at last to the Canadian tundra to see the birds on their nesting grounds, and was able to feel that at least I had begun to understand some of their secrets.

The Nature of Nebraska: Ecology and Biodiversity (Johnsgard, 2001)

At some point between 10,000 and 15,000 years ago, the vast Wisconsin phase of the glacier sheet that covered much of what is now the Dakotas and eastern Nebraska ground to a halt and slowly began to melt. The leading edges of the glacier stalled out near what is now the eastern edge of the Missouri River valley. As they did, shearing stresses in the ice resulted in large amounts of sediment that had been transported south by the glacier being shifted about. During melting, these sediments, including rocks and boulders as large as small cars, were deposited haphazardly. The resulting hilly moraines associated with the static ("dead ice") glacier produced a region of small hills and intervening valleys extending from southern Alberta to northeastern Nebraska. Farther west, unglaciated parts of North and South Dakota eroded over time to form buttes, badlands, and gullies that are often rich in Cenozoic fossils.

The valleys in the hilly "coteau" region (French for "little hill") that formed south of the retreating glacial boundary filled with glacial meltwaters and subsequent seasonal precipitation, producing the thousands of prairie wetlands for which the region is famous. These shallow cattail- and rush-lined marshes, regionally known as "potholes" or "sloughs," now attract countless nesting waterfowl and other water-dependent birds, and constitute the so-called "duck factory" region of the northern Great Plains.

Over time, the meltwaters of central North American glaciers also produced many large lakes, of which glacial Lake Agassiz was much the largest. It formed during mid-Pleistocene times about 2.6 million years ago, in what is now Saskatchewan, Manitoba, Ontario, eastern North Dakota and western Minnesota. Up to 400 feet deep and occupying an area of up 110,000 square miles, or almost as large as Hudson Bay, Lake Agassiz lasted until less than 10,000 years ago. Then melting ice allowed it to gradually drain into the Mississippi River, Lake Superior, and, lastly, Hudson Bay. However, it has left several substantial remnants that have persisted to the present-day, such as lakes Winnipeg, Winnipegosis, Manitoba, and Lake of the Woods. Many large rivers developed along the glacier's boundaries as the ice melted and retreated northward, such as the Missouri and Mississippi Rivers. Other, now much smaller rivers also were born from the melting ice, such as North Dakota's James and Sheyenne Rivers. The Red River valley represents the vestiges of the ancient lakebed of southernmost Lake Agassiz, formed as the lake retreated northward. The current-day Red River is one of the few US rivers that flows almost directly north, now draining into Lake Winnipeg, whereas the James River, 100 miles to the west, flows almost directly south, into the Niobrara River and thence into the Missouri River.

The Sheyenne River now originates inconspicuously from local rainfall and snowmelt near the geographic center of North Dakota and, like a drunken cow, trudges erratically through the eastern half of the state. Along its route it passes slowly eastward through moraine-sculpted landscapes near Lakota in Nelson County, then confusingly turns southward, then eastward again, and finally northward, where it at last empties into the Red River north of Fargo.

During the period of glacial melting in North Dakota, about 12,000 years ago, the Sheyenne River drained into the western edge of Lake Agassiz, forming a broad, sandy delta (the glacial Sheyenne Delta). This is the largest of more than 30 such deltas that developed around Lake Agassiz and comprises about 450,000 acres in southeastern North Dakota. The sandy delta extends over much of northern Richland County and eastern Ransom County, and is now largely preserved as the Sheyenne National Grassland. Although Lake Agassiz was once the largest glacial lake in North America, it existed in North Dakota only from about 11,790 to 9,000 years ago.

Sheyenne National Grassland is America's largest federally owned region of tallgrass prairie, at about 71,000 acres, and includes most the 127,000 acres of native habitats that still survive on the delta, such as wet meadows, wetland fens, sand dunes, and ancient beaches. More than 800 species of plants and wildlife have been documented here, including one of the world's largest known populations of the western prairie fringed orchid (*Plantanthera praeclara*). It is also one of only two remaining locations in North Dakota where greater prairie-chickens still survive (Johnsgard, 2002, *Grassland Grouse*).

The fertile land that my maternal grandparents acquired in the 1880s and were farming when I was a child lies within this beautiful region. There I first saw and learned to identify many native prairie plants, and

came to love such grassland birds as the marbled godwit, upland sandpiper, and bobolink. About a decade later, while attending high school at Wahpeton, North Dakota, hunting for places to photograph waterfowl, I serendipitously encountered an equally wonderful paradise of prairie wetlands. It is located about 30 miles south of Wahpeton, near Rosholt, South Dakota, and along the northern edge of Lake Traverse, another wonderful glacial relict.

Lake Traverse and its associated marshy wetlands are probably fragmentary remnants of glacial Lake Agassiz, which formed with glacial meltwaters and initially flowed southward. However, with further melting, Canadian lands to the north became ice-free. Thereby, an alternative route became available for meltwaters to flow north into Canada, and eventually into Hudson Bay. Lake Traverse and its nearby wetlands remain behind today as tiny souvenirs of these momentous changes in North America's climatic and geographic history.

The small present-day Bois des Sioux ("Woods of the Sioux") River originates by receiving overflow water from the Lake Traverse basin. It then flows north to join the Ottertail River at Wahpeton, and their combined flow, now called the Red River, forms the boundary between North Dakota and Minnesota. The Red River continues northward into Manitoba and eventually into Lake Winnipeg. The northern outlet of Lake Winnipeg in turn drains into the Nelson River, which finally empties into Hudson Bay. Contrarily, south of the shallow Lake Traverse basin, water drains southward through Big Stone Lake into the Minnesota River, and these waters eventually reach the Gulf of Mexico via the Mississippi River.

The Lake Traverse region thus inconspicuously but importantly divides the Great Plains into two widely separated continental drainage destinations, the Gulf of Mexico (via the Minnesota and Mississippi Rivers) and Hudson Bay (via the Bois des Sioux, Red, and Nelson Rivers). It also marks the approximate halfway point for tens of millions of waterfowl and shorebirds that winter along the Gulf Coast and breed in the Canadian Arctic.

In that marvelous wetland environment, I gradually learned to identify the common marshland birds. I also tried ineffectually to photograph them, using an ancient German prototype version of the modern single-lens reflex camera (a 1939 Kine Exacta), which I bought at a secondhand store, along with an equally ancient

180 mm f/6.3 telephoto lens that had obviously already undergone hard use.

During the all-too-brief North Dakota April migration periods of my high school years, I joyfully waded through these wetlands. Often gigantic flocks of snow and Canada geese passed directly overhead, sometimes flying only a few yards above the bed of cattails and rushes among which I would hide. While wading in these icy waters I sometimes also flushed great blue herons, great egrets, black-crowned night-herons, and American bitterns that had been hidden by the dense emergent vegetation.

Of all the marsh birds I encountered there, none was more entrancing than the western grebe. I saw it only infrequently, as it was as elusive as Sir Walter Scott's Lady of the Lake, and seemed the very essence of grace. I called it the "swan grebe," for it has an impossibly long and gracefully curved neck, as well as a bicolored black-and-white head pattern, a rapier-like yellow beak, and flaming crimson eyes.

Although I was never able to photograph western grebes during my high school years, I sometimes saw two adults swimming side by side, performing synchronized preening and bowing displays to one another. Both birds would frequently utter soft calls that have been perfectly described as sounding like the tinkling of silver bells. At times two of the grebes would also madly rush over the water for 20 or 30 yards, churning the water behind them, and end this amazing display with simultaneous dives.

It wasn't until almost a half-century later that I first successfully photographed, and later held, a live western grebe. On a spring visit to Nebraska's Crescent Lake National Wildlife Refuge in the 1970s I once noticed an adult western grebe beached on the shore of a large alkaline marsh. Grebes never willingly venture onto dry land, as their legs are positioned so far back that the birds are virtually helpless out of water. When I picked up the grebe, I saw that one of its legs had been recently and cleanly amputated, almost certainly by a snapping turtle. As a result, the bird was doomed and likely to starve, or to be killed by another predator. Yet, in looking into its laser-red eyes I was unable to bring myself to mercifully end this marvelous creature's life. With tears in my eyes, I carefully placed it back where I had found it, and walked quickly to my car without looking back.

In the spring of 2014 I received a letter from Deb Hanson, a resident of Grand Forks, North Dakota. She described herself as an avid bird photographer and, from her reading, had learned of my love for North Dakota and its wetland birds. She told me that northeastern North Dakota had been receiving record-breaking rainfall over the two previous decades, and the region's countless wetlands were overflowing. She told me that her favorite birding area was about 70 miles west of Grand Forks near the town of Lakota in Nelson County, and urged me to visit it.

Although I couldn't arrange to get to North Dakota in 2014, during the following spring I asked her if water and bird conditions were still comparable. She affirmed that hope and said that she had at times seen as many as 83 bird species during a single spring day, including 5 species of grebes and almost uncountable numbers of shorebirds and waterfowl. I soon convinced a friend we should travel to North Dakota for a week of birding in late May. Driving north, we endured two days of cold rain, and occasional snow or ice pellets with high winds, but took hope in the stoic and confident opinion of local Dakotans that things could only improve.

At last we arrived at Lakota, a town of about 800 residents and the only town with a motel in the general area. We devised a rectangular auto survey route, using Lakota at its southeastern corner, driving north eight miles, east for five miles, then back south and west to Lakota, the entire route totaling 26 miles. The several days of freezing weather that occurred just before we arrived had forced swallows and other aerial insect-eaters such as kingbirds into near-starving conditions. We saw many barn swallows, western kingbirds, and Swainson's thrushes, as well as upland sandpipers, willets, and marbled godwits, foraging on the county roads in search of dead or moribund insects. As the weather improved, flying swallows and black terns became more evident, as did flying insects.

During three days of mostly car-window birding we saw more than 70 species, including 11 species of waterfowl and 22 species of shorebirds, gulls, and wading birds. On our last morning we did an hour-long, car-window survey at 25 miles per hour, counting both wetlands and bird "encounters." Each encounter represented a sighting of a single bird, or a cluster of birds of the same species.

In descending relative abundance, our summed bird encounters along the survey route were: eared grebe, American coot, western grebe, mallard, blue-winged teal, Canada goose, gadwall, lesser scaup, double-crested cormorant, Forster's tern, Franklin's gull, black-crowned night-heron, redhead, and (with single encounters each) pied-billed grebe, American white pelican, northern pintail, ruddy duck, American bittern, white-faced ibis, and black tern.

As we were nearing the last wetland on our last bird survey route, we happened to see a male bittern only about 20 yards away, standing in clear view at the water's edge and uttering his strange low-pitched "thunder-pump" call. Unlike the other American herons, which are monogamous, the little-studied American bittern is evidently at least occasionally polygamous, with several females sometimes nesting within a male's large territory. Males of the European bittern have been reported to have as many as five mates. Most polygamous bird species are easily identified sexually their distinctive colors or plumage pattern, but bitterns lack any such features that identify their sex. Instead of making themselves as visible as possible, displaying male bitterns usually remain well-hidden in marsh vegetation. Their distinctive low-pitched courtship/territorial call, sounding like the groaning of an old hand-operated water pump, is seemingly achieved by the male calling while inflating his esophagus, resulting in a low-frequency but far-carrying vocalization.

In addition to his repeated calling, the male we watched would periodically make his otherwise fully camouflaged presence known by unexpectedly exposing a pair of fan-shaped clusters of immaculate white plumes emerging vertically from just in front of its folded wings, resembling two airy "angel wings" waving in the wind above the bird's shoulders. This astonishing behavior had never been illustrated in the ornithological literature until I made some drawings of it, from observations and photos I made in Grand Teton National Park during the 1970s (Johnsgard, 1970; 2016b, "Bittern Surprise"). Similar behavior has been described for the European bittern species.

On both of the occasions when I have observed this amazing behavior a female was visible and standing within about 30 to 40 yards of the male. On the earlier occasion that I witnessed, the male's displays soon resulted in a mating. We thus waited and watched the North Dakota pair in anticipation for about 20 minutes, when the pair flushed and flew out of sight into the marsh, leaving its outcome a secret.

A week is far too short a time to visit all the magnificent grassland and wetland habitats of North Dakota. With nearly 80 national wildlife refuges and nine wetland management districts, North Dakota leads the nation in the total number of nationally preserved wetlands. The nine North Dakota wetland management districts total more than a million acres and include more than 1,000 waterfowl production areas and 37 wildlife development areas. There are also tens of thousands of conservation easements in the state.

Sadly, several of the wildlife refuges we visited in North Dakota showed signs of neglect and had reduced or no staffing, the result of federal budget cutting. Unfortunately, the current (2017) federal administration would rather invest in incredibly expensive and quickly outmoded weapons rather than protect our most treasured resources, and would reduce or even eliminate federal land holdings such as national monuments, rather than making long-term investments in infrastructure and careful management of these priceless lands.

The Sites: Badlands, Bluestem, and Bobolinks

MINNESOTA

Minnesota (MN) is blessed with one national park, one national monument, one national forest, and 13 national wildlife refuges; federally owned acreage in Minnesota comprises 6.8 percent of the state's total land area. There are also 1,440 public wildlife areas, 67 state parks, 59 state forests, and 9 state recreation areas, totaling 1.29 million acres of public-access lands. Having grown up a stone's throw from Minnesota, namely just across the Red River, I love that state with an intensity equal to my affection for North Dakota. During my early teenage years, I spent a few weeks every summer at my parents' lake cottage near Pelican Rapids, which greatly shaped my life's hopes and goals.

It was in the lake country of central Minnesota where I wandered through the maple-basswood woods behind our cottage, searching for birds as well as trilliums, wild orchids, and other plants to add to my wildflower garden. I sometimes heard pileated woodpeckers, or found their tree excavations, but was never able to see one. I also once found a wood duck nesting in a tree cavity and saw a few nests of common loons and red-necked grebes while paddling in secluded bays of our lake. Lacking binoculars, I carried with me a huge 1840s-era telescope that my maternal great-grandfather had "liberated" while participating in General Sherman's famous march through Georgia and that had been handed down for generations through my mother's family. Given a choice of receiving his Civil War rifle, his officer's sword, or the antique telescope when these items were divided up between me and my two brothers, I happily chose the telescope. Even though its front lens was cracked, and its magnifying power was only about three times my naked-eye view, it served me well in my pre-binocular teenage years. Now, some 70 years after my first birdwatching, and in view of the ever-increasing number of naturalists and birders, Minnesota has established a *Pine to Prairie Birding Trail*. This collection of highways links 45 birding sites along a 223-mile route from Warroad, near the Manitoba border, south to Fergus Falls, and includes diverse habitats that support more than 250 bird species. It extends from northern areas with many boreal species, through the deciduous woods of north-central Minnesota, to remnant prairies and prairie wetlands of western Minnesota, including some sites only a few miles from our cabin. Important Bird Areas (IBAs) that have been named within this region include Kittson/Roseau Aspen Parkland, Lake of the Woods, Agassiz National Wildlife Refuge, Felton Prairie Composite, Bluestem Prairie/Buffalo River Composite, and Hamden Slough National Wildlife Refuge. See www.mnbird-trail.com. A PDF version of the trail can be downloaded free at https://www.gov.mb.ca/watchablewildlife/pdf/minnesota_pine_prairie_trail.pdf. Recently, this Minnesota trail has been extended into Canada as Manitoba's *Pine to Prairie International Birding Trail* (see the Manitoba section).

Agassiz National Wildlife Refuge. 61,500 acres. Situated 11 miles east of Holt in Marshall County, Minnesota, this area, once a part of glacial Lake Agassiz, contains grasslands with hardwood groves, potholes, and lakes at the eastern transition zone between tallgrass prairie and northern forest. Moose and wolves are occasional. At least 86 bird species are common to abundant during spring versus 69 species during fall and just 8 during winter (Jones, 1990). There are at least 132 nesting birds among the 248 listed for the refuge by Jones, including 17 nesting waterfowl. They also include Franklin's gull (North America's largest population), black tern, and five species of grebes. A total of 18 bird species were reported present year-round by Jones, so an estimated minimum of 93 percent of the refuge's total bird diversity is migratory. The refuge is considered to be one of the 100 best birding sites in North America and is identified as a globally Important Bird Area. A recent checklist of 294 species reported on the refuge is available from the refuge manager at 22996 290th St., Middle River, MN 56737 (218-449-4115). It is also available online at https://www.fws.gov/uploadedFiles/Agassiz%20Bird%20List%202008(1).pdf.

Bell Museum of Natural History. This museum, long a landmark on the University of Minnesota's Minneapolis campus, is moving into a new 80-million-dollar building on the St. Paul campus. It opens the summer of 2018. The museum has more than 4 million specimens, is famous for its wildlife dioramas, and will have a new planetarium. *Address:* 2088 Larpenteur Ave. W, Falcon Heights, MN 55108.

Big Stone National Wildlife Refuge. 10,000 acres. Located on the Minnesota River near the South Dakota border, with over 1,700 aces of native prairie. There is a 5.2-mile auto tour road through the refuge. At least 101 bird species are common to abundant during spring versus 89 species during fall and 15 during winter (Jones, 1990). The area is an important stopover for migrant warblers in spring. There are at least 107 nesting birds among the 237 listed for the refuge by Jones. A total of 57 bird species were reported present year-round by Jones, so an estimated minimum of 76 percent of the refuge's total bird diversity is migratory. Spring and summer dryland birds include northern harrier, marbled godwit, grasshopper sparrow, dickcissel, and bobolink. Wetland species include western grebe, black tern, sedge and marsh wrens, and yellow-headed blackbird. A recent checklist of 240 species reported on the refuge is available from the refuge manager at 25 NW 2nd St., Ortonville, MN 56278 (512-839-3700).

Buffalo River State Park. 1,300 acres. Adjacent to *Bluestem Prairie Scientific and Natural Area*, a Nature Conservancy prairie area, this state park and the SNA together cover more than 4,600 acres. They are located 15 miles east of Moorhead off Hwy. 10. These native tallgrass prairie areas are rich in prairie species, such as greater prairie-chicken, upland sandpiper,

Shortgrass songbirds, including adult male (A) and female (B) lark bunting, and males of (C) McCown's and (D) chestnut-collared longspurs.

marbled godwit, loggerhead shrike, chestnut-collared longspur, and grasshopper and LeConte's sparrows. The Bluestem SNA is known to have more than 300 plant species and over 70 bird species. *State park contact:* Regional Manager, DNR Ecological Services, 2115 Birchmont Beach Rd. NE, Bemidji, MN 56601 (218-755-3634). *SNA contact:* The Nature Conservancy, 15337

28th Ave. S, Glyndon, MN 56547 (218-498-2679). www.dnr.state.mn.us/snas/sna00996 or www.nature.org (search "Bluestem Prairie")

Felton Prairie Wildlife Management Area and **Felton Prairie Scientific and Natural Area.** 2,117 acres. Located about 30 miles northeast of Moorhead in

Clay County, near Felton, and part of the Lake Agassiz beach-ridge prairie complex. From Felton drive south two miles on Hwy. 9 and east three miles on RCR 108. This splendid Nature Conservancy tract (the SNA) of tallgrass prairie hosts at least 151 species of prairie birds, such as greater prairie-chicken, northern harrier, upland sandpiper, marbled godwit, loggerhead shrike, chestnut-collared longspur, LeConte's sparrow, and bobolink. *WMA address:* MN Hwy. 9 and CR 34, Felton, MN 56536 (218-449-4115).

Fergus Falls Wetland Management District. This federal multicounty WMD is located at the edge of the Red River valley and along the shoreline area of glacial Lake Agassiz. It includes Douglas, Grant, Otter Tail, Wadena, and Wilkin Counties. The Prairie Wetlands Learning Center, part of the WMD, is located at 602 State Hwy. 210E, Fergus Falls, MN 56537 (218-998-4480). A recent checklist of 290 species reported at this WMD is available from the district manager, Rte. 1, Box 76, Fergus Falls, MN 56537. It is also available online at https://www.fws.gov/uploadedFiles/FFWBirdView.pdf.

Glacial Ridge National Wildlife Refuge. 27,400 acres. Located north of Thief River Falls along Hwy. 32, this recently established refuge includes land obtained by the Nature Conservancy (TNC) and the US Fish and Wildlife Service. In Minnesota, less than one-tenth of 1 percent of the state's original tallgrass prairie remains; this refuge represents the nation's single largest restoration project for tallgrass prairie. Glacial Ridge NWR supports many grassland birds, such as the sandhill crane, greater prairie-chicken, marbled godwit, Nelson's sparrow, and bobolink. The nearby Nature Conservancy *Pankratz Memorial Prairie* is about six miles east of Crookston and includes two units, one of 468 acres and the other of 452 acres. It has more than 100 recorded bird species. A similar mesic prairie, the 376-acre *Burnham Creek Wildlife Management Area*, is three miles northeast of Melville and immediately west of Glacial Ridge NWR. Another 840-acre tallgrass prairie, *Tympanuchus Wildlife Management Area*, is located three miles east of Harold on County Rd. 45 and has about 200 reported wildlife species. The WMA office is at 304 S. Main St., Crookston, MN 56716 (218-281-6063). For general TNC information, contact the Nature Conservancy, Glacial Ridge Project, 31077 MN Hwy. 32S, Mentor, MN 56736 (218-637-2146) and search at www.nature.org.

Hamden Slough National Wildlife Refuge. 3,200 acres. Located about 20 miles northeast of Detroit Lakes, this is a prairie wetland in the prairie-hardwood transition zone. Summer birds include sedge and marsh wrens; Nelson's, Henslow's; and LeConte's sparrows; dickcissel; bobolink; and yellow-headed blackbird. A bird checklist is available. *Contact:* Detroit Lakes Wetland Management District, 26624 N. Tower Rd., Detroit Lakes, MN 56501 (218-847-4431). https://www.fws.gov/refuge/hamden_slough/

Heron Lake Wetlands. These famous wetlands are located on North Heron Lake and South Heron Lake, between the towns of Heron Lake and Lakeland. They are what remains of one of the largest prairie wetlands in North America, which once covered 8,000 acres. There is a now a state-owned wildlife management area of 150 acres, a Lindgren-Traeger-Bird Sanctuary (The Nature Conservancy) area of 91 acres, and an R. and J. Traeger (TNC) Preserve of 237 acres. In addition to attracting great numbers of migrating waterfowl, these wetlands are a breeding area for the western grebe, Forster's and black terns, Canada goose, American white pelican, and double-crested cormorant. Franklin's gulls once had an enormous nesting colony here until fluctuating water levels destroyed the vegetation base needed for their floating nests. The lakes and marshes still attract great blue herons, black-crowned night herons, American and least bitterns, American avocets, marsh wrens, yellow-headed blackbirds, spotted sandpipers, and ospreys. Limited walk-in access is permitted. For information, contact the Minnesota Department of Natural Resources, Wildlife Area Office, Windom, MN 56101 (507-831-2917).

Lac Qui Parle Wildlife Management Area/State Park. 31,238 acres. Located between Appleton and Montevideo on the Minnesota River, this WMA is a major stopping point for Canada geese (up to 150,000), tundra swans, snow geese, and other migrating waterfowl. It is also a nesting area for American white pelicans (up to 30,000 birds), double-crested cormorants, ring-billed gulls, American bald eagles, and many prairie birds. Adjacent to the WMA and two miles northwest of Big Stone NWR is *Plover Prairie*, an 894-acre Nature Conservancy property with nesting upland sandpipers and marbled godwits. Nearby, on the South Dakota border south of Marietta, is *Salt Lake Wildlife Management Area*. This area is the largest saline wetland in Minnesota and a magnet for shore-birds such as American avocets, which sometimes nest. More than 140 bird species have been identified here, including 25 species of warblers. Lac Qui Parle State Park contains 1,057 acres and includes Lac Qui Parle Lake, Minnesota River floodplain, and prairie hillsides. For information, contact Minnesota Department of Natural Resources, Wildlife Area Office, Lac Qui Parle WMA, RR 1 Box 23, Watson, MN 56295 (320-734-4451).

Morris Wetland Management District. This WMD includes 244 waterfowl production areas encompassing about 53,000 acres (77 square miles) scattered throughout an eight-county area, including Big Stone, Chippewa, Lac Qui Parle, Pope, Stevens, Swift, Traverse, and Yellow Medicine Counties. A recent checklist indicates 282 bird species have been reported in this multicounty wetland district. The list is available from the district manager at 43875 230th St., Morris, MN 56267. It is also available online at https://www.fws.gov/uploadedFiles/Bird%20List%20Apr2012.pdf.

Pipestone National Monument. 282 acres, including 260 acres of restored prairie. This famous historic site was the source of pipestone (catlinite) for Plains Native Americans. Pipestone formed from clay exposed to heat and pressure over geologic time. The resulting blood-red stone had great symbolic significance to many tribes and was highly prized. There is also an interpretive center and nature trail at the monument, just at the northern edge of the town of Pipestone. Birds of the area include some prairie-dependent species such as the northern harrier, short-eared owl, upland sandpiper, Savannah sparrow, grasshopper sparrow, and bobolink. Nearby, the 60-acre *Blue Mounds State Park* (four miles north of Laverne, MN) also has some excellent prairie, a nature trail, and an interpretive center. *Address of Pipestone NM:* 36 Reservation Ave., Pipestone, MN 56164 (507-825-5464). *Address of Blue Mounds State Park:* 1410 161st St., Luverne, MN 56156 (507-283-6050). https://www.nps.gov/pipe/index.htm

Roseau River Wildlife Management Area. 62,025 acres. Located 20 miles northwest of Roseau, this is one of Minnesota's most important waterfowl migration and breeding areas. Known breeding species number 149, and the area is an important stopover

for Arctic-breeding sandhill cranes, tundra swans, and shorebirds. A 27-mile wildlife drive winds through the area. This area and the *Lost River State Forest* to the east along the Ontario border supports such boreal species as great gray owls, black-backed woodpeckers, gray jays, and boreal chickadees. *Contact:* Minnesota Department of Natural Resources, Wildlife Area Office, HCT 5 Box 103, Roseau MN 56751 (218-463-1557).

Rydell National Wildlife Refuge. 2,200 acres. This refuge, west of Erskine, has a mixture of marshes, bogs, and deciduous woodlands. It supports nesting trumpeter swans, grassland sparrows, and deciduous forest songbirds. A bird list is available. *Address:* Rydell and Glacial Ridge NWR, 17788 349th St. SE, Erskine, MN 56535 (800-841-0172). https://www.fws.gov/refuge/rydell/

Talcot Lake Wildlife Management Area. 4,000 acres. Located between Westbrock and Dundee. This lake and marshy wetland on the Des Moines River attracts large flocks of waterfowl, especially Canada geese of the eastern prairie flock, during fall migration. The area is one of the largest protected wildlife areas in southwestern Minnesota and a magnet for marsh and prairie birds. *Contact:* Minnesota Department of Natural Resources, Wildlife Area Office, Talcot Lake WMA, RR 3 Box 534, Dundee, MN 56131 (507-468-2248).

Tamarac National Wildlife Refuge. 43,000 acres. Located about 15 miles northeast of Detroit Lakes off Hwy. 34, this refuge has a mixture of tallgrass prairie, bogs, hardwood forests, and pine forest. Breeding birds include the trumpeter swan, common loon, American bald eagle, red-shouldered and broad-winged hawks, peregrine falcon, ruffed grouse, American woodcock, and golden-winged warbler. *Contact:* Tamarac NWR, 35704 Co. Hwy. 26, Rochert, MN 56578 (218-847-2641). https://www.fws.gov/refuge/tamarac/

MONTANA

Of all the Great Plain states, Montana (MT) probably has the largest amount of land still covered with mixed and shortgrass prairies. The state has about 8 million acres managed by the Bureau of Land Management and 1.2 million acres in national park and national monument lands. There are also 2 national parks, 2 national forests, 17 national wildlife refuges, 4 wetland management districts, and a national bison range. There are eight Indian reservations in Montana, most of which are still vegetated with native grasslands and occupy more than 4 million acres. Additionally, there are 17.2 million acres in national forest lands, the largest number of acres of any state, an unknown percentage of which contain grasslands and meadows. Federally owned acreage in Montana composes 29.92 percent of the state's total land area, ranking it fourth from the highest percentage among all the states covered in this book. In addition to 52 state parks, Montana also has eight state forests (250,000 acres) and hundreds of state trust lands. Trust land typically includes sections 16 and 36 of every township, with some exceptions, and is open to general recreational use with appropriate recreational use licenses (see http://dnrc.mt.gov/index/divisions/trust/recreational-use-of-state-land).

American Prairie Reserve. About 123,000 acres. This prairie reserve is a World Wildlife Fund project in northeastern Montana. Plans are to eventually expand to 3 million contiguous acres of grasslands and then to connect with the Charles M. Russell National Wildlife Refuge (see section). The reserve stretches for 125 miles along the upper Missouri River and contains shortgrass prairie, wooded coulees, river-bottom woods, and badlands. The mammals include reintroduced bison, elk, pronghorn, mule deer, and probably all other typical shortgrass wildlife, although no species lists are yet available. *Address:* American Prairie Reserve, 7 E. Beall St., Suite 100, Bozeman, MT 59715 (PO Box 908, 59771) (877-273-1123).

Benton Lake National Wildlife Refuge. 12,383 acres. This marsh-and-wetland federal refuge is situated 14 miles north of Great Falls. Go north from Great Falls on US Hwy. 87 and turn left on State Hwy. 225 to reach the refuge entrance. At least 33 bird species are common to abundant during spring versus 35 species during fall (Jones, 1990). There are at least 59 nesting birds among the 167 listed for the refuge by Jones. A total of 10 bird species were reported present year-round by Jones, so an estimated minimum of 94 percent of the refuge's total bird diversity is migratory. Some of the major migrants are snow goose, tundra swan, northern pintail, American wigeon, and many shorebirds. Nesting shorebirds include upland sandpiper, marbled godwit, and willet. The refuge has been recognized as an internationally significant shorebird site by the Western Hemisphere Shorebird Reserve Network. A recent checklist of 199 bird species is available from the refuge manager, 922 Bootlegger Rd., Great Falls, MT 59404 (406-727-7400). It is also available online at https://www.fws.gov/uploadedFiles/BNL_Wildlife-List_PDF(1).pdf.

Bowdoin National Wildlife Refuge. 15,337 acres. This refuge is located seven miles east of Malta. At least 98 bird species are common to abundant during spring versus 87 species during fall, and 10 during winter (Jones, 1990). There are at least 102 nesting birds among the 266 listed for the refuge by Jones. A total of 9 bird species were reported present year-round by Jones, so an estimated minimum of 97 percent of the refuge's total bird diversity is migratory. A recent checklist of 248 bird species is available from the refuge manager, PO Box J, Malta, MT 59538 (406-654-2863). It is also available online at https://www.fws.gov/uploadedFiles/Bowdoin_bird_List.pdf.

Canyon Ferry Reservoir and Wildlife Management Area. 3,500 acres. This wildlife management area and Bureau of Reclamation recreation area surrounds Canyon Ferry Reservoir (33,500 acres) at the base of the Rocky Mountains about 21 miles east of Helena on US Hwy. 12-287. No specific species lists are available. *Address of recreation area:* Bureau of Reclamation, Canyon Ferry Reservoir, 7700 Canyon Ferry Rd., Helena, MT 59602 (406-475-3310).

Charles M. Russell National Wildlife Refuge. 1,094,301 acres. This vast shortgrass prairie-and-badlands federal refuge is the third largest in the United States. It occupies both sides of Fort Peck Reservoir over a distance of 125 miles. The refuge has a bird checklist of 252 species and a mammal list of over 40 species. Typical Great Plains species include the golden eagle, greater sage-grouse, long-billed curlew, American avocet, willet, common poor-will, and black-billed magpie. Large mammals include pronghorns, mule deer, white-tailed deer, elk, and bighorn sheep. Smaller mammals that are present include the black-tailed prairie dog, bushy-tailed woodrat, and white-tailed jackrabbit. There were an approximate

4,500 acres of prairie dog towns in 2000, providing potential food for the critically endangered black-footed ferrets, which have been released here in a restoration effort. One major access route to the western part of the refuge is available by traveling northeast from Lewiston for 67 miles via US Hwy. 191. Interior refuge roads are unimproved and often impassable for most vehicles. Camping is permitted. Along the mouth of the Musselshell River is the UL Bend National Wildlife Refuge (see section), which is continuous with the C. M. Russell NWR and is administered by it. *Address of refuge complex:* PO Box 110, Airport Rd., Lewistown, MT 59457 (406-538-7521).

First Peoples Buffalo Jump State Park. 1,500 acres. This state park (including the previously named Ulm Piskun State Park) has a mile-long "piskun," a place where bison were stampeded into confined corrals or forced to jump from steep cliffs. This is probably the largest reported such site in the United States and has a 30-foot cliff face. A captive bison herd is present on this shortgrass habitat. The location is about five miles west of the Great Falls airport (Ulm exit of I-15). *Address:* 342 Ulm Vaughn Rd., Ulm, MT 59485.

Fort Belknap Indian Reservation. 650,000 acres. This reservation in north-central Montana is home to two

Adult black-footed ferret.

tribes, the Gros Ventre (A'aninin) and Assiniboine (Nakoda). The reservation population in 2010 was about 4,000 members. Bison were introduced onto the reservation land in 2013 and numbered about 300 head in 2017. Black-footed ferrets were introduced in 1991 but eventually died out. In 2013 and 2014 more than 50 ferrets were again introduced, the success of which is uncertain as of 2017. *Address:* 656 Agency Main St., Harlem, MT 59526 (406-353-2205).

Fort Peck Indian Reservation. About 2,000,000 acres. This enormous reservation was established in 1888 and is home to the Lower Assiniboine and some Sioux (Yanktonai, Oglala, and Hunkpapa) tribes. The reservation was named for a trading post that is now flooded by Fort Peck Reservoir. Several annual powwows are open to the public. Bison from Yellowstone National Park have recently been released to establish a reservation herd. *Address:* Fort Peck Assiniboine and Sioux Tribes, 501 Medicine Bear Rd., PO Box 1027, Poplar, MT 59255 (406-768-2300).

Freezout Lake Wildlife Management Area. 11,350 acres. Freezout Lake WMA is located ten miles southeast of Choteau. This area is mainly of interest for its great spring concentrations of migrating waterfowl, which peak in late March when up to 300,000 snow and Ross's geese from wintering grounds in California and the southern Great Plains stage prior to leaving for breeding grounds in the northwestern corner of Canada's Northwest Territories. There are also up to 12,000 tundra swans, and many migrating ducks, at times totaling a million waterfowl. The area is hunted during fall, so the numbers are less impressive then, but tundra swans move through in good numbers during late October and early November. For information, contact Montana Fish, Wildlife and Parks, PO Box 488, Fairfield, MT 58426 (406-467-2646).

Giant Springs Heritage State Park. 216 acres. This is a state park located in Great Falls, with one of the largest freshwater springs in the world. Nearby is Sulfur Springs, whose mineral-rich waters reputedly saved Sacagawea from a life-threatening illness. The Giant Springs were discovered by William Clark on June 18, 1805, and represent the downstream end of the portage around Great Falls, historically a series of five separate falls and intervening rapids, representing a collective vertical height of nearly 200 feet. At the upper

end of the falls were several islands named the White Bear Islands by Lewis and Clark because of the numerous grizzly bears they found there. Also located at the state park is the *Lewis and Clark National Historic Trail Interpretive Center*, operated by the US Forest Service and home to the *Lewis and Clark Trail Heritage Foundation*. *Address of state park:* 4803 Giant Springs Rd., Great Falls, MT 59405 (406-727-1212).

James Kipp Recreation Area. This undeveloped recreation area is located off US Hwy. 191 near the western end of C. M. Russell National Wildlife Refuge (see section) and at the east end of the federally designated Upper Missouri National Wild and Scenic River segment (see section). It also provides an access point for the *Missouri Breaks National Back Country Byway*. The name is for an early Indian Affairs agent who was a great friend of the northern tribes. Campsites are provided. *Address:* Bureau of Land Management, PO Box 1389, Fort Benton, MT 59442 (406-622-4000).

Little Bighorn Battlefield National Monument. 770 acres. This famous battlefield near Crow Agency, Montana, has been preserved in a way that closely resembles its appearance at the time of Gen. George Custer's final battle, except for markers showing where many of the cavalry men fell and were temporarily buried. There is an associated small memorial for the Native Americans, a military cemetery, and a visitor center that recounts the battle. *Address:* PO Box 39, Crow Agency, MT 59022-0039 (406-638-2621), www.nps.gov/libi/.

Medicine Lake National Wildlife Refuge. 31,457 acres. This wildlife refuge is located one mile south of Medicine Lake. At least 69 species are common to abundant during spring versus 56 species during fall and 6 during winter (Jones, 1990). There are at least 96 nesting birds among the 219 listed for the refuge by Jones. A total of 15 bird species were reported present year-round by Jones, so an estimated minimum of 93 percent of the refuge's total bird diversity is migratory. Migrants that regularly visit the refuge are sandhill and whooping cranes, tundra swan, and many other waterfowl and shorebirds. The areas around the refuge lakes are a mixture of tallgrass and short-grass prairies, with associated birds. A recent checklist of 228 species is available from the refuge manager, HC 51, Box 2, Medicine Lake, MT 59247 (406-799-2305). It is also available online at https://www.fws.gov/upload-edFiles/BirdList(4).pdf.

Missouri Headwaters State Park. 527 acres. Located at Three Forks, this state park is located at the confluence of the Gallatin, Madison, and Jefferson Rivers. The site was first described by Lewis and Clark as representing the primary origin of the Missouri River, although the actual snowmelt headwaters derive from many small sources high in the mountains. The state park has interpretive exhibits with information on Lewis and Clark. Camping is permitted. *Address:* 1585 Trident Rd., Three Forks, MT 59752 (406-285-3610).

Museum of the Rockies. Associated with Montana State University in Bozeman, this museum is most famous for its paleontological collections, which contain the largest assemblage of dinosaur remains in the United States, including the largest *Tyrannosaurus* skull ever found, and a total of 13 *T. rex* specimens. *Address:* 600 W. Kagy Blvd., Bozeman, MT 59717 (406-994-2251).

Pompeys Pillar National Monument. 51 acres. Located near the Yellowstone River, Pompeys Pillar is 28 miles east of Billings, off Exit 23 on I-94. This 200-foot sandstone promontory was named "Pompy's Tower" by Captain Clark after Sacagawea's son, Jean Baptiste ("Pompy") Charbonneau, who was then about eight months old. Clark's dated, carved signature is still visible in the soft rock. Nearby is the Pompeys Pillar Visitor Center. *Address:* Bureau of Land Management, 5001 Southgate Dr., Billings, MT 59101 (406-647-2540).

UL Bend National Wildlife Refuge. 50,048 acres. This refuge (named for the river's meandering course there) is continuous with the C. M. Russell NWR (see section) and is administered by it. The UL Bend NWR is even more remote than the C. M. Russell refuge. Here are at least 98 nesting bird species among the 252 that Jones (1990) listed for the refuge. A total of 35 bird species were reported present year-round, so an estimated minimum of 86 percent of the refuge's total bird diversity is migratory. A recent checklist of 240 species is available from the refuge manager at PO Box 110, Lewistown, MT 59457 (406-538-8707). It is also available online at https://www.fws.gov/uploadedFiles/CMRBirdList(1).pdf (Charles M. Russell NWR bird list).

Upper Missouri National Wild and Scenic River. This is a 149-mile stretch of free-flowing river, extending downstream from Fort Benton to US Hwy. 191 and James Kipp Recreation Area (see section). It flows through the Upper Missouri River Breaks National Monument (see section). The castlelike sandstone formations found here (the famous "white Cliffs" of Lewis and Clark) rise 200 to 300 feet above the river and are the most spectacularly beautiful part of the entire Missouri River system. They remain much as they were when Lewis and Clark described them, and as they were later painted by Karl Bodmer in 1833. They extend from near the mouth of the Marias River east for about 40 air miles (55 river miles) and are not visible by normal land access. A scenic area of similar length called the Missouri River Badlands occurs downstream. An 81-mile road loop starting and ending at Winfred is called the *Missouri Breaks National Back Country Byway*, but this unimproved road is suitable only for high-clearance vehicles during good weather. About nine miles west of the mouth of the Judith River, and about 1.5 miles downstream from the mouth of Arrow Creek ("Slaughter Creek" of Lewis and Clark), is the site of the buffalo jump described by Lewis and Clark, where they found more than a hundred dead bison, the animals having been stampeded by Native Americans off the brink of the steep cliffs. There is a local bird checklist of 233 species, including many of the same species that are found in the Charles M. Russell NWR. *Address of Upper Missouri National Wild and Scenic River:* Bureau of Land Management, Lewistown Field Office, 920 NE Main St., Lewistown, MT 59457 (406-622-4000).

Upper Missouri River Breaks National Monument. 774 square miles (375,000 acres). This remote area in north-central Montana stretches for 150 miles along the scenic upper Missouri River (see previous section) and was made famous by the stunning paintings of Karl Bodmer made during the Maximilian expedition. The monument has been reported to have 233 species of birds, 60 species of mammals, 20 species of reptiles and amphibians, and 49 species of fish. Large mammals include pronghorns, white-tailed and mule deer, and bighorn sheep, in addition to mountain lions, coyotes, and red foxes. *Address:* 920 NE Main St., Lewistown, MT 59457 (406-538-1900).

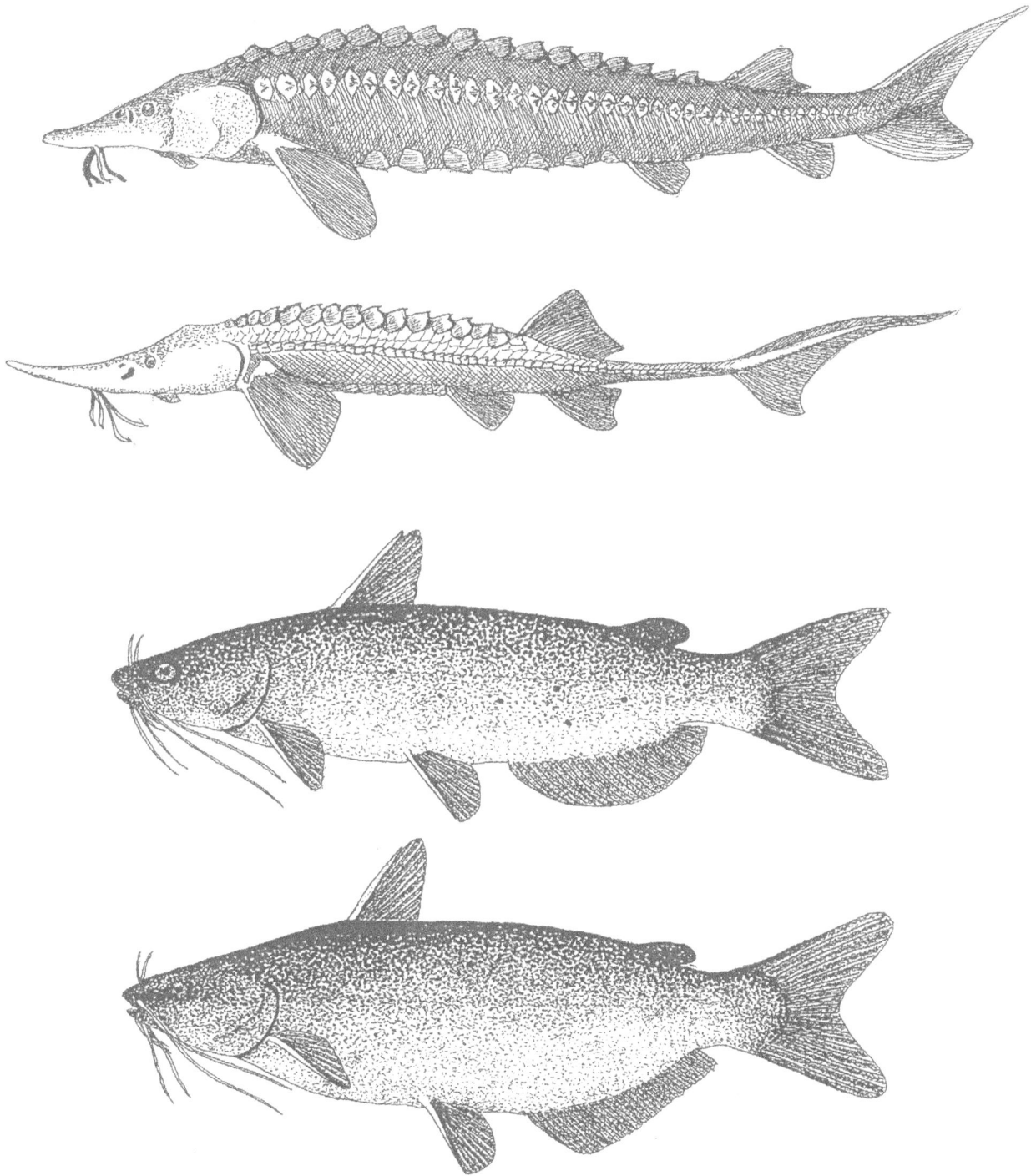

Typical fish of the Great Plains, including (top to bottom) lake sturgeon, pallid sturgeon, channel catfish, and blue catfish.

NORTH DAKOTA

North Dakota (ND) is notable for naturalists in at least two important ways. First, it has the largest number of national wildlife refuges of any state—77. In addition, it has a national park of 70,000 acres and a national game preserve that totals nearly 500,000 acres. The state also has three national grasslands that total 1.2 million acres of federally preserved lands, and 11 wetland management districts (WMDs), which contain most of the state's waterfowl production areas (WPAs), all open to public use. The state's 1,100 WPAs account for about 40 percent of the nation's total number and represent a total of 263,000 acres. Additionally, 823,000 acres of privately owned wetlands are protected through wetland easements. The state also has about 190,000 acres in 150 state-managed wildlife management areas that are also open to public use. Nearly all of the state's national wildlife refuges are also open to public use, although some might have restricted areas or restricted activities. Federally owned acreage in North Dakota composes 2.67 percent of the state's total land area.

Also of historic interest, the region that 85 years later became the state of North Dakota is where Lewis and Clark had some of their most important early interactions with Native Americans. There they built their first fort (Fort Mandan) and endured the expedition's first winter (1804–5), one of the region's coldest winters in history. There too they obtained the critically important assistance of their Lemhi, Idaho, Shoshone guide, Sacagawea. (In North Dakota, the preferred spelling of her name is Sakakawea, based on the dialect of the Hidatsa tribe, who kidnapped her from the Shoshones when she was 10 or 12 years old and adopted her.) Without her presence, knowledge, and abilities to communicate with her own and other regional tribes, the expedition might well have failed disastrously. The *Lewis and Clark Trail* is a scenic highway route that follows the expedition's river route as closely as possible through the state, from the South Dakota to the Montana borders. Conveniently for travelers' memory, North Dakota Hwy. 1804 traces the expedition's 1804 outward-bound route along the east and north side of the Missouri River, while Hwy. 1806 similarly follows the expedition's return route in 1806, along the south and west side of the river. This same highway numbering arrangement applies in South Dakota.

Arrowwood National Wildlife Refuge. 15,934 acres. Situated about 14 miles north of Jamestown (5.5 miles east of Edmunds), this NWR consists of lakes, marshes, grasslands, wooded areas, and fields and straddles the James River for 14 miles. About 6,000 acres remain in native grasslands that are surrounded by wooded coulees. At least 64 bird species are common to abundant during spring versus 59 species during fall and 25 during winter (Jones, 1990). There are at least 105 nesting bird species among the 246 listed for the refuge by Jones. Among them are 5 species of grebes, 13 ducks, Forster's and black terns, willet, marbled godwit, American avocet, and Wilson's phalarope. A total of 19 bird species were reported present year-round by Jones, so an estimated minimum of 92 percent of the refuge's total bird diversity is migratory. A recent checklist of 266 species is available from refuge manager at RR 1, Box 65, Pingree, ND 58476 (701-285-3341). It is also available online at https://www.fws.gov/uploadedFiles/ArrowwoodBirdList_Web.pdf.

Audubon National Wildlife Refuge. 24,700 acres. Situated at the east end of Lake Sakakawea, between Minot and Bismarck (three miles west and one mile north of Coleharbor), this NWR contains about 13,500 acres administered by the federal government and 11,200 acres supervised by the state. The refuge mostly consists of short-grass prairie and reservoir shoreline as well as prairie potholes and marshes. At least 78 bird species are common to abundant during spring versus 61 species during fall and 6 during winter (Jones, 1990). There are at least 85 nesting birds among the 205 listed for the refuge by Jones. A total of 25 bird species were reported present year-round by Jones, so an estimated minimum of 88 percent of the refuge's total bird diversity is migratory. It provides an important fall staging area for sandhill cranes, returning from breeding areas during October, and for lesser Canada geese. Sharp-tailed grouse and marbled godwits are common; burrowing owls are rare. Among the 37 reported mammal species are such grassland species as pronghorns, white-tailed jackrabbits, and three different ground squirrels. Five reptiles, 3 amphibians, and 37 fish have also been reported. About 15 miles east of Audubon NWR, and east of Turtle Lake, is the *John E. Williams Nature Preserve*, with several alkali lakes and one of the nation's largest populations of piping plovers. A refuge checklist is available from the manager

Typical amphibians of the Great Plains, including (top to bottom) tiger salamander, spadefoot toad, northern leopard frog, and Plains leopard frog.

at RR 1, Coleharbor, ND 58531 (701-442-5474). It is also available online at https://www.fws.gov/upload-edFiles/Wildlife%20Checklist.pdf.

Big Gumbo. 20,000 acres. This federally owned area overseen by the Bureau of Land Management is undeveloped, with sometimes impassable roads. Located south of Marmarth near the northwestern South Dakota and southwestern North Dakota borders in Bowman County, the area extends along the West River Road and Camp Crook Road, and follows the Little Missouri River valley. It includes *Cedar Ridge*, a 1,900-acre area of shortgrass and sagebrush prairie at the northeastern limits of woody sagebrush in the United States. The wildlife includes the long-billed curlew, ferruginous hawk, golden eagle, lark bunting, and chestnut-collared longspur. Several sage-dependent species, such as the pronghorn, greater sage-grouse, and Brewer's sparrow, are also present. *Address of BLM office:* 2933 3rd Ave. W, Dickinson, ND 58601.

Cedar River National Grassland. 6,237 acres. This federally owned shortgrass and mixed-grass prairie is along the South Dakota line near Grand River National Grassland (see section) and lies mostly within the Standing Rock Indian Reservation. The area is largely inaccessible by car. No species checklists are available. *Address:* USFS, Box 390, Lemmon, SD 57638 (605-374-3592).

Chase Lake National Wildlife Refuge. 4,385 acres. Administered through Arrowwood National Wildlife Refuge, this refuge is classified as a Globally Important Bird Area and is notable for its enormous nesting colony of American white pelicans (up to about 30,000 birds), along with nesting double-crested cormorants, ring-billed gulls, and California gulls. Rare grassland bird species such as Sprague's pipits and Baird's sparrows, as well as piping plovers, nest here. About 35 species of butterflies have also been reported. Most of the refuge (3,155 acres) is classified as a wilderness area and has had no development. East of Chase Lake and near Woodworth is the *Woodworth Waterfowl Production Area* (managed through the Chase Lake Wetland Management District), and south of Chase Lake near Crystal Springs are two state-owned lakes, *Alkali Lake* and *George Lake*. Both are alkaline wetlands with abundant growths of pondweeds and wigeongrass that attract huge numbers of tundra swans, redheads,

canvasbacks, other waterfowl, and shorebirds. For information about the refuge or the WPA, contact the Arrowwood NWR manager: 5924 19th St. SE, Woodworth, ND 58496 (701-752-4218). (The *Chase Lake Wetland Management District* office has the same address and phone number.)

Crosby Wetland Management District. This WMD oversees 20,000 acres in Burke, Divide, and Williams Counties, including Lake Zahl National Wildlife Refuge in northern Williams County. Many alkali lakes are in this region, providing nesting habitat for piping plovers. The extensive wetlands—as many as 600 per square mile—provide important breeding habitat for waterfowl and shorebirds. The area is also often used by migrating whooping cranes. *Address:* PO Box 148, Crosby, ND 58730 (701-965-6488).

Cross Ranch Nature Preserve. 6,000 acres. This Nature Conservancy preserve is located about ten miles south of Washburn, off State Hwy. 200A, or six miles southeast of Hensler. It is largely mixed-grass prairie with typical high plains wildlife. A managed herd of about a hundred bison is present. A total of 147 bird species (with at least 33 nesters) have collectively been reported for the preserve and the state park. The sharp-tailed grouse and upland sandpiper are common. More than 100 species of wildflowers are known to occur at the preserve, and a preliminary plant list of more than 250 species has been developed. There is a nine-mile hiking and nature trail. Ancient sites of Mandan and Minitari villages are also present. *Address of nature preserve:* 1401 River Rd., Hensler, ND (791-794-8741). *Address of the Nature Conservancy state office:* 2000 Schafer St., Ste. B, Bismarck, ND 58501-1204. Nearby is the state-owned *Cross Ranch State Park* (589 acres). This park is located 9 miles south of Washburn and 22 miles east of Center, and extends along 7 miles of the Missouri River. Camping is permitted in the state park. *State park address:* 1403 River Rd., Center, ND 58530 (701-794-3721). Four miles south of the state park is *Smith Grove Wildlife Management Area* (25 acres), with massive old-growth riparian woods of gigantic cottonwoods, prairie, and woody draws. Information about both the state park and WMA can be obtained from the North Dakota Game and Fish Department, 100 N. Bismarck Expressway, Bismarck, ND 58650-5095 (701-328-6300).

Des Lacs National Wildlife Refuge. 19,500 acres. Located one mile west of Kenmare, this refuge encompasses a chain of lakes that extend from the Canadian border 26 miles south. At least 92 bird species are common to abundant during spring versus 69 species during fall and 8 during winter (Jones, 1990). One of the country's largest and most diverse populations of grebes breed here, including western, eared, horned, red-necked, and pied-billed. There are at least 145 nesting birds among the 266 listed for the refuge complex by Jones. A total of 25 bird species were reported present year-round by Jones, so an estimated minimum of 91 percent of the refuge's total bird diversity is migratory. A collective bird checklist of 308 species, including 150 nesters, reported from all three refuges in the "Souris loop" (Des Lacs, J. Clark Salyer, and Upper Souris), is available from the manager at Des Lacs Refuge, PO Box 578, Kenmare, ND 58746 (701-385-4046). It is also available online at https://www.fws.gov/uploadedFiles/BirdList(9).pdf.

Devils Lake Wetland Management District. 221,989 acres. This vast WMD in northeastern North Dakota includes Benson, Nelson, Grand Forks, Walsh, Ramsey, Towner, Cavalier, and Pembina Counties. It averages 40 to 80 wetlands per square mile and has 187 waterfowl production areas totaling 40,113 acres, 10 easement refuges totaling 15,891 acres, and 2,521 conservation easements totaling 154,000 acres. The WMD also includes Lake Alice National Wildlife Refuge (12,179 acres) northwest of Devils Lake (see section) and Sullys Hill National Game Preserve (1,674 acres) southwest of Devils Lake (see section). *Stump Lake National Wildlife Refuge* (27 acres), south of Lakota, has long been a major shorebird magnet during spring and fall. Stump Lake was flooded in 2005, and the refuge was temporarily closed. It is managed by the Devils Lake Wetland Management District. For information about the WMD, contact the district office: PO Box 908, Devils Lake, ND 58301 (701-662-8611).

Double Ditch Indian Village State Historic Site. This unrestored Mandan village, seven miles north of Bismarck on State Hwy. 1804, dates back to about 1500 and was abandoned after a smallpox epidemic in the early 1780s. There is a self-guided walk and a 116-acre buffer zone between the site and the river. The state-owned site has been seriously flooded in recent years and is badly eroded. It is managed by the State Historical Society of North Dakota, 612 E. Blvd., Bismarck, ND 58505 (701-328-2566), email histsoc@nd.gov.

Fort Abraham Lincoln State Park. 1,006 acres. This state park is seven miles south of Mandan on State Hwy. 1806. Nearby is the partially restored *On-A-Slant Indian Village*, an ancient Mandan site occupied at the mouth of the Heart River for two centuries, or until about 1740, and supporting a maximum population about 1,500 Mandans. By 1764 the villagers had moved north to join the Hidatsas near the Knife River. Smallpox struck the Upper Missouri tribes in 1837, when it was brought upstream by an American Fur Company's supply ship, reducing the Mandan population to only about 150. At the time of Lewis and Clark, the entire Mandan tribe numbered perhaps 3,600 people, as compared with about 2,500 Hidatsas (the "Minnetaree" of Lewis and Clark). Compared with the Mandans, the Hidatsas were relatively fierce, often fighting at the extreme western end of their range with the Shoshones. In one of these encounters, they captured Sacagawea, then still only about 10 or 12 years old. Four full-sized Mandan earth lodges have been reconstructed, and there is evidence of 75 ancient lodge sites. A visitor center displays Mandan cultural objects and replicas of some Lewis and Clark items. During the Indian wars of the 1870s, Gen. George Armstrong Custer and the Seventh Cavary were stationed here prior to their disastrous military campaign of 1876. The fort was built in 1872 and abandoned in 1891 after the Indian wars, but many buildings have been reconstructed. Located eight miles south of Mandan on State Hwy. 1806, it is near the Lewis and Clark outward-bound campsite of October 20, 1804, which was used again during the return phase of the expedition on August 18, 1806. From about this point north to the Garrison Dam there are nearly 100 miles of fairly free-flowing river. Camping is permitted at the state park. *Address:* 44880 Ft. Lincoln Rd., Mandan, ND 58554 (701-667-6340).

Fort Berthold Indian Reservation. About 1 million acres. This very large reservation occupies much of both sides of Lake Sakakawea, which has impounded 368,000 acres and measures 1,600 miles of shoreline. It is home to Mandans, Arikaras, and Hidatsas, collectively called the MAH Nation. Fort Berthold was built in

1845 by the American Fur Company as a trading post, to be near the Mandan and Hidatsa villages then being established about 60 river miles upstream from Fort Mandan. Near the north end of the reservation and 11 miles west of New Town on US Hwy. 23 is *Four Bears Park*. A reservation museum (the *Three Tribes Museum*) near New Town is run by the Three Affiliated Tribes. It details the history of the Hidatsas, Arikaras, Mandans, including their encounters with Lewis and Clark, and features a reconstructed full-sized earth lodge. Three miles south of New Town on North Dakota Hwy. 23 is *Crow Flies High Butte Historic Site* and associated exhibits. The top of this butte provides a panoramic view of the nearby badlands and upland topography; the river valley itself is now entirely impounded. The butte is named for a Hidatsa chief who founded a nearby village. No information is available on native fauna of the reservation's extensive areas of prairie. In 2003 the total reservation acreage suitable for prairie dogs in North Dakota was estimated at 20,500 acres. *Address:* Three Affiliated Tribes, 404 Frontage St., New Town, ND 58763 (701-627-4781).

Fort Burford State Historic Site. This site is located 6 miles west, 14 miles southwest, and 1 mile south of Williston on State Hwy. 1804. The fort replaced the rather short-lived Fort Williams in 1866. Only a few remnants of Fort Burford are still visible, including the stone powder magazine, the Officer of the Day building, a restored field officer's quarters that is now a museum, and a military cemetery. It was to Fort Burford that Chief Joseph was brought with 400 of his Nez Perce tribe after their failed attempt to escape into Canada. Fort Burford is also where Sitting Bull surrendered in 1881 after returning with his 187 surviving Hunkpapa Sioux followers (mostly women and children) from Canada. The *Confluence Area Interpretive Center* at Fort Burford describes the early exploration of the Upper Missouri region. Camping is permitted.

Fort Mandan Historic Site and **Lewis and Clark Interpretive Center.** Fort Mandan Historic Site is located 2.5 miles west of Washburn on North Dakota County Road 17, close to the junction of US Hwy. 83 and State Hwy. 100a, and 1.5 miles west of the Lewis and Clark Interpretive Center. The fort was contracted by and the winter home of the L. & C. party in 1804–5. It was destroyed by a prairie fire before the expedition's return in 1806 and has since been replaced by a modern replica. The exact site of the original fort is not known, but it is probably now inundated. The interpretive center has a cottonwood dugout canoe of the type used by Lewis and Clark as well as other items similar to those used by the expedition. *Address:* 838 28th Ave. SW, Washburn, ND 38577 (702-463-8535).

Fort Stevenson State Park. 600 acres. This park is a state-owned site managed by North Dakota Parks and Tourism located 3 miles south of Garrison in McLean County. It is a peninsula along the shore of Lake Sakakawea and consists mostly of rolling hills and upland prairie, including a prairie dog town. Coyotes, jackrabbits, sharp-tailed grouse, and other grassland animals are present. *Address:* 1252 41st Ave. NW, Garrison, ND 58540-9229 (701-337-5576). A few miles south of the east end of Garrison Dam and between the dam spillway and the river is the *Riverdale Wildlife Management Area* (2,197 acres). It has a sharp-tailed grouse display ground and a bird checklist of more than 100 species. It is managed by the North Dakota Game and Fish Department, 100 N. Bismarck Expressway, Bismarck, ND 58650-5095 (701-328-6300).

Fort Union Trading Post National Historic Site. This site is located 24 miles southwest of Williston on ND Hwy. 1804. Fort Union (built in 1828) has been recreated on a 443-acre site, with reconstructed walls, bastions, and a trade house. The Bourgeois House serves as a museum and visitor center. This trading post was built by John J. Astor's American Fur Company in 1828 and remained active until 1867. It was then 1,776 river miles from St. Louis and a major frontier fur-trading center. The Fort Union Trading Post was the largest in the American West and was often visited by Native Americans. It also hosted such illustrious visitors as George Catlin (1830), Karl Bodmer and Prince Maximilian (1833), and John J. Audubon (1842). There is a bird checklist of 138 species. Two now-rare mixed-grass-prairie bird species, the Sprague's pipit and Baird's sparrow, were both discovered here by Audubon about four decades after Lewis and Clark had passed through. *Address:* 15550 Hwy. 1804, Williston, ND 58801 (701-572-9083).

J. Clark Salyer National Wildlife Refuge (formerly Lower Souris NWR). 58,700 acres. Salyer NWR is located two miles north of Upham. More than 23,000 acres of wetlands are in this refuge, as well as 5,000 acres of woodlands. Over 250,000 ducks and 300,000 snow geese visit this refuge annually. At least 92 bird species are common to abundant during spring versus 69 species during fall and 8 during winter (Jones, 1990). There are at least 145 nesting birds among the 266 listed for the refuge complex by Jones. All of the typical mixed-grass sparrows breed in this largest of North Dakota's national wildlife refuges, including LeConte's, Baird's, and Nelson's sparrows, plus the other usual northern prairie and prairie wetland species. A total of 25 bird species were reported present year-round by Jones, so an estimated minimum of 91 percent of the refuge complex's total bird diversity is migratory. The reported mammals include white-tailed deer, red fox, coyote, mink, beaver, and porcupine, plus a small population of moose and occasional elk and mule deer. The refuge has been named a Globally Important Bird Area by the American Bird Conservancy and is a regional site in the Western Hemisphere Shorebird Reserve Network. A bird checklist of 308 species, including 150 nesters, collectively reported from all three refuges in the so-called "Souris loop" (Des Lacs, J. Clark Salyer, and Upper Souris), is available from the J. Clark Salyer refuge manager at Box 66, Upham, ND 58799 (701-768-2548). It is also available online at https://www.fws.gov/uploadedFiles/BirdList(9).pdf.

J. Clark Salyer Wetland Management District. 6,543 square miles. This large WMD is in Renville, Bottineau, Rolette, McHenry, and Pierce Counties. It includes the Turtle Mountains and the regions known geologically as the Souris Lake Plain and glacial Lake Caddo, where two relatively small glacial lakes existed during the late Pleistocene period of glacial melting. The Souris Lake Plain has some of the best quality waterfowl habitat in the entire prairie pothole region, with breeding duck densities up to 180 pairs per square mile. *Address:* J. Clark Salyer NWR, PO Box 66, 681 Salyer Rd., Upham, ND 58789 (701-268-2548).

Kelly's Slough National Wildlife Refuge. 1,270 acres. This refuge is located eight miles west and three miles north of Grand Forks. Kelly's Slough is fed by an intermittent stream that flows into the Turtle River and has been developed into a series of ponds. In 2000 there were nearly 40,000 shorebirds using the area, the most abundant being semipalmated sandpiper followed by lesser yellowlegs, Wilsons's phalarope, American avocet, stilt sandpiper, pectoral sandpiper, and dunlin. The American avocet, killdeer, Wilson's phalaropes, and spotted sandpiper nest in the refuge. The Kelly's Slough National Wildlife Refuge complex of regionally preserved lands is an extremely important migration stopover point for shorebirds and has been designated as a Globally Important Bird Area and a Western Hemisphere Shorebird Research Site. These wetlands in northeastern North Dakota's moist prairie region area are also of great importance to migratory waterfowl. The Kelly's Slough bird list of 280 species has ten breeding ducks and seven breeding shorebirds. Several sparrows, including Nelson's and LeConte's, breed here. *Address:* Kelly's Slough NWR, c/o Devils Lake WMD, PO Box 908, Devils Lake, ND 58301 (701-662-8611, ext. 329). The bird list is available from the refuge office at 21st St. NE, Emeraldo, ND 58301.

Knife River Indian Villages National Historic Site. 1,758 acres. This federally owned historic site is managed by the National Park Service and is located on ND Hwy. 31 half a mile north of Stanton in Mercer County. Grasslands and river bottom forests plus a restored Mandan earth lodge are present. A major Mandan and Hidatsa village was located here during the time of the Lewis and Clark expedition. A bird checklist (212 species) is available. Locally occurring grassland birds include sharp-tailed grouse, black-billed magpie, bobolink, and loggerhead shrike. *Address:* National Park Service, PO Box 9, Stanton, ND 58571-0009 (701-745-3309).

Kulm Wetland Management District. 42,352 acres. This WMD in south-central North Dakota encompasses several small federal refuges in Logan, Lamoure, McIntosh, and Dickey Counties. It also oversees 109,000 acres of wetlands on 1,379 conservation easements that are important for migratory waterfowl and shorebirds. Geologically, it includes parts of North Dakota's Southern Drift Plain, the Missouri Coteau, and the Coteau Slope. Of these, the Missouri Coteau is most productive and attracts up to 80 duck pairs per square mile. No bird list is yet available. *Address:* 1 First St. SE, Box E, Kulm, ND 58456 (701-647-2866).

Lake Alice National Wildlife Refuge. 12,157 acres. Located 9 miles west and 1.5 miles north of Garske, Lake Alice NWR is a shallow marsh of 3,500 acres surrounded by other wetlands. Lake Alice attracts some

200,000 snow geese in spring and has nesting colonies of American white pelican, double-crested cormorant, black-crowned night-heron, and Franklin's gull. It is used heavily by migrating sandhill cranes, geese, and ducks, and a variety of gulls, terns, grebes, and ducks breed there. Public observation platforms, an auto tour route, and information stations are available. *Address:* Lake Alice NWR, PO Box 908, Devils Lake, ND 58301 (701-662-8611, ext. 323).

Lake Ilo National Wildlife Refuge. 4,033 acres. Located one mile east of Dunn Center, Lake Ilo NWR is a reservoir that was impounded during the 1930s, with waterways that can be manipulated to form wetlands. The uplands are native mixed-grass prairie (1,200 acres) plus planted grasslands. The refuge list includes 226 birds, 36 mammals, 9 reptiles and amphibians, and 11 fish. At least 79 bird species are common to abundant during spring versus 61 species during fall and 6 during winter (Jones, 1990). There are at least 83 nesting bird species among the 205 listed for the refuge by Jones. A total of 27 species were reported as present year-round, so an estimated minimum of 87 percent of the refuge's total bird diversity is migratory. Shorebirds, including piping plovers, upland sandpipers, and marbled godwits, all breed commonly; burrowing owls are uncommon breeders. The area was used 11,000 years ago by Paleo Indians to obtain Knife River flint that they used for making tools and weapons. A bird checklist is available from the refuge manager at PO Box 127, Dunn Center, ND 58626 (701-385-4046). It is also available online at https://www.fws.gov/lakeilo/birdlist.pdf.

Lewis and Clark State Park. 490 acres. This state-owned site is managed by North Dakota Parks and Tourism and is located 16 miles east and 3 miles south of Williston, in Williams County, along one of the northern bays of Lake Sakakawea. This rather remote park has one of the largest intact areas of native mixed-grass prairie of all the North Dakota state parks. No species checklists are available. *Address:* 4904 119th Rd. NW, Epping, ND 58843 (701-859-3071).

Little Missouri National Grassland. 1,027,852 acres. Two separate units—the McKenzie and Medora Ranger Districts, each more than 500,000 acres—make up the Little Missouri National Grassland. This grassland is now included as one of the collective *Dakota Prairie Grasslands* and is part of a vast region of federally owned shortgrass prairies and badlands that in part extend to the south shore of Lake Sakakawea. Bison occasionally occur in the grassland, as escapees from the adjoining Theodore Roosevelt National Park (see section). Bighorn sheep were reintroduced in 1956 and numbered about 200 animals by the early 2000s. Elk have also been reintroduced, and pronghorns are present. Predators include golden eagles, coyotes, mountain lions, and bobcats (Moul, 2006). The relatively small northern section is located generally to the north of Keene and is best reached by taking ND Hwy. 1806 east and north from Watford City. A larger section of this enormous national grassland, the largest federally owned grassland in the United States, lies along the Little Missouri River and is headquartered in Dickinson. A 95-mile hiking trail, the *Maah Daah Trail*, connects the two units. Camping is permitted on both units of the national grassland. Managed by the US Forest Service, 161 21st St. W, Dickinson, ND 58601. *McKenzie Ranger District address:* HC02, Box 8, Watford City, ND 58854 (701-842-2343). *Medora Ranger District address:* 99 23rd Ave. W, Suite B, Dickinson, ND 58501 (701-227-7800).

Long Lake National Wildlife Refuge. 22,300 acres. Situated about four miles southeast of Moffitt, North Dakota, this refuge is mostly prairie grasslands, ravines, fields, trees, and shrubs, plus marshes or shallow lakes. At least 67 bird species are common to abundant during spring versus 66 species during fall and 5 during winter (Jones, 1990). There are at least 78 nesting birds among the 203 listed for the refuge by Jones. A total of 18 bird species were reported present year-round by Jones, so an estimated minimum of 91 percent of the refuge's total bird diversity is migratory. This is one of North Dakota's most important stopover sites for migrants, the more common species including tundra swans, Canada and greater white-fronted geese, sandhill cranes, both yellowlegs, a half-dozen "peep" (*Calidris*) sandpipers, and three gulls. Regular shorebird migrants total at least 16 species. The willet, piping plover, marbled godwit, Wilson's phalarope, and upland sandpiper are also regular nesters. Many prairie birds occur here, including the northern harrier, sharp-tailed grouse, and 20 species of grassland sparrows, such as the chestnut-collared longspur, Baird's sparrow, lark bunting, and clay-colored sparrow. A checklist of 289 bird species is available from the refuge manager at RR 1, Moffitt, ND 58560 (701-387-4397).

Lostwood National Wildlife Refuge. 27,647 acres. Located 16 miles southwest of Kenmare, this beautiful prairie refuge is a mixture of rolling hills and many small, shallow "pothole" wetlands, some of which are alkaline. Recognized as a Globally Important Bird Area, the refuge supports upland mixed grasses (22,000 acres, about two-thirds being original mixed-grass prairie), aspen grovelands, and alkaline lakes and marshes or prairie potholes. The spring and fall migrations include tundra swans, snow and greater white-fronted geese, and dozens of duck species. Mixed-grass species, such as Sprague's pipit and Baird's sparrow, are common, as are sharp-tailed grouse, marbled godwit, McCown's and chestnut-collared longspurs, and most other grassland birds of the northern High Plains. At least 13 species of ducks probably nest on the refuge as well as 4 grebes, 3 herons, 3 terns, 2 rails, and 2 gulls. The piping plover, Wilson's phalarope, California gull, and American avocet nest in alkaline areas, and other prairie-nesting shorebirds include the spotted sandpiper, willet, and marbled godwit. A vertebrate list includes 234 birds (104 breeders), 37 mammals, 3 reptiles, and 4 amphibians. *Address:* Lostwood NWR, RR 2, Box 93, Kenmare, ND 58746 (701-848-2722).

Lostwood Wetland Management District Complex. This large WMD includes five North Dakota counties in northwestern North Dakota that extend from the Canadian border to the Montana border. It includes four national wildlife refuges and two wetland management districts, 56 waterfowl production areas, 13,500 acres of private lands, and 1,815 acres (450 acres of them wetlands) in *Shell Lake National Wildlife Refuge* in Montrail County. Three species of terns, ring-billed and California gulls, western grebes, and Wilson's phalaropes all breed at Shell Lake NWR. Lostwood WMD attracts up to 10,000 sandhill cranes during migration but is then closed to public access. The district is part of the vast glaciated Prairie Pothole Region, where up to 12 waterfowl species nest and might have 100 to 150 nesting pairs per square mile. Another part of the complex is the 2,700-acre *Coteau Prairie Waterfowl Production Area*, which is believed to be the largest tract of native mixed-grass prairie in any WPA and has up to 150 wetlands per square mile. The district's total waterfowl production areas encompass about 35,000 acres of wetland easements and 20,000 acres in grassland easements. *Address:* 8315 Hwy. 8, Kenmore, ND 58746 (701-848-2466).

Adult male greater prairie-chicken.

Prairie Chicken Management Areas. About 4,000 acres. These scattered management areas consist of several tracts of land west of Grand Forks that are owned by the North Dakota Department of Game and Fish. They are managed for greater prairie-chickens but also support LeConte's and Nelson's sparrows and the very rare yellow rail. Two are located north and northwest of the towns of Mackinock and Manvel, respectively. The nearby *Oakville Prairie* is a 900-acre prairie only 12 miles from Grand Forks that is managed by the University of North Dakota. It is situated on 9,500-year-old beach ridges of glacial Lake Agassiz and supports many tallgrass bird species. Call the University of North Dakota for further information (703-777-2623). Information on prairie-chickens can be obtained from the North Dakota Game and Fish Department at 100 N. Bismarck Expressway, Bismarck, ND 58650-5095 (701-328-6300).

Sheyenne National Grassland. 70,180 acres. This grassland consists of sandhills tallgrass prairie and riverine hardwoods on a sandy, glacial-age delta of the Sheyenne River; it is the largest area of federally owned tallgrass prairie in the United States. The plant life is very diverse, with eight different habitat types, including late Pleistocene-age sand dunes, 25,000 acres of tallgrass prairie, many wetlands and potholes, oak savanna, aspen parkland, and river terraces. Special species include two rare butterflies (Dakota skipper and regal fritillary), a population of the threatened western prairie fringed orchid, and North Dakota's last major surviving population of the greater prairie-chicken. Moose and elk are occasionally seen, and there are rare records of wolves and black bears. Apparently no species checklists are available, although 280 species of birds have been reported (Moul, 2006). Now managed as part of the Dakota Prairie Grasslands. *Address:* Sheyenne Ranger District, PO Box 946, 701 Main St., Lisbon, ND 58054 (701-683-4342).

Slade National Wildlife Refuge. 3,000 acres. Slade NWR is situated between Jamestown and Bismarck near Moffitt, North Dakota, and consists of prairie pothole habitat with many marshes and small lakes. It is managed through Long Lake NWR (see section). A recent checklist of 202 bird species, including 88 breeders, is available from the refuge manager of Long Lake NW Refuge at RR 1, Moffitt, ND 58560 (701-387-4397).

Standing Rock Indian Reservation. Standing Rock is the largest North Dakota Indian reservation, covering some 3,500,000 acres. In 2010 the Sioux population on the reservation was 8,200. Treaty lands have recently been seriously affected by construction of the Dakota Access Pipeline and have been at the center of associated legal and activist protests. Including the South Dakota acreage, the reservation had about 137 prairie dog colonies on 1,000 acres as of 2002 (Johnsgard, 2005). *Address:* Standing Rock Agency, Bureau of Indian Affairs, PO Box E, Fort Yates, ND 58535 (701-854-3433).

Sullys Hill National Game Preserve. 1,674 acres. This century-old national game preserve (the only so-named federal refuge) was established in 1902 to help preserve declining populations of native big game, such as bison and elk. Their introduction in the early 1900s supplemented the native white-tailed deer and occasional moose. The refuge consists of deciduous woodlands (especially aspens), grasslands, and brushlands on glacial moraine. There is a 1.5-mile nature trail, an auto tour route, and an education center. *Lake*

Metigoshe State Park (1,200 acres; 701-263-4651) is nearby in North Dakota's scenic Turtle Mountains region (the "mountains" are glaciated hills). A bird list of 267 species is available from the manager. *Address of game preserve:* c/o Devils Lake WMD, PO Box 908, Devils Lake, ND 58301 (702-766-4272).

Tewaukon National Wildlife Refuge. 8,442 acres. Situated in southeastern North Dakota near Cayuga, Tewaukon NWR consists of nearly 8,000 acres of prairie grassland, marshes, and larger water areas. The refuge includes four large wetlands that seasonally attract 100,000 or more snow geese, and its remnant tallgrass prairie contains a wide diversity of prairie wildflowers. Eared, western, and pied-billed grebes nest here, as do willet; marbled godwit; upland sandpiper; northern harrier; the Nelson's, LeConte's, and swamp sparrows; and bobolink. At least 84 species are common to abundant during spring versus 72 species during fall and 8 during winter (Jones, 1990). There are at least 98 nesting birds among the 236 listed for the refuge by Jones. He reported a total of 29 bird species were reported present year-round, so an estimated minimum of 88 percent of the refuge's total bird diversity is migratory. There is an eight-mile auto tour route and a visitor center. A recent bird checklist of 236 species (98 nesters) is available from the refuge manager at RR 1, Cayuga, ND 58103 (701-724-3598).

Theodore Roosevelt National Park. 70,416 acres. This park has been recognized by the National Geographic Society (2011) as one of the nation's ten best national parks for seeing prairie dogs, charismatic megafauna, and evidence of "presidential footprints" and for having wonderfully scenic campgrounds. It consists of two separate sections within part of the Little Missouri National Grassland (see section). These grasslands and eroded badlands provide habitat for a wide array of other high plains mammals and birds. The large mammals include reintroduced bison (250–400 head), reintroduced bighorn sheep, elk, and mule deer. Seabloom et al. (1978) published a list of 50 mammal species reported from this general region that included the white-tailed jackrabbit, black-tailed prairie dog, bushy-tailed woodrat, and swift fox. About 4,000 acres of prairie dog colonies existed in 2003, and about a third of these colonies supported burrowing owls (Johnsgard, 2005). Golden eagles and prairie falcons are regular nesters. A checklist of 286 bird species occurring in southwestern North Dakota (covering the entire region southwest of the Missouri River) was compiled by Rich (1992). *Address:* Dakota Prairies Grasslands, 2 Miriam Circle, Bismarck, ND 58501 (701-989-7300).

Upper Souris National Wildlife Refuge. 32,000 acres. This refuge is located seven miles north of Foxholm and extends along more than 35 miles of the Souris River valley. Lake Darling, a 9,900-acre impoundment, is the largest wetland. At least 92 bird species are common to abundant during spring versus 69 species during fall and 8 during winter (Jones, 1990). The yellow rail and piping plover nest here, as do the Baird's sparrow, Sprague's pipit, marbled godwit, upland sandpiper, and LeConte's and Nelson's sparrows. Recognized as an Important Bird Area by the American Bird Conservancy, there are at least 145 nesting birds among the 266 listed for the refuge complex by Jones. A total of 25 bird species were reported present year-round by Jones, so an estimated minimum of 91 percent of the refuge complex's total bird diversity is migratory. There are four nature trails and a 3.5-mile scenic drive. A collective three-refuge bird checklist of 308 species, including 150 nesters, is available from any of the three refuges in the "Souris loop" (Des Lacs, J. Clark Salyer, and Upper Souris) or by mail from Upper Souris NWR, 1775 212th Ave., Berthold, ND 58718 (701-468-5467). It is also available online at https://www.fws.gov/uploadedFiles/BirdList(9).pdf.

Valley City Wetland Management District. This WMD includes 17,000 acres of waterfowl production areas, 55,400 acres of wetland easements, and 5,500 acres of easement refuges in Barnes, Cass, Griggs, Steele, and Trail Counties. The district oversees wetlands and grasslands managed for waterfowl. Hundreds of waterfowl production areas are located in this rich "prairie potholes" region of central North Dakota. *Address:* 11515 River Rd., Valley City, ND 58072 (701-845-3466).

SOUTH DAKOTA

South Dakota (SD) boasts one national monument, two national parks, two national forests, three national grasslands, four wetland management districts, and five national wildlife refuges. National forest lands cover 2.4 million acres, national grasslands total 1.9 million acres, and US Fish and Wildlife Service lands occupy 206,000 acres. Federally owned acreages in South Dakota compose 6.19 percent of the state's total land area, the highest percentage of any of the central Great Plains states between North Dakota and Texas. State lands include 11 state parks, 45 state recreation areas, and 5 state nature areas or nature preserves.

The Black Hills of western South Dakota and adjacent Wyoming destroy the topographic uniformity of the northern Great Plains by rising up out of the plains a few thousand feet, to a maximum of 7,242 feet. These isolated and ancient mountains have an origin dating back to nearly a billion years ago, when an igneous uplift first began to form them. Their ancient eroded tops terminate well below the alpine zone but are the highest North American elevations east of the Rocky Mountains and north of New Mexico. Besides lacking tundra plants and animals, the present-day Black Hills also lack such typical high montane trees as subalpine fir and Engelmann spruce, and instead white spruce ("Black Hills spruce" variant) occurs at higher elevations. Instead of the widespread mid-montane Douglas-firs of the Rockies, ponderosa pines have long been the dominant coniferous trees over much of the Black Hills, although, like Douglas-fir, they are declining rapidly as a result of bark beetle infestations.

In spite of these obvious botanical differences, the Black Hills flora closely resembles that of Wyoming's Bighorn and Rocky Mountains. Studies of more than 1,000 species of Black Hills plants indicated that 30 percent had Rocky Mountain associations, 17 percent were Great Plains species, 9 percent were eastern deciduous forest species, 6 percent had northern associations, 4.5 percent were southwestern, and the rest were widespread or introduced taxa (Froiland, 1990).

Although much of the Black Hills flora is thus very similar to that of the Rocky Mountains, there are strong echoes of the eastern deciduous forest flora as well. These include such typical eastern trees as ironwood (*Ostrya virginiana*) and bur oak (*Quercus macrocarpa*), and shrubs such as the beaked hazelnut (*Corylus cornuta*) and honeysuckle (*Lonicera dioca*) (Dorn, 1977). In contrast, the Bighorns lack such eastern and boreal species as bur oak, ironwood, paper birch (*Betula papyrifera*), and white spruce (*Picea glauca*) (Despain, 1973).

Lodgepole pine has long been a dominant tree over vast areas of the central Rockies, especially after forest fires, but its range and abundance are quickly declining throughout the Rocky Mountains because of beetle infestations. Lodgepole pine in the Black Hills is limited to a single stand of about 150 acres (Froiland, 1990; Larson and Johnson, 1999). All together, the Black Hills flora has a lower degree of coniferous tree diversity than is found in Wyoming's Bighorns and Rocky Mountains. Such botanical diversity differences probably affect the range of available foraging and breeding niches for conifer-dependent birds such as finches and woodpeckers (Canterbury, Johnsgard, and Dunning, 2011).

Comparing mammals, the red squirrel (*Tamiasciurus hudsonicus*) occurs in both the Bighorns and Black Hills. The subalpine- and tundra-adapted pika (*Ochotona princeps*) is present in the Bighorns but not in the Black Hills, as are the boreal-adapted snowshoe hare (*Lepus americanus*), water vole (*Microtus richardsoni*), and montane vole (*Microtus montanus*). Contrarily, the northern flying squirrel (*Glaucomys sabrinus*) occurs in the mountains of northwestern Wyoming and the Black Hills but not in the Bighorns (Clark and Stromberg, 1987). The elk was eliminated from the Black Hills in 1877 but has been locally reestablished at Custer State Park. The mountain goat was also introduced in the 1920s and can occasionally be seen around Mount Rushmore, Crazy Horse Memorial, and the northern parts of Custer State Park. All told, at least 62 species of mammals occur in the Black Hills, including 59 indigenous forms, at least 4 of which were reintroduced after their local extirpation (bison, pronghorn, bighorn sheep, and elk).

At least 139 species of birds regularly occur in the Black Hills, and at least 87 more are occasionally present. Of all the regular Black Hills birds, 61 species are summer residents, 37 are permanent residents, 26 are spring and fall transients, and 13 are winter residents (Froiland, 1990). Relatively few cold-blooded vertebrates are present in the Black Hills. Of 15 species of reptiles, there are 10 snakes, 3 turtles, and 2 lizards, and the amphibians consist of 3 frogs, 2 toads, and 1 salamander (Froiland, 1990).

Badlands National Park. This park covers a vast 244,000-acre region and is located south of I-90 with easy highway access south from Wall. The park's north unit adjoins Buffalo Gap National Grassland (see section), while the south unit lies within the Pine Ridge Indian Reservation (see section) and is jointly managed by the Park Service and the Oglala Sioux. The sedimentary beds of materials eroded from the nearby Black Hills began to be deposited about 37 million years ago and were formed over a period of about 14 million years. As the sediments grew, erosion also occurred, producing buttes, peaks, terraces, arroyos, and scarps of varied sizes and colors, depending on the mineral sources. The oldest and lowest beds are of Pierre Shale, of late Cretaceous times, deposited from ancient marine sediments as early as 80 million years ago and ranging in color from black to red and yellow. The later Chadron Formation consists of gray claystone, with deposits as early as 35 million to 40 million years ago and from 30 to 50 feet in thickness. The Brule Formation was deposited during the latter half of the Oligocene and is often from 330 to 450 feet thick. It ranges in color from pinkish red to yellow-beige and is notably rich in mammalian fossils, such as titanotheres. More than 100 fossil species of mammals have been found in the Badlands, mostly dating from the Oligocene, when most modern orders of mammals first arose. Bison were reintroduced into the park in 1963, and about 800 were present by 2010. Rocky Mountain bighorn sheep were also reintroduced to replace the extirpated Great Plains (Audubon's) race of bighorns, and they had increased to about 150 by the 1990s. Robert Prairie Dog Town is located along the Sage Rim Road, five miles west of the Pinnacles. This park has been recognized by the National Geographic Society (2011) as one of the nation's ten best national parks for stunning landscape views from hiking trails. *Address:* PO Box 6, Interior, SD 57750-0006 (605-433-5361).

Black Hills National Forest. 1,235,453 acres. This national forest includes the highest elevation of any point in the northern Great Plains, Black Elk Peak (previously known as Harney Peak), at 7,242 feet. It is in the *Black Elk Wilderness* and the *Norbeck Wildlife Preserve*. A bird checklist of 190 species may be obtained from the Forest Service headquarters at PO Box 792, Custer, SD 57730 (605-763-9200).

Buffalo Gap National Grassland. 591,771 acres. Buffalo Gap is a shortgrass and mixed-grass prairie that extends south from Wall and encloses part of Badlands National Park. Prairie dogs are abundant, and a black-footed ferret reintroduction program into Conata Basin (see section) resulted in 264 ferrets present by 2003 after an initial introduction of 161 kits. As of 2017, this remains one of a very few successful ferret introductions. Swift foxes have also been released. Species lists include 230 birds, 47 grasses, and 199 forb and tree species. A bird checklist for Buffalo Gap National Grassland is available from the US Forest Service. A *National Grassland Visitor Center* is at the park's headquarters in Wall. *Address:* USFS, Wall Ranger District, PO Box 425, 708 Main St., Wall, SD 57790 (605-279-2125) or USFS, Fall River Ranger District, 209 N. River, Hot Springs, SD 57747 (605-745-4107).

Cedar River National Grassland. 6,237 acres. This federally owned site consists of shortgrass and mixed-grass prairie along the South Dakota line and is mostly inaccessible by car. It is located near Grand River National Grassland (see section) and the Standing Rock Indian Reservation. No species checklists are available. *Address:* USFS, Grand River Ranger District, Box 390, Lemmon, SD 57638 (605-374-3592).

Cheyenne River Indian Reservation. 1,400,000 acres. The enormous Cheyenne River Indian Reservation borders the west side of Lake Oahe for much of its length and is home to four bands of Lakotas. Prior to the Civil War, all of South Dakota west of the Missouri was made part of a vast Sioux Indian Reservation, but in the 1870s the federal government violated its own treaty and subdivided it. Much of this region was then taken from the Sioux, including their sacred Black Hills, where gold had been discovered during General Custer's military survey in 1874. There are still nearly 5 million acres of reservation lands in South Dakota, totaling nine reservations and supporting about 62,000 residents as of 2000, including three reservations whose boundaries extend into Nebraska or North Dakota. The Pine Ridge and Rosebud Indian Reservations (see sections) of southwestern South Dakota support the state's largest number of reservation members, the Oglala and Brule, both composing part of the Lakotas. Other groups live on the Cheyenne River, Standing Rock, and the Wood Mountain (in Canada) reservations. The western Lakota group comprised seven major subgroups or tribal bands, including such famous names as the Oglala, Brule, and Hunkpapa. Under the leadership of chiefs like Crazy Horse and Sitting Bull, these bands took their long-awaited revenge on General Custer at the Battle of Little Bighorn. The more easterly Lakota group included the Yankton and the Yanktonai subgroups. The major tribal subgroups of the northern Dakota group included the Sisseton, Wahpeton, Wahpekute, and Mdewakantonwon. *Address:* Cheyenne River Sioux Tribe, PO Box 590, East Hwy. 212, Eagle Butte, SD 57625 (605-964-7812).

Conata Basin. 148,000 acres. This vast shortgrass prairie ecosystem consists of a large tract of 142,000 acres in Buffalo Gap National Grassland just south of Badlands National Park and a smaller tract of 6,188 acres owned by the Nature Conservancy. It has long held a very large population of prairie dogs and is the site of one of a very few so-far successful reintroductions of black-tailed ferrets. It also supports reintroduced bison, bighorn sheep, and swift foxes, and probably all of South Dakota's other shortgrass wildlife. Bird species lists are available for Buffalo Gap National Grassland (see section). *Address:* The Nature Conservancy, Southwest South Dakota (605-342-4040) or TNC, Central US Conservation Region, 1101 West River Parkway, Suite 200, Minneapolis, MN 55415-1291 (612-331-0700).

Crazy Horse Memorial. This gigantic and still unfinished mountain sculpture is located four miles north of Custer City on US Hwy. 16/385. Naturalists are most likely to be more interested in the visitor center's associated *Indian Museum of North America* and its *Native American Education and Cultural Center* (605-673-4681).

Custer State Park. 75,000 acres. This state park, one of the largest in the United States, is operated by the South Dakota Game, Fish and Parks Department. It is located south of Hill City on Hwy. 87. The vegetation is mostly shortgrass prairie but with ponderosa pine and white spruce forests at upper elevations and hardwoods in valleys and coulees. Animals include more than 1,500 free-ranging bison, numerous elk, mule and white-tailed deer, and Rocky Mountain bighorn sheep (the Great Plains Audubon's race was extirpated in the 1920s but has been replaced by Rocky Mountain bighorns). Mountain goats were also introduced to the park, but most of them escaped and moved to higher altitudes, such as around Mount Rushmore and the Needles. Coyotes, mountain lions, and bobcats also occur. More than 180 bird species have been documented. As at Wind Cave and Badlands National Parks, prairie dogs are common. *Address:* HC 83, Box 70, Custer, SD 57730 (605-255-4464).

Farm Island State Recreation Area. 1,235 acres. This state-owned nature preserve and recreational area is just south of Pierre. A hiking trail extends from Pierre to the recreation area along the east shoreline of the Missouri River. Camping is permitted. *Address:* 1301 Farm Island Rd., Pierre, SD 57501 (605-773-2885).

Fort Pierre National Grassland. 115,996 acres. This is an enormous federally owned area of shortgrass and mixed-grass prairie, with an associated bird checklist of more than 200 species. Many gravel roads intersect the grassland, where western meadowlarks, chestnut-collared longspur, upland sandpipers, longbilled curlews, and marbled godwits are among the more characteristic breeding birds. Lark buntings are usually very common, and loggerhead shrikes and short-eared owls are also present. Both greater prairie-chickens and sharp-tailed grouse are present, and viewing blinds are available for public use. Ferruginous hawks and burrowing owls are often found near prairie dog colonies. No published mammal list is available, but the white-tailed jackrabbit, thirteen-lined ground squirrel, black-tailed prairie dog, bushy-tailed woodrat, coyote, mule deer, and pronghorn all occur in this general area. Camping is permitted. The northern boundary is located about ten miles south of Fort Pierre and may be reached via US Hwy. 83. *Address:* PO Box 417, 124 S. Euclid Ave., Pierre, SD 57501 (605-224-5517).

Grand River National Grassland. 156,000 acres. This national grassland consists of shortgrass and mixed-grass prairie in Perkins and Corson Counties, and adjoins the Standing Rock Indian Reservation. Bisected by the Grand River, the shortgrass prairie has prairie dogs and burrowing owls, and there are extensive river bottom woodlands. *Headquarters address:* PO Box 390, Lemmon, SD 57638 (605-374-3592).

Huron Wetland Management District. 87,500 acres. This wetland district manages 62 waterfowl production areas (WPAs) in eight central counties: Beadle, Buffalo, Hand, Hughes, Hyde, Jeraud, Sanborn, and Sully. Three of the notable WPAs in the district are *LeClair WPA*, 13 miles northwest of Iroquois; *Bauer WPA*, 13 miles east of Huron; and *Campbell WPA*, 15 miles southeast of Miller. *District office address:* Room 308, Federal Building, 200 4th St. SW, Huron, SD 57360 (805-353-5894).

Jewel Cave National Monument. Located 13 miles west of Custer City, this is one of the world's longest known caves, with more than 180 miles of mapped passages. The cave's rock formations are unusually diverse, with "nailhead" crystals, frostwork, and ribbons of rare red scintillate. *Address:* National Park Service, EE 1, Box 60AA, Custer, SD 57730 (605-673-8300).

Karl Mundt National Wildlife Refuge. 1,100 acres. Karl Mundt NWR is a small federal refuge located immediately below Fort Randall Dam and Lake Francis Case. It was established to protect wintering American bald eagles, and public access is restricted. However, an eagle-watching platform is located at *Randall Creek Recreation Area*, about three miles north of the refuge and near the south end of Fort Randall Dam. Karl Mundt NWR is located near the now-impounded Lewis and Clark campsite of September 8,1804, and is managed by Lakes Andes NWR (see section). The first section of the *Missouri National Recreational River* extends 39 miles from Fort Randall Dam south to Running Water; the second section extends 59 miles from Gavins Point Dam to Ponca Park, Nebraska. *Address of recreational river:* 508 E. 2nd St., Yankton, SD 57078 (605-665-0209). See also www.nps.gov/mnrr.

Lacreek National Wildlife Refuge. 16,250 acres. Situated about 15 miles southeast of Martin, South Dakota, this refuge at the northern edge of the Nebraska Sandhills consists of extensive marshes and shallow lakes in the Lake Creek valley along the South Fork of the White River. Trumpeter swans are present during most seasons, but many move south into spring-fed, ice-free creeks in the Nebraska Sandhills during winter. There are at least 93 nesting bird species among the 213 listed for the refuge by Jones. The refuge produces 15 to 20 trumpeter swans each summer as well as up to 6,000 ducks and 800 Canada geese. It also has one of the state's three nesting colonies of American white pelicans. At least 77 species are common to abundant during spring versus 53 species during fall and 15 during winter (Jones, 1990). Migrating sandhill cranes pass through during late March and early April and again in October. There are also spring and fall records of whooping cranes using the refuge. A total of 56 bird species were reported present year-round by Jones, so an estimated minimum of 74 percent of the refuge's total bird diversity is migratory. A recent checklist of 273 bird species (46 breeders) seen on the refuge since 1936 is available from the refuge manager at 29746 Bird Rd., Martin, SD 57551 (605-685-6508). It is also available online at https://www.fws.gov/refuge/lacreek/wildlife_and_habitat/bird_list.html.

LaFramboise Island Nature Area. 1,280 acres. This recreational area and nature preserve includes an eight-mile nature trail loop. Its entrance is located near Steamboat Park off Poplar Avenue in Pierre. It was at the nearby mouth of the Bad ("Teton") River, along the west shore of the Missouri River (now a Fort Pierre city park), that the Lewis and Clark Corps of Discovery met three Lakota (Brule) chiefs and their warriors. It proved to be a danger-fraught encounter that led to threats and near-bloodshed over gifts and trading procedures, probably caused or at least exacerbated by translation problems. *Address:* 28563 Powerhouse Rd., Pierre, SD 57501 (605-224-5862). Also in Pierre is the *South Dakota Cultural Heritage Center*, which exhibits such items as an Arikara bullboat, a tipi, a stunning war-pony effigy, examples of Native American beadwork, and a replica of the Jefferson peace medals carried by Lewis and Clark. *Address:* 900 Governors Dr., Pierre, SD 57501 (605-773-3458).

Lake Andes National Wildlife Refuge. 5,450 acres. This refuge is located north of Fort Randall Dam in Charles Mix County. It includes Lake Andes, a shallow Pleistocene glacial lake and marsh, which occupies 4,700 acres of open water and marsh. The nearby Karl E. Mundt National Wildlife Refuge (see section) is located below Fort Randall Dam. It occupies less than 1,000 acres but is an important wintering area for American bald eagles. At least 113 species are common to abundant at the Lake Andes refuge complex during spring versus 94 species during fall and 17 during winter (Jones, 1990). There are at least 85 nesting birds among the 214 listed for the area by Jones. A total of 45 bird species were reported present year-round by Jones, so an estimated minimum of 79 percent of the area's total bird diversity is migratory. The state-controlled *Lake Andes Wetland Management District* encompasses 34,682 acres of wetlands and grassland easements over a 13-county area of southeastern South Dakota, including Aurora, Bon Homme, Brule, Charles Mix, Clay, Davison, Douglas, Hanson, Hutchinson, Lincoln, Turner, Union, and Yankton Counties. A recent checklist for the complex (including both refuges and the wetland management district) has 213 species, with 97 wetland species (37 breeders), and is available from the refuge manager at Box 391, Lake Andes, SD 57356 (605-487-7603).

Lewis and Clark Keelboat Information Center. This state-operated tourist information center is located in Chamberlain just off I-90 near the bridge crossing Lake Francis Case. It is devoted largely to Lewis and Clark. Exhibits feature some of the supplies carried on the expedition, its regional discoveries, and murals showing historical aspects of the expedition. The information center also has surrounding native vegetation and provides a spectacular overview of Lake Francis Case. Chamberlain's other historic and cultural attractions include the *Atka Lakota Museum and Cultural Center* at St. Joseph's Indian School at 1301 Main St. (1-800-798-3452). This is a modern Native American museum and art gallery with both historic and recent Lakota cultural items. Two miles north of town on South Dakota Hwy. 50 is *Roam Free Park*, with two nature trails and native grassland vegetation.

Lewis and Clark State Recreation Area. 1,227 acres. This small state recreation area adjoins the 32,000-acre Lewis and Clark Lake and Gavins Point Dam. Calumet Bluff, where Lewis and Clark met formally with the Yankton Sioux, is located on the Nebraska side of the river, about two miles east of Gavins Point Dam. This bluff, about 180 feet high, is part of a series of steep-sided reddish to brownish loess promontories that appear on both sides of the river. Calumet Bluff is now the site of a Lewis and Clark Visitor Center (see section in Nebraska), which contains exhibits on the river, the Lewis and Clark expedition, and the council held with the Yankton Sioux. A nearby nature trail is 1.5 miles long. At the western end of the reservoir on the Nebraska side is a lowland area of woods and wetlands, the *Bazille Creek Wildlife Management Area*, totaling 4,500 acres. Camping is permitted at the state recreation area. *Address:* 43349 Hwy. 52, Yankton, SD 57078 (605-668-2985).

Lower Brule Indian Reservation and **Crow Creek Indian Reservation.** These large reservations—the Lower Brule Indian Reservation is 132,601 acres and the Crow Creek Indian Reservation is 125,591 acres—border both sides of the impounded Missouri River (Lake Sharpe) in the region of the Big Bend for about

80 miles of shoreline distance. These reservations are home to the Lower Brule and Crow Creek components of the Lakota Sioux. There are summer powwows in August, and the reservation lands support large tribal bison herds. A *Native American National Scenic Byway* (the Bureau of Indian Affairs Hwy. 10 and 4) crosses both reservations, linking Chamberlain and Pierre. This near-wilderness road passes scenic rolling hills that are often capped with blackish Pierre shale of Cretaceous age. Fort Kiowa, built in 1822, was located just south of the Lower Brule Reservation, and Fort Defiance, built in 1842, was located within it, as was Fort Hale. These forts, as well as Fort Thompson and Fort Pierre, were once important jumping-off points for prospectors headed for the Black Hills.

Madison Wetland Management District. 52,000 acres. This wetland district, in the heart of the glaciated pothole region of eastern South Dakota, manages wetlands ranging in size from 40 to 400 acres and includes more than 36,000 acres preserved in waterfowl production areas. It includes eight east-central counties: Brookings, Deuel, Hamlin, Kingsbury, Lake, McCook, Minnehaha, Moody, Sanborn, and Sully. A recent checklist containing 297 bird species, including 96 wetland bird species (42 breeders) that have been observed in the district, is available from the Madison Wetland District Office, Box 48, Madison, SD 57042 (605-256-2974).

Mammoth Site of Hot Springs. This enclosed facility contains a 26,000-year-old site of at least 60 mammoth skeletal remains that are now under excavation. Wolves, camels, pronghorns, rabbits, and hares are among a total of at least 85 species of fossil animals and plants that have also been found, including a giant short-faced bear that was larger than present-day grizzly bears. The bookstore is notably strong in geology and paleontology. *Address:* PO Box 692, Hot Springs, SD 57747-0692 (605-745-6017).

Mobridge. The name Mobridge is a shortened version of the Missouri River Bridge and was first used by telegraph operators. It was here, at the mouth of the Grand River, that the first Arikara ("Rikara") village was encountered by Lewis and Clark. A smallpox epidemic in 1780–81 had already killed most of the population of perhaps, originally, as many as 30,000 people. By 1800 the Arikaras were about 3,800 persons. Like

Adult male bison.

the Pawnees, they were part of the Caddoan language group. The quite different Siouan-Catawba language group comprised a large, multitribal assemblage, including the Lakota, Dakota, Mandan, Hidatsa, Ponca, Omaha, Missouria, and Kansa tribes.

Mount Rushmore National Memorial. 1,277 acres. Located east of Hill City on Rte. 244, this world-famous group of presidential faces cut into the granite face of Mount Rushmore is probably mainly of interest to naturalists because of the mountain goats that were released here in 1924. The mountain goats can often be seen on the mountain slopes as well as on Black Elk (previously Harney) Peak and in the Needles area. *Address:* 13000 Hwy. 244, Building 31, Ste. 1, Keystone, SD 57751 (605-574-2523).

Museum of Geology. This museum is located in Rapid City at the South Dakota School of Mines and Technology and is noted for its excellent displays of fossils, rocks, and minerals. Its collections include 350,000 specimens from around the world. *Address:* 501 E. Saint Joseph St., Rapid City, SD 57701 (605-394-2467).

Pine Ridge Indian Reservation. 1,700,000 acres. This reservation in southwestern South Dakota includes Shannon, Washabaugh, and part of Jackson Counties. It is home to most of the Oglala branch of the Lakota-speaking group, or about 15,000 people in 2000. The village of Wounded Knee was the site of the December 29, 1890, massacre by the Seventh Cavalry, during which Minneconjou Chief Big Foot (who had been returning to the Pine Ridge agency to surrender), at least 50 men, and more than 200 women and children were killed. During the killing spree, about 25 of the cavalrymen were also killed. Probably most of them died from inept crossfire, since a good deal of drinking had been done by the cavalry while they were waiting for the dawn to attack. Afterward, the soldiers scoured the hillsides to hunt out and kill any surviving women and children who had managed to flee. Incredibly, about 20 Congressional Medals of Honor were given to cavalry participants of this infamous event. In 1973 there was a 71-day standoff between federal law enforcement agents and Native Americans (from various tribes representing the newly formed American Indian Movement) who were occupying Wounded Knee in protest of reservation living conditions. During the standoff, a Cherokee and an Oglala man were killed and a US marshal was wounded. In 1980 the US Supreme Court offered eight Sioux tribes a settlement payment for the treaty-breaking seizure of the tribe's sacred Black Hills. The offer, now worth more than $750 million, was refused. In 2000, 110 years late, the US Congress passed a resolution expressing "deep regret" for the Wounded Knee massacre. However, the Pine Ridge IR still remains among the most poverty-stricken Indian reservations in America, with rampant malnutrition, alcoholism, diabetes, and other diseases, high infantile mortality, record unemployment and suicide rates, and abysmally low life expectancies (Johnsgard, 2008, *Wind Through the Buffalo Grass*). Only four sitting US presidents have visited an Indian reservation or tribal headquarters. These were Calvin Coolidge in 1927 (Pine Ridge Reservation, celebrating the granting of long-deferred citizenship to Native Americans); Franklin Roosevelt in 1936 (Cherokee Nation Headquarters, North Carolina); Bill Clinton in 1999 (Pine Ridge Reservation, South Dakota); and Barrack Obama in 2014 (Standing Rock Reservation, North Dakota). Our current (2017) president has not been invited to any.

Pocasse National Wildlife Refuge. 2,540 acres. Located in Brown County just north of Pollock off US Hwy. 83 and bordering the east side of the Missouri River, this NWR is mostly marshes and open water (1,045 acres of wetland). The refuge is an important stopover area for migrating sandhill and whooping cranes as well as for waterfowl. No bird list for Pocasse NWR is yet available. Administered from Sand Lake NWR (see section), general information may be obtained from that refuge manager. Address: c/o Sand Lake NWR, RR 1, Box 253, Columbia, SD 57433 (605-885-6320).

Rosebud Indian Reservation. 900,000 acres. This reservation is in Todd County in south-central South Dakota, where the Brule (Sicango) branch of the Lakota-speaking Sioux were interred at the end of the Indian Wars. About 10,000 Brules were living there in 2,000. Three other branches of the Sioux (San Arcs, Minneconjous, and Oohenonops) were moved to the 1.4 million-acre Cheyenne River Indian Reservation, which had a population of about 8,500 residents in 2000 (Johnsgard, 2008, *Wind Through the Buffalo Grass*).

Sacagawea Monument and **Sitting Bull Monument.** After the Lewis and Clark expedition, Sacagawea evidently spent the last part of her about 25 years in the vicinity of Fort Manuel, a Missouri Fur Company post that was located in what is now Corson County, South Dakota, near the present North Dakota border. She died in December 1812, not long after giving birth to a daughter, Lizette. Although her exact burial site is unknown, it has probably since been covered by Lake Oahe. A monument to Sacagawea is located on the west side of Lake Oahe near Mobridge. It is on the Standing Rock Indian Reservation (see sections in both the South Dakota and North Dakota listings) about six miles west of Mobridge on US Hwy. 12, then four miles south on South Dakota Hwy. 1806. After the death of his mother, Jean Baptiste spent a few years with Captain Clark in St. Louis but later traveled abroad, became a mountain man and guide, and eventually died of pneumonia at the age of 61 in Oregon.

About a hundred yards from the Sacagawea memorial is a seven-ton granite bust of Sitting Bull, the great Lakota chief of the Indian wars, who was reburied here in 1953 after an initial interment at Fort Yates, North Dakota. He had surrendered in 1880, several years after fleeing to Canada with the few survivors of his Hunkpapa tribe, and been brought to Fort Union, North Dakota, for indefinite semiconfinement. In 1890, after having been falsely accused of fostering the messianic Ghost Dance ritual that had been sweeping the western plains, Sitting Bull was shot and killed, along with his son, while he was being detained by American Indian police.

Samuel H. Ordway, Jr. Memorial Preserve. 7,800 acres. The Ordway Prairie is a tallgrass prairie and wetlands—the largest tallgrass prairie in South Dakota and an important grassland/wetland preserve for migrating and nesting birds. More than 300 plant species have been found here, and up to 2,000 pairs of ducks nest during a good year. A small herd of bison is also present. Owned by the Nature Conservancy: 35333 115th St., Leola, SD 57456 (605-439-3475).

Sand Lake National Wildlife Refuge. 45,000 acres. This refuge is located 25 miles northeast of Aberdeen, Brown County, in the James River valley, and was part of the shoreline of glacial Lake Dakota until about 10,000 years ago. It consists of more than 21,000 acres of marshes, grasslands, shallow impoundments, shelterbelts, and fields. Sand Lake NWR has the world's largest nesting colony of Franklin's gulls and has been identified as a Ramsar Wetland of International Importance. It attracts hundreds of thousands of snow geese and other waterfowl during migration, and four breeding grebe species (eared, western, Clark's, and pied-billed) as well as nesting canvasback, redhead, lesser scaup, and ruddy duck. Notable nesting shorebirds include the marbled godwit, Wilson's phalarope, and three terns (common, Forster's, and black). This refuge also administers Pocasse NWR (see section) and is located among more than 150,000 acres of regional state-owned wildlife management areas in the glaciated pothole region of northeastern South Dakota. At least 91 bird species are common to abundant at Sand Lake NWR during spring versus 60 species during fall and 10 during winter (Jones, 1990). There are

at least 111 nesting birds among the 239 species listed by Jones. A total of 49 bird species were listed as present year-round, so an estimated minimum of 80 percent of the refuge's total bird diversity is migratory. A recent checklist for Sand Lake NWR totals 263 species, including 106 wetland species (of which 55 are breeders), and is available from the refuge manager at 39650 Sand Lake Dr., Columbia, SD 57433 (605-885-6320).

Sand Lake Wetland Management District. 9,000 square miles. Sand Lake WMD is the largest wetland management district in the country, encompassing thousands of square miles. The WMD includes ten of South Dakota's north-central counties: Brown, Campbell, Corson, Dewey, Edwards, Faulk, McPherson, Potter, Spink, and Walworth. It contains 45,000 acres of land under federal protection, involving 162 waterfowl production areas, and includes an additional 550,000 acres protected by conservation easements. *Address:* See Sand Lake NWR section.

Snake Creek State Recreation Area. 735 acres. This recreation area is located on the shoreline of impounded Lake Francis Case. It is directly west of Platte via State Hwy. 44, near the now-flooded Lewis and Clark campsite of September 11, 1804. Camping is permitted. The *Platte Creek State Recreation Area* is located about eight miles farther south, near the Lewis and Clark campsite of September 10, 1804. Camping is also permitted here. *Address:* 35316 SD-44, Platte, SD 57369 (605-337-2587).

Spirit Mound State Park. 240 acres. Spirit Mound is seven miles north of Vermillion on the west side of State Hwy. 19. It is a low, treeless promontory that was climbed by Captain Clark and a small party on August 25, 1804, from which they saw large herds of elk and bison. A restoration of the original prairie vegetation has been underway since 2001. In Vermillion, the *W. H. Over Museum* has a Lewis and Clark–Spirit Mound Learning and Information Center. Associated with it is a Heritage Garden featuring plants observed or collected by Lewis and Clark. The Vermillion River's name comes from the red clay pigments along its banks. The nearby 39-mile section of the Missouri River from Fort Randall Dam south to the confluence of the Niobrara River is also part of the *Missouri National Recreational River* (see Karl Mundt NWR section). About 30 miles north of Vermillion is Sioux Falls, home to the *Center* *for Western Studies* at Augustana University and the *Washington Pavilion of Arts and Sciences*, which house both Native American and regional art galleries. *Address:* Spirit Mound State Park, 31148 SD-19, Vermillion, SD 57069 (605-987-2263).

Standing Rock Indian Reservation. 2,328,534 acres. This massive reservation is centered on the Missouri River and extends from northern South Dakota into southern North Dakota. The Standing Rock IR is home to some of the Dakota- and Lakota-dialect branches of the Sioux Nation and extends along the west shoreline into southwestern North Dakota, north to about 25 miles beyond Fort Yates. The reservation was named for a rock sacred to the Arikaras and Lakotas whose form resembles that of a seated woman. It is located across from the Indian Agency headquarters at Fort Yates. Sitting Bull, chief of the Hunkpapa branch of the Sioux, spent most of the period from 1883 to 1890 at the Standing Rock Reservation. (See also the North Dakota section on this reservation and the Sacagawea Monument and Sitting Bull Monument section.)

Waubay National Wildlife Refuge. 4,600 acres. This refuge is situated eight miles north of Waubay, Day County, in the glaciated till region of northeastern South Dakota, the heart of South Dakota's pothole country. It contains nearly 5,000 acres of marshlands, lakes, grasslands, brush, and woodlands. It has all the species of nesting grebes as those mentioned for Sand Lake NWR plus horned and occasional red-necked grebes. It also attracts the same nesting species of diving ducks, shorebirds, and terns. At least 106 bird species are common to abundant at Waubay NWR during spring versus 105 species during fall and 7 during winter (Jones, 1990). There are at least 109 nesting birds among the 244 listed for the refuge by Jones. A total of 29 bird species were reported present year-round by Jones, so an estimated minimum of 88 percent of the refuge's total bird diversity is migratory. A recent bird checklist containing 244 species, including 103 wetland species (52 breeders), is available from the refuge manager at RR 1, Waubay, SD 57273 (605-947-4695).

Waubay Wetland Management District. About 5,000 acres. This district includes more than 300 waterfowl production areas in six wetland-rich northeastern counties: Clark, Codington, Day, Grant, Marshall, and Roberts. It is headquartered at Waubay, South Dakota, in the glaciated Coteau Hills of northeastern South Dakota, and contains marshlands, lakes, grasslands, brushy areas, and oak timber. The bird list for Waubay NWR (see section) is probably applicable here. *Address of district office:* 44401 134A St., Waubay, SD 57273 (605-947-4521).

West Bend State Recreation Area. 154 acres. This state-owned recreational site is along the famous Big Bend of the Missouri, now a part of impounded Lake Sharpe, which formed behind Big Ben Dam. The historic river length of Big Bend was 30 miles, but the overland distance between the two ends of the loop was only about 2,000 yards. The SRA is located 35 miles southeast of Pierre, off SD Hwy. 34. Camping is permitted. *Address:* 22154 W. Bend Rd., Harrold, SD 57536 (605-773-2885).

Wind Cave National Park. 33,000 acres. Located 11 miles north of Hot Springs, this park is mostly mixed-grass prairie, with bison, white-tailed and mule deer, elk, pronghorn, prairie dogs, and other plains wildlife. It has been recognized by the National Geographic Society (2011) as one of the nation's ten best national parks for seeing charismatic megafauna, such as bison and elk. There are more than 30 miles of hiking trails. Wind Cave is the third-largest cave in North America and the fifth largest in the world, with about 136 miles of explored caverns, yet perhaps as little as 10 percent of the cave has so far been mapped. The cave is noted geologically for its rare "boxwork" calcite formations and unusual popcorn and frostwork stalactites. Open daily, entrance prices vary with type and length of tour. *Address:* Wind Cave National Park, 26611 US Hwy. 385, Hot Springs, SD 57747 (605-745-4600), www.nps.gov/wica.

WYOMING

Wyoming (WY) is a state of superlatives for naturalists, having two of our most wildlife-rich and most beloved of our national parks, Yellowstone and Grand Teton (Johnsgard, 1982; 2013, *Yellowstone Wildlife*), and having seemingly endless amounts of open vistas and the lowest human population of any state. Wyoming also has ten state parks and 450,000 acres of wildlife habitat management areas that are public-access along with 225 miles of public-access streams and 21,000 lake acres. Wyoming also has 18.5 million acres of Bureau of Land Management (BLM) properties, 1.9 million acres of national grasslands, 2.4 million acres of national forests, and 2.3 million acres of National Park Service lands. Federal acreage in Wyoming composes 42.3 percent of the state's total land area, and the highest percentage of public-access lands among all the states discussed in this book.

Wyoming likewise supports the largest remaining state population of pronghorns, which declined one third from about 550,000 in 2006 to 360,000 in 2013. Wyoming also has the best remaining population of the increasingly threatened greater sage-grouse (Johnsgard, 2002, *Grassland Grouse*). Its population declined in the state by 56 percent between 2007 and 2013, but, in a deep bow to ranchers and oil/coal industry, the US Fish and Wildlife Service (USFWS) decided in 2015 to exclude it from further consideration as an endangered species.

The Greater Yellowstone–Teton ecosystem of western Wyoming and parts of Idaho and Montana supported about 700 grizzly bears by 2017. This is the largest regional population south of Canada, and one whose positive response to long-term protection from hunting has increased their population from fewer than 150 in the 1960s. In June 2017, federal officials decided to remove federal protection for grizzly bears as a threatened species in the greater Yellowstone region, which will open a floodgate of applications from would-be hunters.

Wyoming also has one of the largest surviving state populations of black-tailed prairie dogs, and is also where the world's last surviving population of black-footed ferret was serendipitously found. This remarkable event occurred in 1981, long after the species had been judged extinct by the mid-1900s. After a ranch dog carried a dead weasel-like animal back to the ranch house, its intrigued owner decided to have the strange mammal identified. The resulting identification of the animal as a ferret proved that a small population of black-footed ferrets was still surviving among white-tailed prairie dog colonies on BLM land near Meeteetse in northwestern Wyoming.

After the USFWS personnel were alerted to the ferret discovery, a massive effort was undertaken to save the species from extinction. This effort began by capturing essentially all the remaining wild ferret population, instigating a long period of captive breeding, and finally performing a series of carefully monitored releases back into the species' historic range. The most successful of these releases were those begun in 1994 in the South Dakota Badlands and Buffalo Gap National Grassland (Higgins et al., 2000).

Starting in 1991, black-footed ferret releases were successfully achieved in Wyoming's Shirley Basin, Carbon County, and by 2008 releases in Thunder Basin National Grassland had begun. As of 2013, the Shirley Basin population was estimated at 39 breeding adults, but had ranged from 203 to 229 individuals between 2006 and 2012. At that time 19 ferrets were also present at Meeteetse.

The number of released and reestablished breeding adult ferrets declined nationally by 40 percent between 2008 and 2015. As of 2015, there were about 296 mature ferrets surviving in nature, of which 206 were in four self-sustaining populations, with two (mostly in Canata Basin of the Badlands/Buffalo Gap region) in Pennington County, South Dakota, one (Aubrey Valley) near Seligman, northwestern Arizona, and one (Shirley Basin) south of Casper, Wyoming, with a collective range of about 190 square miles.

As of 2015 there were also four ferret populations having limited survival success in South Dakota, Kansas, Utah, and New Mexico. There were also six recently initiated populations of uncertain status in Montana, Colorado, and Arizona. Finally, there were six declining or extirpated populations in South Dakota, Montana, Colorado, and New Mexico, and two extirpated populations in Canada and Mexico (*IUCN Red List of Threatened Species,* 2017).

As to prairie dogs, a 1998 survey by the National Wildlife Federation concluded that a 99.5 percent reduction in US black-tailed prairie dog colony acreage occurred between 1870 and 1998, from an estimated 116 million acres and over a billion animals to about 635,000 colony acres and perhaps 8 million to 16 million animals. A somewhat more optimistic 2011 estimate of the black-tailed prairie dog population by the USFWS was 24 million animals occupying an estimated range of 2.4 million acres. In 1998 there were possibly 136,000 additional acres of occupied habitat in northern Mexico and about 1,000 acres in southern Alberta.

During the past four to five decades, the USFWS has spent hundreds of thousands of dollars in trying to save the black-footed ferret from extinction, a species whose survival is dependent on large populations of prairie dogs, which the US Department of Agriculture has ironically been indefatigably attempting to

Adult black-tailed prairie dog uttering jump-yip call.

eliminate by massive poisoning campaigns for more than a century (Johnsgard, 2005). A 2015 estimate of the US black-tailed prairie dog population by the Defenders of Wildlife was 10 million to 20 million animals in 11 states occupying 1 million to 2 million acres, or about 1 percent of its original range.

Bighorn Canyon National Recreation Area. 120,000 acres. This steep-sided, 1,000-foot-deep canyon in northern Wyoming north of Lovell was partly impounded by the construction of Yellowtail Dam on the Bighorn River in Montana, forming a 71 square-mile lake. From the top of the canyon, turkey vultures, golden eagles, and other raptors can often be seen in flight or perched along the canyon's steep walls. There is a visitor center in Lovell. North of Lovell is also the *Pryor Mountains Wild Horse Range*, a 40,000-acre area where horses that reportedly were descended from those of early Spanish conquistadors run free. There is also a good chance of seeing Rocky Mountain bighorn sheep in this region. The horse herd is managed by the Bureau of Land Management (contact 866-468-7826 or wildhorse@blm.gov). *Address of recreation area headquarters:* 5 Ave. B, PO Box 7458, Fort Smith, MT 59035 (406-666-2412).

Bighorn Mountains. This isolated north-south mountain range in north-central Wyoming is geologically similar to the Rocky Mountains and includes the second-highest peak—Cloud Peak at 13,167 feet—in Wyoming. The range is about 120 miles long and is bounded by shortgrass plains and two northern-flowing rivers, to the west the Bighorn River and to the east the Powder River. Bighorn National Forest (1,107,000 acres) surrounds almost the entire range (see the South Dakota introduction, which compares Bighorn Mountain and Black Hills flora and fauna). The birds of the Bighorn Mountains have been documented by Canterbury, Johnsgard, and Dunning (2013), who reported more than 320 regional species and provided some suggested birding routes. Canterbury and Johnsgard (2017) also described the common birds of the Bighorn Mountains foothills and the vicinity of the *Brinton Museum* (600 acres), a historic ranch converted into a major western art museum near Big Horn. *Address of Brinton Museum:* 239 Brinton Rd., Big Horn, WY 82833 (307-672-3273). *Address of Bighorn National Forest:* 1949 S. Sheridan Ave., Sheridan, WY 82801 (307-672-0751).

Boysen State Park. 39,545 acres. The Wyoming State Parks Department manages Boysen State Park. Located north of Shoshoni, in Fremont County, the park surrounds a reservoir and has about 20,000 land acres, including some native grasslands. No species checklists are available. *Address:* State Parks, Historic Sites and Trails Department, 2301 Central Ave., Cheyenne, WY 82002 (307-777-6323).

Buffalo Bill Center of the West. This large complex in Cody consists of five separate western-oriented museums and art galleries. One, the *Plains Indian Museum*, has one of the world's best collections of Plains Indian art and artifacts from many tribes, including the Arapaho, Blackfeet, Comanche, Crow, Cheyenne, Kiowa, Pawnee, Shoshone, and Sioux. Another, the *Draper Museum of Natural History*, concentrates on the biology and ecology of the Greater Yellowstone ecosystem. *Address:* 720 Sheridan Ave., Cody, WY 82414-3428 (307-587-4771), www.bbhc.org.

Bureau of Land Management. The BLM controls 17.5 million acres of land in Wyoming (28 percent of the state's total land area), much of which is arid upland habitat that supports shortgrass or scrub-steppe species, including prairie dogs (both white-tailed and black-tailed). In Sheridan County, a 560-acre *BLM Recreation and Public Purposes site* had 268 acres of black-tailed prairie dog colonies in 1979, and a coal-lease site (the *Wildcat Preference Right Lease Application Site*) of 4,500 acres in Campbell County had 1,166 colony acres of prairie dogs. Among seven prairie dog sites surveyed, 34 associated species of mammals were seen as well as 62 bird species, 8 reptiles, and 2 amphibians. One example of the BLM's large sage-steppe holdings in east-central Wyoming (48,400 acres) occurs along the Middle Fork of the Powder River, Johnson County, and is administered by the regional BLM office (PO Box 670, Buffalo WY 82834). Greater sage-grouse, golden eagles, and other sage-adapted species are present along with species more typical of ponderosa pine forest. In the same county and having similar habitats are the state-managed *Bud Love Wildlife Management Area* (8,000 acres), northwest of Buffalo, and *Taylor Wildlife Management Habitat Area* (10,158 acres), west of Kaycee, both with shortgrass prairie, scrub, and coniferous woodlands. For information contact the Wyoming Game and Fish Department, Cheyenne WY 82002 (207-777-4600). For information on specific Wyoming BLM holdings, contact the state BLM headquarters, 2515 Warren Ave., PO Box 1828, Cheyenne WY 82003, or the BLM Casper District, 1701 East E St., Casper WY 82601.

Devils Tower National Monument. 1,347 acres. Devils Tower is a federally owned site managed by the National Park Service. The 1,200-foot column of volcanic basalt is surrounded by ponderosa pines, scrubby thickets, and grasslands. A bird species checklist (158 species, 75 nesters) is available. Burrowing owls have not been reported, but prairie dogs have long been common (19 colony acres in 1994). *Address:* Box 10, Devils Tower WY 82714 (307-467-5283), www.nps.gov/deto/. *Keyhole State Park* (15,674 acres) is nearby, with 6,256 acres of prairie. It is managed by the Wyoming State Parks, Historic Sites, and Trails, 2301 Central Ave., Cheyenne WY 82002 (307-777-6323).

Glendo State Park. 22,430 acres. This state park is located near Glendo in Platte County. The 9,930 acres of land surrounding an impoundment include some grasslands. No species checklists are available. *Address:* Wyoming State Parks, Historic Sites, and Trails, 2301 Central Ave., Cheyenne, WY 82002 (307-777-6323).

Guernsey State Park. 6,227 acres. Located north of Guernsey in Platte County, this area is partly an impoundment with about 4,000 acres of surrounding land, including some prairie and sage-steppe as well as pines and juniper woodlands. No species checklists are available. *Address:* Wyoming State Parks, Historic Sites, and Trails, 2301 Central Ave., Cheyenne, WY 82002 (307-777-6323).

Hutton Lake National Wildlife Refuge. 1,968 acres. Located about ten miles south of Laramie at about 7,000 feet elevation, this small refuge's arid grassland supports a population of white-tailed prairie dogs (and attracts raptors such as ferruginous hawks and golden eagles), mountain plovers, McCown's and chestnut-collared longspurs, and grassland sparrows such as lark buntings, chipping sparrows, and lark sparrows. Several small lakes that vary in size and depth are present, with the one nearest the refuge entrance the largest and deepest. It often has a variety of migrant ducks, plus grebes (eared and western). The most distant wetlands include a marshy area that attracts many migrant shorebirds and dabbling ducks. Managed from the Arapahoe NWR in Colorado, the refuge roads are barely passable rutted trails, and there is no available water or toilet facilities. In the same general region (off Hwy. 230) is Hattie Lake, a flood-control reservoir. Depending on the amount of water present, it may attract large numbers of diving ducks, and many shorebirds, gulls, and American white pelicans. Nearby (12 miles northwest of Laramie) is the smaller *Bamforth National Wildlife Refuge* (1,166 acres). It is mostly alkaline-adapted greasewood shrub-steppe, with only a small amount of grasslands. This NWR is also managed through Colorado's Arapaho NWR. *Address:* PO Box 457, Walden, CO 80480 (303-482-5155).

Lake DeSmet. Lake DeSmet is a historic 258-acre lake near the eastern slope of the Bighorns, between Buffalo and Story, and one of the few natural lakes in eastern Wyoming. Clear Creek provides the lake's water supply, and for many years the Texaco Oil Company controlled its levels. During the 1970s, the lake levels were raised 40 feet, covering the mudflats and sandbars that had long been used by shorebirds and wading birds. Nevertheless, it is a still magnet for migrating loons, diving ducks, and gulls. Western grebes stage here in substantial numbers during migration, and four species of migrant loons have been seen.

Ocean Lake Wildlife Habitat Management Area. 12,750 acres. Located 17 miles northwest of Riverton, off Hwy. 134, about half of the area consists of a large, shallow lake with marshy edges that attract many migrating ducks and grebes. The site also attracts sandhill cranes, about 400 of which stage here during spring and fall, and some remain to nest. Up to 3,000 geese and 10,000 ducks stop here during migration. Owned by the Wyoming Game and Fish Department. *Address:* 5400 Bishop Blvd., Cheyenne, WY 82006 (307-777-4600).

Seminoe State Park. 16,970 acres. Located 34 miles north of Sinclair in Carbon County, this park is situated around a reservoir with about 5,000 acres of grassland and scrub uplands. *Address:* Wyoming State Parks, Historic Sites, and Trails, 2301 Central Ave., Cheyenne, WY 82002 (307-777-6323).

In the same area are the *Morgan Creek Wildlife Habitat Management Area* (4,125 acres), 30 miles north of Sinclair, and the *Laramie Peak Wildlife Habitat*

Management Area (11,000 acres), 40 miles west of Wheatland, Platte County. Both sites have extensive grasslands and sage-steppe and are within the Great Basin ecoregion of the Nature Conservancy. No species checklists are available. The two WHMA sites are managed by the Wyoming Game and Fish Department, 5400 Bishop Blvd., Cheyenne, WY 82006 (307-777-4600).

Table Mountain Wildlife Habitat Management Unit. 1,716 acres. Located about 15 miles southeast of Torrington, this state-owned area is a major migration stopover point for waterfowl in spring. During fall it is open to controlled waterfowl hunting. The marsh attracts thousands of snow geese and hundreds of American white pelicans as well as Canada, Ross's, and greater white-fronted geese, plus dozens of duck species. Migrant shorebirds include many "peep" (*Calidris*) sandpipers, especially stilt sandpipers. About ten miles to the west (and about five miles south of Yoder) is *Bump Sullivan Reservoir* and nearby *Springer Lake*, the latter owned by the Wyoming Game and Fish Department. Bump Sullivan Reservoir's migrant birds are much like those of Table Mountain, but the reservoir lacks marshy habitats. Springer Lake is an alkaline wetland that is notable for its migrant shorebirds, American white pelicans, double-crested cormorants, Canada and snow geese, sandhill cranes, and grebes. For more information, contact the Wyoming Game and Fish Department headquarters at 5400 Bishop Blvd., Cheyenne, WY 82006 (307-777-4600).

Thunder Basin National Grassland. 572,211 acres. This federally owned site consists of shortgrass and shrub-steppe plains at 3,600–5,200 feet elevation. This is the largest area of federally protected grasslands in Wyoming, which support the state's biggest herd of pronghorns as well as mule deer and other sage-steppe species. Prairie dog colonies in this grassland once had the largest collective colony acreage of any

of the national grasslands (about 18,200 acres in 1998). However, sylvatic plague in 2001 caused great losses here. The Douglas office of the US Forest Service has maps of the prairie dog colonies at Thunder Basin. A bird species checklist (231 species) is available, with the burrowing owl, greater sage-grouse, mountain plover, long-billed curlew, and both longspurs shown among the regular breeders. In addition, there are 72 species of mammals, including elk, pronghorn, mule deer, mountain lion, bobcat, coyote, and swift fox. *Address:* USFS, 2550 E. Richards St., Douglas, WY 82633 (307-358-4690).

University of Wyoming Geological Museum. This museum on the University of Wyoming campus in Laramie is rather small but, nevertheless, large enough to hold a 75-foot-long *Apatosaurus* (brontosaurus) skeleton and the most complete specimen of an *Allosaurus* ever found. *Address:* 200 N. 9th St., Laramie, WY 82072 (307-766-2646).

Whitney Preserve. 4,600 acres. This Nature Conservancy prairie preserve in the northern Black Hills is located southwest of Hot Springs near the South Dakota border and includes about 2,000 acres of prairie. Entrance is by permission only. For information contact The Nature Conservancy, 258 Main St., Suite 200, Lander WY 82520, or 822 Main St., Rapid City SD 57701 (605-342-4040).

Wyoming Dinosaur Center. This new museum centers on Wyoming's dinosaurs with more than 30 mounted skeletons and hundreds of displays and dioramas. There is a *Supersaurus* skeleton, one of the largest dinosaurs ever mounted, and a 35-foot *Tyrannosaurs rex* charging a *Triceratops*. It also has on display the only *Archaeopteryx* specimen exhibited outside of Europe, one of only 12 known specimens of this famous Cretaceous-era feathered reptile. *Address:* 110 Carter Ranch Rd., Thermopolis, WY (307-864-2997).

IV

The Central Plains

March Wings and April Drums

*Skeins of snow geese can still etch a March
   Nebraska sky from dawn to dusk,
Prairie-chickens still annually greet the
   spring sunrises with their ancestral
   rituals,
And the spine-tingling cries of sandhill
   cranes coming to roost on the Platte
Still bring with them the distant echoes
   of thundering bison, trumpeting
   mammoths,
And even of times before recorded time.
We can still totally lose ourselves in their
   grace and beauty,
Imagining that we have discovered some
   other Eden,
And hopefully resolve to act in such a way
That these birds might still be able to cast
   their marvelous spells
Just as strongly on our descendants a
   century hence as they do today.*

"A Century of Ornithology in Nebraska"
(Johnsgard, 2001)

For Nebraska naturalists, March is a time for rejoicing, for on its soothing south winds sweep wave after wave of northbound migrant birds. By the first of March, the Platte River has usually fully thawed, although thin ice shelves might line its edges on frosty mornings, and dying snow patches are usually confined to deeper ditches and the shady sides of buildings.

Western meadowlarks are appearing on fence posts along country roads and are tentatively starting to re-claim old territories or establish new ones. In towns and cities, northern cardinals have been singing enthu-siastically from trees and shrubs for nearly two months. Wintering sparrows, such as tree sparrows and juncos, and horned larks are now abandoning their foraging grounds in weedy edges, stubble, and plowed fields and are disappearing. They are quickly replaced by countless red-winged blackbirds, whose loose flocks dance over the fields like restless spirits, searching for brief resting places.

Early March is a time in Nebraska when the natu-ral world changes on an almost day-to-day basis, with spring arriving in erratic fits and starts, as bone-chilling north and welcome south winds blow across the plains in regular alternation. Nevertheless, day lengths dur-ing early March are increasing at a perceptible rate, and the sunrises and sunsets creep ever closer toward marking exact eastern and western compass points on the horizon.

As recently as 40 years ago, the first of March rep-resented the average arrival date for sandhill cranes at the Platte River. Recent warmer winters and ear-lier thaws have tended to shift their first arrival date back into mid-February, the birds being driven ever northward by a combination of hormones, experi-ence, and melting ice. Thus, by the middle of Feb-ruary a few flocks of cranes are now usually braving the possibility of late blizzards and icy Platte River waters, giving them early opportunities at the waste grain scattered across the harvested cornfields of the Platte valley. During a recent mild winter, a thousand or more even overwintered along the Platte from Grand Island west to Scottsbluff. Those cranes stopping on the Platte's eastern reaches around Grand Island are mostly headed for breeding areas in northeastern Can-ada, while the westernmost flocks staging along the North Platte River are headed to western Alaska and Siberia, as far as 3,000 to 4,000 miles distant.

The sandhill cranes arrive in the Platte valley none too soon. By the time they have arrived, a million or so more cold-tolerant snow geese are already present, and thousands of overwintering Canada geese are harvesting corn from fields all along the central and western Platte valley. Overwintering by Canada geese in the Platte valley has greatly increased in recent decades, so that tens of thousands of birds now often sit out the winter there on ice-free springs, creeks, and rivers, rather than pushing farther south. The snow goose flocks, which now number less than 3 million and that until about the 1960s migrated northward along the Missouri valley, have shifted westward to the Platte valley, perhaps because of greater foraging opportunities. Scattered among the snow geese, and composing less than 5 percent of the flocks, are nearly identical Ross's geese, miniature versions of snow geese that are also headed toward similar high-Arctic nesting grounds.

Add to these multitudes the tens of thousands of tiny cackling geese and the even larger numbers of greater white-fronted geese staging in the Platte. The March goose population in the Platte valley and adjoining Rainwater Basin to the south may easily thus approach 5 million birds. And, adding to the mix, mallards and northern pintails are the vanguards of up to 20 species of ducks that pour into the Platte valley and Rainwater Basin during March. All in all, it is an avian spectacle possibly unmatched anywhere in North America, with perhaps 10 million waterfowl and half a million sandhill cranes concentrating in the Platte valley at peak numbers.

And, if rarity rather than uncountable numbers is the naturalist's goal, then the possibility also exists of seeing a few whooping cranes, one of North America's rarest and most beautiful upland birds. Probably all of the historical Great Plains flock of whooping cranes, which now numbers more than 300 birds, pass through Nebraska each spring. Whooping cranes normally arrive later in spring than do the sandhill cranes, and very few historically appeared before the first of April. However, with climate change, whooping cranes are now arriving at least two weeks earlier in spring than historically was the case, and likewise migrating south about two weeks later in the fall (Jorgensen and Brown, 2017). They typically migrate in small, family-sized groups, and, to avoid unnecessary disturbance and harassment (which is highly illegal), their exact stopping points are never publicized by state and

federal agencies. As a result, it takes great luck to encounter any whooping cranes in the state.

Even rarer than whooping cranes are the Eurasian, or "common," cranes that breed from northwestern Europe to northeastern Asia and have been reported in North America less than a dozen times. Most of these sightings have occurred in the Platte valley, where single birds have unexpectedly appeared among flocks of sandhill cranes. Probably during fall migration out of Siberia, these birds headed east rather than turning south upon reaching the Bering Strait and followed sandhill cranes to the sandhills' Great Plains wintering areas.

Unlike waterfowl and songbirds, which often migrate at night, cranes are daylight migrants, mainly because they rely on soaring ability to carry them from point to point. By using thermal updrafts, which develop during warm days as sun-warmed air rises up from the ground, the birds can ascend thousands of feet with little physical effort and then glide on a slight downward flight path for many miles, until they locate another thermal.

At a flight speed of 45 to 50 miles per hour, sandhill cranes can cover up to five hundred miles in a single ten-hour day, or nearly the entire distance from their Texas and New Mexico wintering grounds to the Platte valley. It is a unique joy to be waiting along the Platte after a warm March day and to hear the distant clarion calls of cranes thousands of feet above, as they recognize their long-remembered roosting sites on the Platte and begin a lazy circling glide downward to land among its protective sandbars and islands.

For the sandhill cranes, the Platte River offers safe nighttime roosting sites on sandy islands and bars that are sufficiently far from shore that coyotes or other land mammals can't reach them without wading through water and alerting the birds to danger. During the daylight hours, from about sunrise until sunset, the birds spend their time in harvested cornfields eating predominantly corn, which is rapidly converted to fat stores needed for completing the long migration to Arctic tundra. A small percentage of the cranes' Platte valley food consists of various invertebrates found in wet meadows, such as snails and earthworms, which provide the protein and calcium that will be needed for egg-laying and other aspects of reproduction.

The middle of March is the peak of goose migration in the Platte valley, with the goose population at or slightly past its peak, and the near peak of the sandhill crane migration. This is the ideal time for venturing to the Platte valley between Grand Island and Kearney, the focal point of goose and crane concentrations. There, visitors can arrange to observe the sandhill cranes' dawn and dusk flights out of and back into the river roosts in the comfort of riverside blinds, such as those provided by Audubon's Rowe Sanctuary near Gibbon and the Crane Trust south of Alda. Visitors can also watch from either of two free public viewing platforms situated along the river at bridges that are about two miles south of I-80 along the Alda road (exit 305) and Gibbon road (exit 285). Or, view from the hike-bike bridge that crosses the Platte at Fort Kearny State Recreation Area (drive south off I-80 at exit 272 for about two miles, then go east on 105A about four miles to the SRA access road). The park has a daily entrance fee, but the gate is usually not manned until about April 1. Recent studies at the University of Nebraska–Kearney have estimated the annual economic impact of 43,000 nonlocal, crane-oriented tourists at about $14 million dollars (Dority et al., 2017), from the roughly 30,000 tourists who now come during the March-to-early-April crane migration period.

Ducks and geese are most highly concentrated during March on the "borrow pit" ponds that were formed during the construction of I-80 and on temporary wetlands of the Rainwater Basin south of the Platte. The Rainwater Basin wetlands vary greatly in number and water depth from year to year, depending on winter and early spring precipitation. The staff at the Crane Trust and Rowe Sanctuary visitor centers can often provide good advice on local waterfowl and crane distribution. The many regional wildlife management areas in the Rainwater Basin are usually affected by spring hunting activities, but often very large numbers of field-feeding geese can be found along country roads. Maps and information on the birds of the Rainwater Basin can be found in Johnsgard (2007, *A Guide to the Natural History*) and on the broader Central Platte valley by Brown and Johnsgard (2013).

During the day, by driving country roads such as the Platte River Road from Doniphan west to the Kearney area, motorists can watch cranes and geese feeding in stubble fields near the river and revel in the countless skeins of geese and ducks spread out overhead from horizon to horizon, like animated strings of Christmas decorations. The best times for doing this

are the first hour after sunrise, when the birds are most actively foraging, or the last hour before sunset, as the birds start to move out of the fields and toward the river. Avoid leaving the car and flushing the flocks during these times, as it not only needlessly disturbs the birds but also robs them of the precious foraging time they must have for replenishing their energy stores. Typically cranes will tolerate open windows, if the car's occupants remain still and quiet. I have personally accompanied visitors from as far away as Europe, Pakistan, and Japan on crane-watching trips. To do so is to provide a gift easily and uniquely given by Nebraskans, and one that I know they will carry in their memories and cherish for a lifetime. It is also a gift that all Nebraskans who love the natural world should consider giving themselves every year, as I have done for more than half a century.

At times I think April is the saddest month. The last of the sandhill cranes are then leaving the Platte valley for northern breeding grounds. As I watch the last flocks disappear into the clouds like departing angels singing a final farewell, I am saddened, knowing that I will not see or hear them again for six months. My primary consolation lies in the fact that I know I will soon be hearing a different chorus, a sunrise serenade of grassland dancers, just as mysterious and magical as the departing cranes. To hear and see this event requires more planning and even more patience than is needed for watching cranes.

At least for Lincoln or Omaha residents, to see prairie-chickens display one must leave by about 3:30 a.m. to drive the 80-odd miles into southeastern Nebraska, where native prairie grasses still grow thick over glacial-molded hills. Then, in total darkness, one must find the right county roads and locate the best stopping point for setting up a blind. After erecting the blind, one must finally insert into it both oneself and all the necessary paraphernalia, such as a flashlight, binoculars, camera, spare lenses, tripod, gloves, a coffee-filled thermos, a stool, and perhaps a small sound recorder.

Almost always the best place for a blind's location is atop a hill covered with low prairie grasses, at least several hundred yards away from tall trees or thick shrubbery, and a quarter mile or more away from any occupied dwellings. An advance scouting the day before, with critical odometer information recorded, and the setting out of a few yellow flag markers to show the best predawn walking route, often makes the difference between finding the exact site and an entire morning's efforts being wasted. Recent bird droppings and scattered grouse feathers provide the best clues to judging the center of mating activity.

If all goes well, one is settled in the blind at least a half-hour or more before sunrise, before the eastern sky begins to brighten and the surrounding landscape features begin to take shape. If there is a full moon, an even earlier predawn arrival is needed, whereas a cloudy sky will mean that the curtain rising for the dawn serenade will be somewhat delayed. Then, one must quietly wait, listening for early-rising coyotes or perhaps the last great horned owl duet of the night. This is a time to be thankful for the preservation of these prairie relicts of the past—almost nowhere else in North America are there still countless locations where, without making reservations or paying a hefty viewing fee, can one watch and hear the dawn drumming and dancing of the greater prairie-chicken.

I have often described the greater prairie-chicken as the spirit of the prairie; few other birds are so closely associated with native tallgrass prairies or are so sensitive to their destruction. It is a bird the color of autumn grasses, its feathers disruptively patterned in vertical stripes of switchgrass buff and Indiangrass brown, so that a motionless prairie-chicken simply fades into its background. Only its normally hidden under tail-coverts are conspicuously white.

Also completely hidden beneath the elongated neck feathers of adult males are two patches of bright orange-red skin. Like secret signals, these areas are exposed only during the dawn and dusk mating ceremonies of prairie-chickens, when the males fill their throats with air, inflating the orange skin "air sacs" on each side of the throats, and causing each side of their necks to resemble half tangerines. As the esophagus is inflated, the male utters a mellow and low-pitched cooing. The sound is something like that produced by blowing across the top of an empty bottle, but it is uttered in a three-part cadence sounding to me something like "Old-Mul-Doooon." Although this "booming" vocalization is soft, it can be heard for a mile or more under ideal conditions.

While booming, the male also simultaneously stamps his feet rapidly, producing a soft drumming sound, and quickly fans and closes his tail feathers during each call sequence. While displaying, the male erects his long neck feathers so that two ear-like feather groups (pinnae) are exposed on the sides of his head. He also tilts his tail vertically, exposing white under-tail feathers. This dramatic transformation of the bird's appearance, movements and sounds produces a hypnotic effect on humans and also, it would seem, on female prairie-chickens, for whom it is intended.

When the females arrive on the mating grounds, usually at about sunrise, they begin to inspect each male carefully, moving around the group like shoppers searching for the best Thanksgiving turkey but giving no outward indication of their possible preferences. The males in turn ratchet up the speed and intensity of their displays as each female approaches, and it is probably the relative vigor and perfection of an individual male's display behavior that helps females make their final mating choices. Not only are the males' minor display variations a possible basis for female choice but of equal or greater importance is each male's relative position among the other males, as a reflection of his ability to defend and maintain a desirable territory. Socially dominant and centrally positioned male grouse ("master cocks") are often at least four years old and are the most effective at attracting and successfully mating with females. Indeed, even among a group of 20 or more interacting males, a single highly experienced and socially dominant male is likely to obtain at least 80 percent of all matings. Clearly, sexual selection works most rapidly and most effectively in nonmonogamous species such as most grouse.

Many other open-country grouse, such as the North American sharp-tailed grouse and sage-grouse perform similar communal courtship ceremonies. These highly localized and strongly competitive congregations of displaying males are called "leks," and their behavior is called "lekking." Lekking behavior appears to function biologically as a means of making certain that only the fittest males are able to attract mates and propagate the species' genetic line. Such a highly selective function requires an unfailing ability by females to rapidly assess all the males accurately, and likewise stimulates individual males to develop ever more effective ways of competing with other males and attracting females.

This selective mating process, which gradually improves the genetic effectiveness of individual birds in selectively attracting and mating with those of the other sex, is called "sexual selection." First described by Charles Darwin, sexual selection accounts for the evolution of such male grouse features as the presence and

Greater prairie-chicken

exhibition of conspicuous feathers or colorful skin, the utterance of complex vocalizations, and performance of extravagant postural displays, by which breeding females might identify and choose specific males for mating. It also explains the comparable presence of such uniquely male traits as antlers, horns, beards, and aggressive behavior among male mammals, especially those that are nonmonogamous. Darwin realized that sexual selection must work reciprocally, with females accurately detecting and choosing the most virile males on the basis of such "secondary" sexual traits.

Over time, males thus evolve increasingly unique traits that allow matings by only the fittest individuals able to outcompete other males, either through intimidation and physical dominance over other males, or by attracting females more effectively than other males. Over time, these interacting mating attributes that improve both intrasexual (male-male) and intersexual (male-female) mating effectiveness result in ever more apparent sexual differences in the social behavior and physical appearance of both sexes.

When watching lek activities over time, one can often detect spatial and behavioral differences among the males, as size and positions of their territorial boundaries become apparent, and realize that some males are more self-assured, more aggressive, and more active than others. Thus, it becomes easier to realize that females are indeed able to choose their most desirable mating partner rapidly, even during the half-light of dawn and the melee of intensely competing males.

Mating itself is brief and might be easily overlooked if one is not paying close attention. After a successful mating—and only a single mating is needed for a female to lay a clutch of 12 or more fertile eggs—the female then quickly leaves the lekking ground and begins to search for a nest site, which may be as far as a mile or so away. She will not interact again with males or other females until her brood is grown and autumn flock formation begins.

In Nebraska, the males continue their daily display activities with diminishing enthusiasm until well into May. Some of the late matings probably are the result of females having lost their original clutch and attempting a second mating and nesting. The males play no role in chick rearing or other familial duties. After a summer of molting and foraging, the older males usually return to the lek in early fall, apparently to reclaim possession of their spring territories, or perhaps to try to expand into space made available by the deaths of others. This fall display activity also attracts the attention of young males, which may become peripheral viewers or even minor participants. As each male grows older and more experienced, he is likely to move his territory ever closer to the middle of the lek, with the potential of eventually becoming a master cock if he lives long enough.

There are several possible options for visiting a prairie chicken lek in Nebraska. Prairie grouse are most common in the eastern and central Sandhills, where optimum survival conditions are provided by a combination of native Sandhills prairie and access to corn and other crops that supplement winter foods. Some commercial businesses in the Sandhills offer guided lek-viewing from preestablished blinds, which are often converted school buses. Such opportunities are provided by Mitch Glidden's uniquely personalized guiding service at the Sandhills Motel in Mullen (308-546-2206 or 888-278-6167) and the family-run Calamus Outfitters ranch near Broken Bow (308-346-4697). Both facilities offer the choice of viewing a lek of greater prairie-chickens or sharp-tailed grouse, or arranging separate viewings of each. Free public-access permanent blinds at grouse leks are available at a few locations, such as the Bessey District of the Nebraska National Forest near Halsey in Thomas County, on a first-come, first-served basis.

No naturalist should consider his or her life complete without experiencing these unique drums of April. Like watching a star-filled Sandhills sky, seeing sandhill cranes in formation above the Platte, or canoeing the Niobrara River, it is a defining experience of life on the Nebraska prairie.

We don't know what originally drew the cranes to the Platte,
But the unique present-day combination of a wide, sandy river,
Nearby wet meadows with a supply of invertebrate foods for a source of calcium,
And an almost unlimited amount of waste corn in nearby fields
For getting abundant carbohydrates that can be converted and stored as fat
Provide the magic attraction now.

Millions of snow geese, Canada geese, and other geese join in on this feast,
As do several million ducks, making March in Nebraska a bird-watcher's paradise.
Its prospect alone is enough to warm the heart during the long days of winter,
And the sounds of cranes filling the sky when they finally do arrive
Is at least as thrilling as hearing a massed choir
Singing the triumphant chorus to Beethoven's Ninth Symphony.

The Nature of Nebraska (Johnsgard, 2001)

The Sites: Playas, Pronghorns, and Prairie-Chickens

COLORADO

There can be no doubt that most naturalists, when thinking about Colorado (CO), imagine high mountains and canyons, with stunning peaks, snowfields, waterfalls, and perhaps glaciers. However, over the entire state, Colorado has six national wildlife refuges totaling 175,000 acres, National Park Service lands totaling 661,000 acres, and national grasslands totaling 193,000 acres. Federally owned acreage in Colorado composes 36.6 percent of the state's total land area, ranking it third among the states covered in this book, behind Wyoming and New Mexico. The state is also third in total Bureau of Land Management acres, at 8.3 million acres. Colorado also has 41 state parks, including a state forest state park of 71,000 acres, and 350 state wildlife areas.

Considering only lands east of Colorado's front range, there is a veritable feast of natural attractions, including two national wildlife refuges, two national grasslands, dozens of state parks, and nearly 100 state wildlife areas. In terms of wildlife viewing opportunities in eastern Wyoming, the Colorado Wildlife Viewing Guide (Gray, 1992) lists 25 prime viewing sites in the northeast and southeast regions of Colorado. Colorado is one of very few states that supports leks of both greater prairie-chickens (Pawnee National Grassland) and lesser prairie-chickens (Comanche National Grassland), and the only state where one might observe lekking behavior by both the greater and Gunnison's sage-grouse as well as by sharp-tailed grouse. With the greatest of luck (and enough time and endurance), one might even observe courtship by dusky grouse and white-tailed ptarmigan.

Alamosa National Wildlife Refuge. 11,168 acres. Located about seven miles northeast of Alamosa (and slightly beyond the mapped western geographic limits of the Great Plains), this wildlife refuge consists of bottomland along the Rio Grande River. At least 58 bird species are common to abundant during spring versus 48 species during fall and 16 during winter (Jones, 1990). American bald eagles are common here in winter. There are at least 70 nesting birds among the 183 listed for the refuge by Jones. A total of 41 bird species were reported year-round by Jones, so an estimated minimum of 78 percent of the refuge's total bird diversity is migratory. More information is available from the refuge manager at PO Box 1148, Alamosa, CO 81101 (303-589-4021). A recent checklist that also includes the birds of Monte Vista National Wildlife Refuge is available online at https://www.fws.gov/uploadedfiles/wildlifelist(1).pdf.

Comanche National Grassland. 435,707 acres. This region of shortgrass prairie is located in the southeastern corner of Colorado and includes short-grass prairie, mixed-grass prairie, and eroded canyonlands. The Purgatoire River separates two units of the area, and exposed sandstone banks on its shore have dinosaur tracks of the Jurassic era, including more than 1,000 brontosaurus (*Apatosaurus*) footprints. There are also Native American petroglyphs and pictographs. Little water is present, but about 275 species of birds have been recorded here, including lesser prairie-chickens (public grouse-viewing blinds are available). Burrowing owls are present among the 6,000 acres of prairie dog towns. In addition to about 60 mammal species, there are records of 40 reptiles, 9 amphibians, and 11 fish species. Some of the Neotropical migrant birds that commonly breed here are the scissor-tailed flycatcher, Cassin's kingbird, black-chinned hummingbird, Mississippi kite, eastern phoebe, and dickcissel—the two last-named species are at the western edge of their breeding ranges. A bird list (345 species and 72 nesters, includes Cimarron NG in Kansas [see section]) is available from the headquarters at 27162 Hwy. 287, PO Box 127, Springfield, CO 81073 (719-523-6591) or from the La Junta office, PO Box 817, 3rd St. and East Hwy. 50, La Junta, CO 81050 (719-384-2181).

Denver Museum of Nature and Science. This enormous 700,000-square-foot repository of more than a million objects is one of the great natural history museums in America. Its public exhibits in natural history include North American and Colorado wildlife dioramas, evolution, North American Indian culture, anthropology, gems and minerals, and others. *Address:* 2001 Colorado Blvd., Denver, CO 80205 (303-370-6000).

Mixed-grass and shortgrass songbirds, including adult males of Savannah (top left), clay-colored (top right), grasshopper (middle), Cassin's (bottom left), and Brewer's sparrows (bottom right).

Jackson Lake State Park. 2,540 acres. This park is located in north-central Colorado near Fort Morgan. To reach it, go north from Exit 66 of I-76 (Wiggins exit) and take Hwy. 30 north to Goodrich. Jackson Lake State Park is a few miles northwest of Goodrich (follow the signs). The park is notable for spring and fall migrations of shorebirds when Jackson Reservoir levels are low, and for American white pelican migrations (up to 400 birds) regardless of reservoir levels. Up to about 20,000 migrating ducks are also typical, and the area is a major stopover point for sandhill cranes during spring and fall. Good numbers of American bald eagles are present during the waterfowl migrations. *Riverside Reservoir* (3,150 acres) is about 15 miles west of Jackson Reservoir (via Colorado Hwy. 133, 34, and 67) and is one of three nesting areas for white pelicans in Colorado. Much of the reservoir if off limits to the public, but there is lakeshore trail access along the southeastern shore that provides views of the pelicans' nesting island, which typically supports about 500 nesting pairs of the birds. Camping is permitted. *Address of Jackson Lake SP:* 26363 County Rd. 3, Orchard, CO 80649 (970-645-2551), http://cpw.state.co.us/placestogo/parks/jacksonlake. The Riverside Reservoir is managed by the Bureau of Land Management (719-836-2031). For information contact Colorado Parks and Wildlife, 1313 Sherman St., 6th Floor, Denver, CO 80203 (303-297-1192).

John Martin Reservoir State Park. 22,000 acres. Located five miles east of Las Animas at the confluence of the Arkansas and Purgatoire Rivers, this vast area supports shortgrass prairies, with prairie dogs and their associated raptor predators such as golden eagles, ferruginous hawks, and other buteos. Wintering and migrant waterfowl use the reservoir, as do nesting great blue herons, double-crested cormorants, and American white pelicans. The *Purgatoire River State Wildlife Area* (950 acres) is nearby on the Purgatoire River, with excellent riparian and marshland habitat. For more information, contact Colorado Parks and Wildlife, 6060 Broadway, Denver, CO 80216 (303-291-7227) or the state park (719-829-1801).

Monte Vista National Wildlife Refuge. 14,188 acres. This refuge includes montane grasslands (7,500–8,000 feet elevation) and mountain-fed streams, plus farmland and about 200 small wetland areas. Located near Alamosa (and slightly beyond the western geographic limits of the Great Plains), this is one of the best locations in Colorado for seeing sandhill cranes during March–April or October–November, while in summer there are Canada geese, several species of nesting ducks, pied-billed grebes, coots, yellow-headed and red-winged blackbirds, and marsh wrens. A bird list (combined with that of Alamosa National Wildlife Refuge) is available (183 species, 70 nesters). *Address:* Box 1148, Alamosa, CO 81101 (719-589-4021).

Pawnee National Grassland. 200,000 acres. One entrance to this federally owned grassland is located two miles north of Briggsdale. The national grassland consists of various-sized parcels of reclaimed arid grasslands from failed homesteads. Two landmark buttes, the Pawnee Buttes, rise as high as 530 feet and provide nesting sites for raptors. Little water is present, and the area is mostly of importance to breeding birds of the short-grass prairie, such as McCown's and chestnut-collared longspurs and mountain plover. Raptors, including the golden eagle, prairie falcon, ferruginous hawk, and burrowing owl, are fairly common, especially near prairie dog colonies. A list of 59 mammal species, including such rarities as the swift fox and other predators such as the coyote, bobcat, and mountain lion, is available. About 400 species of plants have been reported (Moul, 2008). A recent checklist of the birds (225 species) of the Pawnee National Grassland is available from the headquarters at 115 N. 2nd Ave., PO Box 386, Ault, CO 80610 (970-834-9270) or from the US Forest Service Supervisor's Office at 2150 Centre Ave., Bldg. E, Ft. Collins, CO 80526 (970-295-6600).

Prewitt Reservoir State Wildlife Area. 2,900 acres. Located four miles southwest of Merino off US Hwy. 6, this reservoir along the South Platte River attracts sandhill cranes, American white pelicans, and many waterfowl during migrations as well as herons and other water birds. For more information, contact Colorado Parks and Wildlife, 6060 Broadway, Denver, CO 80216 (303-291-7227).

Queens State Wildlife Area. 4,426 acres. This site is actually made up of several eastern Colorado reservoirs ("Queens reservoirs"): Neenoshe, Neeskah, Neesopah, Negrande, Thurston, and Upper Queens. They are scattered near the towns of Lamar and Eades. The reservoirs attract large numbers of

Canada, cackling, snow, and Ross's geese from fall to spring and a great variety of shorebirds from April through October. For locations and more information, contact Colorado Parks and Wildlife, 2500 S. Main St., Lamar, CO 81052 (719-336-6600) or online at http://cpw.state.co.us/placestogo/parks/Pages/WildlifeAreaMap.aspx.

IOWA

Iowa (IA) is a state with 72,000 acres of US Fish and Wildlife Service land (six national wildlife refuges and a wetland management district) and 2,700 acres of National Park Service land. Federally owned acreage in Iowa comprises only 0.76 percent of the state's total land area, the least of any of the states or provinces covered in this book. This tiny fraction reflects the fact that some of America's most fertile and agriculturally valuable soils are found in Iowa; Iowa is thus one of the country's most intensively farmed states. However, an enormous amount of state, county, and private effort has gone into preserving prairie remnants. As of the early 1990s, 84 natural areas totaling about 8,900 acres had been set aside as state preserves (Fleckenstein, 1992). These include archeological, geological, and historic sites. Of these, 26 sites are prairie preserves, 35 are forest preserves, and 13 are wetland preserves. Iowa also has 10 state forests, 18 state parks, and 20 wildlife management areas, as well as a state recreation area.

Broken Kettle Grasslands Preserve. About 3,000 acres. This expansive Loess Hills Nature Conservancy prairie is located about 20 miles north of Sioux City in Plymouth County, and it is the largest parcel of native prairie left in Iowa. The location is almost adjacent to *Stone State Park*, which has a 90-acre prairie. From Exit 151 on I-29, go 10 miles north on Hwy. 12 to county road K18, then north 4 more miles to Butcher Road. Turn right and go two miles to the top of the hill. The office is a half mile north of the Butcher Road crossing. For more information, contact the Nature Conservancy at 24764 Hwy. 12, Westfield, IA 51062 (712-568-2596). Stone State Park's nature center is managed by the Woodbury County Conservation Board (park: 712-255-4698; nature center: 712-258-0838).

DeSoto National Wildlife Refuge. 7,823 acres. This refuge can be reached by driving five miles east of Blair, Nebraska. It consists of a 750-acre oxbow cutoff of the Missouri River (DeSoto Lake) and encompasses floodplain lands including river-bottom forest and adjacent grasslands, marshes, and cultivated lands. The refuge has historically been a spring and fall staging area for snow geese and other migratory waterfowl. A visitor center contains panoramic viewing windows and a diverse collection of artifacts from a large freight steamboat, the *Bertrand*, which sunk when it hit a snag in 1865. It had been filled with household goods and mining supplies intended for the Montana goldfields. The refuge has a bird checklist that includes species seen in this general region by Lewis and Clark, such as the great blue heron, American bald eagle, wild turkey, and western meadowlark. DeSoto NWR has extensive riparian and bottomland woods that make for fine spring birding; 21 species of warblers are on the spring list, and at least 4 (yellow, black-and-white, American redstart, and common yellowthroat) have been reported to nest. A total of 187 species are present on DeSoto's spring bird list, including 5 that were classified as abundant. One of these, the snow goose, no longer occurs in large numbers during spring, but other still-abundant spring species include the mallard, ring-necked pheasant, mourning dove, and red-winged blackbird. A checklist of 240 bird species is available from the refuge manager. There is a small daily admission fee. *Address:* 1434 316th Ln., Missouri Valley, IA 51555 (712-388-4800). It is also available online at https://nebraskabirdingtrails.com/wp-content/uploads/pdf/Desoto.pdf.

Five Ridge Prairie. 964 acres. This site is woodlands and native prairie on loess hills near Sioux City. The property was purchased by the Nature Conservancy and is now owned by the Plymouth County Conservation Board. For tours, contact the preserve office (712-568-2596) or Iowa's Nature Conservancy headquarters at 303 Locust St., Suite 402, Des Moines, IA 50309 (515-244-5044).

Forneys Lake Wildlife Management Area. 1,800 acres. This wetland is located at the base of the loess hills just east of the Missouri River, near the towns of Bartlett and Thurman. Formerly an old Missouri River oxbow lake, it is now a shallow cattail and tule marsh with wonderful spring habitat for migratory waterfowl (especially snow geese) and other wetland birds. It is reached by taking the Bartlett exit from I-29, about 15 miles north of Waubonsie State Park (see section). It is most noted for its spring concentrations of up to 100,000 snow geese and other waterfowl in early March, accompanied by up to 100 American bald eagles. American white pelicans migrate through about a month later, and various herons and egrets are common throughout summer. Trumpeter swans nested here in 2012. About 400 acres of this state-owned wildlife area is a refuge, and the rest is open to sport hunting and closed to nonhunters. Managed by the Iowa Department of Natural Resources (Sidney office: 712-374-3133). For more information, contact the Iowa DNR (headquarters) at Wallace State Office Building, 502 E. 9th St., 4th Floor, Des Moines, IA 50319-0034 (515-282-5145).

Hitchcock Nature Center. 582 acres. This Pottawattamie County educational facility, located about eight miles north of Crescent, lies at the crest of the loess hills east of the Missouri River. The loess hills, here up to about 300 feet high, provide a natural migration route for raptors that use the updraft winds for lift and form a narrow north-south migration corridor used by thousands of vultures, hawks, and other raptors annually. It is noted as an important site for watching fall raptor migrations along the Missouri valley (*Hitchcock Nature Center HawkWatch*), where an average of 13,000 raptors of about 20 species are counted every fall, when a peak migration period of September 20 to October 20 occurs. During one fall, more than 6,900 raptors of 19 species were counted, of which the 8 most common species were red-tailed hawk (41%), Swainson's hawk (22%), sharp-shinned hawk (14%), American bald eagle (5%), broad-winged hawk (4%), northern harrier (3%), Cooper's hawk (3%), and American kestrel (2.5%). Hitchcock has been identified as one of the top five eagle-watching sites in the world, with November being the prime viewing period. Large numbers of turkey vultures also pass through early in the fall. For information, contact the Pottawattamie County Conservation Board, 223 S. 6th St., Council Bluffs, IA 51501 (712-328-5638).

Lewis and Clark Monument. This 40-acre site on the north side of Council Bluffs, commemorates the formal meeting of Lewis and Clark with the Otoe-Missourias. Natural habitats include oak-dominated woods and hillside prairies. On July 28, 1804, Captain Clark reported seeing "high prairie and hills, with timber" near present-day Council Bluffs. *Folsom Point Preserve*, a 281-acre Nature Conservancy prairie in the loess hills, is located at the south side of Council Bluffs off Brohard Avenue. Council Bluffs is also home to the *Western Historic Trails Center*, which has information on the Lewis and Clark Historic Trail and other western trails such as the Oregon and Mormon Trails. About eight miles north of Council Bluffs, off State Hwy. 183, is Hitchcock Nature Center (see section). The "Councile Bluff" site that was selected by Lewis and Clark for their historic meeting with the Otoe-Missourias is located about 15 miles north of the city of Council Bluffs, Iowa, on the Nebraska side of the river (see Fort Atkinson section in Nebraska).

Lewis and Clark State Park. 176 acres. This small state park is situated five miles west of Onawa on State Hwy. 15. Its oxbow lake is surrounded by cottonwoods and other riverine hardwoods, with a reconstructed full-sized keelboat and two pirogues on view during the summer months. *Address:* 21914 Park Loop, Onawa, IA 51040 (712-423-2829). Just east of Onawa is *Sylvan Runkel State Preserve*, a 330-acre tallgrass prairie within the 2,742-acre *Loess Hills Wildlife Management Area*. Monona County has two other public-access natural areas, *Loess Hills State Forest*, with more than 100 acres of prairie, and *Turin Loess Hills Nature Preserve*, with 220 acres.

Loess Hills region. The loess hills in western Iowa (Woodbury and Monona Counties) may approach 400 feet in height and range up to ten miles wide, the loess caps themselves adding as much as about 200 feet to the underlying sedimentary substrate. The silt-sized particles that were deposited here originated much farther west, and a layer of loess several feet thick covers all of Iowa except for the north-central section. The hills still support up to 20,000 acres of native tallgrass prairies, most of which exists in small, diminishing patches that tend to be replaced by red cedars over time. There are also at least 39 native species of trees and larger shrubs in the loess hills. This region of Iowa and adjacent Missouri supports more than 100 nesting species of birds, 54 mammals, 24 reptiles, and 10 amphibians, according to a summary by Cornelia Mutel (1989). Mutel listed nearly 50 public-use areas in the Loess Hills region between northwestern Iowa and northwestern Missouri. Iowa sites include *Loess Hills Wildlife Area*, *Turin Loess Hills Nature Preserve*, and *Sylvan Runkel Preserve* (collectively about 3,500 acres), all in Monona County, near Turin. For information, contact the Monona County Conservation Board, Box 209, Onawa, IA 51040 (712-423-2426). There is also *Loess Hills Pioneer State Forest* (17,190 acres, under acquisition) in Harrison County, administered by the Iowa Department of Natural Resources (712-423-2400). A patchwork of mixed-grass prairie and hardwood forest occur on loess bluffs. The entire loess hills region is part of a *Loess Hills Scenic Byway* system, with maps available through the state's Welcome Centers at highway rest areas. Not far to the east is *Cayler Prairie State Preserve* (640 acres, near Spirit Lake), now being restored to tallgrass prairie by the Iowa Natural Heritage Foundation (Insurance Exchange Bldg., Suite 444, 505 Fifth Ave., Des Moines, IA 50309 (515-288-1846). A list of state-owned preserves was published by the Iowa State Preserves Board in 1978. Other useful sources of information on Iowa prairie preserves are provided by Roosa (1984), Wolf (1991), and Fleckenstein (1993). A list of 103 probable nesting loess hills bird species, including 7 grassland endemics, was provided by Mutel (1989). The similar loess hills prairies of Nebraska were described by Nagel (1998).

Neal Smith (previously Walnut Creek) **National Wildlife Refuge.** 8,654 acres. Located near Prairie City, this refuge is an example of restored and entirely reconstructed prairie habitat. It is managed partly for bison, with 70 to 90 head in a 700-acre enclosure, along with a small herd of elk. There is an excellent modern interpretive center (Prairie Learning Center) that emphasizes prairie ecology and restoration. A bird list is in preparation; 69 species have been seen during breeding bird count surveys. *Address:* PO Box 399, 9981 Pacific St., Prairie City, IA 50228 (515-994-3400).

Prairie preserves. In addition to the Nature Conservancy's two largest Iowa prairies, Broken Kettle Grasslands Preserve and Five Ridge Prairie (see sections), 8 of Iowa's other 24 state-recognized prairie preserves are of at least 100 acres. These include *Bushy Creek Prairie* (279 acres, Webster County), *Turin Loess Hills Prairie* (230 acres, Monoma County), *Steele Prairie* (200 acres, Cherokee County), *Anderson Prairie* (200 acres, Emmet County), *Cayler Prairie* (160 acres, Dickinson County), *Kaslow Prairie* (160 acres, Pocahontas

County), *Gitchie Manitou Prairie* (144 acres, Lyon County), and *Rolling Thunder Prairie* (123 acres, Warren County). Not included here are a few other Iowa prairies also owned by the Nature Conservancy, but most are owned by individual counties or the state of Iowa. Information on the state-owned prairies can be obtained from the Bureau of Preserves and Ecological Services, Iowa Department of Natural Resources, Wallace State Office Bldg., 502 E. 9th St., 4th Floor, Des Moines, IA 50319 (515-281-8676). County-owned prairies (for example, Five Ridge, Rolling Thunder, and Steele Prairies) are managed by the relevant county conservation boards.

Riverton Wildlife Management Area. 2,700 acres. This is a large, state-owned wetland located about a mile north of Riverton in the Nishnabotna River valley that is notable for its large concentrations of migratory waterfowl, especially snow geese, as well as their frequently associated American bald eagles. Waterfowl numbers peak in March and again in late November to mid-December, when snow goose numbers may reach 200,000 and the eagles up to 50 or more. Depending on spring water levels, up to 20 or more species of shorebirds may also be present, including Hudsonian godwit, Baird's and stilt sandpipers, and Wilson's phalarope. The wildlife area is managed by the Iowa Department of Natural Resources (712-374-32133). For more information, contact the Iowa Department of Natural Resources headquarters in the Wallace State Office Building, 502 E. 9th St., 4th Floor, Des Moines, IA (515-725-8200).

Sioux City. This city, built near the Lewis and Clark campsite of August 20, 1804, has a *Lewis and Clark Interpretive Center* in Chris Larsen Park as well as the Sergeant Floyd Monument, which is placed on a hilltop south of town near where Sgt. Charles Floyd, the only expedition fatality, was buried. Floyd River runs nearby, and the *Sergeant Floyd Riverboat Welcome Center*, a dry-docked diesel inspection ship, has been converted into a small museum of Missouri River history, including information on Lewis and Clark. At the northern edge of Sioux City, at 5001 Talbot Road, is *Stone State Park*, a 1,069-acre prairie and woodland reserve situated on loess hills overlooking the confluence of the Big Sioux and Missouri Rivers. It has a nature trail, a demonstration prairie, and an available list of local wildflowers (712-255-4698). *Dorothy Pecaut*

Nature Center, with exhibits on the loess hills region, is within the park (712-258-0838). Nearby is *Sioux City Prairie*, a 150-acre tallgrass prairie west of Briar Cliff College, and *Mount Talbot State Preserve*, off Talbot Road. About ten miles north of Sioux City is the Five Ridge Prairie (see section), and near there is the Broken Kettle Grasslands Preserve (see section), the largest of the tallgrass prairie preserves in Iowa. Both are Nature Conservancy preserves. Iowa has a total of 19 Nature Conservancy preserves. For information, contact the Iowa Field Office, 303 Locust St., Ste. 402, Des Moines, IA 50309 (515-244-5044).

Union Slough National Wildlife Refuge. 2,845 acres. This refuge consists of marsh, grassland, and timber. During March and April, thousands of waterfowl pass through, especially Canada and snow geese, plus mallards, blue-winged and green-winged teal, gadwall, and American wigeon. Other common migrants are American white pelicans, American bald eagles, Franklin's gulls, Forster's terns, and great egrets as well as many shorebirds and passerines. At least 91 bird species are common to abundant during spring versus 97 species during fall and 18 during winter (Jones, 1990). There are at least 96 nesting birds among the 217 species listed for the refuge by Jones. A total of 30 species were reported present year-round by Jones, so an estimated minimum of 86 percent of the refuge's total bird diversity is migratory. A more recent checklist of more than 240 bird species is available from the refuge manager at Rte. 1., Box 52, Titonka, IA 50480 (515-928-2523).

University of Iowa Museum of Natural History. This Iowa City museum is best known for its bird, mammal, and Native American collections. There is a geological, cultural, and ecology section in Iowa Hall; a Mammal Hall; and a Hageboeck Hall of Birds as well as evolution and ecological exhibits. *Address:* 17 N. Clinton St., University of Iowa, Iowa City, IA (319-335-0606).

Waubonsie State Park. 1,247 acres. This prairie and hardwood forest park is located on steep loess hills overlooking the Missouri River. At least one of the bur oaks in the park is known to be more than 300 years old, so it was already mature when Lewis and Clark passed by in 1804 and described these "bald-pated hills." Isolated patches of the park are still in prairie vegetation, usually on the drier south-facing slopes.

The park is nine miles north of Hamburg, off I-29 on State Hwy. 2. Camping is permitted. Located near the Lewis and Clark campsites of July 16–17, 1804. *Address:* 2585 Waubonsie Park Rd., Hamburg, IA 51640 (712-382-2786).

KANSAS

Kansas (KS) is the very definition of a flat state, and was once reportedly proven to be flatter than a pancake when the two were measured at a comparable scale. Its highest elevation, Mount Sunflower, in western Kansas, is an inconspicuous hill barely breaking 4,000 feet above sea level and is only 3,360 feet higher than the state's lowest elevation in southeastern Kansas. However, Kansas has five national wildlife refuges, one national grassland, and the only national prairie preserve in the United States. The Flint Hills of eastern Kansas support what collectively represent the largest remaining vestiges of tallgrass prairie in the United States. Federally owned acreage in Kansas comprises 1.2 percent of the state's total land area. Kansas also has 26 state parks, covering some 32,000 acres, with 500 miles of trails and more than 130,000 acres of surface water, so there is an abundance of places and spaces that should please any naturalist. For the convenience of birders, county checklists of the birds of any of the state's 103 counties can be downloaded at http://www.ksbirds.org/checklist/checklist_index.htm.

Baker Wetlands. 927 acres. This restored prairie and wetland is at the south edge of Lawrence, east of the intersection of US Hwy. 59 and the South Lawrence Trafficway. It is the site of the *Baker University Discovery Center*. There are more than ten miles of trails and paths through prairie, wetlands, and riparian habitats along the Wakarusa River as well as observation blinds and picnic sites. At least 480 plant and 376 vertebrate species have been reported, including 278 bird species (Rose, 2017).

Benedictine Bottoms Wildlife Area. 2,000 acres. This wetland along the Missouri River northeast of Atchison has a mixture of timber, seasonal wetlands, and native grasses. It is managed by the Kansas Department of Wildlife, Parks and Tourism and was constructed by the US Corps of Engineers. The area is used by nearby Benedictine College for field research. It can be reached from Doniphan by traveling north on the gravel road or from Atchison by driving east toward the river on Commercial Street. This street turns north and becomes River Road. Drive about 1.5 miles to the end of the pavement, then turn right and cross Independence Bridge, where you will have reached the Bottoms.

Cheyenne Bottoms Waterfowl Management Area. 27,000 acres. This famous state-owned wildlife area is about five miles north of Great Bend, within a larger area of about 60 square miles of bottomlands that comprise the largest inland wetland complex in the United States (Rose, 2017). It consists of marshland as well as adjacent bottomlands associated with the Arkansas River. The site is partly managed by the Kansas Department of Wildlife, Parks and Tourism (19,000 acres) and partly by the Nature Conservancy (8,000 acres). Cheyenne Bottoms is recognized as being of international importance for migratory shorebirds, at peak holding as many as 200,000 or more migrants. Notable breeding species include some relatively rare species, such as the least bittern, yellow-crowned night-heron, king rail, common gallinule, and snowy plover. Whooping cranes stop fairly often here on migration. About 50 miles east of Cheyenne Bottoms (and 20 miles southwest of Salina) is Kanopolis Lake, a 1940s flood-control impoundment, and associated *Kanopolis State Park*, where whooping cranes have also been recently seen on its associated 12,500-acre wildlife area. Cheyenne Bottoms' birding attractions were described by Zimmerman and Patti (1988) and also by Gress and Janzen (2008). For general information, contact the Kansas Department of Wildlife, Parks and Tourism (316-793-7730). A checklist of 325 species was included by Zimmerman (1990) in his book on the area's ecology. Among the long-distance migrants are 34 species of waterfowl, 39 shorebirds, 12 flycatchers, 6 vireos, and 24 warblers. A bird species list is available from the area manager at 204 NE 60 Rd., Great Bend, KS 67530 and online at http://ksoutdoors.com/ KDWPT-Info/Locations/Wildlife-Areas/Southwest/ Cheyenne-Bottoms.

Chisholm Creek Park. This urban park in northeastern Wichita (entrances off Hwy. 96 at N. Woodlawn St. and N. Oliver Ave.) contains the modern (2000) *Great Plains Nature Center*, with a large auditorium, habitat exhibits, and a 2,000-gallon aquarium. Nearby long walking trails pass through wetlands and woodlands and restored prairie. *Address:* Great Plains Nature Center, 62323 E. 29th St. N, Wichita, KS 67220-2200 (316-683-5499) (Rose, 2017).

Cimarron National Grassland. 108,175 acres. This multiparcel national grassland (mixed shortgrass prairie and sagebrush-yucca prairie) is located a few miles north of Elkhart in the southwestern corner of Kansas. Considering the region's aridity, a remarkably long bird list of 342 species was published by Cable, Seltman, and Cook (1996). Among them are 27 waterfowl, 35 shorebirds, 9 gulls and terns, 9 herons and egrets, and 16 hawks, eagles, and falcons. Lesser prairie-chickens are fairly common, and two public viewing blinds are present. Abundant overwintering nonbreeding species include the Lapland longspur, American tree and white-crowned sparrows, dark-eyed junco, and pine siskin. Common breeding short-distance migrants or permanent residents include the ring-necked pheasant, mourning dove, horned lark, Cassin's sparrow, grasshopper sparrow, red-winged blackbird, and western meadowlark. Breeding Neotropical migrants include the Mississippi kite, Swainson's hawk, common nighthawk, chimney swift, and yellow-billed cuckoo, plus 3 swallows, 7 vireos, 35 warblers, 3 tanagers, and 2 orioles. Breeding bird surveys have documented at least 58 species. *Address:* 242 E. Hwy. 56, PO Box 300, Elkhart, KS 67950 (620-697-4621), https://www.fs.usda. gov/main/psicc/home.

Cross Timbers State Park. 1,075 acres. This park near Toronto in east-central Kansas lies in the transitional Cross Timbers ecologic region, where a band of post oaks once stretched hundreds of miles in a north-south direction across the tall prairies. Some of these old-growth trees still exist along the Ancient Oaks Trail. The adjacent 4,600-acre *Toronto Wildlife Area* is a mixture of forests, grasslands, and farmlands. *Address:* 144 Hwy. 105, Toronto, KS 66777 (620-637-2213).

Flint Hills National Wildlife Refuge. 18,500 acres. This refuge is at the upper end of the John Redmond Reservoir on the Neosho River in Coffey County. Most of the refuge consists of the reservoir itself and is managed primarily for waterfowl with 2,500 acres of wetlands. Notable breeding birds include the wood duck, least bittern, and upland sandpiper. During migration up to 100,000 waterfowl may be present. Many waterfowl overwinter here, which attracts substantial numbers of American bald eagles. At least 123 species are common to abundant during spring versus 114 species during fall and 38 during winter (Jones, 1990). There are at least 86 nesting birds among the 285 species listed for the refuge by Jones. A total of 62 bird species were reported present year-round, so an estimated minimum of 78 percent of the refuge's total bird diversity is migratory. The site's birding aspects were described by Zimmerman and Patti (1988), Gress and Potts (1993), and Gress and Janzen (2008). A recent checklist of more than 290 bird species, including 113 wetland species (21 breeders), is available from the refuge manager at 530 W. Maple Ave., PO Box 128, Hartford, KS 66854 (620-392-5553). The list is also available online at https://www.fws.gov/uploadedFiles/20130320103941.pdf.

Gardner Wetlands (Kansas City Power and Light Company Wetland Park). 55 acres. This suburban site was described by Gress and Janzen (2008). It is notable for its migratory shorebirds and other migratory species that use its 23-acre wetland. Located just west of Gardner at the intersection of US Hwy. 50 and South Waverly Rd. (first road west of the Catholic church) in Johnson County. A boardwalk leads to a large viewing blind (Rose 2017).

Highland, Kansas. This small town in northeastern Kansas houses the *Native American Heritage Museum* and the *Sac and Fox Tribal Museum*. They contain exhibits documenting the impact of the Lewis and Clark expedition on the Native Americans then living along the Missouri River, including the Iowa and Sac and Fox tribes. The relatively small, adjoining *Iowa Indian Reservation* and *Sac and Fox Indian Reservation* are located along the Nebraska-Kansas border, south of the Big Nemaha River. Clark observed that the Big Nemaha ("Ne-Ma-Haw") was then a meandering stream of clear water about 80 yards wide at its mouth. It is now little more than a narrow, muddy creek with eroded silt banks. On the Nebraska side, about four miles south of Rulo, is a community hall of the Iowa tribe, housing some artifacts and historic as well as more recent Native American images. Not far north, along the Big Nemaha River and about 1.5 miles upstream from its mouth, is an ancient Iowa-Missouri burial ground. It was discovered on July 12, 1804, by Captain Clark, who

described them as "Artificial Mounds." Traces of these ancient burial mounds still exist, but they have been largely obscured by more recent interments and agricultural activities.

Kansas Department of Wildlife, Parks and Tourism miscellaneous wetlands. This group of state-owned wetlands includes half a dozen that typify the Great Plains. (1) *Turkey Playa Wetland* (157 acres, 50 of which are wetlands) is located 12 miles southwest of Dodge City. To reach it, drive west from Dodge City on Hwy. 50 for 7 miles to Howell, turn south on Road 102, cross the Arkansas River, and continue 4 miles to the intersection of Road 102 and Nickle Road. Seasonally closed, the area can be viewed from the north and west roads. Nearby in Ford County are (2) *Herron Lake Playa Wetland* (160 wetland acres), 4.5 miles southwest of Spearville, and (3) *Stein Playa Wetlands* (73 wetland acres, 260 acres of native grassland), which is 2.5 miles west and a half mile south of Spearville. East of Dodge City are (4) *Isabel Wildlife Area*, with 41 wetland acres, a few miles north of Isabel on Hwy. 42, and (5) *Texas Lake Wildlife Area*, northeast of Wellesford on NW 130th Ave., with a natural wetland. Southwest of Oxford in Sumner County is (6) the *Slate Creek Wetlands* (947 acres). To reach the Slate Creek site, drive south out of Oxford on South Sumner Avenue, which becomes South Oxford Road. Continue to East 70th Street and turn west onto a gravel road that terminates at Greenwich Road and a parking area. From there, walk to the observation tower. Other access points occur along East 80th Street (Rose, 2017). Benedictine Bottoms Wildlife Area, McPherson Valley wetlands, and Neosho Wildlife Area (see separate sections) are also administered by the state of Kansas.

Kirwin National Wildlife Refuge. 10,800 acres. This refuge is about ten miles southeast of Phillipsburg in Phillips County. It consists mostly of marshes, grasslands, croplands, and a 5,000-acre reservoir impounded on the north fork of the Solomon River. Large numbers of ducks (especially mallards) and Canada geese winter here. Flocks of migrating sandhill cranes regularly stop here, and whooping cranes have been seen on rare occasions. At least 60 species are common to abundant during spring versus 61 species during fall and 20 during winter (Jones, 1990). There are at least 46 nesting birds among the 191 species listed for the refuge by Jones. He reported that a total of 56 bird species are present year-round, so an estimated minimum of 71 percent of the refuge's total bird diversity is migratory The site's birds and favored birding locations were described by Zimmerman and Patti (1988) and by Gress and Janzen (2008). A recent checklist includes 234 total bird species, including 131 wetland species (10 breeders, mostly ducks and the least tern). The list is available from the refuge manager at 702 E. Xavier Rd., Kirwin, KS 67644 (785-543-6673).

Marais des Cygnes National Wildlife Refuge and **Marais des Cygnes Wildlife Area.** 15,000 acres, collectively. These two adjoining "Marsh of the Swans" sites encompass a wide diversity of wetlands, tallgrass prairie, deciduous upland and riparian woodland, and transitional habitats. At least 321 bird species, including 117 breeders, have been identified here, but published species lists for these sites are apparently not yet available. More than 30 warblers have been seen; breeding species include the yellow-breasted chat, American redstart, northern parula, and the yellow-throated, Kentucky, black-and-white, prothonotary, and cerulean warblers. There are also more than 200 species of plants, 58 reptiles and amphibians, and 31 mussel species that have been documented. These two sites and their birds were described by Gress and Janzen (2008). *Address of NWR:* 24141 Kansas Hwy. 5, Pleasanton, KS 66075 (913-352-8956). *Address of wildlife area:* 16382 US Hwy. 69, Pleasanton, KS 66075 (913-352-8956).

Maxwell Wildlife Refuge. 2,254 acres. Located seven miles north of Canton on County Road 304 to Pueblo Road in McPherson County, this grassland refuge had its origins in the 1940s, when H. I. Maxwell bought the land with the purpose of establishing a wildlife refuge. In 1944 the property was turned over to what is now the Kansas Department of Wildlife, Parks and Tourism, and in 1951 the first ten bison were released. There are now about 200 bison and 50 elk that roam free on the refuge. Tram rides can be arranged, and there is a 30-foot observation tower. *Address:* 2565 Pueblo Rd., Canton, KS 67248 (620-628-4455).

McPherson Valley wetlands. 4,335 acres. This state-owned area is located northeast of Inman in McPherson County. It includes Lake Inman, the largest natural lake in Kansas (about 100 acres), as well as many relict marshes that developed at the end of the Pleistocene epoch and comprised more than 9,000 acres

until they were drained during the past century. The area now contains 51 independently managed marsh units covering 1,760 acres of wetlands and is important for migrating water birds (Gress and Potts, 1993). It is located within 50 miles of both Quivira NWR and Cheyenne Bottoms Wildlife Area, and has been visited periodically by migrating whooping cranes. No bird list is yet available. For more information, contact the Kansas Department of Wildlife, Parks and Tourism (620-241-7669).

Natural History Museum, University of Kansas. This biology/geology museum on the University of Kansas campus in Lawrence is notable for its fossil holdings and displays, especially of fossils found in the Mesozoic chalk beds of western Kansas, such as pterosaurs, plesiosaurs, and mosasaurs, as well as the late Cretaceous flightless diving bird, *Hesperornis*, first discovered there. The museum also has a panorama of dioramas illustrating a wide range of North American habitats. *Address:* 1345 Jayhawk Blvd., Lawrence, KS 66045 (785-864-4450).

Neosho Wildlife Area. 3,246 acres. This state-owned wildlife area, located one mile east of St. Paul in Neosho County, is the largest wetland in southeastern Kansas. It was formed by placing levees in an old oxbow and consists of wetlands and riparian woodlands in the Neosho River valley. It is especially important for migrating waterfowl and shorebirds, and has been described by Gress and Potts (1993) and Gress and Janzen (2005). Summer resident wading birds include snowy, great, and cattle egrets as well as both night-herons. Notable breeding Neotropical passerines include the Acadian flycatcher, yellow-throated vireo, prothonotary warbler, northern parula, and summer tanager. For more information, contact Kansas Department of Wildlife, Parks and Tourism at 8705 Wallace Rd., Saint Paul, KS, 66771 (620-449-2539) or see http://ksoutdoors.com/KDWPT-Info/Locations/Wildlife-Areas/Southeast/Neosho.

Perry Reservoir and **Perry Lake State Park.** This site in the Delaware River valley consists of Perry Reservoir (11,000 acres), marshes, mudflats, prairie, old fields, and riparian woodlands. The area and its birds have been described by Gress and Potts (1993) and Gress and Janzen (2005). Its nearby associated wetlands of importance to birds include Kyle, Lassiter, and

Ferguson Marshes. Summering migrants include a variety of buntings, vireos, tanagers, thrushes, and warblers, while during fall and spring migration, ducks, snow geese, and American bald eagles are abundant. No bird lists are yet available. *Address of reservoir:* US Army Corps of Engineers, 10419 Perry Park Dr., Perry, KS 66073 (785-597-5144). *Address of Perry State Park:* 5441 West Lake Rd., Ozawkie, KS 66070 (785-246-3449).

Prairie Dog State Park. 1,150 acres. This state park near Norton in northwestern Kansas is on the shores of Keith Sebelius Reservoir and home to a colony of about 300 prairie dogs, some of the lucky survivors of Kansas's endless war on prairie dogs. An adjacent 6.500-acre *Norton Wildlife Area* supports both white-tailed and mule deer as well as pheasants, turkeys, and other grassland wildlife. *Address:* 13037 State Hwy. 261, Norton, KS 67654 (785-877-2953).

Quivira National Wildlife Refuge. 21,800 acres. Named for the mythical city of gold that was unsuccessfully searched for by early Spanish explorers, Quivira is nevertheless very real and an ornithological gold mine. Located along Rattlesnake Creek in central Kansas, about ten miles southwest of Raymond (or 25 miles southeast of Great Bend), it includes two large salt marshes fed by a system of dikes and canals that result in about 5,000 acres of shallow wetlands. These wetlands are major spring staging areas for 200,000 waterfowl, plus thousands of American white pelicans and sandhill cranes, and have been designated as critical habitat for whooping cranes. The refuge is on the Ramsar list of wetlands of international importance and is notable for its diverse wetland birds, including consistent use by both sandhill and whooping cranes. Whooping cranes regularly stop here; more than 100 were seen during the fall of 2016. Notable breeding birds include hooded merganser, eared grebe, least bittern, great egret, snowy egret, yellow-crowned night-heron, white-faced ibis, rails (black, king, sora, and Virginia), snowy plover, and black-necked stilt. Some of the rare spring birds that sometimes have nested include the least tern, snowy plover, American avocet, black-necked stilt, and white-faced ibis. It is much harder to find the black, king, and Virginia rails and the common moorhen. At least 112 species are common to abundant during spring versus 110 species during fall and 39 during winter (Jones,

1990). There are at least 88 nesting birds among the 252 species listed for the refuge in 1990 by Jones, but a more recent total exceeds 310. A total of 67 bird species were reported present year-round by Jones, so an estimated minimum of 74 percent of the refuge's total bird diversity is migratory. A checklist is available from the refuge manager at 1434 NE 80th St., Stafford, KS 67578 (620-486-2304). It is also available online at https://www.fws.gov/uploadedFiles/Bird%20Checklist%202011.pdf.

Tallgrass Prairie National Preserve. 10,900 acres. This tallgrass prairie near Strong City was preserved through purchase by the National Park Trust in 1994. Later the trust purchased about 32 more acres, including a historic house, barn, and outbuildings. Then in 2005, the entire ranch was sold to the Nature Conservancy. Bison were reintroduced in 2009 and now (in 2017) number about 70 to 100 head. Bird and other species lists are not yet available. *Address:* 2480B Kansas Hwy. 177, Strong City, KS 66869 (620-273-8494), https://www.nps.gov/tapr/index.htm.

Tuttle Creek Lake region. 28,500 acres. This largest of Kansas reservoirs is north of Manhattan and has public lands and wetlands associated with Tuttle Creek Lake (19 square miles) and *Tuttle Creek State Park* (1,250 acres). Significant regional wetlands with public access include *Fancy Creek Wildlife Area, Olsburg Marsh, Carnahan Creek Park, Outlet Park, Tuttle Creek Park, Stockdale Park,* and *River Pond State Park*. The last-named area is noted for its winter American bald eagle population. Information on these sites and their locations can be obtained from the US Corps of Engineers Visitor Center at Tuttle Creek Dam (785-539-8511). No species lists are yet available. *Address of Tuttle Creek State Park:* 5800 River Pond Rd., Manhattan, KS 66502 (785-539-7941).

Weston Bend Bottomlands. Access to the bottomlands is through the Fort Leavenworth Visitor Control Center at the intersection of Metropolitan Avenue and North 4th Street in Leavenworth. After entering the Fort Leavenworth Military Reservation, find the one-way Chief Joseph Loop Road and drive into a 200-year-old bottomland forest with several hiking trails. Checklists of vertebrates and plants compiled by the Kansas Biological Survey are available at https://biosurvey.ku.edu/field-station/brochures (Rose, 2017).

MISSOURI

Missouri (MO) is notable in having four major national wildlife refuges (two of which are located within the Great Plains region), a national forest, a national scenic waterway, 38 state parks and state historic sites, and several hundred state conservation areas and state nature and wildlife preserves. Missouri has 1.5 million acres of National Forest Service land, 60,000 acres of US Fish and Wildlife Service land, and 54,000 acres of National Park Service land. Federally owned acreage in Missouri comprises 5.61 percent of the state's total land area. Missouri is also notable for the educational efforts of its Department of Conservation, including its publication of numerous identification guides to the state's plants and animals. They include books on the state's fossils, birds, mammals, amphibians and reptiles, fishes, wildflowers, mushrooms, grasses, trees, and shrubs and woody vines. Missouri also recently established an online birding trail that divides the state into six regions and describes more than 30 sites that fall within the geographic limits of the Great Plains. Individual site accounts include an area map, area website, a detailed site description, comments on birds likely to be found, and a description of the surrounding area's places of potential interest to a naturalist. See http://greatmissouribirdingtrail.com/Wordpress/.

Brickyard Hill Conservation Area. 2,610 acres. This conservation area is in Atchison County, extreme northwestern Missouri, off I-29 at Exit 116. Mostly forested, with some very old bur oaks, the site also has old fields and some loess hills shortgrass prairie, which represents a unique regional shortgrass community type. Created in 1962, the area has been enlarged over the years and includes the Brickyard Hill Loess Mound Natural Area. For more information, contact the Missouri Department of Conservation, Northwest Regional Office, 701 James McCarthy Dr., St. Joseph, MO 64507 (816-271-3100).

Dunn Ranch–Pawnee Prairie. 3,258 acres. The Nature Conservancy's Dunn Ranch is located along the Iowa border about ten miles northwest of Eagleville in north-central Missouri. The nearby 900-acre tallgrass Pawnee Prairie is jointly owned by the Nature Conservancy (476 acres) and the Missouri Department of Conservation (about 500 acres) and lies two miles northwest of Dunn Ranch. The Nature Conservancy also owns about 5,000 acres of the nearby *Grand River Grasslands*, which are also adjacent to the ranch. The area is open to hiking, bird watching, and nature viewing. Henslow's sparrows, bobolinks, and upland sandpipers are among the breeding birds. A herd of bison was introduced in 2011; the bison area is closed to the public. The Dunn Ranch also has a public-access prairie-chicken viewing blind that likely requires advance arrangement for use. The Dunn Ranch–Grand River Grasslands restoration project is a prairie restoration effort that includes grasslands in both Iowa (Ringgold County) and Missouri (Harrison County). About 60 private landowners are also participating in the restoration project, as well as federal agencies and the National Audubon Society. The grasslands will eventually total more than 80,000 acres, with Iowa protecting about 13,000 acres and Missouri about 70,000 acres. An associated prairie-chicken restoration project has also been initiated by the Missouri Department of Conservation (MDC) and the Iowa Department of Natural Resources (IDNR). Aided by repeated translocations of birds from Nebraska, in 2017 a total of 61 male prairie-chickens were found on leks at the Dunn Ranch, Pawnee Prairie, and the Grand River Grasslands. The combined Missouri-Iowa population was then estimated at slightly over 200 birds. For more information about prairie-chickens in Missouri, visit https://nature.mdc.mo.gov/discover-nature/field-guide/greater-prairie-chicken. Information about MDC's Pawnee Prairie is available at https://nature.mdc.mo.gov/discover-nature/places/pawnee-prairie. For information about the Grand River Grasslands and the Conservancy's Dunn Ranch, visit http://bit.ly/RmQ4Rr. To visit the Dunn Ranch, call in advance at 660-867-3866. *Address of Dunn Ranch/Pawnee Prairie Project and Osage Plains Nature Conservancy office:* 16970 W. 150th St., Hatfield, MO 64458 (660-867-3866).

Lewis and Clark State Park. Located five miles south of Rushville off State Hwy. 45, this park has mature riverine woodlands and an oxbow lake (Sugar Lake), a onetime channel in the Missouri River that was cut off from the main flow at least two centuries ago. It was first described by Lewis and Clark, who called it "Gosling Lake" because of all the goose families they observed there. Although now largely developed for

Tallgrass songbirds, including adult males of western (top left) and eastern (right) meadowlarks, and (bottom left) Henslow's sparrow and (right) dickcissel.

summer camping and recreational activities, the lake sometimes attracts very large flocks of migrating snow geese from nearby Loess Buff National Wildlife Refuge. *Address:* 807 Lake Crest Blvd., Rushville, MO 64484 (816-579-5564).

Loess Bluffs National Wildlife Refuge. 7,350 acres. This refuge, previously known as Squaw Creek NWR, is five miles south of Mound City in extreme northwestern Missouri. It consists of shallow marshes, Missouri River bottomlands, wooded loess bluffs, and farmlands. The wetlands are at the base of 200-foot-high bluffs of wind-blown silts that form the Loess Hills region along the west banks of the Missouri River valley from northern Iowa to northern Missouri, and are part of an aerial highway for thousands of migrating raptors each spring and fall. The refuge lies a few miles east of the Missouri River, in rich prairie bottomland, and its large (3,400 acres) shallow marsh is fed by two small creeks and ditches. At least 90 bird species are common to abundant during spring versus 71 species during fall and 25 during winter (Jones, 1990). There are at least 104 nesting birds among the 268 listed for the refuge by Jones. A total of 65 bird species were reported present year-round by Jones, so an estimated minimum of 76 percent of the refuge's total bird diversity is migratory. Depending on the severity of the winter, up to 400,000 snow geese, other geese, and ducks may be present. Nearly 900 trumpeter swans have been seen here, with the numbers of migrant and wintering American bald eagles varying with the waterfowl numbers but often approaching 200 (Johnsgard, 2013, *Birds of Nebraska*). The refuge is part of a series of important migratory stopping points for the more than 10 million snow geese that arrive from vast colonies in Hudson Bay and the central Canadian Arctic en route to wintering areas that extend from Missouri and Kansas southward. Phenomenally large flocks of snow geese (up to 1.5 million birds at peak) have been reported in late fall and early spring in recent years. The refuge's bird list includes at least 277 total species, with more than 100 nesting species and a spring list of more than 260 species. Beyond this very high overall spring diversity, 12 species are listed as abundant during spring. Other abundant spring birds include the Canada goose, mallard, northern pintail, American coot, bank swallow, red-winged blackbird, and

brown-headed cowbird. Large numbers (up to about 475 as of 2017) of American bald eagles follow the migrating snow goose flocks, with some remaining until the geese depart in March, and a few nest locally. At least two pairs of greater sandhill cranes have nested on the refuge in recent years, and since then a few have either overwintered locally or returned very early in the spring. Many other marsh birds also nest here, as do pileated woodpeckers in the heavily wooded lowlands. A recent checklist of 268 species is available from the refuge manager at PO Box 158, Mound City, MO 64470 (660-442-3187) or online at https://www.fws.gov/uploadedFiles/Squaw-CreekBirdList.pdf.

McCormack Loess Mounds Natural Area. 112 acres. McCormack Loess Mounds NA is about 1.5 miles south of Loess Bluff (Squaw Creek) NWR (see section). This site is near the southern end of the ridge of loess hills that extends north-south along all of extreme western Iowa. This NA is also part of the state-owned 227-acre *J. C. McCormack Wildlife Area*, and both overlook the refuge's lowlands. Both sites are mostly relict upland prairies and woodlands covering loess hills that rise nearly 250 feet above the surrounding lowlands.

Missouri prairies and prairie-chickens. Very few greater prairie-chickens were surviving in Missouri as of 2017, the population having declined from several thousand in 2000 (Johnsgard, 2002, *Grassland Grouse*) to at most a few hundred. The state's total 2013–17 average count was only 121 birds on nine leks and at three locations, with most of the birds at the Dunn Ranch–Pawnee Prairie (see section). In 2017 Wah'Kon-Tah Prairie had only a single active prairie-chicken lek, with four males present. *Wah'Kon-Tah Prairie* occupies 5,000 acres and is located ten miles southeast of Appleton and about five miles northeast of El Dorado Springs. It is owned by the Missouri Department of Conservation (MDC) and the Nature Conservancy (TNC). A few prairie-chickens were also still present in 2017 at *Taberville Prairie* (1,680 acres, TNC), eight miles north of Taberville and ten miles southeast of Appleton, a richly diverse prairie where some 400 plant species have been documented. Other important relict prairies in western Missouri are *Diamond Grove Prairie* (611 acres of prairie, MDC), located five miles southwest of Diamond; *Golden Prairie* (500 acres,

Missouri Prairie Foundation), located five miles south-west of Golden City; *Marmaton River Bottoms Prairie* (609 acres of wet prairie and riverine forest, TNC); and *Osage Prairie Conservation Area* (1,517 acres, TNC), about six miles south of Nevada (Jones and Cushman, 2008). *Address of state TNC office:* 2816 Sutton Blvd., Ste. 2, St. Louis, MO 63144 (314-968-1105). *Address of MDC:* 2901 W. Truman Blvd., Jefferson City, MO 65109 (573-751-4115). *Address of Missouri Prairie Foundation:* PO Box 200, Columbia, MO 65205.

Prairie State Park. About 4,000 acres. This state park, located west of Lamar near the Kansas border in southwestern Missouri, protects one of the best prairies in the state, with four prairie parcels classified as Star Natural Areas. More than 500 species of wildflowers have been documented here. There is also a herd of captive bison. *Address:* 128 NW 150th Ln., Minden-mines, MO 64769 (417-843-6711).

Star School Hill Prairie Natural Area. 70 acres. This state-owned native prairie site is located about 1.5 miles south of the Iowa state line and 12 miles north of Rockport. It is also about 5 miles northeast of the Brickyard Hill Conservation Area (see section). It lies within the *Star School Hill Prairie Conservation Area*, the two totaling 359 acres. Both are upland prairies situated on steep loess hills adjacent to the Missouri floodplain. For more information, contact the Missouri Department of Conservation, Northwest Regional Office, 701 James McCarthy Dr., St. Joseph, MO 64507 (816-271-3100).

Swan Lake National Wildlife Refuge. 10,795 acres. About half of the acreage at Swan Lake NWR is covered by shallow lakes. Located two miles south of Sumner, this refuge has long been an important wintering area for Canada geese, which typically number well over 200,000 annually. More than 100 American bald eagles also usually overwinter. March–April and October–November are the peak months for waterfowl numbers. Jones (1990) listed 233 bird species, of which 83 were nesters. A more recent summary reported 241 bird species as well as 14 additional species with only very rare ("accidental") occurrences. There is a 1.5-mile hiking trail and a visitor center. *Address:* Rte. 1, Box 29A (Swan Lake Drive), Sumner, MO 64681 (660-856-3323), email swanlake@fws.gov

NEBRASKA

Nebraska (NE) has five national wildlife refuges totaling 174,000 acres, two national forests totaling 257,000 acres, two national monuments totaling 5,900 acres, and one national grassland totaling 94,000 acres. Nebraska also has eight state parks, nine state historical parks, nearly 60 state recreation areas, and about 300 wildlife management areas. Federally owned acreage in Nebraska comprises 1.36 percent of the state's total land area. About 800,000 acres are public-access state and federal lands in the state; Nebraska's state and federal public lands represent about 2 percent of the state's total area. County checklists of the birds of any of the state's 93 counties can be downloaded at www.noubirds.org/Birds/CountyChecklists.aspx. An online source to locating more than 300 birding sites in Nebraska can be found at http://nebraskabirdingtrails.com/, and a county-by-county online guide to birding in Nebraska exists at http://digitalcommons.unl.edu/biosciornithology/51/.

One of Nebraska's greatest natural treasures is its Platte River. Although the Platte River's headwaters consist of two mountain-fed courses in Colorado and Wyoming, these streams merge in western Nebraska near North Platte, and the resulting river soon settles into a placid 70- to 80-mile stretch that extends from about Lexington to Grand Island in central Nebraska. There the river meanders slowly from west to east through the lower half of the state like a slightly sagging blue belt supporting a well-fed Cornhusker fan. The sand-bottom stream flows comfortably within a barely discernable 13-mile-wide and highly fertile valley, methodically if randomly and simultaneously depositing and eroding away countless sandy bars and islands during its seasonal flow fluctuations.

This otherwise inconspicuous stretch of the Platte River annually hosts one of the world's greatest bird spectacles during the month of March, because the river here intercepts the middle of a north-south, roughly hourglass-shaped Central Flyway migration route that is used by nearly 30 species of waterfowl, 2 species of American cranes, and up to about two dozen species of shorebirds (Johnsgard, 1979; 1984; 2005; 2011, *Nebraska Bird-Finding Guide*; 2012, *Wetland Birds*; 2012, *Wings*). At least 373 bird species have been reported from the Central Platte valley (Brown and Johnsgard, 2013), representing over 80 percent of the state's total recorded species list, the largest regional checklist for any Nebraska location, and perhaps the largest for anywhere in the entire Great Plains north of Texas.

In early spring up to about 9 million waterfowl and a half million sandhill cranes descend into the Platte valley and the adjoining Rainwater Basin south of the valley (Johnsgard, 2012, *Wetland Birds*; Brown and Johnsgard, 2013). Estimates of waterfowl vary greatly. Actual numbers depend on water conditions, but it is commonly estimated that 7 million snow geese may be here in mid-March, along with hundreds of thousands each of Canada geese and greater white-fronted geese. Probably at least 100,000 cackling geese are also present, and perhaps as many as 40,000 Ross's geese (in 2016 more than 21,000 were calculated to be present within a mostly snow goose flock that was estimated at 1,074,000 birds). The numbers of ducks are equally impressive, with mallards and northern pintails usually the most common and numbering in the tens or hundreds of thousands, and usually (along with common mergansers and common goldeneyes) the earliest ducks to arrive, competing with the cranes and geese for unharvested corn. By the end of March, 20 or more duck species will have arrived in the Platte valley, while the geese and sandhill cranes will have begun to leave.

By mid-April the central Platte's sandhill cranes (mostly Arctic tundra–breeding lesser sandhills headed for Alaska and Siberia) are being replaced by the earliest of the shorebird migrants and family-sized groups of whooping cranes. The approximately two dozen species of shorebirds usually peak by the end of April or mid-May, their totals being estimated at 200,000 to 300,000 birds. The birds of this 10,000-square-mile region have been described by Brown and Johnsgard (2013) with a total of over 390 species documented. There are no federal refuges on this important section of the Platte River, but much of it is now protected as a result of efforts by the Nature Conservancy, Platte River Recovery Implementation Program, National Audubon Society, Crane Trust, and other conservation organizations.

Agate Fossil Beds National Monument. 11,617 acres. This site is located in Sioux County, 22 miles south of Harrison, or 34 miles north of Mitchell, on NE Hwy. 29. This world-famous fossil site has been the source of vast numbers of early Miocene mammals, from sediments dating about 20 million to 22 million years ago

(Maher, Engelmann, and Shuster, 2003; Johnsgard, 2015, "Secrets"). The fossil beds were discovered in 1904 by Capt. James Cook, a local rancher, one-time Indian Wars scout, and a friend of the Lakota Sioux. Since then the site has produced almost countless numbers of mammalian fossils that are represented in museums around the world, among them the Carnegie Museum of Natural History and the University of Nebraska State Museum (see section). The fossils include such early mammals as *Miohippus* (horse), *Monceras* (rhino), *Amphycion* (bear-dog), *Daeodon* (antelodont), *Stenomylus* (camel), *Moropus* (chalcothere), and *Paleocaster* (land beaver). The visitor center has several reconstructed skeletons of *Moropus* and other fossils, and it also houses Captain Cook's personal collection of Native American (Sioux) artifacts. Prairie rattlesnakes commonly sun themselves on the nearly mile-long trail to the old dig sites during summer, so caution is advised in selecting one's path. Carrying a canteen of drinking water on hot days is important too. *Address:* 301 River Rd., Harrison, NE 69346 (308-668-2211), www.nps.gov/agfo.

Ashfall Fossil Beds State Historic Park. 260 acres. This park is located in Antelope County, two miles west and six miles north of Royal on 517th Avenue. This world-famous fossil site includes the exposed, *in situ*, fossil remains from dozens of mid-Miocene mammals, mostly rhinos, which died after a fallout of volcanic ash that originated from eruptions in the Yellowstone region about 12 million years ago (Voorhies, 1981; Maher, Engelmann and Shuster, 2003; Johnsgard, 2014, "Secrets"). There are also one- and three-toed horses (5 genera), camels (three genera), canids (three genera), saber-toothed deer (one genus), and a few birds—including a crane very similar to the modern African crowned cranes but distantly related to the two North American cranes. Operated by the University of Nebraska and the Nebraska Game and Parks Commission. Open Memorial Day to Labor Day; limited hours from May to October. *Address:* 86930 517th Ave., Royal, NE 68773 (402-893-2000).

Boyer Chute National Wildlife Refuge. 3,300 acres. This relatively new and still uncompleted refuge is located about five miles east of Fort Calhoun. It is a reconstructed side channel ("chute") on the west side of the Missouri River, managed by the nearby DeSoto NWR (see section in Iowa list). The refuge

Black-billed magpie

is still under development, with an additional 8,000 acres planned for acquisition. There is no local bird checklist, but the DeSoto NWR list is probably applicable. *Address:* 3720 Rivers Way, Fort Calhoun, NE 68023 (712-388-4800).

Chimney Rock National Historic Site. 83 acres. This famous spire stands about 300 feet above the surrounding grasslands in western Nebraska and was one of the most mentioned landmarks on the Oregon Trail. There is a small visitor center with historic exhibits, a video presentation, and a variety of books for sale dealing with western and Oregon Trail history. Golden eagles have sometimes nested on bluffs to the south, prairie dogs are often also present near these bluffs, and burrowing owls might still sometimes be found among the prairie dogs. A small alkaline marsh, *Facus Springs*, along the south side of NE Hwy. 28/92 about five miles east of Chimney Rock often has migrant or nesting shorebirds, such as the Wilson's snipe, American avocet, and Wilson's phalarope. *Address:* PO Box F, Bayard, NE 69334 (308-586-2581), https://www.nps.gov/nr/travel/scotts_bluff/chimney_rock.html.

The Crane Trust. The Crane Trust (originally known as the Platte River Whooping Crane Critical Habitat Maintenance Trust) was formed in the 1970s as a result of a legal settlement over the environmental costs of building an upstream dam in Wyoming and manages several thousand acres of riparian wetlands along the Platte River of importance to cranes. Its biologists perform annual surveys of sandhill crane usage, habitat surveys, and other avian and ecological research. Bison have recently been added to the site's attractions, and there are eight miles of walking trails (not available during crane season). The Crane Trust's headquarters is one mile east of the Alda Road bridge (about a mile south of I-80 at Exit 305); turn east and continue approximately 1.5 miles on Whooping Crane Drive (limited access, call 308-384-4633). The Trust's Nature and Visitor Center (308-382-1820) is located just south of the I-80 interchange at Exit 305, where free talks and videos are often offered during spring crane season and a gift shop is available. The Crane Trust and its Visitor Center also provide information on cranes and other wildlife to tourists and, like Rowe Sanctuary, offer low-cost guided sunrise and sunset trips to crane-viewing blinds in the vicinity of the Alda Road bridge from late February to early April. Excellent (and free) public-access crane-viewing is also possible from a raised platform beside the Alda Road bridge, with a downstream crane roost often visible toward the east. See the Crane Trust website at https://cranetrust.org.

Crescent Lake National Wildlife Refuge. 45,818 acres. Located 28 miles north of Oshkosh, in Garden County (or 20 miles south of Lakeside, Sheridan County), this enormous refuge can be reached only via sand, gravel, and deteriorated hardtop roads. About 20 wetland complexes are contained in this sandhills refuge; these total 8,251 acres and comprise almost 20 percent of the refuge. Crescent Lake NWR is in the central Nebraska Sandhills region, which extends over about 19,000 square miles and is the largest region of (mostly stabilized) dunes in North America (Johnsgard, 1995). At least 32 species of waterfowl have been reported at the refuge, and 14 are known or suspected breeders. Three grebes (western, eared and, pied-billed) are also breeders. Other common wetland breeders include the double-crested cormorant, great blue heron, black-crowned night-heron, American bittern, sora and Virginia rail, and Forster's tern. The common yellowthroat, sedge wren, and marsh wren are abundant breeders, and the American avocet, white-faced ibis, and black-necked stilt breed regularly. The marshes and shallow lakes in this large and remote Sandhills refuge vary greatly as to their relative alkalinity. At the western edge of the refuge, Border Lake marks the eastern boundary of a multicounty (Garden, Morrill, and Sheridan) regional area of hypersaline water conditions; the Wilson's phalarope and American avocet are common breeders here, and cinnamon teal perhaps also breed occasionally. At least 66 bird species are common to abundant during spring versus 56 species during fall and 6 during winter (Jones, 1990). There are at least 83 nesting birds among the 233 listed in 1990 for the refuge by Jones. A total of 40 bird species were reported present year-round by Jones, so an estimated minimum of 83 percent of the refuge's total bird diversity is migratory. The refuge and its birds have been described by Farrar (2004) and Johnsgard (1995; 2011, *Nebraska Bird-Finding Guide*). Bullsnakes and ornate box turtles may often be seen along roadsides or crossing roads. The refuge headquarters has the only source of drinking water and public facilities on the refuge. A recent refuge bird list includes 273 species, with many wetland species, and is available from the refuge manager at 10630 Rd. 181, Ellsworth, NE 69340 (308-762-4893). A bird checklist is also available online at https://www.fws.gov/refuge/Crescent_Lake/wildlife_and_habitat/index.html (scroll to Birds and "bird list").

The Cupola. This treeless, sedimentary cone of grayish yellow clays, about 70 feet high, was discovered on September 7, 1804, and named "The Cupola" by Lewis and Clark expedition members. Locally known as "Old Baldy," the site is seven miles north of Lynch, Nebraska, on privately owned land. The nearest public road (unnumbered but easily found) passes within about a half mile of the promontory and offers an excellent view of it and several miles of the nearby river valley, which is still fairly pristine. A colony of black-tailed prairie dogs was discovered here by Lewis and Clark, providing the first specimens of this iconic shortgrass plains mammal known to science. The colony is long gone, but others in the general vicinity have survived. Several prairie dogs and four black-billed magpies that Lewis and Clark had captured alive were sent back to Washington, DC, in April of 1805 from Fort Mandan, along with many other acquisitions, before the group departed upstream. One of the prairie dogs and a magpie survived the thousand-plus-mile trip, and the prairie dog was Jefferson's White House guest for a time. Both animals were later preserved and displayed at Charles W. Peak's Philadelphia Museum, which eventually received nearly all the Lewis and Clark specimens. The museum was housed in Independence Hall until 1838, when it was moved the first of two times. Finally, in 1850 its contents were sold, some to P. T. Barnum and the rest to the Boston Museum. Some of the materials from the museum eventually were passed on to Harvard University, but most have since disappeared, including the prairie dog. However, the plant materials mostly survived, and the more than 200 herbarium specimens brought back to Philadelphia were the basis for the naming of more than 100 new plant species (Phillips, 2003).

DeSoto National Wildlife Refuge. (See section in Iowa.)

Fort Atkinson State Historical Park. 196 acres. This historical site is located one mile north of Fort Calhoun on County Rd. 34. Fort Atkinson was founded in 1820 but was abandoned in 1827, when western overland routes farther south made the Missouri River corridor less vital to national interests. Fort restoration began in the 1960s, with several restored buildings as well as a visitor center. The fort was situated on the summit of Council Bluff, the place where Lewis and Clark met with the Otoe-Missourias on August 3, 1804, Lewis and Clark's first formal meeting with any tribe of Native Americans. It is now on the Nebraska side of the river as a result of channel shifting; the river has shifted some three miles east of the bluff summit, and because of timber growth the river is no longer visible from the bluff. The nearby *Lewis and Clark National Historic Trail Visitor Center* and its headquarters are located at 601 Riverfront Dr., Omaha, NE 68102 (402-661-1804). During resettlement in 1854, the Otoe-Missourias ceded their land back to the US government and were initially confined to a reservation area of 160,000 acres along the present-day Nebraska-Kansas border. By 1880 most of the tribe had left the reservation to join the Sac and Fox Nation in Indian Territory. In 1881 the remainder relocated to Indian Territory (now parts of Noble and Pawnee Counties, Oklahoma). It was the Otoe (historically also spelled Oto) who were responsible for giving Nebraska its name, from an Otoe word meaning "flat water," referring to the Platte River.

Fort Niobrara National Wildlife Refuge. 19,122 acres. This refuge, located about five miles east of Valentine along Nebraska Hwy. 12, includes approximately 4,350 acres of mostly riparian woods and 375 acres of wetlands. Riparian hardwood forest occurs along the Niobrara River, and the uplands are sandhills prairie, with some spring-fed ponds. Notable wetland breeding species include the wood duck, upland sandpiper, and long-billed curlew. The most abundant Neotropical migrants nesting in the refuge area are the common yellowthroat, ovenbird, black-and-white warbler, and red-eyed vireo. At least 71 species are common to abundant during spring versus 67 species during fall and 14 during winter (Jones, 1990). There are at least 76 nesting birds among the 201 species listed for the refuge by Jones. A total of 25 bird species were reported present year-round by Jones, so an estimated minimum of 88 percent of the refuge's total bird diversity is migratory. The most recent refuge bird list includes 230 species, many of which are riparian woodland species with primarily eastern zoogeographic affinities, but some western species also occur, along with some hybrids between eastern and western counterpart species (Johnsgard, 2007, *Niobrara*). The bird list is available from the refuge manager at 39983 Refuge Rd., Valentine, NE 69201 (402-376-3789). The refuge website is at https://www.fws.gov/refuge/fort_niobrara/.

Fort Robinson State Park. 22,673 acres. Located three miles west of Crawford, at 3200 US Hwy. 20, this largest of Nebraska's state parks is one of special historic interest. Established in 1874 to protect the Red Cloud Indian Agency, this is where the Lakota chief Tasunke Witco (Crazy Horse) was murdered after he had surrendered. His body was taken away and buried by his parents at a secret and still unknown location, but an unimpressive stone memorial is present on the fort grounds. In 1891 the last remaining free-living Oglalas also surrendered at South Dakota's nearby Pine Ridge Agency, marking the end of the Indian Wars on the northern plains. Besides a general history museum on the grounds, there is also a *Trailside Museum of Natural History* that describes the geology and rich fossil history of the region. The park is situated on the Arikaree geologic group of the late Oligocene and early Miocene epochs, below which are earlier sediments dating from the Oligocene's White River group (Maher, Engelmann, and Shuster, 2003). One of the more interesting museum displays is the skeletal heads of two Pleistocene-age Columbian mammoths that had died with their tusks intertwined in combat. *Address:* 3200 Hwy. 20, Crawford, NE 69339-0392 (308-665-2900), http://outdoornebraska.gov/fortrobinson/.

Homestead National Monument of America. 195 acres. Located four miles west of Beatrice on Nebraska Hwy. 4, this is the site of the first homestead acreage awarded through the 1862 Homestead Act. The property includes a restored log cabin of the 1860s and a modern heritage and education center where visitors can research family histories online by using microfilms of early US census information and immigration data from Ellis Island. There are about 100 acres of tallgrass prairie, largely restored from original local prairie remnants, and an approximate quarter-mile stretch of the Blue River's riparian woodland. A local bird list is available. *Address:* 8523 W. State Hwy. 4, Beatrice, NE 68310 (402-223-3514), https://www.nps.gov/home/index.htm.

Iain Nicolson Audubon Center at Rowe Sanctuary. 2,400 acres. This National Audubon Society sanctuary and nature center are located about five miles southwest of Gibbon on Elm Island Road (drive south off I-80 at Exit 285 for 2.1 miles, then drive west on Elm Island Road for 2.1 miles). The sanctuary protects nearly five miles of prime crane feeding and roosting habitat, and up to 70,000 roosting cranes can often be seen from its blinds. Least terns and piping plovers often nest on barren sandbars that are also used by roosting cranes. Summer breeding birds include the dickcissel, upland sandpiper, and bobolink as well as riparian wooded habitat species such as the rose-breasted grosbeak and willow flycatcher. Rowe is also immediately north of the western Rainwater Basin (see section), a region of seasonal wetlands of great importance to shorebirds and waterfowl. The sanctuary is located along the Platte River in the heart of the sandhill crane's spring staging area, about five miles southwest of Gibbon. The Iain Nicolson Audubon Center is open year-round and provides guided sunrise and sunset crane-viewing blind tours from early March until early April. Audubon's "Crane Cam" provides year-round live-streaming video of crane roosting areas and river views via the internet. The largest blind accommodates up to 40 people and overlooks a roost attracting as many as 70,000 cranes during peak migration in late March. Single- or two-person blinds can also be rented for overnight use by photographers able to tolerate the cold. Others might use a free elevated public viewing platform at the Platte River bridge on Gibbon Road (2 miles south of Exit 285 on I-80, just north of the turn onto Elm Island Road), which provides excellent free sunset and sunrise crane-viewing. (A similar viewing platform is present south of I-80 exit 305, see the Crane Trust section.) A hike-bike trail bridge across the Platte at the *Fort Kearney State Recreation Area*, about ten miles to the west of Rowe off Nebraska Hwy. L-50A (the Platte River Road), also offers an alternate viewing choice, although a daily entrance fee to the park might be collected, especially late in the crane migration season. An Audubon-sponsored celebration of the cranes and Platte valley natural history has been held annually for more than forty years around the first day of spring in March. *Rowe Sanctuary address:* 44450 Elm Island Road, Gibbon NE 68440 (308-468-5282), http://rowe. audubon.org/.

Indian Cave State Park. 2,831 acres. This site is a mature riverine hardwood forest park about ten miles east of Shubert on Nebraska Hwy. 64E and located near the Lewis and Clark campsite of July 14, 1804. The park's centerpiece is a shallow, water-scourged Cretaceous-era limestone cave of upper Permian (Pennsylvanian) age, deposited during the major coal-forming period of early Paleozoic geologic history (Maher, Engelmann,

and Shuster, 2003). The exposed rock surfaces also contain a few Native American animal petroglyphs, made during an unknown period of Native American or Paleo-Indian habitation, that are now mostly overwhelmed by recent scribbles. There are 20 miles of hiking trails and camping is permitted. *Address:* 65296 720 Rd., Shubert, NE 68437 (402-883-2575).

Joslyn Art Museum. Omaha's Joslyn Art Museum has the entire collection of the 359 magnificent watercolors made by Karl Bodmer during his trip up the Missouri River during the early 1830s with Alexander Philipp Maximilian, Prince of Wied-Neuwied, just three decades after the Lewis and Clark expedition. Many of these original paintings were later converted into hand-colored aquatint engravings and published in Europe. *Address:* 2200 Dodge St., Omaha NE 68102 (402-342-3300).

Lake McConaughy State Recreation Area. 41,192 acres. This largest of Nebraska's reservoirs (over 30,000 acres when full), was developed for flood control, irrigation, and recreational use. It is about 22 miles long, 3 miles wide, up to 140 feet deep, and has 105 miles of shoreline when full. Including the adjacent *Lake Ogallala State Recreation Area*, the site totals about 5,500 land acres. Mostly bare sandy shorelines are on the northern side, but extensive wetlands exist at *Clear Creek Wildlife Management Area*, at the lake's western end. The lake is an important nesting area for both piping plovers and least terns, and also hosts many nonbreeding double-crested cormorants and American white pelicans throughout summer. Western and Clark's grebes summer and breed here, and about 20,000 to 30,000 western grebes stage here during fall migration. Large numbers of waterfowl, gulls, other water birds, and eagles winter here. A recent bird checklist for the Lake McConaughy region has 362 species (Brown, Dinsmore, and Brown, 2012), a high percentage of which are wetland-dependent species. Lake McConaughy is located nine miles north of Ogallala on Nebraska Hwy. 61. A daily or seasonal state park entry permit is required to enter the area (308-284-8800). See https://ilovelakemac.com/.

Lewis and Clark Visitor Center. This center is located on Calumet Bluff, off NE Hwy. 121, about four miles west of Yankton, South Dakota. It focuses on the ecology and history of the Missouri River, including the

Lewis and Clark expedition. A regional bird checklist of about 240 species covers several counties and should be available at the visitor center (402-667-2546).

Missouri National Recreational River (southern unit). The lower 59-mile section of this nationally designated part of the Missouri River encompasses the locations of the Lewis and Clark campsites of August 22–25, 1804. This segment stretches from about Yankton, South Dakota, to Ponca State Park (see section) and still somewhat resembles the river conditions probably seen by Lewis and Clark. The *Yankton Sioux Indian Reservation* (about 36,000 acres) is located directly north of the river. It has been home to the Nakota-dialect (Yankton) Sioux, who first formally met Lewis and Clark in the vicinity of the present-day city of Yankton. The reservation-based population in 2000 was about 3,000 people, with another 3,000 living off the reservation. At the time of Lewis and Clark, the Sioux (Lakota, Dakota, and Nakota) were the most numerous of the Plains tribes, at one time numbering perhaps as many as 27,000 people.

Missouri River Basin Lewis and Clark Interpretive Trail and Visitor Center. About 80 acres. Located off Hwy. 2 at the eastern edge of Nebraska City on a wooded bluff overlooking the Missouri River, this center contains exhibits on the Lewis and Clark expedition, especially the natural history aspects. It also has modern replicas of a 55-foot keelboat and a Plains Indian earth lodge. *Address:* 100 Valmont Drive, Nebraska City, NE 68410 (402-874-9900).

Niobrara State Park. 1,632 acres. This state park is located one mile north of the town of Niobrara and mostly consists of mature riverine hardwood forest, not greatly altered from the area's natural state. It is situated at the now-impounded mouth of the Niobrara River, 20 miles of which is part of the Missouri National Recreational River system (see section). A two-mile trail traverses the entire northern boundary of the park, and an interpretive center has Lewis and Clark exhibits. Camping is permitted. East of Niobrara State Park is the *Santee Sioux Indian Reservation*, whose members' ancestors were brought there in 1869 from the Crow Creek Reservation in western South Dakota. Still earlier, they had been removed from Minnesota, where they had engaged in a bloody uprising against the white settlers in 1862, after which

1,800 Santees were imprisoned and 33 were executed. The Santee Sioux Reservation in Nebraska originally consisted of 117,000 acres but was later substantially reduced. The current reservation population numbers about 600 residents.

Niobrara Valley Preserve. 56,000 acres. This Nature Conservancy preserve north of Springview in Keya Paha County is in the transition zone between western ponderosa pine forest and eastern deciduous forest. It includes 23 miles of shoreline along the Niobrara River and the northern edge of the Nebraska Sandhills (Johnsgard, 1995). The preserve is largely managed for bison, and research on bison foraging ecology and fire ecology is conducted here. A fire in 2012 burned 76,000 acres of this general region, including 29,000 acres of the preserve. Almost no tree regeneration has developed since that time. A list of 105 summering bird species has been published, and several of the breeding birds have east-west counterpart species or races (buntings, orioles, grosbeaks, flickers) that hybridize in this important continental ecological transition zone (Johnsgard, 2007, *Niobrara*). A largely pristine 76-mile section of the Niobrara River that passes through the preserve has been designated as the *Niobrara National Scenic River* and is one of Nebraska's most popular rivers for canoeing and floating. *Address of the preserve:* 42269 Morel Rd., Johnstown, NE 69214 (402-722-4440). *Address of the scenic river park:* 214 W. US Hwy. 20, Valentine, NE 69201 (402-376-1901).

North Platte National Wildlife Refuge. 5,047 acres. Once part of the Crescent Lake NWR (see section), although distant from it, the North Platte NWR now includes Lake Alice (1,500 acres when full, but usually dry), Lake Minatare (737 acres), and Winter's Creek Lake (536 acres). The best wetland bird habitat is at Winter's Creek, which seasonally supports many waterfowl and sandhill cranes. The location is four miles north and eight miles east of Scottsbluff. The refuge bird list totals 228 species, including 85 wetland species (13 breeders), and is available from the refuge manager at 10630 Rd. 181, Ellsworth, NE 69340 (308-762-4893) or online at https://www.fws.gov/refuge/north_platte/wildlife_and_habitat/birds.html.

Oglala National Grassland. 94,344 acres. This enormous grasslands in Sioux and Dawes Counties is seven miles north of Crawford on Nebraska Hwy.

71. It consists of shortgrass prairie over badlands of eroded clay and Cretaceous-age Pierre shale. Toadstool Geological Park (see section), also administered by the US Forest Service, is within the grassland, north of Fort Robinson State Park (see section). The *Hudson-Meng Bison Kill Research and Visitor Center* (20 acres) is also in the area (four miles north of Crawford on Nebraska Hwy. 2 and west on Toadstool Road, or about two miles southwest of Toadstool Park by trail). Here about 600 bison skeletal remains dating back 8,000 to 10,000 years (Alberta Culture period) have been excavated. About 50 mammal species have been reported from Oglala National Grassland (Moul, 2008). A bird list of 302 species (covering the nearby Nebraska National Forest and entire associated Pine Ridge region of northwestern Nebraska) is available from the USFS at 270 Pine St., Chadron, NE 69337 (308-432-3367 or 308-432-4475).

Omaha Indian Reservation and **Winnebago Indian Reservation.** The Omaha and Winnebago Reservations, located between Decatur and Homer, Nebraska, were established in 1856 and 1866, respectively, the Winnebagos having been moved here from South Dakota and, still earlier, from Minnesota. Blackbird Hill, on the Omaha Indian Reservation (12,421 acres), is the gravesite of Omaha chief Blackbird, which was visited by Lewis and Clark on August 11, 1804. Chief Blackbird had died of smallpox in 1800 and was buried sitting erect on a horse. A wooden pole decorated with all the scalps he had taken was planted in the soil above. His gravesite is situated on the highest of the river bluffs between Decatur and Macy and is easily visible from nearby roads. The 300-foot-high and now mostly tree-covered promontory can best be observed about one mile east of Blackbird Scenic Overview at a site three miles north of Decatur (milepost 152 on US Hwy. 75). The Omahas had moved into the region from the Ohio River valley by the 1700s, and by 1775 the tribe had a large village in this immediate area. During the smallpox epidemic of 1800, the Omaha population was reduced from about 700 to 300, and its previous reputation as a powerful warrior society disappeared. During the later period of displacement of Native Americans to reservations in the mid-1800s, the Omahas were allowed to remain on part of their original homeland (originally 300,000 acres). The northern part of their ceded land was later given to the Winnebagos, and some of the remainder was later sold to white settlers.

In spite of their peaceful nature, the Omahas were not accepted as US citizens until 1887, and their full rights of citizenship were not attained until 1924. Similarly, the Pawnees of eastern Nebraska (the "Pani" or "Pania" of Lewis and Clark) were sent in the 1850s to a relatively tiny preserve (now part of Nance County) of about 300 square miles along the Loup River, an area representing less than 1 percent of their original vast homeland that centered on the Platte valley. After their land was sold to settlers in 1872, the Pawnees were relocated in 1874 to a part of Indian Territory (Oklahoma), in a region between the Arkansas and Cimarron Rivers. At the time of Lewis and Clark, the Pawnees were probably second only to the Lakotas in population size among Plains tribes, numbering perhaps 10,000 people. By comparison, the Omahas may have historically numbered about 2,800 at maximum, the Otoes about 1,800, and the Missourias about 500. By the year 2000, nearly 8,000 Native Americans were still living on reservations in Nebraska, including about 5,100 Omahas, 2,600 Winnebagos, and about 400 Santees.

Ponca State Park and **Ponca Indian Reservation.** The 2,400 acres of Ponca State Park are situated four miles north of Ponca on NE Hwy. 12. The park consists of mature and old-growth riverine hardwood forest at the downstream end of the federally designated Missouri National Recreational River (see section), with 17 miles of hiking trails and a recently added adjoining *Elk Point Wildlife Management Area* to the north. The park was named for the Ponca tribe, which had settled on the west bank of the Missouri River in present-day South Dakota during the early 1700s. At the time of Lewis and Clark, the Poncas numbered perhaps 800 people. Their initial reservation was established in 1858 and enlarged to 96,000 acres in 1865. However, it was taken over abruptly in 1868 by the federal government and was made part of the Great Sioux Reservation. The resulting conflicts with the Lakota Sioux, together with a government eviction order in 1876, forced the Poncas to resettle about 600 miles south in Indian Territory (now Oklahoma). Hundreds of adults and, later in spring, the children, were all forced to walk the entire distance with their few possessions. The Poncas were first assigned to the then-existing Quapaw Agency. During that winter of 1877–78, nearly one in five tribal members died of starvation or illnesses, including the daughter, Prairie Flower, of Chief Standing Bear, and then his eldest son, Bear Shield. However,

Chief Standing Bear and 26 members of his tribe returned to Nebraska the following spring to bury his son in an ancestral Ponca graveyard. Their trip took ten weeks, pulling three wagons. Their arrival in Nebraska was soon discovered and led to the entire group's arrest and detention in Omaha. At that time, Native Americans were not legally regarded as US citizens and had no rights of *habeas corpus* that might have achieved their release from prison. The resulting quandary over Standing Bear's captive status produced one of the most famous courtroom scenes in American history. It was centered on the critical legal question as to whether a Native American was a "person" under the interpretation of constitutional law and thus entitled to basic constitutional rights. During the trial, Standing Bear argued emotionally that indeed, like white men, he too was a person. The case against him was eventually dismissed by the US Supreme Court and, after a presidential commission reviewed the tribe's sad history, a restoration of 26,236 acres of Ponca tribal land in the Niobrara valley was also granted in 1881. In 1884 the Indian Territory population was moved to a new reservation in the Salt Fork River region, and later was moved again into what is now Oklahoma's Kay and Noble Counties. Adding to the tribe's endless difficulties, the Ponca Indian Reservation in Nebraska was dissolved in 1954, and for nearly 50 years the tribe was not recognized by the federal government, until it was officially restored in 1990. The *Missouri National Recreational River Resource and Educational Center* is located in Ponca State Park, at the end of Hwy. Spur 26 E; it describes the ecology and history of the Missouri River. *Ponca State Park address:* 88090 Spur 26 E, Ponca, NE 68770 (402-755-2284).

Rainwater Basin. This diffuse region of seasonal playa wetlands is spread widely across central and eastern Nebraska. It occurs south of the Platte River from Gosper and Dawson Counties in the west to Seward County in the east, and south from Franklin to Jefferson Counties. This region once held an estimated 4,000 wetlands, of which more than 90 percent have been ditched and drained. However, some 22,000 acres are still protected as waterfowl production areas, and 12,000 acres are state-owned wildlife management areas (Johnsgard, 2012, *Nebraska's Wetlands*). The *Rainwater Basin Wetland Management District* is a multicounty region south of the central Platte River that contains hundreds of temporary to seasonal playa

wetlands. The Rainwater Basin Joint Venture coordinates the Rainwater Basin's wetland management, which involves the approximately 50 federally owned waterfowl production areas, and about 30 state-owned wildlife management areas, extending from Phelps County east to Butler and Saline Counties, and geographically divided into eastern and western components. The Rainwater Basin's importance to Great Plains migrating shorebirds during April and early May is probably second only in the Great Plains to Cheyenne Bottoms in Kansas (Jorgensen, 2012; Brown and Johnsgard, 2013). During wet springs, it also often holds millions of migrating geese (mostly snow geese, plus Ross's, greater white-fronted, Canada, and cackling geese) in March. At least 29 species are common to abundant in the basin during spring versus 122 species during fall and 28 during winter (Jones, 1990). There are at least 102 nesting birds among the 256 species listed for the region by Jones. A total of 49 bird species were reported present year-round by Jones, so an estimated minimum of 81 percent of the district's total bird diversity is migratory. A collective bird list for the Rainwater Basin and adjacent central Platte River valley has more than 300 species, including 120 wetland species, and is available from the US Fish and Wildlife Service, 2610 Ave. Q W, Kearney, NE 68847 (308-236-5015). The address for the Rainwater Basin Wetland Management District is 73746 V Road, PO Box 8, Funk, NE 68940 (308-263-3000), https://www.fws.gov/refuge/rainwater_basin_wmd/. The Rainwater Basin Joint Venture's address is 2550 N. Diers Ave., Suite L, Grand Island, NE 68803 (308-395-8586). Nebraska's playa wetlands are included within the multistate Playa Lakes Joint Venture program, which extends geographically from Nebraska to western Texas. The Playa Lakes Joint Venture address is 103 E. Simpson St., LaFayette, CO 80026 (303-926-0777).

Rulo Bluffs Preserve. 424 acres. Rulo Bluffs is a Missouri valley forest, about six miles southeast of Rulo, that contains mature hardwood forests and some prairie vegetation on high, steep loess bluffs overlooking the Missouri River. It is noted for its high botanical diversity but, because the area is undeveloped with no amenities or marked trails, access is restricted. Owned and managed by the Nature Conservancy, permission to enter must be obtained from the Omaha field office, 1007 Leavenworth St., Omaha, NE 68102 (402-342-0282).

Scotts Bluff National Monument. 4.7 square miles. This famous landmark on the Oregon Trail is located just west of the city of Scottsbluff and refers to a promontory that rises 750 feet above the surrounding land. The face of the bluff exposes geological strata from the Tertiary period dated from 33 million to 22 million years ago. The top of the bluff is well vegetated with ponderosa pines and can be reached by a scenic summit road. From the bottom of the bluff, travelers pass sequentially through pink and tan siltstone of the early Oligocene's upper Brule formation of the White River group, two white volcanic ash layers also of the White River group, and lastly the even-bedded sandstones of the late Oligocene to early Miocene-age Gering and Monroe Creek formations of the Arikaree group (Maher, Engelmann, and Shuster, 2003). From the bluff's summit, it is often possible to see flying raptors such as prairie falcons, red-tailed hawks, and ferruginous hawks as well as white-throated swifts and violet-green swallows that nest on the sheer sides of the monument. The visitor center is notable for holding the world's largest collection of drawings, photographs, and watercolor paintings of western scenes done by famed geologist and explorer William Henry Jackson in the latter 1800s. *Address:* PO Box 27, Gering, NE 69341 (308-436-9970).

Spring Creek Prairie Audubon Center. About 850 acres. Located about 20 miles south of Lincoln and three miles south of Denton, this mostly virgin tallgrass prairie is on rolling glacial moraine (including a hilltop having the highest elevation in Lancaster County) and is one of the largest such preserved tallgrass prairies in Nebraska. There are also wetlands, riparian edges, and deciduous woods. The property is owned by the Nebraska office of the National Audubon Society. It has a recently built visitor/interpretive center (of hay-bale construction), many miles of trails, and nearly 400 documented species of plants, along with more than 200 birds, 30 mammals, and about 50 butterflies. Of the 200 or so prairie-adapted (nontree and nonaquatic) plant species, native grasses compose about 20 percent of the flora, broad-leaved forbs about 70 percent, and shrubs and vines about 8 percent. Open daily year-round, except for major holidays. *Address:* 11700 SW 100th St., PO Box 117, Denton, NE 68339 (402-797-2301), http://springcreekprairie.audubon.org/.

Toadstool Geological Park. Toadstool is part of the Oglala National Grassland and is located 15 miles north of Crawford, Nebraska. To get there, go four miles north from Crawford on Nebraska Hwy. 2 and 71. Turn northwest on Toadstool Road and go about ten miles. Turn left at the sign to Toadstool Park and go another 1.5 miles. The badland topography here consists of eroded sandstones and siltstones formed from streambed sediments deposited about 45 million to 25 million years ago, as well as more recent volcanic ash deposits, with most of the park's area exposing highly eroded sediments from the Orella member of the Oligocene's Brule formation from 35 million to 25 million years ago (Maher, Engelmann, and Shuster, 2003). Fossil remains of several now long-extinct mammalian groups, such as oreodonts, brontotheres, entelodonts, and hyaenodons, have been found. Some fossils of still-surviving or post-Oligocene extinct groups, such as three-toed horses, saber-tooth cats, early rhinos, and other animals, have also been also discovered. A one-mile loop trail circles through the formations, and a three-mile Bison Trail leads hikers to the Hudson-Meng Bison Kill bone bed (see Oglala National Grassland section). Small groups of pronghorn are often seen in the vicinity, and prairie rattlesnakes and bull snakes are common. When hiking in hot weather carry water because none is available at this remote site. *Address:* US Forest Service, Nebraska National Forest, 125 N. Main St., Chadron, NE 69337 (308-432-0300).

University of Nebraska State Museum. Public exhibits of the museum's collections are located in Morrill Hall on the University of Nebraska–Lincoln main campus (approximately on the southwest corner of 14th and Vine Streets). This museum has the world's most complete collection of fossil mammoths and mastodons, including the largest known complete fossil reconstruction of *Archidiskodon imperator*, a 14-foot-tall Columbian mammoth (Maher, Engelmann, and Shuster, 2003). A full-sized bronze version of this same mammoth as it might have appeared in life stands near the museum's entrance. There is also a series of mounted animals in dioramas representing many examples of Nebraska wildlife and habitats, an exhibition of Native America plains culture, exhibits of Paleozoic and Mesozoic life, and a planetarium. *Address:* 645 N. 14th St., University of Nebraska–Lincoln, Lincoln, NE 68588-0338 (402-472-2642), http://museum.unl.edu/.

Valentine National Wildlife Refuge. 71,516 acres. Located 22 miles south of Valentine, this location is Nebraska's largest national wildlife refuge, consisting mostly of sandhills prairie with sand dunes and intervening depressions that contain many shallow, sometimes lake-sized, marshes. The native plants are a mixture of local sand-adapted species (including a state-endemic penstemon species, *Penstemon haydenii*) and others from the more general mixed-grass and tallgrass Nebraska floras. The refuge includes more than 30 shallow and mostly small lakes, plus numerous marshes, surrounded by sand dunes up to 200 feet high. Many typical grassland birds, such as the long-billed curlew and upland sandpiper, are abundant on this enormous refuge. Four grebes (eared, western, Clark's, and pied-billed) have regularly nested here, as well as the white-faced ibis, long-billed curlew, upland sandpiper, Wilson's phalarope, and American avocet. Up to 150,000 migrant ducks can be found on the refuge, with peak numbers occurring in May and October. At least 67 species are common to abundant during spring versus 66 species during fall and 8 during winter (Jones, 1990). There are at least 95 nesting birds among the 233 species listed for the refuge in 1990 by Jones. A total of 35 bird species were reported present year-round by Jones, so an estimated minimum of 85 percent of the refuge's total bird diversity is migratory. A more recent refuge checklist of 272 species includes 100 wetland species: 31 shorebirds, 24 waterfowl, 10 gulls and terns, 5 grebes, and 4 rails. The list is available from the refuge manager at 39679 Pony Lake Rd., Valentine, NE 69201 (402-376-1889); it is also available online at https://www.fws.gov/uploadedFiles/ValentineWildlifeList.pdf.

The refuge website can be explored from https://www.fws.gov/refuge/valentine/.

Wildcat Hills State Recreation Area and Nature Center. 1,094 acres. This modern center is managed by the Nebraska Game and Parks Commission and is ten miles south of Gering off Nebraska Hwy. 71, in the middle of the Wildcat Hills. Some 30,000 acres of land are open for public use in the Wildcat Hills. This east-west ridge of sandstone, siltstone, volcanic ash, and limestone in western Nebraska has many of the same geological and biological features as Scotts Bluff and the Pine Ridge escarpment of northwestern Nebraska (see Scotts Bluff National Monument section). In driving south on Hwy. 71 to the ridge summit, visitors pass through the Brule formation of the Oligocene epoch (34 million to 30 million years ago) on the lower slopes, followed by Miocene (Arikaree) deposits at the crest, where the nature center is located (Maher, Engelmann, and Shuster, 2003). Hiking trails at the nature center and a half-mile boardwalk extend out from the center, where pygmy nuthatches, red crossbills, common poorwills, and other western species might be encountered. Large mammals of the area include introduced bighorn sheep and elk, plus pronghorns, mule and white-tailed deer, bobcats, and mountain lions. The center includes samples of fossil mammals from the Oligocene epoch from about 30 million years ago that have been found locally during highway excavations. These include a four-horned deer (*Syndyoceras*), a hippo-like anthracothere, a tapir, weasel, camel, and bear. *Address:* 210615 Hwy. 71, Gering, NE 69341 (308-436-3777).

V

The Southern Plains

Sobering Lessons in Conservation Ecology

Perhaps no North American species of bird has come closer to extinction and yet managed to survive into the twenty-first century than has the whooping crane. The ratification and activation of the Migratory Bird Treaty in 1918 had brought the whooping cranes of Canada and the United States into complete protection, but by then there were probably no more than about 60 of these birds still surviving. And, at least 25 more were killed over the next four years. By then it was apparent that most of the surviving birds were wintering in coastal Texas and migrating north to unknown breeding grounds somewhere in Canada. It was not until 1955 that the species' breeding grounds were located in a remote but already protected area, Wood Buffalo National Park. This park, along the border of Alberta and Northwest Territories, was established in 1922 to protect a remnant population of a forest-adapted race of bison, the "wood buffalo," and not until the mid-1950s was it discovered to be the only breeding grounds of whooping cranes.

In Texas, a second group of whooping cranes that had wintered on the vast King Ranch of southern Texas disappeared by 1937, leaving the last known major population of about a few dozen birds that wintered on the Blackjack Peninsula of coastal Texas north of Corpus Christi, between San Antonio and Aransas Bays. A small group then also survived in southwestern Louisiana, where a dozen or so birds had been found around White Lake during the construction of the Intracoastal Waterway in 1929.

Ironically, Professor Myron Swenk, Nebraska's premier (and only) ornithologist of the 1930s, was responsible for the sadly mistaken belief that there were still perhaps three hundred whooping cranes still surviving during the 1930s. This belief was based on unverified reports by volunteer birds watchers tallying spring migrants, and who may have mistaken white pelicans or sandhill cranes for whooping cranes. These reports were subsequently published in the state's ornithological journal, *The Nebraska Bird Review*, and were accepted by professional ornithologists of the American Ornithologists' Union, who thus failed to understand the gravity of the species' actual precarious status.

In a better turn of irony, the Great Depression of the 1930s had the beneficial effect of stimulating the federal government to employ thousands of out-of-work people in the Civilian Conservation Corps. This workforce undertook innumerable conservation-oriented activities, such as constructing more than 800 local parks nationwide, planting millions of trees, and developing roads and facilities for sites that were or were to become national parks and national wildlife refuges.

One of the many locations studied by the Department of Interior and recommended for inclusion in the rapidly expanding system of national wildlife refuges during the 1930s was the Blackjack Peninsula. This area was not only the single known winter home of the entire remnant migratory whooping crane flock but also the wintering ground of a great variety of shorebirds and waterfowl. It additionally supported a resident population of the already rare Attwater's prairie chicken, a race of the greater prairie-chicken endemic to the coastal prairies of Texas, which by 1937 had already lost 93 percent of its original habitat, and its population had plummeted from nearly a million birds to less than 9,000.

In December of 1937, President Franklin D. Roosevelt signed an executive order creating the Aransas Migratory Waterfowl Refuge (later renamed the Aransas National Wildlife Refuge), purchasing land that

Whooping crane

encompassed much of Blackjack Peninsula, totaling over 47,000 acres at about ten dollars per acre. The area's bargain-basement purchase unfortunately excluded control of grazing and mineral rights, both of which would later cause serious problems in refuge management. Additionally, shooting rights by a local hunting club extended to the refuge's boundaries, threatening the safety of any cranes straying beyond the refuge. To make matters still worse, in 1940 the US Army Corps of Engineers began to dredge a channel for the expanding Gulf Intracoastal Waterway, cutting a three-hundred-foot-wide ditch and associated right-of-way through a previously isolated part of the refuge.

During the area's initial fall and winter of 1938–39, the refuge manager counted 14 whooping cranes, including 2 juveniles, causing him to estimate that a total of no more than 18 birds might be present, assuming that as many as 2 birds might have been overlooked.

In the following fall five pairs returned with young, two of the pairs tending twins, and five other adults were also present, for a total of 22 birds.

In 1940 oil drilling began just outside the refuge's limits, and the Army Air Corps took over nearby Matagorda Island for military use. Along with nearby San José Island, this large barrier island was an important foraging area for the cranes and had been recommended for inclusion in the refuge, but the federal budget hadn't permitted its purchase.

During the fall of 1941, only 14 adult whooping cranes and 2 young returned to Aransas, a total that marks a historic population low point for the species, although 6 additional birds were then still surviving in Louisiana. The Louisiana flock was extirpated by 1950–51, probably as a result of coastal storms. By that time the Wood Buffalo–Aransas flock had reached a total of 34, but this number represented an average population gain of only 2 birds annually.

By the end of the next decade (1959–60), the Wood Buffalo–Aransas flock still hovered precariously at only 33 birds, but a decade later by the fall of 1969–70 it had gained another 23 birds, totaling 56. By 1979–80 the total was 76, and by 1989–90 the flock had reached 146. At the turn of the twenty-first century, the autumn refuge total was 188 birds.

In concert with the whooping cranes' painfully slow population growth during the past century, the Aransas refuge has had more than its share of disappointments. Oil drilling, illegal shooting, and other disturbances along the Intracoastal Waterway became serious problems during the 1940s and still persist. During World War II, the 56,000-acre Matagorda Island was used as a practice bombing range by the Air Force, causing an unknown amount of disturbance and damage to the cranes.

It was not until 1955, a year after the crane's nesting grounds in Canada's Wood Buffalo Park were finally discovered, that the Air Force agreed not to undertake nighttime bombing practice on Matagorda Island, which would have caused an even greater wildlife disturbance. In 1973 the Aransas National Wildlife Refuge finally acquired management jurisdiction over much of Matagorda Island. In 1995 the entire island was named Matagorda Island Wildlife Management Area, to be managed jointly by the state and federal government for conserving rare and endangered birds and supporting migratory bird management.

Periodic hurricanes have also ravaged the area. In August of 1965 a major hurricane passing up the Texas coast slammed into Matagorda Island, illuminating the region's vulnerability to such storms. Luckily these increasingly frequent late-summer storms have so far occurred before the cranes are present on the refuge. Another developing ecological problem is the invasion of black mangroves into the region, which is likely to impact foraging opportunities for both whooping cranes and other marshland foraging birds.

Other chronic problems have long existed at Aransas. By 1970 heavy grazing by up to 4,000 cattle on the refuge had a negative impact on grassland-dependent birds such as the Attwater's prairie-chicken, and it eventually was extirpated from the area. Since then, grazing has been terminated and the prairie conditions have improved, although invasive growth by a scrubby species of shinnery oak (*Quercus havardi*) is a significant problem.

By 2008 the flock had increased by about 16-fold

cranes in 70 years, and a record total of 283 birds arrived at Aransas that fall. Disaster struck the Wood Buffalo–Aransas flock in the winter of 2008 with the onset of a prolonged drought in Texas. The major source of fresh water to Aransas National Wildlife Refuge is the Guadalupe River, which maintains the salinity of the coastal wetlands and allows for the survival of blue crabs, the whooping crane's major winter food. Increased drought-related diversions of this river water by Texas water management authorities (the ironically named Texas Commission on Environmental Quality) resulted in an increased salinity of water around the Aransas refuge. These salinity changes decimated the local population of blue crabs and led to the death of at least 23 whooping cranes during the winter of 2008–9, reducing the crane population to 263 by the spring of 2009. A later lawsuit filed in US District Court in 2010 resulted in the development of a "Habitat Conservation Plan for Whooping Cranes."

By 2011, the Wood Buffalo–Aransas flock had reached a record high breeding population of 75 nests and had fledged about 37 young at Wood Buffalo Park. The flock has continued to increase in recent years. In the fall of 2016 a total of 329 whooping cranes arrived at Aransas, with 38 juveniles among them, continuing an upward population trend. A record 98 nests were found at Wood Buffalo Park in 2017, an increase of 16 over the prior record number of 82 in 2014. More than 400 cranes arrived at Aransas in the fall of 2017, having fledged 63 juveniles, indicating a strong upward population trend. Given the average minimum winter territory size of whooping cranes (about 425 acres, according to the refuge's ex-manager Tom Stehn), Aransas and its contiguous areas that are now being used by the flock are approaching an estimated carrying capacity of about 576 birds.

Since the establishment of Aransas National Wildlife Refuge, many other major conservation efforts have been undertaken to preserve and restore whooping cranes, and to initiate a second flock independent of the Wood Buffalo–Aransas population. These have included an unsuccessful effort to hatch and raise whooping cranes using wild sandhill cranes as foster parents in Idaho, and a similarly unsuccessful effort to establish a resident whooping crane flock in the Kissimmee Prairie of Florida.

A different and innovative approach used an ultralight aircraft to train hand-reared and imprinted whooping cranes raised in Wisconsin to follow it and thus be guided to wintering areas in Florida. Over more than a decade, this time-intensive and highly expensive technique resulted in a new migratory population numbering more than 100 whooping cranes, but the breeding success of these birds has been extremely limited.

In 2011 ten hand-reared whooping cranes were introduced into the White Lake region of southwestern Louisiana, the start of a multiyear effort to reestablish a resident flock in that state. By the beginning of 2014 that flock had increased to about 35 birds as a result of supplemental introductions. Since 2014 at least five pairs of these birds have nested and laid eggs, although as of 2016 only one pair had successfully hatched and raised a chick through its first year of life. In the spring of 2017, 11 juvenile cranes were released in the White Lakes Wetlands Conservation Area, resulting in a potential current total of about 70 wild cranes living in southwest Louisiana.

In spite of these promising trends, considering the recent warming and drying climate trend in the Great Plains, and consequent increased losses of wetlands, the future of these introductions and the Wood Buffalo–Aransas flock of whooping cranes is still by no means secure. Additionally, Wood Buffalo Park has been increasingly threatened by oil-drilling activities nearby. However, without the establishment of Aransas National Wildlife Refuge at a critical time, the species would almost have gone extinct.

Like the whooping cranes' narrow brush with extinction, and its still-precarious state, the black-tailed prairie dog and burrowing owl offer other examples of how rapidly the fortunes of a common to once-superabundant Great Plains species can change. It is probable that as recently as the late 1800s there may have been more than a billion prairie dogs living in the Great Plains. Indeed, if ever a single keystone animal species were to be identified with the Great Plains grasslands, the black-tailed prairie dog would probably most easily qualify. Keystone species are those animals that tend to hold an ecosystem together, and whose presence or absence has the greatest effect on the well-being of the other species. In various ways it can be argued that predators such as the black-footed ferret, swift fox, coyote, ferruginous hawk, golden eagle, and prairie rattlesnake all largely or partly depended historically on the black-tailed prairie dog as important prey.

The ecological effects of prairie dog towns on the surrounding vegetation are also exploited by many grassland birds and mammals, such as mountain plovers, horned larks, ground squirrels, and grasshopper mice. The prairie dogs' abandoned burrows are inhabited by horned lizards, spadefoot toads, tiger salamanders, and a wide variety of insects and other invertebrates. Probably no other North American animal can claim to accept so many uninvited guests as the prairie dog, and perhaps the most charismatic of these is the burrowing owl.

Few birds will bring birders screeching their cars to a halt faster than will a burrowing owl perched quietly on a fencepost or peering quizzically over a prairie dog mound. Whether standing solemnly beside a prairie dog hole or perched on a low fencepost, a miniature owl standing erect and in plain view during the middle of the day somehow seems to be such an unlikely apparition that it demands prolonged and extensive study. There is something in the animal's intense yellowish green eyes that demands to be watched with equal intensity, and the burrowing owl's comical, not-quite-erect stance might remind birders of a spindly legged, feather-clad leprechaun still trying to recover from a late-night hangover.

Burrowing owls are every western bird-watcher's favorite owl, simply because they won't follow all the accepted rules of owldom. First, they are one of the few North American species that are most active during the day, when they often conveniently stand on fenceposts along gravel roads, where they can be easily spotted by birders, rather than hiding all day long in thick vegetation. Second, they typically are found near prairie dog "towns," whose vacant dwellings they are happy to take over and occupy, imparting no real danger to the prairie dogs, since the owls mostly forage during the summer on large, slow-moving insects, such as dung beetles and ground beetles, which are abundant around dog towns.

The seemingly curious if not actually friendly manner of the burrowing owl when approached by humans is probably the reason that in some parts of the American West the species is known as the "howdy" owl. The usual rules of owl decorum do not apply to burrowing owls. First, they are not as highly nocturnal as most other owls, but instead are active mainly during broad daylight. In fact, their retinas lack the reflective surface that increases nocturnal visual sensitivity and produces the "eye shine" typical of most owls. Secondly, unlike the larger owls of the grasslands, burrowing owls are surprisingly insectivorous, at least during the summer months.

Burrowing owls are also unusual among owls in that they seem to lack the acute binaural hearing and precise sound-source localization abilities that owls as a group are primarily noted for, and instead appear to rely on their keen daytime vision for prey-finding. In correlation, their faces have only poorly developed facial disk feathers surrounding their ears, which help funnel extremely faint sounds into the ear canals of the most highly nocturnal owls.

When an approaching human confronts a burrowing owl, it is more likely to stay put than to fly away immediately. Often, after a few slight horizontal or vertical head movements by the bird, as if trying to shake its head clear of a foggy memory, but which are probably designed to get a better distance-estimating fix on the new intruder into its personal space, the owl will probably retreat back into its hole. Or, if perched on a post, the owl may take silent flight over the prairie dog town and land near its burrow entrance.

When cornered in its burrow, a burrowing owl will utter a sound that mimics a rattlesnake's rattle, and at such times may also spread and tilt its wings vertically, apparently to make itself appear larger and more dangerous. The male's courtship call is usually soft and dove-like, but adults of both sexes also utter a rapid chatter when alarmed or while defending their nest.

Although a pair of burrowing owls are perfectly content to take over a prairie dog burrow without making major structural changes or other renovations, they are likely to gather fragments of dried bison or cattle dung, break them into small pieces, and line the entrance area in front of its burrow with these bits of debris. Such markings help birders recognize an active burrowing owl burrow, as do the dried owl pellets that are usually rich in insect fragments such as the undigested remnants of grasshopper and beetle exoskeletons.

The biological function of the scattered droppings is uncertain, but they may help mask the odors of an active owl burrow, for burrowing owls are highly vulnerable to badgers and coyotes. In a 1989 study, G. Green and R. Anthony found that, next to desertion, badgers were the most significant source of burrowing owl nesting mortality, and that nests lined with livestock dung were significantly less susceptible to predation than were unlined nests. Additionally, it has been suggested that the presence of dung may help attract dung beetles to the nest, where the owls can easily capture them.

The burrowing owl is the only strongly migratory owl of the northern plains, presumably because its insect foods become progressively unavailable in fall. Then it turns increasingly to relatively small rodents,

Burrowing owl

such as pocket mice, for food. Although small mammals and birds make up a low percentage of the summer diet as measured by their sheer number (about 5–20 percent), the much larger body mass of mammals relative to insects tends to make mammals compose the predominant portion (about 80–95 percent) of the biomass of all foods taken.

There is also some hunting activity at night, especially during bright moonlit nights, and at these times small nocturnal rodents such as voles and pocket mice would be the most likely targets. R. Poulin (2003) determined that in Saskatchewan the primary long-term burrowing owl foods are deer mice and meadow voles. Frogs, toads, lizards, snakes, and even turtles have also been reported as burrowing owl prey, and so have birds, at least as large as horned larks.

Besides using prairie dog burrows, burrowing owls have also occasionally adapted to living in burrows made by ground squirrels, marmots and woodchucks, badgers, foxes, coyotes, skunks, armadillos, kangaroo rats, and tortoises. They may also dig their own burrows in the absence of housing provided by these animals. They have even been known to use natural rock cavities and to accept human-made artificial burrows where natural excavations are not possible.

On the Great Plains, it is primarily the black-tailed prairie dog that offers the owls housing. According to a study by S. Conrad, J. Dose, and D. Svingen, an estimated 95 percent of all the burrowing owls nesting on the Comanche, Cimarron, Rita Blanca, and Kiowa National Grasslands—all in the southern Great Plains—were directly associated with prairie dog towns. They reported that only 3 of 114 prairie dog towns supporting burrowing owls lacked active prairie dog burrows, indicating the importance of recent "dog" activity in making good owl breeding sites. The three inactive towns that supported burrowing owls had apparently been inactive for only one year.

Likewise, among 543 burrowing owl nests surveyed in the Oklahoma Panhandle by K. Butts and J. Lewis, two-thirds were located within black-tailed prairie dog colonies. Besides being able to exploit inactive dog burrows, the owls favor the combination of low shrub coverage, short vegetation, and high percentage of bare ground that is typically present in prairie dog colonies. When the ground-level vision is variously obstructed, the birds find suitable nearby observation posts to use, such as fenceposts or boulders.

Within prairie dog towns, burrowing owls favor larger and active colonies; typically, a town that has been abandoned by prairie dogs will also be abandoned by burrowing owls within three years, perhaps largely as a result of encroachment of dense vegetation but also because of the gradual deterioration of the burrows themselves. In active towns, the owls often choose nests near the periphery of the colony, where there may be a greater abundance of insects, more available nearby perches, and a proximity to foraging areas. Burrowing owls may also favor sites that provide additional "satellite" burrows. Both adults and young use these, perhaps to avoid the buildup of nest parasites or loss of an entire family to predators. As many as five such satellite burrows might be used by a single owl family, which could contain a half dozen or more owlets of varying ages and sizes.

The owls were found in one study to use active dog towns at a rate 6.3 times greater than at inactive ones, indicating the need for active prairie dog colonies to maintain breeding habitat for burrowing owls. The presence of live prairie dogs not only means there will be a ready supply of newly abandoned but structurally intact burrows available to the owls but also that the owls may exploit the efficient warning system of the prairie dogs. There is no proof that prairie dogs directly benefit from the presence of burrowing owls, and the ever-alert rodents sometimes utter alarm notes when the owls fly overhead, suggesting that prairie dogs are at least somewhat wary of the owls, and very young pups might be vulnerable to them.

For the Great Plains as a whole, burrowing owl occupancy rates of active prairie dog colonies are substantially lower in the northern Great Plains national grasslands than in those of the southern Great Plains. Great Plains naturalists who want to see burrowing owls firsthand have many, if rapidly declining, choices. As of 2017 there are progressively more burrowing owls to be found southward from the Dakotas into the southwestern plains. A range-wide survey of burrowing owl populations by the National Wildlife Federation in 1997 suggested that as of the early 1990s there might have been 20,000 to 200,000 breeding pairs in the United States. Texas had an estimated population in excess of 10,000 pairs in the 1990s, and states with population estimates of 1,000 to 10,000 pairs were Wyoming, Colorado, Nevada, and New Mexico. States then having 100 to 1,000 estimated pairs included Montana, North Dakota, Nebraska, Kansas, and Oklahoma.

In western Nebraska, one population study (Desmond, Savidge, and Eskridge, 2000) indicated that a 58 percent population decline of burrowing owls occurred between 1990 and 1996, during a period of intensive prairie dog poisoning and their associated rapid population declines. The owl's greatest population declines have occurred in the northern Great Plains. Burrowing owls have been essentially extirpated from Iowa and Minnesota. The species is state-endangered in Minnesota, threatened in Colorado, and considered to be a species of special concern in Arizona, California, Montana, Oklahoma, Oregon, Utah, Washington, and Wyoming. Other populations exist in Florida, Mexico, the West Indies, and South America.

Although there have also been a few apparent regional increases of burrowing owls in the southwestern desert grasslands and the interior northwestern grasslands, their greatest population declines have occurred in the northern Great Plains. Sadly, the familiar and friendly "howdy" owl is in increasing danger of having to say "adios" across most of its Great Plains homeland, along with its endlessly persecuted partner, the black-tailed prairie dog.

> *Probably no single grassland bird species is as fascinating to observe for hours on end than is the burrowing owl. It is an owl that doesn't seem to accept the fact that owls should sleep during the day and hunt at night. Instead it sits interminably on fence posts or large boulders, carefully surveying its daytime surroundings with all the solemnity of a spindly-legged Bible-belt preacher on his pulpit, constantly scanning his flock to make certain they are all paying proper attention. Also like many such self-righteous preachers, the owl typically produces a large, unmanageable brood of youngsters in progressive stair-step sizes, who seem too prone to leave the confines of their burrow and wander away at the earliest opportunity, thereby often encountering trouble enough on their own.*
>
> *Prairie Birds* (Johnsgard, 2001)

The Sites: Caprock, Coyotes, and Cacti

NEW MEXICO

New Mexico (NM) has one national park, one national recreation area, one national grassland, and five national forests. It also has eight national wildlife refuges totaling 332,000 acres, and 23 Indian reservations or pueblos. New Mexico's National Park Service lands total 466,000 acres, and national grasslands total 137,000 acres. Regionally, the state is second only to Wyoming in the Bureau of Land Management's total state acreage, at 14.1 million acres. Federally owned acreage in New Mexico collectively composes 41.7 percent of the state's total land area, making it one of the region's top three states in its percentage of federal land ownership. New Mexico also has 34 state parks and other state game commission lands that allow wildlife viewing, hiking, photography, and other wildlife-associated activities.

New Mexico is the only state in the Great Plains that contains a representative portion of the Chihuahuan Desert. It is also home to one of the largest known cave complexes in the world, Carlsbad Caverns National Park in Eddy County, a county with a 5,000-foot elevational gradient from about 3,000 feet to 8,000 feet of elevation. However, New Mexico is also in part a land of boundless flatness; in southeastern New Mexico and adjacent Texas is a region called the *llano estacado*, or staked plains, a landscape so featureless and flat that early Spanish explorers reputedly had to pound stakes into the ground to visually navigate their way across it.

Bitter Lake National Wildlife Refuge. 23,310 acres. The Bitter Lake refuge is located ten miles northeast of Roswell. At least 68 bird species are common to abundant during spring versus 60 species during fall and 35 during winter (Jones, 1990). This refuge has long been one of the major wintering grounds for sandhill cranes in the Great Plains, with as many as 72,000 reported in earlier decades. But recent numbers have been trending far lower, as crane wintering trends have shifted eastward into Texas, probably because of changes in farming. A recent checklist of 285 bird species recorded on the refuge is available from the refuge manager at 4200 E. Pine Lodge Rd., Roswell, NM 88201 (575-622-6755). It is also available online at https://www.fws.gov/refuge/Bitter_Lake/wildlife_and_habitat/species_list.html.

Bosque del Apache National Wildlife Refuge. 57,191 acres. Located 93 miles south of Albuquerque, near Socorro, this refuge is a major wintering area for greater sandhill cranes and also for snow and Ross's geese. At least 95 nesting birds are among the 252 listed for the refuge by Jones (1990). A total of 83 bird species were reported present year-round by Jones, so an estimated minimum of 67 percent of the refuge's total bird diversity is migratory The refuge offers some of the country's best opportunities for observing large flocks of wintering greater sandhill cranes (up to 20,000) from mid-November to mid-February, as well as very large numbers of snow geese, Ross's geese, and other waterfowl. More than 10,000 sandhill cranes have been reported at Bosque during Audubon Christmas Bird Counts. At least 83 bird species are common to abundant during spring versus 76 species during fall and 55 during winter (Jones, 1990). During the 1980s the refuge served as the wintering grounds for whooping cranes that had been foster-reared by sandhill cranes at Grays Lake National Wildlife Refuge, Idaho, in an early but eventually failed restoration effort. The refuge hosts an annual *Festival of the Cranes* celebration during the third week of November. *Address:* 1001 Highway 1, PO Box 280, San Antonio, NM 87832 (575-835-1828), https://www.fws.gov/refuge/bosque_del_apache/.

Capulin Volcano National Monument. 793 acres. This small national monument is three miles north of Capulin, Union County. It is centered on an inactive volcanic cinder cone and crater that is nearly 1,000 feet tall and rises to 8,182 feet above sea level. It was last active 58,000 to 62,000 years ago. The surrounding area consists of grassland and various forest communities, including pines, junipers, oaks, and scrub, including chokecherry (*capulin* is Spanish for chokecherry). On the southeastern horizon is Sierra Grande, at 8,720 feet the highest North American mountain east of longitude 104° W. Also, 12 miles to the northwest is the *Folsom Man* archeological site, where the distinctive Folsom stone points were made by Paleo-Indians to hunt giant bison between 9000 and 8000

BC. A 1970s bird checklist contained 104 species. *Address:* 44 Volcano Rd., Capulin, NM 88418 or PO Box 40, Des Moines, NM 88418 (575-278-2201), https://www.nps.gov/cavo/index.htm.

Carlsbad Caverns National Park. 73 square miles. This famous park has more than 100 separate caves that were formed within an ancient limestone ridge (Capital Reef) at the edge of an inland sea some 250 million years ago. Not only are the caverns amazing but a half-million Mexican free-tailed bats enter and leave the caverns every dawn and dusk between May and October. They are one of 67 mammal species reported from the park, which include the javelina, black bear, spotted skunk, and even introduced Barbary sheep. More than 300 bird species have also been found, of which the cave swallow is one of the more abundant and typical species. This park has been recognized by the National Geographic Society (2011) as one of the nation's ten best national parks for seeing "quirky creatures," free-tailed bats in this case. There are also about 900 species of vascular plants, 55 reported species of reptiles and amphibians, and 5 fish. *Address:* 3225 National Parks Hwy., Carlsbad, NM 88220 (505-785-2232), https://www.nps.gov/cave/index.htm.

Grulla National Wildlife Refuge. 3,235 acres. This refuge is located a few miles east of Arch. Most of it is covered by a salt lake, with the rest in grassland. The refuge is primarily managed to provide winter habitat for sandhill cranes (*grulla* means "crane" in Spanish), and 100,000 or more may be present by December. Shorebird numbers and diversity depend on water conditions. At least 46 bird species are usually common to abundant during spring versus 60 species during fall and 31 during winter (Jones, 1990). There are at least 21 nesting birds among the 88 species listed in 1990 for the refuge by Jones. A total of 42 bird species were reported present year-round by Jones, so an estimated minimum of 52 percent of the refuge's total bird diversity is migratory. A checklist of bird species recorded on the refuge is available from the refuge manager. *Address:* c/o Muleshoe National Wildlife Refuge, PO Box 549, Muleshoe, TX 79347 (806-946-3341). It is also available online at https://www.fws.gov/refuge/Grulla/wildlife_and_habitat/index.html.

Kiowa National Grassland. 136,505 acres. This grassland consists of shortgrass upland plains in two units separated by 85 miles. One unit, east of Clayton, borders the Texas boundary line. The western unit, north of Roy, lies mostly east of the Canadian River, which flows through a steep 900-foot canyon lined with pinyon and ponderosa pines. Playa lakes are present seasonally. A bird list is available (226 species and 60 residents or summer residents). *Address:* 714 Main St., Clayton, NM 88415 (575-374-9652).

Las Vegas National Wildlife Refuge. 8,700 acres. This wildlife refuge near Las Vegas is a mixture of shortgrass prairie, timbered canyons, pinyon-juniper woodlands, spring-fed wetlands, and riparian areas. The wetlands attract large numbers of migrating and wintering sandhill cranes during wet years. Nesting birds include long-billed curlew, American avocet, and a variety of ducks. No species lists are available. *Address:* Route 1, Box 399, Las Vegas NM 87701 (505-425-3581), https://www.fws.gov/refuge/las_vegas/.

Maxwell National Wildlife Refuge. 3,600 acres. This high plains refuge is mostly shortgrass prairie, with three playa lakes, located in an open mountain basin at 5,000 feet. It is primarily managed for migrating waterfowl but also attracts wintering bald and golden eagles, other raptors, and about 290 total bird species. Among 42 mammals there are both mule and white-tailed deer, black-tailed prairie dogs, and occasional pronghorns and elk. Additionally, 14 reptiles (including two rattlesnakes) and 9 amphibians have been found on the refuge. *Address:* 168 Lake 13 Rd., PO Box 276, Maxwell, NM 87728 (505-375-2331).

New Mexico Museum of Natural History and Science. This museum is a natural history and science museum in Albuquerque, near Old Town. A Jurassic "Super Giants" exhibit features complete skeletons of *Stegosaurus*, *Seisomosaurus*, *Saurophanax*, and one leg of a *Brachiosaurus*. A specimen of the second largest *Tyrannosaurus rex* ever found measures 40 feet in length and 12 feet in height. Bronze statues of a *Pentaceratops* and an *Albertosaurus* are at the museum entrance. *Address:* 1801 Mountain Rd. NW, Albuquerque, NM 87104 (505-841-2800).

Rita Blanca National Grassland. (See section in Oklahoma and Texas.)

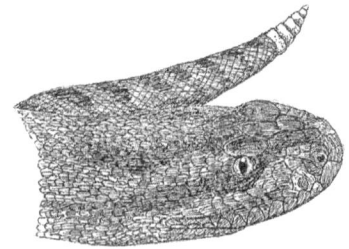

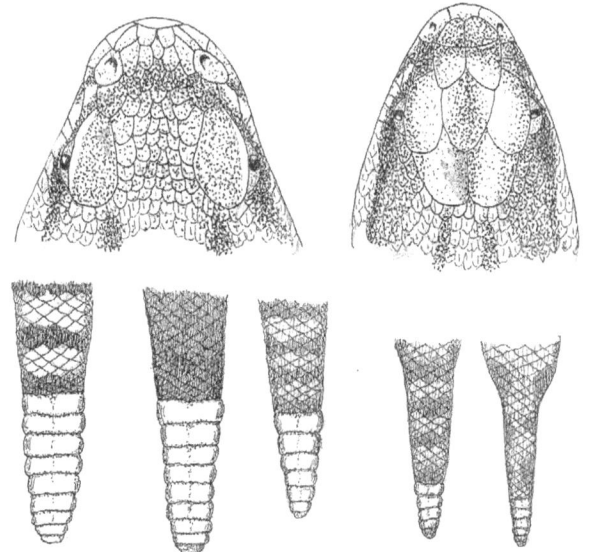

Rattlesnakes of the Great Plains, including (top to bottom) massasauga; scale patterns of Crotalus (left) and Sisturus (right) snakes; and (left to right) diamondback, timber, prairie, massasauga, and pygmy rattlesnake rattles.

OKLAHOMA

Oklahoma (OK) has nine national wildlife refuges occupying 107,000 acres, a national recreation area of 9,800 acres, and parts of two national grasslands totaling 46,000 acres. Federally owned acreage in Oklahoma comprises 3.6 percent of the state's land area. Oklahoma also has 33 state parks totaling about 80,000 acres, and about 70 wildlife management areas, which collectively, including federal lands, total more than 1.6 million acres open for public use. Prior to its statehood, Oklahoma was known as Indian Territory because so many Native American tribes were involuntarily translocated there, mostly between the time of the Civil War and the end of the Indian wars during the late 1800s. Oklahoma now has only a single Indian reservation, the Osage Indian Reservation, but 39 tribal governments are located in the state.

Altus-Lugert Wildlife Management Area. 10,400 acres. This wildlife management area is located two miles east of Granite in Greer and Kiowa Counties, and consists of prairie uplands, river bottom, and slough areas along the shoreline of Lake Altus. The slough areas are dominated by cattail and other aquatic species. The bottomlands are heavily wooded with cottonwood, American elm, willow, Kentucky coffeetree, honey locust, cedar, and saltcedar. No species checklists are available. For more information, contact Oklahoma Department of Wildlife Conservation, PO Box 53465, Oklahoma City, OK 73152 (405-521-3851).

Beaver River Wildlife Management Area. 15,600 acres. This WMA is located 11 miles west of Beaver in Beaver County. It is mostly sandsage grassland, with prairie dogs, burrowing owls, swift foxes, and probably some lesser prairie-chickens. *Address:* Oklahoma Department of Wildlife Conservation, PO Box 53465, Oklahoma City, OK 73152 (405-521-3851).

Black Kettle National Grassland. 31,300 acres (30,724 acres in Oklahoma; 576 acres in Texas). This federally owned site consists of holdings in Roger Mills County bisected by the Washita River. There are also several impoundments, springs, and seasonal streams among the mixed-grass and tallgrass prairies, shrublands (including shinnery oaks), and upland woods. No species checklists are available. *Address:* US Forest Service, 18555 Hwy. 47A, Ste. B, Cheyenne, OK 73628 (580-497-2143).

Black Mesa Preserve. 1,600 acres. This shortgrass and juniper woodland preserve is owned by the Nature Conservancy but managed by the Oklahoma Tourism and Recreation Department (OTRD). Golden eagles, prairie falcons, and pronghorns are present in this transition zone between the shortgrass prairie and the Rocky Mountains. It is contiguous with *Black Mesa State Park* (549 acres). Like Black Mesa Preserve, Black Mesa State Park includes juniper woodlands and shortgrass prairies. The park has a large prairie dog town with burrowing owls present. No species checklists are available for either area, but reported lists for the entire Oklahoma panhandle include more

than 290 bird species. Both sites are located in Cimarron County, about 27 miles northwest of Boise City and southeast of Kenton in the extreme northwestern Oklahoma panhandle. *Preserve information:* OTRD, 900 N. Stiles Ave., Oklahoma City, OK 73104 (405-521-2409). *State park information:* HCR 1, Box 8, Kenton OK 73946 (580-426-2222).

Canton Reservoir and Wildlife Management Area. 16,775 acres. This federally owned site is managed by the US Army Corps of Engineers and is located about two miles northwest of Canton in Blaine County. Mixed-grass prairies, with bottomland and cross timber upland forests, and a prairie dog town and nature trail are located near Canton Reservoir. No species checklists are available. *Address:* Oklahoma Tourism and Recreation Department, 900 N. Stiles Ave., Oklahoma City, OK 73104 (405-521-2409).

Ellis County Wildlife Management Area. 4,800 acres. Located 15 miles southeast of Arnett (Ellis County) on Hwy. 46, this area contains shinnery oak grasslands, with lesser prairie-chickens and other arid grassland species, plus wooded bottomlands along a lake. No species checklists are available. This WMA is a state-owned site managed by the Oklahoma Department of Wildlife Conservation, PO Box 53465, Oklahoma City, OK 73152 (405-521-3851).

Fort Cobb Wildlife Management Area and **Fort Cobb State Park.** This wildlife management area and state park are 8,020 acres and 1,872 acres, respectively, and consist of native mixed-grass prairie and blackjack oak woodlands. They are located around the Fort Cobb Reservoir six miles north of Fort Cobb in Caddo County. No species checklists are available. The sites are jointly managed by the Bureau of Reclamation and the Oklahoma Department of Wildlife Conservation, the latter of which can be reached at PO Box 53465, Oklahoma City OK 73152 (405-521-3851). *Address of state park:* 27022 Copperhead Rd., Fort Cobb, OK 73038 (405-643-2249).

Fort Supply Wildlife Management Area. 5,418 acres. This federally owned site is managed by the US Army Corps of Engineers and is located one mile south of Fort Supply in Woodward County. The WMA consists of sandsage grasslands and riparian hardwoods, with a variety of grassland species. No species checklists are available. For more information, contact Oklahoma Tourism and Recreation Department, 900 N. Stiles Ave., Oklahoma City, OK 73104 (405-521-2409).

Optima National Wildlife Refuge. 4,333 acres. This federally owned refuge is located two miles northwest of Hardesky in Texas County (15 miles east of Guymon). It consists of shortgrass and mixed-grass prairies, sage-dominated shrubsteppe, and hardwoods in the Beaver River valley. A total of 63 bird species were reported present year-round by Jones, so an estimated minimum of 74 percent of the refuge's total bird diversity is migratory. Burrowing owls are occasional nesters, and pronghorns also occur. The nearby *Optima Wildlife Management Area* (about 8,000 acres) is managed jointly by the US Army Corps of Engineers and the Oklahoma Department of Wildlife Conservation (ODWC), PO Box 53465, Oklahoma City, OK 73152 (405-521-3851). Five miles south and a mile east of Hardesky is *Schultz Wildlife Management Area* (306 acres), also managed by the ODWC. This area consists of shortgrass prairie along a wooded stream, which attracts golden eagles and ferruginous hawks during winter. A bird species checklist (246 species, 106 nesters) is available. *Manager's address:* Rte. 1, Box 68, Butler, OK 73625 (405-473-2205).

Packsaddle Wildlife Management Area. 19,659 acres. This state-owned site is located 17 miles south of Arnett in Ellis County and consists of shortgrass, sandsage, and shinnery oak grasslands, along with riparian woodlands. No species checklists are available. It is managed by the Oklahoma Department of Wildlife Conservation, PO Box 53465, Oklahoma City, OK 73152 (405-521-3851).

Rita Blanca National Grassland/Wildlife Management Area. The Rita Blanca National Grassland occupies 15,800 acres in Oklahoma; the WMA occupies 15,575 acres. These sites are located about 17 miles southwest of Boise City in Cimarron County on Hwy. 56. Both consist of shortgrass prairie with prairie dogs, ferruginous hawks, golden eagles, mountain plovers, and other associated shortgrass species. (See also the Rita Blanca National Grassland entry in the Texas section.) The federally owned national grassland is managed by the US Forest Service, 714 Main St., Clayton, NM 88415 (575-374-9652).

Salt Plains National Wildlife Refuge. 31,997 acres. This refuge is three miles southeast of Jet, Oklahoma, in Alfalfa County, and is associated with the Salt Plains Reservoir on the Salt Fork of the Arkansas River. Most of the area is covered by the Salt Plains Reservoir, but there is upland forest, rangeland, and extensive salt flats that provide a unique habitat. Nesting snowy plovers are among the refuge's rarities. At least 131 bird species are common to abundant during spring versus 110 species during fall and 43 during winter (Jones, 1990). There are at least 98 nesting birds among the 243 listed for the refuge by Jones. Burrowing owls are rare in summer. A total of 67 bird species were reported present year-round by Jones, so an estimated minimum of 73 percent of the refuge's total bird diversity is migratory. Large flocks of American white pelicans use the refuge during migration, and whooping cranes are regular transients. About 25,000 sandhill cranes have been reported during Audubon Christmas Bird Counts. A mammal list of 30 species includes coyotes and badgers. *Great Salt Plains State Park* (8,890 acres) is nearby and has similar habitats. A recent checklist of 296 species is available from the refuge manager at Rte. 1, Box 76, Jet, OK 73749 (405-626-4794). It is also available online at https://www.fws.gov/refuge/Salt_Plains/wildlife/species.html. *State park address:* 23280 S. Spillway Dr., Jet, OK 73749 (580-626-4731).

Sam Noble Museum. This modern University of Oklahoma museum was completed in 2000 and is a 198,000-square-foot structure with 50,000 feet of public galleries. Its many galleries include a Hall of the World, Hall of Natural Wonders, Hall of Ancient Life, and Hall of the People of Oklahoma, among others. The paleontology exhibits include the world's largest *Apatosaurus* specimen and a fully articulated *Pentaceratops* with the world's largest known skull. The many dioramas in the natural history section include a walkthough limestone cave and a walk-through shortgrass prairie. *Address:* 2401 Chautauqua Ave., Norman, OK 73072-7029 (405-325-4712).

Sandy Sanders Wildlife Management Area. 16,400 acres. This state-owned site is located ten miles south of Erick in Beckham County. The WMA consists of rolling to rugged terrain extending north from the Elm Fork of the Red River. Mesquite, juniper, and mixed grasses dominate. The central third of the WMA contains dense stands of redberry juniper. Extending outward from the center, there is a transition to mesquite savanna and mixed-grass prairie. No bird details or species checklists are available. For more information, contact the Oklahoma Department of Wildlife Conservation, PO Box 53465, Oklahoma City, OK 73152 (405-521-3851).

Sequoyah National Wildlife Refuge. 20,800 acres. This refuge is in east-central Oklahoma, around the western part of the Robert S. Kerr Reservoir, and about half of the acreage is water. Most of the rest is shoreline or river bottomland, with many ponds and sloughs. At least 78 bird species are common to abundant during spring versus 71 species during fall and 57 during winter (Jones, 1990). There are at least 96 nesting birds among the 250 species listed for the refuge by Jones. A total of 56 bird species were reported present year-round, so an estimated minimum of 78 percent of the refuge's total bird diversity is migratory. A more recent checklist of 256 species seen since 1970 is available from the refuge manager at 107993 S. 4520 Rd., Vian, OK 74962-9304 (918-773-5251 or 918-773-5252). It is also available online at https://www.fws.gov/refuge/Sequoyah/wildlife/species.html.

Tallgrass Prairie Preserve. This enormous Nature Conservancy preserve in Osage County five miles north of Pahuska and surrounded by the *Osage Indian Reservation* contains 39,000 acres, with an additional 6,000 acres are under leased management. Except perhaps for North Dakota's Sheyenne National Grassland (see section), this is the largest preserved area of tallgrass prairie in the world and is probably the largest that is contiguous. The Tallgrass Prairie Preserve introduced a herd of 300 bison in 1993, which has since multiplied to more than 3,000 head, probably the largest herd in any nonprivate ranch or nature preserve in the Great Plains. The preserve is open daily with free admission. A local bird list that has 173 species, of which 86 are nesters, is available at the headquarters. Notable common nesters include the cattle egret, Mississippi kite, northern harrier, broad-winged hawk, red-shouldered hawk, king rail, yellow-billed cuckoo, chuck-wills-widow, loggerhead shrike, Acadian flycatcher, scissor-tailed flycatcher, fish crow, northern parula, summer tanager, indigo and painted buntings, and blue grosbeak. *Address:* 15316 Co. Rd. 4201, Pawhuska, OK 74056 (918-287-4803).

Tishomingo National Wildlife Refuge. 16,600 acres. This refuge is six miles southeast of Tishomingo on Lake Texoma in eastern Oklahoma. It includes about 4,000 acres of reservoir as well as marshes, cropland, and grassland. At least 113 bird species are common to abundant during spring versus 94 species during fall and 65 during winter (Jones, 1990). There are at least 81 nesting birds among the 243 listed for the refuge by Jones. A total of 72 bird species were reported present year-round by Jones, so an estimated minimum of 70 percent of the refuge's total bird diversity is migratory. A recent checklist of 252 species is available from the refuge manager at 12000 S. Refuge Rd., Tishomingo, OK 73460 (580-371-2402). It is also available online at https://www.fws.gov/refuge/Tishomingo/wildlife/species.html.

Washita National Wildlife Refuge. 8,200 acres. This federal wildlife refuge is located about seven miles northwest of Butler in Custer County and contains approximately 3,000 acres of mixed-grass prairies plus wooded creeks and a reservoir. An older bird species checklist (220 species, 67 nesters) indicates that 58 species are common to abundant during spring versus 54 species during fall and 40 during winter (Jones, 1990). There are at least 67 nesting birds among those listed for the refuge by Jones. A total of 59 bird species were reported present year-round, so an estimated minimum of 73 percent of the refuge's total bird diversity is migratory. Prairie dogs are present, and burrowing owls are rare in summer. This wildlife refuge and associated state park support large numbers of sandhill cranes during late fall and early winter. A recent refuge checklist of 229 bird species is available from the refuge manager at 20834 E. 0940 Rd., Butler, OK 73625-5001 (580-664-2205). It is also available online at https://www.fws.gov/refuge/Washita/species_lists.html.

The state-owned *Foss State Park* (1,749 acres) is nearby (13 miles west of Clinton). It has similar habitats and adjoins the 8,800-acre Foss Reservoir. *Address:* 10252 Hwy. 44, Foss, OK 73647 (580-592-4433).

Waurika Wildlife Management Area. 10,600 acres. The US Army Corps of Engineers (580-963-2111) manages some of this site on Lake Waurika, located four miles south of Corum in southwestern Stephens County. The Oklahoma Department of Wildlife Conservation also manages the area's mixed-grass prairie and hardwoods around the northern end of the lake. No bird details or species checklists are available.

Wichita Mountains National Wildlife Refuge. 59,020 acres. Located northwest of Lawton in Comanche County, this federal wildlife refuge contains about 30,000 acres of mixed-grass prairie. Juniper and scrub oak uplands rise up to about 1,400 feet in elevation. The uplands are the eroded remnants of Paleozoic mountains some 300 million years old and are sprinkled with more than a hundred small wetlands. The refuge has managed herds of bison (500–600 head), elk (about 500–700), and longhorn cattle (about 300), and an unmanaged population of pronghorns. A bird species checklist is available with 278 species, including 78 nesters, along with refuge lists of 50 mammals, 64 reptiles and amphibians, 36 fish, and 806 plants (see https://www.fws.gov/refuge/Wichita_Mountains/wildlife/species_list.html). Prairie dog colonies are present (on about 150 acres in 2000), and burrowing owls are rare residents. (Within the city of Lawton is a small prairie dog colony in Elmer Thomas Park.) *Address:* 32 Refuge Headquarters, Indiahoma, OK 73552 (580-429-3222). Immediately south of the refuge is the federally owned *Fort Sill Military Reservation*, with 93,000 acres of mostly mixed-grass prairie. The reservation provides major habitat for some rare shrub-dependent species such as the black-capped vireo. Access to the military facilities is restricted and traffic may be limited to public roads. *Visitors Center address:* 4700 Mow-Way Rd., Fort Sill, OK 73503-0000 (580-442-3217).

TEXAS

Texas (TX) is not only huge, covering almost 287,000 square miles, but it also has the largest diversity of bird habitats and greatest species diversity to be found in the Great Plains. For naturalists, Texas has 114 state parks, 47 wildlife management areas, 16 national wildlife refuges, seven state forests, five national grasslands, four national forests, three Indian reservations, two national parks, two national recreation areas, and a national seashore. Federally owned acreage in Texas composes 1.86 percent of the state's land area. All together, federal lands in Texas include 1.3 million acres in National Park Service lands, 107,009 acres in US Fish and Wildlife Service lands, 532,000 acres in national grasslands, and 32,000 acres in national forest lands.

Because of the great number of public-access lands in Texas, it has been difficult to select only about 60 sites that seem to be both among the most important and that illustrate the high degree of the state's ecological and biological diversity. However, in keeping with its unparalleled diversity, there are dozens of splendid books on the natural history of Texas and its wildlife, especially its birds and birding opportunities (see references). Additionally, there is a set of nine viewing guides, the *Great Texas Wildlife Trails*, with interactive maps that are available online and collectively cover the entire state. The regional maps include Far West Texas, Upper Texas Coast, Central Texas Coast, Lower Texas Coast, Heart of Texas West, Heart of Texas East, Panhandle Plains, Prairies and Pineywoods West, and Prairies and Pineywoods East. The mapped regions and birding sites can be purchased in hard copy or viewed free online at https://tpwd.texas.gov/huntwild/wildlife/wildlife-trails/.

Alibates Flint Quarry National Monument. 1,333 acres. This site, located between Fritch and Amarillo, consists of native short grasses and a quarry where flint (agatized dolomite) for making flint implements such as Clovis spear points was obtained by pre-Columbian ("Panhandle Aspect") Paleo-Indians as early as about 11,000 years ago. To get there, from the Amarillo Business I-40 and Texas Hwy. 136 junction, take Hwy. 136 north 26.4 miles; turn left on Cas Johnson Road into Bates Canyon; after 2.4 miles (at the Y-intersection), take the right fork to the quarry visitor center. Common breeding birds include Mississippi kite, burrowing owl, painted bunting, indigo bunting, rock wren, and both rufous-crowned and Cassin's sparrows (Kutac, 1998). No national monument bird checklist is available, but a checklist for the entire Lake Meredith National Recreation Area (see section) is available from the area office at PO Box 1460, Fritch, TX 79036 (806-857-3151). *Monument address:* (also) PO Box 1460, Fritch, TX 79036 (806-857-6680). https://www.nps.gov/alfl/index.htm

Anahuac National Wildlife Refuge. 24,356 acres. This important coastal estuary is located about ten miles southeast of Anahuac. At least 100 bird species are common to abundant at the refuge during spring versus 100 species during fall (Jones, 1990). There are at least 40 nesting birds among the 252 listed for the

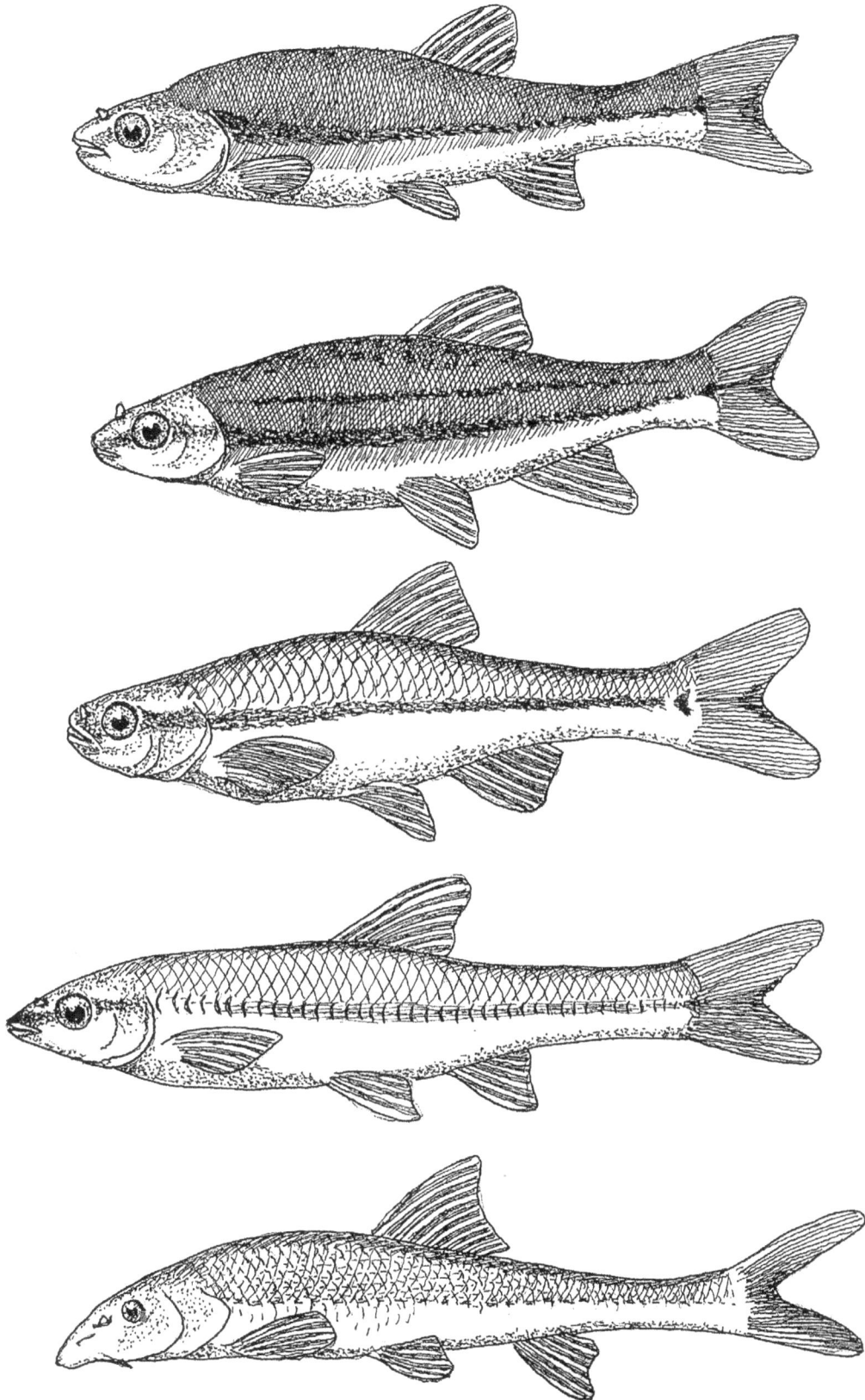

Typical rare minnows of the Great Plains, including (top to bottom) finescale dace, northern redbelly dace, blacknose shiner, Topeka shiner, and sturgeon chub.

refuge by Jones. A total of 49 bird species were reported present year-round by Jones, so an estimated minimum of 81 percent of the refuge's total bird diversity is migratory. Anahuac NWR also administers McFaddin NWR (see section) and Texas Point NWR (see section), which provide important winter estuarine habitats for vast numbers of wintering ducks and geese. Up to 100,000 ducks of 23 species winter at Texas Point, as well as large numbers of geese (snow, Ross's, Canada, cackling, and greater white-fronted). Texas Point is located 17 miles south of Port Arthur and has no vehicular roads, so public access is very limited. Progressively farther to the west are Sabine Woods Bird Sanctuary (see section), Sea Rim State Park (see section), and McFaddin NWR. A recent checklist of 279 bird species is available from the Anahuac refuge manager at Trinity St. and Washington Ave., PO Box 278, Anahuac, TX 77514 (409-267-3337). It is also available online at https://www.fws.gov/nwrs/threecolumn.aspx?id=2147487775.

Aransas National Wildlife Refuge. 54,829 acres. Located seven miles south of Austwell, this refuge was originally established to protect the whooping crane's primary wintering grounds. Aransas NWR is one of the most important of Texas's coastal protected habitats. Jones (1990) listed 252 bird species for the refuge, of which at least 92 species are common at the refuge during spring versus 76 species during summer, 74 during fall, and 69 during winter. Nesting birds include the pauraque, white-tailed hawk, crested caracara, purple gallinule, common moorhen, and Cassin's sparrow (Kutac, 1998). A total of 79 bird species were reported present year-round by Jones, so an estimated minimum of 69 percent of the refuge's total bird diversity is migratory. Essentially the entire population of the highly endangered whooping crane that breeds in Alberta's Wood Buffalo National Park winters here, the early arrivals usually appearing by late October and all leaving by early April (Johnsgard and Gil-Weir, 2010; Johnsgard, 2014, "Aransas"). By late 2017, this slowly recovering population numbered more than 400 birds, but Hurricane Harvey did substantial ecological damage to the refuge habitat in September of 2017, including a storm surge that filled freshwater ponds with salt water and caused salinity changes in the estuary that may have long-term effects on crane foods such as blue crabs. A checklist of 392 bird species, with 37 waterfowl, 28 shorebirds, 42 warblers, and 29 sparrows, is available from the refuge manager at PO Box 100, Austwell, TX 77950 (361-286-3559). It is also available online at https://www.fws.gov/nwrs/threecolumn.aspx?id=2147490512.

Attwater Prairie Chicken National Wildlife Refuge. 3,400 acres. This coastal prairie refuge seven miles northeast of Eagle Lake was established to preserve and restore the critically endangered and nearly extinct Attwater's race of the greater prairie-chicken. Now probably extinct in the wild, the refuge has a small resident population, which currently (2017) is entirely dependent on artificial incubation and hand-rearing to maintain the flock (Johnsgard, 2002, *Grassland Grouse*). More than 250 bird species are reported for the refuge, such as the white-tailed hawk, crested caracara, king rail, common moorhen, black-necked stilt, and both whistling-ducks (Kutac, 1998). Larger mammals on the refuge include bison, white-tailed deer, armadillos, coyotes, and bobcats. *Address:* PO Box 519, Eagle Lake, TX 77434 (979-234-3021).

Austin and vicinity. *Austin City Park* is a good place to look for endangered golden-cheeked warblers, the only warbler that nests exclusively in Texas. It inhabits stands of mature Ashe juniper and oaks, over a narrow region extending from Dinosaur Valley State Park (see section) southwest to Del Rio. A bird checklist with 223 species is available at the park office at 5805 McKinney Falls Parkway Austin, TX 78744 (512-243-1643). Many state parks occur within 60 miles of Austin, and a bird checklist for this general area, with 393 species, can be obtained at small cost from the Travis Audubon Society at 3710 Cedar St., Box 5, Austin, TX 78705 (512-300-2473). *McKinney Falls State Park* (640 acres) is located at the southern edge of Austin and has a mixture of grasslands, underbrush, and trees (Kutac, 1998). Another of these parks is *Pedernales Falls State Park* (5,211 acres), 14 miles east of Johnson City off FM 3232. The golden-cheeked warbler is often seen at the top of the bluff along the river on the Pedernales Hill Country Nature Trail and along the trail to the Primitive Camping Area.

Balcones Canyonlands National Wildlife Refuge. 71.8 square miles. This huge refuge is about 30 miles northwest of Austin, in the Texas hill country on the limestone-based Edwards Plateau. Nesting birds include the local and endangered golden-cheeked warbler and black-capped vireo. Other more common breeding-season species are the ladder-backed woodpecker, ash-throated flycatcher, vermilion flycatcher, western scrub-jay, painted bunting, canyon towhee, and lesser goldfinch. A bird checklist for the refuge has more than 300 species, with 10 hawks, 7 vireos, 19 warblers, and 21 sparrows (Kutac, 1998). It is available at the headquarters or online at https://www.fws.gov/refuge/Balcones_Canyonlands/wildlife_and_habitat/species_list.html. *Address:* 24518 FM 1431, Marble Falls, TX 78654 (512-339-9432).

Big Bend National Park. 801,163 acres. This enormous park is largely desert, but the bordering Rio Grande River provides a limited water source. The park's bird checklist is remarkable for its huge number of wintering and nesting birds, with at least 388 documented species, plus 59 hypothetical species. This park has been recognized by the National Geographic Society (2011) as one of the nation's ten best national parks for birding. Some 50 species of warblers (essentially all of the US species) have been reported, of which 43 are migrants or accidentals. The warblers include one rare nesting species, the Colima warbler, which is endemic to the park and is most often seen in Boot Canyon. Some notable birds are Hutton's vireo, acorn woodpecker, Mexican jay, zone-tailed hawk, white-throated swift, bushtit, and blue-throated hummingbird. Other nesters include zone-tailed hawk, elf owl, lesser nighthawk, black-tailed gnatcatcher, crissal thrasher, varied bunting, and Scott's oriole (Kutac, 1998). The adjoining *Big Bend Ranch State Park* is smaller (269,714 acres) and has more water in the form of springs, tanks, and waterfalls as well as associated riparian habitats. It has no bird checklist, but the national park checklist is probably applicable. The *Rio Grande Wild and Scenic River* is a 198-mile stretch of the Rio Grande, of which 69 miles are within Big Bend National Park. *Address of Big Bend National Park:* PO Box 129, Big Bend National Park, TX 79834-0129 (432-477-2251) https://www.nps.gov/bibe/index.htm. *Address of Big Bend Ranch State Park:* Sauceda Ranger Station (Northern Unit), 1900 Sauceda Ranch Rd., Presidio, TX 79845 (432-358-4444). *Address of Rio Grande Wild and Scenic River:* PO Box 129, Big Bend National Park, TX 79834-0129 (432-477-2251).

Big Boggy National Wildlife Refuge. 4,216 acres. Located along the Gulf Coast south of Bay City and Wadsworth, this wildlife refuge is a major rookery for colonial breeding birds such as roseate spoonbills, reddish egrets, and snowy egrets. It currently (2017) is open only for waterfowl hunting and is off-limits to the general public.

Big Spring State Park. 370 acres. Big Spring State Park is at the west end of the city of Big Spring in Howard County and is managed by Texas Parks and Wildlife. It is a relatively small park with native vegetation that has long supported a prairie dog town and burrowing owls. A bird checklist is available online at https://tpwd.texas.gov/state-parks/big-spring/nature. *Address:* No. 1 Scenic Dr., Big Spring, TX 79720 (432-263-4931). (Another western Texas city that had prairie dogs within its city limits was Lubbock, with a colony in Mackenzie Park and others on farmlands just east of the city. Lubbock was cited by the Texas Commission on Environmental Quality in 2002 for endangering the groundwater by allowing effluent from cattle operations to drain into prairie dog burrows. City officials responded by poisoning the approximately15,000 prairie dogs then living on the city's lands. By early 2003 most had been killed, but some surviving animals were translocated. Statewide, the prairie dog population dropped from an estimated 56,833,000 acres in 1870 to 22,500 acres by 1998, representing a 99.96 percent population reduction.)

Big Thicket National Preserve. 84,500 acres. This national preserve north of Beaumont includes eight land units and four river or stream corridor units in five counties. There is a great diversity of ecosystems, such as pine-hardwood forest, longleaf pine–savanna forest, beech-magnolia-loblolly pine forest, American bald cypress–tupelo swamps, bog wetlands, riparian hardwoods, and others. The Turkey Creek Unit (7,800 acres) has the greatest plant diversity, with mature stands of bald cypress, sweetgum, and loblolly pine. Twenty species of oaks live in the preserve, as do carnivorous pitcher plants and orchids. A checklist with 235 bird species is available at the preserve headquarters in Beaumont or the North Ranger District Office in Woodville on US Hwy. 287. Many migratory species nest here, including many Neotropical migrants (at least 13 warblers and 3 vireos). There are also five breeding woodpeckers, including the pileated woodpecker. Many more northerly nesting migrants also winter here (Kutac, 1998). *Address:* 6044 FM 420, Kountze, TX 77625 (409-951-6800).

Black Kettle National Grassland. 3,005 acres in Texas; 30,724 acres in Oklahoma (see also the Black Kettle NG section in Oklahoma). This small Texas portion of Black Kettle National Grassland is located in Hemphill County east of the city of Canadian and just north of the Canadian River. Its mixed shinnery oak–shortgrass habitat is similar to that of the Oklahoma section, with shrub-sized oaks growing in groups ("motts") among the grasses. The name Black Kettle is based on a Southern Cheyenne chief who was killed, along with his entire village, during the Washita Massacre in an unprovoked attack led by George Custer in 1868.

Bolivar Flats Shorebird Sanctuary. 615 acres. This area of tidal mudflats, salt marsh, beach, and uplands is located at the south end of the Bolivar Peninsula at the head of Galveston Bay in the unincorporated community of Port Bolivar. It is managed by the Houston Audubon Society and provides resting, feeding, and breeding habitats for hundreds of thousands of shorebirds and other water-dependent birds annually. It is also heavily used by thousands of wading birds, such as reddish egrets and roseate spoonbills, for resting or foraging. Large numbers of piping and snowy plovers use this area as a migratory stopover and wintering area. Several herons and egrets are permanent residents, and a wide variety of gulls and terns are often present. It has been designated a nationally recognized Important Bird Area. It is also recognized as a Wetland of International Importance by the Western Hemisphere Shorebird Reserve Network. For more information contact the Houston Audubon Society, 440 Wilchester Blvd., Houston, TX 77079 (713-932-1639).

Brazoria National Wildlife Refuge. 10,407 acres. This refuge is located about ten miles northeast of Freeport. At least 98 bird species are common to abundant at the refuge during spring versus 86 species during fall and 81 during winter (Jones, 1990). Wintering birds include large numbers of snow, Ross's, Canada, cackling, and greater white-fronted geese; concentrations of up to 100,000 geese and 80,000 ducks of 24 species have been seen. It is an important wintering area for sandhill cranes from October to late February. The cranes can usually be found foraging on the upper prairies. At least 71 nesting birds are among the 272 listed for the refuge by Jones in 1990. A total of 99 bird species were reported present year-round by Jones, so an estimated minimum of 64 percent of the refuge's total bird diversity is migratory. The refuge is open to the public on the first full weekend of each month, and on the third weekend from November through April, with limited access during the week. A recent Brazoria NWR bird checklist with 301 species (including San Bernard and Big Boggy NWR) is available from the refuge manager at 24907 FM 2004, Angleton, TX 77515 (979-922-1037). It is also available online at https://www.fws.gov/refuge/brazoria/wildlife_and_habitat/species_list.html.

Brazos Bend State Park. 4,900 acres. This park is on the Brazos River 35 miles south of Houston. It includes a wooded river bottom, grasslands, marshes, and lakes. Nesting birds include the hooded, northern parula, prothonotary, and Swainson's warblers; the red-eyed, yellow-throated, and white-eyed vireos; and both painted and indigo buntings. Wetland birds include the purple gallinule, common moorhen, and anhinga (Kutac, 1998). A bird checklist with 274 species is available at the headquarters at 21901 FM 762, Needville, TX 77461 (979-553-5101). It is also available online at https://tpwd.texas.gov/state-parks/brazos-bend/nature.

Buffalo Lake National Wildlife Refuge. 7,700 acres. Situated 30 miles southwest of Amarillo, this refuge includes about 1,000 acres of surface water (resulting from the impoundment of Tierra Blanca Creek) as well as adjoining grasslands. Buffalo Lake is shallow and often disappears when the creek becomes dry The refuge's alkaline wetlands are a major wintering area for lesser sandhill cranes. At least 28 bird species are common to abundant at the refuge during spring versus 19 species during fall and 20 during winter (Jones, 1990). There were at least 42 nesting bird species among the 246 that were listed for the refuge by Jones in 1990. At least 36 shorebirds have been documented on the refuge, and 13 sparrows also have been reported, along with all four longspurs. A total of 28 warblers are on the 1990 refuge list, and at least 5 nest. A total of 42 bird species were reported present year-round by Jones, so an estimated minimum of 83 percent of the refuge's total bird diversity is migratory. Alibates Flint Quarry National Monument is nearby (see section). A recent refuge bird checklist contains 344 species and is available from the refuge manager at PO Box 179,

Umbarger, TX 79091 (806-499-3382). It is also available online at https://www.fws.gov/refuge/Buffalo_Lake/wildlife/species.html.

Caddo Lake State Park (480 acres) and **Caddo Lake Wildlife Management Area** (7,000 acres). Caddo Lake is on the Texas-Oklahoma border, northeast of Marshall. It is notable for its flooded bald cypress trees and nesting birds such as the anhinga, Mississippi kite, several herons and egrets, and 13 warblers. The park's nesting warblers include the northern parula and Louisiana waterthrush as well as the black-and-white, pine, prothonotary, and yellow-throated warblers. A bird checklist is available at the park office at 245 Park Rd. 2, Karnack, TX 75661 (903-679-3351).

Caddo National Grasslands Wildlife Management Area. 17,796 acres. This national grasslands of mixed prairies and hardwoods is distributed between two units, both of them north of Dallas and near the Oklahoma border. The larger Bois d'Arc Unit surrounds several impounded lakes, and the smaller Ladonia Unit consists of open blackland prairie. No species lists are available. *Address:* US Forest Service, 1400 US Hwy. 81/287, PO Box 507, Decatur, TX 76234 (940-627-5475).

Candy Cain Abshier Wildlife Management Area. 207 acres. Located near Smith Point, a few miles west of Anahuac National Wildlife Refuge (see section), this WMA is best known as a viewing point for the fall raptor migrations. From early September to mid-October, tens of thousands of broad-winged hawks as well as hundreds of other buteos, accipiters, falcons, eagles, kites, and vultures can be seen from mid-August to mid-November. A hawk-watching tower (*Smith Point Hawk Watch Tower*) is operated by the Texas Parks and Wildlife Department and the Gulf Coast Bird Observatory. Fall raptor totals in 2016 at Smith Point exceeded 54,000 birds and included more than 43,000 broad-winged hawks. *WMA address:* 10 Parks and Wildlife Dr., Port Arthur, TX 77640 (409-736-2551).

Caprock Canyons State Park and Trailway. 15,310 acres. This park is located near Quitaque in Briscoe County. Some native arid grasslands are present as well as badlands and scrubby mesquite and juniper thickets. Caprock is a flat, impervious limestone layer

(caliche) that is resistant to erosion and thus often forms the tops of hills and bluffs. There are also high red cliffs of sandstones and shales from the Pliocene Ogallala formation, crossed by bands of white gypsum. Caprock Canyons supports the largest (and relatively free-roaming) herd of bison in the state as well as Barbary sheep (introduced), pronghorns, and deer (mule and white-tailed). An introduced prairie dog town attracts golden eagles in winter. Over 175 species of birds have been reported. Managed by Texas Parks and Wildlife, PO Box 204, 850 Caprock Canyon Park Rd., Quitaque, TX 79255 (806-455-1492).

Colorado Bend State Park. 5,328 acres. Located six miles south of Bend, this park is notable for the fact that both golden-cheeked warblers and black-capped vireos nest here. The warbler is best found along the Colorado River or Spicewood Creek, but the vireo is most common in an area that has been closed to the public. However, accessible parts of the park also have common poorwill, golden-fronted woodpecker, ash-throated flycatcher, cactus and canyon wrens, bushtit, summer tanager, and indigo and painted buntings (Kutac, 1998). A bird species list with 157 species can be obtained at the headquarters. *Address:* PO Box 118, Bend, TX 76824 (325-628-3240).

Connie Hagar Wildlife Sanctuary. Rockport, on the central Gulf Coast, is a birding "hotspot," in part because of the vast numbers of ruby-throated hummingbirds that pass through during fall migration (they are the basis for a birding celebration each September). At least 413 bird species have been tallied in this central Gulf Coast region. Connie Hagar Wildlife Sanctuary extends on Broadway Street along Little Bay to include a coastal woodland that reaches from northern Rockport to the mouth of Fulton Harbor. *Connie Hagar Cottage Sanctuary* (6 acres) is the location where the Hagars had a group of rental cottages. Rockport is a major "fallout" location for migrating songbirds, and it also attracts herons, egrets, and many other wading birds. The location is 1001–1838 Broadway St., Rockport. For more information, contact the Rockport Chamber of Commerce, 319 Broadway, Rockport TX 78382 (361-729-6445).

Copper Breaks State Park. 1,933 acres. This park is located 12 miles south of Quanah in Hardeman County.

It features mesquite and juniper thickets plus restored shortgrass and mixed-grass prairie over eroded, red-tinted sedimentary Paleozoic rocks of Permian age along the Pease River. The park is managed in large part for longhorn cattle, but mule deer, armadillos, bobcats, coyotes, opossums, and raccoons are prevalent. No species checklists are available. Managed by Texas Parks and Wildlife, 777 Park Rd. 62, Quanah, TX 79252 (940-839-4331).

Dallas Museum of Natural History. Now a part of the Perot Museum of Nature and Science, the original Dallas Museum of Natural History remains a major research collection and reference library. The Fair Park location also has some dioramas of Texas's natural history. *Address:* 3535 Grand Ave., Dallas, TX 75210 (214-428-5555). The *Cedar Ridge Nature Preserve*, formerly known as the *Dallas Nature Center*, is located southwest of the city, going west on I-20, then south off Exit 458 for three miles. The preserve has a butterfly garden and seven miles of trails through varied habitats. *Address:* 7171 Mountain Creek Pkwy., Dallas, TX 75249 (972-709-7784). A heron rookery, usually containing breeding great, snowy, and cattle egrets, is about 3.5 miles northwest of central Dallas at the University of Texas Southwestern Medical Center, 5323 Harry Hines Blvd. The birds are present from mid-March to early October (Kutac, 1998). *Cedar Hills State Park* is 16 miles southwest of Dallas off FM 1382. It has hiking trails with woodlands, ponds, and grasslands, and a bird list of 193 species is available from the office, 1570 W. FM 1382, Cedar Hill, TX 75104 (972-291-3900).

Davis Mountains State Park. 2,677 acres. Located near Fort Davis in the montane foothills, the mountains here rise to 8,382 feet, with mature forests and grassy meadows. The park is a good place to look for the increasingly rare Montezuma quail as well as for scrub and grassland birds such as the scaled quail, common poorwill, western scrub-jay, Cassin's kingbird, bushtit, curve-billed thrasher, and pyrrhuloxia (Kutac, 1998). A bird list with 189 species is available from the park headquarters at PO Box 1707, Fort Davis, TX 79734 (432-426-3337).

Dinosaur Valley State Park. 1,274 acres. This park is located about 60 miles southwest of Dallas and 5 miles west of Glen Rose. In addition to preserving the

footprints of sauropods, theropods, and ornithopods, this park is one of the best locations for finding both the golden-cheeked warbler and black-headed vireo, both at the northern edges of their ranges. The ridge trails offer the best chance for seeing both. There are also many western species at or near the eastern limits of their ranges, such as the common poorwill, black-chinned hummingbird, and canyon wren (Kutac, 1998). A bird checklist with 151 species is available at the park office. *Address:* 1629 Park Rd. 59, Glen Rose, TX 76043 (254-897-4588).

Fort Worth Nature Center and Refuge. 3,412 acres. The prime Fort Worth location for naturalists is probably the Fort Worth Nature Center and Refuge located on Lake Worth. There are 20 miles of trails through diverse habitats and a 900-foot boardwalk over Lotus Marsh. An interpretive center includes a library, herbarium, and bird checklists for the refuge as well as for surrounding regions (Kutac, 1998). *Address:* 9601 Fossil Ridge Rd., Fort Worth, TX 76135 (817-392-7410).

Franklin Mountains State Park. 23,867 acres. This park is located at the northern edge of El Paso. Its bird checklist of more than 150 species is available at the headquarters and includes such western species as the golden eagle, common poorwill, white-throated swift, Say's phoebe, violet-green swallow, verdin, and crissal thrasher (Kutac, 1998). *Address:* 1331 McKelligon Canyon Rd., El Paso, TX 79930 (915-566-6441).

Galveston Island State Park. 1,950 acres. This park begins at 13 Mile Road where Stewart Road meets FM 3005 and includes 1.6 miles of beach. The park supports a host of nesting marsh and beach-nesting birds, including the least bittern, reddish egret, black-crowned night-heron, roseate spoonbill, clapper rail, purple gallinule, common moorhen, American oystercatcher, Wilson's plover, willet, six tern species, black skimmer, marsh wren, and seaside sparrow. A list of 297 bird species is available from the park office at 14901 FM 3005, Galveston, TX 77554 (409-737-1222). *Laffite's Cove Nature Preserve* (19 acres), on West Galveston Island, is a city-owned preserve and consists of a free-access interpretive trail through an oak hammock and a boardwalk over a swamp. *Address:* 3503 Eckert Dr., Galveston, TX 77554 (281-255-3055).

Gene Howe Wildlife Management Area. 5,896 acres. This WMA consists of high plains and canyons in the northeastern Texas panhandle. In two units, the Murphy Unit (889 acres) is mostly shortgrass prairie and old fields located in Liscomb County near Glazier. The larger Main Unit (about 5,000 acres) is in Hemphill County, seven miles northwest of Canadian. Prairie dogs and other sandsage-adapted species occur here, including burrowing owls, pronghorns, and horned lizards. Lesser prairie-chickens are perhaps more common in the Main Unit than anywhere else in Texas, and no other wildlife management area in Texas supports prairie dogs. No species checklists are available. Managed by Texas Parks and Wildlife, 15412 FM 2266, Canadian, TX 79014 (806-323-8642).

Typical lizards of the Great Plains, including (top to bottom) collared lizard (top left), slender glass lizard (top right), Great Plains skink (middle), and short-nosed horned lizard (bottom).

Goose Island State Park. 314 acres. This park is located 12 miles northeast of Rockport, at the southern tip of Lamar Peninsula. Nesting birds include the reddish egret; black-crowned night-heron; roseate spoonbill; clapper rail; American oystercatcher; black skimmer; Forster's, royal, and Caspian terns; and seaside sparrow (Kutac, 1998). A bird checklist with 274 species is available at the office: 202 S. Palmetto St., Rockport, TX 78382 (361-792-2858).

Guadalupe Mountains National Park. 86,415 acres (with almost 47,000 acres of wilderness area). This park on the New Mexico border contains the highest mountain in Texas (Signal Peak, 8,749 feet) and an overall elevation range of more than 8,000 feet from the Chihuahuan desert floor. The mountains are the top of an exposed reef (Permian Reef Complex) deposited by an ancient sea some 200 million years ago. The park has a wide variety of climates and habitats, ranging from subalpine pine forests and grassy meadows to wooded deciduous canyons and arid scrub desert. There are no food, lodging, or gas facilities within the park. Hiking is the only way to explore the park; the McKittrick Canyon hike is the best for bird diversity and also the easiest, relative to its length (Kutac, 1998). Over 300 bird species have been reported, including many western-oriented Neotropical migrants. A bird checklist is available at the visitors center at refuge headquarters: 400 Pine Canyon, Salt Flat, TX 79847 (915-828-3251). https://www.nps.gov/gumo/index.htm

Hagerman National Wildlife Refuge. 11,320 acres. Located 15 miles northwest of Sherman, Texas, on the Texas-Oklahoma border, this refuge is situated around Lake Texoma and includes habitats similar to those in the Tishomingo National Wildlife Refuge in Oklahoma (see section). The winter refuge bird list includes 5 geese, 21 ducks, and 36 species of shorebirds. At least 63 species are common to abundant at the refuge during spring versus 67 species during fall and 46 during winter, including all four longspurs. A total of 76 bird species were reported present year-round by Jones, so an estimated minimum of 72 percent of the refuge's total bird diversity is migratory. There are at least 86 nesting birds among the 272 listed for the refuge in a 1990 checklist (Jones, 1990), with 17 sparrows and nearly 30 warblers. A more recent bird checklist containing 316 species is available from the refuge manager at 6465 Refuge Rd., Sherman, TX 75092 (903-786-2826). It is also available online at https://www.fws.gov/refuge/Hagerman/wildlife/species_lists.html.

Hazel Bazemore Park. This 78-acre park south of Sinton is located on the Nueces River. Average recent annual fall raptor counts are 730,000. During one fall, hawk-watchers at Hazel Bazemore Park tallied more than 690,000 individuals of 24 raptor species that included more than 678,000 broad-winged hawks. Operated by the Nueces County Parks and Recreation Department. *Address:* 4343 County Rd. 69, Corpus Christi, TX 78410 (361-387-4231).

Heard Natural Science Museum and Wildlife Sanctuary. 287 acres. This sanctuary, located about 30 miles north of Dallas on US Hwy. 75, is a combination of wetlands, tallgrass prairie, and riparian woodlands. The wetlands support nesting habitat for about 2,000 herons and egrets of seven species. The museum operates the oldest bird-banding station in Texas, a raptor rehabilitation station, and educational programs. *Address:* 1 Nature Place, McKinney, TX 75069 (972-562-5566).

High Island Audubon sanctuaries. The town of High Island is 30 miles northeast of Galveston and is slightly higher in elevation than surrounding areas of coastal prairie that support tree growth. Several groves of live oaks are in town, and they are vital temporary resting ("fall-out") points for Neotropical migrants that have just crossed the Gulf of Mexico. The four free-access sanctuaries at High Island are all owned and managed by the Houston Audubon Society. These are *Smith Oaks Sanctuary* (142 acres), *Louis B. Smith Woods Sanctuary* (50+ acres), *Eubank Woods Sanctuary* (9.5 acres), and *S. E. Gast Red Bay Sanctuary* (8.8 acres). Great numbers and a wide variety of warblers, vireos, orioles, buntings, and other migrants can be seen here from mid-April to mid-May, especially after a cold front accompanied by rain has passed. For more information contact Houston Audubon Society, 440 Wilchester Blvd., Houston, TX 77079 (713-932-1639).

Houston Museum of Natural Science. This major museum features sections on natural history, geology, and archeology. The Earth Science section is notable for its mineral exhibits, and the Cockrell Butterfly Center has a remarkable walk-through exhibit of living butterflies. The paleontology exhibits include a reconstructed full-size representation of *Quetzalcoatlus northropi*, the largest of all known pterodactyls, with an estimated wingspan of about 36 feet, that was found in Big Bend National Park. Address: 5555 Hermann Park Dr., Houston, TX 77030 (713-639-4629). *The Houston Arboretum and Nature Center* has more than 155 acres of woodlands, ponds, and prairie, and an environmental education center. It is located in Memorial Park at 4501 Woodway Dr., Houston, TX 77024 (713-681-8433).

Hueco Tanks State Park. 860 acres. This is a small park located about 32 miles northeast of El Paso that is notable for Native American pictographs present on cave walls and rock formations. Notable nesting western birds include the lesser nighthawk, black-chinned hummingbird, ash-throated flycatcher, crissal thrasher, Scott's oriole, and common poorwill (Kutac, 1998). A bird list with 211 species is available from the park headquarters at 6900 Hueco Tanks Rd., #1, El Paso, TX 79938 (915-857-1135).

Laguna Atascosa National Wildlife Refuge. 45,187 acres. This important NWR is located 25 miles east of Harlingen. At least 97 species are common to abundant at the refuge during spring versus 95 species during fall and 67 during winter (Jones, 1990). There are at least 90 nesting birds among the 329 listed for the refuge by Jones. A total of 122 bird species were reported present year-round by Jones, so an estimated minimum of 63 percent of the refuge's total bird diversity is migratory. Seven vireos and 35 warblers have been reported; two of the warblers remain to nest. There is a small reintroduced population of aplomado falcons and great numbers of wintering ducks, especially redheads. A recent bird checklist containing 369 species is available from the refuge manager at 22817 Ocelot Rd., Los Fresnos, TX 78566 (956-748-3607). It is also available online at https://www.fws.gov/refuge/Laguna_Atascosa/wildlife_habitat/species_list.html.

Lake Meredith National Recreation Area. 44,951 acres. This National Park Service NRA is made up of the grasslands around a large impoundment of the Canadian River. Species lists (225 birds, 38 reptiles, and 11 amphibians) are available. Pronghorns, swift foxes, and prairie dogs are among the area's 65 reported mammals. Nesting birds include the Mississippi kite,

burrowing owl, rock wren, rufous-crowned sparrow, Cassin's sparrow, painted bunting, indigo bunting, and both eastern and western meadowlarks. The manager's address is 419 E. Broadway St., PO Box 1460, Fritch, TX 79036 (806-857-3151).

Lost Maples State Natural Area. 2,174 acres. This state area, four miles south of Vanderpool, preserves an isolated stand of big-toothed maple, as well as other typical vegetation and wildlife of the Edwards Plateau. The golden-cheeked warbler, black-headed vireo, and green kingfisher all nest, along with other more generally widespread birds, such as the greater roadrunner, western scrub-jay, pyrrhuloxia, and Scott's oriole (Kutac, 1998). A list of 197 bird species is available from the park office at 37221 FM 187, Vanderpool, TX 78885 (830-966-3413).

Lower Rio Grande Valley National Wildlife Refuge. 90,000 acres. Located seven miles south of Alamo, this still-developing refuge shares a headquarters with Santa Ana National Wildlife Refuge. The refuge follows the lower Rio Grande in Starr, Hidalgo, Cameron, and Willacy Counties and may eventually be expanded to include up to 132,500 acres. The bird list is the largest of any refuge in the Great Plains and totals 402 species. The list contains 39 shorebirds, 24 New World flycatchers, and 40 warblers, of which the flycatchers and warblers are nearly all Neotropical migrants. The list is online at https://www.fws.gov/refuge/Lower_Rio_Grande_Valley/wildlife_and_habitat/species_list.html or for more information, contact the refuge manager at 3325 Green Jay Rd., Alamo, TX 78516 (956-784-7500).

Lyndon B. Johnson National Grassland (formerly Cross Timbers National Grassland). 20,320 acres. Located near Decatur, or 35 miles northwest of Fort Worth in Wise County, this grassland consists of mixed-grass prairies with interspersed blackjack and post oak savanna. About 230 bird species have been reported from this grassland, as well as 88 butterfly species (Moul, 2008). This site is managed by the US Forest Service, PO Box 507, Decatur, TX 76234 (940-627-5475).

Matador Wildlife Management Area. 28,183 acres. This state-owned site is located in Cottle County, eight miles north and two miles west of Paducah. It consists of shinnery oak grasslands, mesquite uplands, gravelly hills, and bottomland. Wild turkeys, mule deer, coyotes, bobcats, and other grassland- and brush-adapted fauna are present. There are 73 miles of (barely) improved roads. No species checklists are available. This site is managed by Texas Parks and Wildlife, 3036 FM 3256, Paducah, TX 79248 (806-492-3405).

McClellan Creek National Grassland. 1,449 acres. This mostly shortgrass prairie had a 2006 fire that burned all but 586 acres of grassland and most trees. It is located in Gray County, near Pampa and Alanreed, and surrounds Lake McClellan. Lake McClellan is a reservoir that was impounded over a natural playa lake; other shallow playa lakes are in the area and attract many migratory birds. No species checklists are available. It is managed through Black Kettle National Grassland (see the Black Kettle National Grassland section in Oklahoma). *Address:* PO Box 266, Cheyenne OK 73628 (508-497-2143).

McFaddin National Wildlife Refuge. 55,000 acres. This refuge protects the largest remaining freshwater marsh in Texas and is adjacent to thousands of acres of variably brackish marshland. The mottled duck is a common year-round resident, and tens of thousands of geese and ducks winter here. McFaddin NWR is located at Sabine Pass, and has 12 miles of beach and 8 miles of interior roads. The refuge is located about 15 miles south of Port Arthur. Parts of the refuge are open to hunting. Information is available at the refuge's field headquarters at 7950 S. Gulfway Dr., PO Box 358, Sabine Pass, TX 77655 (409-971-2909) and https://www.fws.gov/refuge/mcFaddin/.

Meridian State Park. 502 acres. This park is located about four miles southwest of Meridian on SG 22. The park is near the northern limits of the golden-cheeked warbler, and additionally many eastern and western species occur in this transitional zone, where the Edwards Plateau meets the western Cross Timbers and Grand Prairie and Plains ecoregions. A bird checklist with 207 species is available from the office at 173 Park Rd., #7, Meridian, TX 76665 (254-435-2536) or online at https://tpwd.texas.gov/publications/pwdpubs/media/pwd_bk_p4503_0021a.pdf.

Muleshoe National Wildlife Refuge. 5,809 acres. Situated 20 miles south of Muleshoe in Bailey County, this refuge contains a variety of lakes, marshes, shortgrass plains, and other minor habitats. Sandy shortgrass and semidesert grasslands with alkaline playa lakes are important for wintering cranes and waterfowl. The sink-type lakes provide the most important wintering habitat in North America for lesser sandhill cranes, which often number more than 100,000. During some winters they have reached as many as 250,000, out of a national population of about 600,000. At least 78 bird species are common to abundant at the refuge during spring versus 82 species during fall and 49 during winter (Jones, 1990). There are at least 59 nesting birds among the 243 listed for the refuge by Jones. A total of 65 bird species were reported present year-round by Jones, so an estimated minimum of 73 percent of the refuge's total bird diversity is migratory. Burrowing owls are common summer nesters; golden eagles, ferruginous and rough-legged hawks, and prairie falcons all occur in winter. A recent bird checklist includes 282 species (59 nesters) and is available from the refuge manager at PO Box 549, Muleshoe, TX 79347 (806-946-3341).

Palo Duro Canyon State Park. 16,402 acres. With a depth of up to 1,000 feet, a maximum width of 20 miles, and a length of 120 miles, this is the second largest canyon in the United States, exceeded only by the Grand Canyon. The park is located in Randall County, 12 miles east of the town of Canyon. The rim of the canyon is the top of the Caprock Escarpment, and its deepest levels are Permian in age (Quartermaster Formation), above which sequentially are the Triassic-age Tecovas Formation, the Triassic Trujillo Formation, and the late Miocene to early Oligocene Ogallala Formation. Fossils found in the last-named formation include saber-toothed cats, bone-crushing dogs, mastodons, long-necked camels, rhinoceroses, and tortoises (Spearing, 1991). Mountain lions and mule deer have been reported in the park. Shortgrass prairie occurs along the canyon rim, and mesquite scrub thickets are widespread. Golden eagles are regular in winter, and a few remain to nest. A bird checklist is available at the park headquarters or online at https://tpwd.texas.gov/publications/pwdpubs/media/pwd_bk_p4506_0007a.pdf. This site is managed by Texas Parks and Wildlife at 11450 Park Rd. 5, Canyon, Texas 79015 (806-488-2227).

Adult ferruginous hawk.

Padre Island National Seashore. 134,000 acres. About 80 percent of Padre Island is preserved as a national seashore. Drivers can reach Padre Island via the Kennedy Causeway, and for the first 14 miles of the seashore travel safely in a normal passenger car, before encountering road conditions that then require a four-wheel-drive vehicle. Padre and Mustang Islands are the longest of the barrier islands in Texas, and these islands and associated estuaries are among the most important natural wetland resources of the entire Gulf region. Nesting shore and marsh birds include five species of terns, eight herons and egrets, snowy and piping plovers, black-necked stilt, and black skimmer (Kutac, 1998). The islands are also important migration routes, with 35 species of warblers reported. A bird list with 329 bird species can be obtained from the seashore office at 20420 Park Rd. 22, Corpus Christi, TX 78418 or PO Box 181300, Corpus Christi, TX 78480 (Malaquite Visitor Center: 361-949-8068).

Perot Museum of Nature and Science. This newly completed Dallas museum has six floors, stands about 14 stories high, and cost 185 million dollars, so it is probably the most expensive natural history museum in the Great Plains. The biology division includes interactive dioramas of three Texas ecosystems. *Address:* 2201 N. Field St., Dallas, TX 75201 (214-428-5555).

Playa Lakes Wildlife Management Area. 1,492 acres (in three units). The only public access units of this WMA are the Taylor Lakes Unit (530 acres, 7 miles southeast of Clarendon in Donley County) and the Armstrong Unit (160 acres, 12 miles southwest of Dimmitt in Castro County). All the units consist of shortgrass prairie and have several seasonal playa lakes that attract many migrating water birds. The WMA is managed by Texas Parks and Wildlife, 3036 FM 3256, Paducah, Texas 79248 (806-492-3405).

Rita Blanca National Grassland. 93,000 acres. This national grassland is made up of shortgrass and mixed-grass prairies in western Texas along the Oklahoma and New Mexico borders (77,463 acres) with a separate unit in Oklahoma (15,800 acres). In addition to the grasslands, there are hundreds of seasonal playa lakes up to several hundred acres in size. The larger mammals include mule and white-tailed deer, pronghorns, coyotes, and swift foxes. Numerous prairie dog towns are also present (Moul, 2006). Breeding

grassland birds include the scaled quail, mountain plover, and grasshopper sparrow, but no bird lists are yet available. The address for both the Kiowa and Rita Blanca Grasslands is 714 Main St., Clayton, NM 88414 (575-374-9652).

Sabine Woods Bird Sanctuary. 30 acres. This sanctuary near Sabine Pass is owned by the Texas Ornithological Society, and its spring bird migration from mid-March to mid-May is reportedly nearly equal to the better-known High Island Audubon sanctuaries (see section). Sabine Woods is four miles west of Sabine Pass on Texas Hwy. 87. At the stop sign in the main square of Sabine Pass turn west where Hwy. 87 turns west. Then proceed about 4.2 miles on Hwy. 87 to a woodlot on the north (right side), immediately past the Petroleum Helicopters base. Note that the site's inconspicuous sign is easily overlooked. Birders are welcome at all times; access is through a marked gate. Mosquitoes can be bad after mid-May.

San Bernard National Wildlife Refuge. 2,414 acres. This NWR is located about ten miles south of Lake Jackson and 12 miles west of Freeport. San Bernard, Brazoria, and Big Boggy refuges collectively winter many migratory waterfowl, especially snow geese, with greater white-fronted, Canada, and Ross's geese present in smaller numbers. A checklist for the three-refuge complex contains 301 bird species and is available from the manager at 2547 CR316, Brazoria, TX 77422 (979-964-4011). It is also available online at https://www.fws.gov/refuge/San_Bernard/wildlife/species.html.

Santa Ana National Wildlife Refuge. 2,088 acres. Located seven miles south of Alamo, this refuge is regarded as one of the best birding sites in the Great Plains because of its great species diversity. About 400 species have been found within its 2,000 acres, including many Mexican species at the edge of their ranges. Neotropical species include great kiskadee, brown-crested flycatcher, rose-throated becard, northern beardless flycatcher, clay-colored robin, and rufous-backed robin. At least 61 species are common to abundant at the refuge during spring versus 53 species during fall and 41 during winter (Jones, 1990). There were at least 87 nesting birds among the 334 listed for the refuge by Jones in 1990. Jones also reported a total of 92 permanent resident bird species, so an

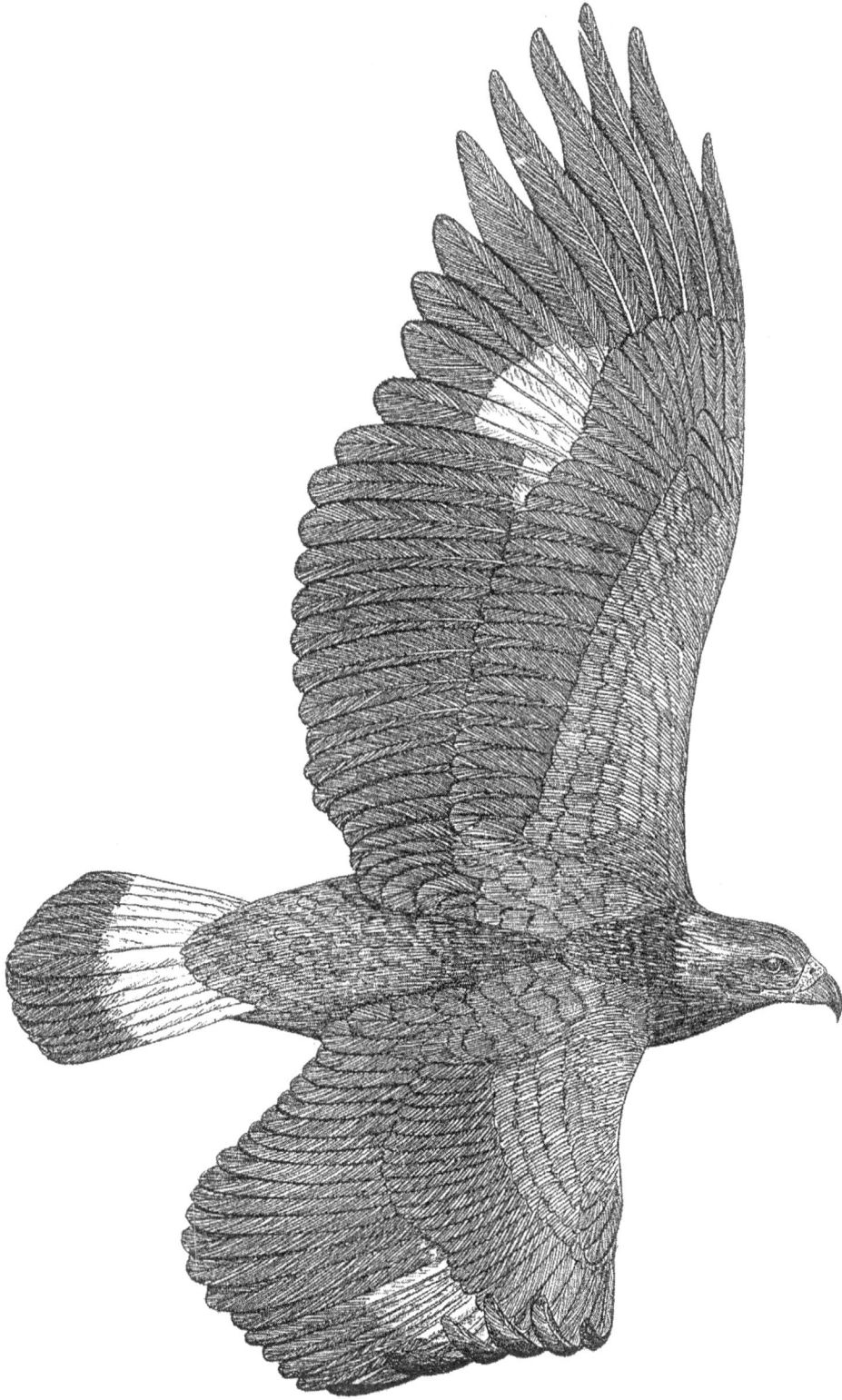

Adult golden eagle.

estimated minimum of 73 percent of the refuge's total bird diversity is migratory. The refuge list has a remarkable 43 warbler species (about 90 percent of the total North American species), most of them migratory. Many other migrants also stop here. During migration, thousands of broad-winged hawks pass overhead. A recent bird checklist included 396 species, and a total of 29 species of mammals and more than 450 species of plants have been reported. The bird list is available online at https://www.fws.gov/refuge/Santa_Ana/wildlife_and_habitat/species_lists.html or from the refuge office. *Address:* 3325 Green Jay Rd., Alamo, TX 78516 (956-784-7500).

Sea Rim State Park. 15,000 acres. Located five miles south of Texas Point NWR (see section), this coastal park has 5.2 miles of shoreline and 4,000 acres of marshlands. There are about 12 miles of hiking trails, observation blinds, and canoes and kayaks for rent. There is also an interpretive center and a 3,640-foot boardwalk extending into the saltwater marsh. The park was heavily damaged in 2008 by Hurricane Rita, so park conditions have perhaps changed considerably. Marsh birds occurring here include great blue heron; great, snowy, and cattle egrets; white and white-faced ibises; and roseate spoonbills (Kutac, 1998). Essentially all the ducks and geese that winter on the Gulf coast can be seen here. The park list has 29 species of waterfowl and 34 warblers. Alligators are also notably common. A checklist with 297 bird species can be obtained at the park office or found online at https://tpwd.texas.gov/state-parks/sea-rim/nature. *Address:* 19335 S. Gulfway Dr., Sabine Pass, TX 77655 (409-971-2559). McFaddin NWR (see section) is also nearby and has similar birds.

Texas Point National Wildlife Refuge. 8,900 acres. This refuge consists of fresh water to saline marshlands, with some wooded uplands and prairie ridges. It is located 12 miles east of McFaddin NWR (see section) along Texas Hwy. 87 and near the Louisiana border. Like McFaddin, it is an important wintering area for geese and ducks. Texas Point NWR is managed from McFaddin NWR at 7950 S. Gulfway Dr., PO Box 358, Sabine Pass, TX 77655 (409-971-2909).

Welder Wildlife Foundation. 7,800 acres. Welder Wildlife Foundation is a privately owned nature preserve and research facility. It is located eight miles north of Sinton and includes coastal plains and uplands habitats. The site's bird list includes 372 species, 96 of which nest or have nested on the preserve, and also includes 41 shorebirds, 24 hawks, and 41 warblers. More than 1,300 plant taxa, 55 mammals, and 55 reptiles and amphibians have also been reported. The facility is normally open to the public each Thursday afternoon at 3 p.m. For more information, contact the staff at PO Box 1400, Sinton, TX 78387 (361-364-2643).

Ord's kangaroo rat

References

General References

Bailey, R. G. 1995. *Descriptions of the Ecoregions of the United States.* Washington, DC: US Department of Agriculture.

Bolen, E. G., L. M. Smith, and H. L. Schramm, Jr. 1989. "Playa Lakes: Prairie Wetlands of the Southern High Plains." *Bioscience* 39: 615–23.

Burroughs, R. D. 1961. *The Natural History of the Lewis and Clark Expedition.* East Lansing: Michigan State University Press. 340 pp.

Elson, J. A., 1967. "Geology of Glacial Lake Agassiz." In *Life, Land and Water*, edited by W. Mayar-Oakes, 37–96. Winnipeg: University of Manitoba Press.

Feldhamer, G. A., B. C. Thompson, and J. A. Chapman. 2003. *Wild Mammals of North America: Biology, Management, and Conservation.* Baltimore: Johns Hopkins University Press. 1216 pp.

Forsberg, M., D. O'Brien, D. Wishart, and T. Kooser. 2009. *Great Plains: America's Lingering Wild.* Chicago: University of Chicago Press. 256 pp.

Gentile, R. J. 2015. *Rocks and Fossils of the Central United States, with Special Emphasis on the Greater Kansas City Area.* 2nd ed. University of Kansas, Department of Geology and Paleontological Institute, Special Publication 8. 221 pp.

Johnsgard, P. A. 1994. *Arena Birds: Sexual Selection and Behavior.* Washington, DC: Smithsonian Institution Press. 330 pp.

Johnsgard, P. A. 2001. "A Century of Ornithology in Nebraska: A Personal View." In *Contributions to the History of North American Ornithology, Vol. II*, edited by W. E. Davis and J. A. Jackson, 329–55. Boston: Nuttall Ornithological Club. http://digitalcommons.unl.edu/biosciornithology/26

Kays, R. W., and D. E. Wilson. 2002. *Mammals of North America.* Princeton, NJ: Princeton University Press. 818 pp.

Küchler, A. W. 1964. *Potential Natural Vegetation of the Conterminous United States.* American Geographical Society, Special Publication No. 36.

Küchler, A. 1977. *Potential Natural Vegetation of the Coterminous United States.* New York: American Geographical Society.

Kurten, B., and E. Anderson. 1980. *Pleistocene Mammals of North America.* New York: Columbia University Press. 442 pp.

Martin, A. C., H. S. Zim, and A. L. Nelson. 1951. *American Wildlife and Plants.* New York: McGraw Hill. 512 pp.

National Geographic Society. 2011. *The 10 Best of Everything National Parks.* Washington, DC: National Geographic Society. 478 pp.

Omernik, J. M. 1987. "Ecoregions of the Coterminous United States." *Annals of the Association of American Geographers* 77: 118–25.

Paleontological Research Institute. n.d. *The Teacher-Friendly Guide to the Earth Science of the Northwest Central US Region Two: The Great Plains.* (Includes MT, ID, WY, ND, SD, and NE.) Ithaca, NY: Paleontological Research Institute.

Paleontological Research Institute. n.d. *The Teacher-Friendly Guide to the Earth Science of the South Central US Region Four: The Great Plains.* (Includes KS, MO, OK, AR, TX, and LA). Ithaca, NY: Paleontological Research Institute.

Phillips, H. W. 2003. *Plants of the Lewis and Clark Expedition.* Missoula, MT: Mountain Press. 277 pp.

Poole, A. 2000–2018. *The Birds of North America Online.* Cornell University Laboratory of Ornithology. (Life histories of more than 600 species of North American bird species, now partly updated online from printed versions of the 1990s and early 2000s.) https://birdsna.org/

Rich, T. C., et al., eds. 2004. *North American Landbird Conservation Plan.* Ithaca, NY: Partners in Flight and Cornell University Laboratory of Ornithology. 84 pp.

Robinson, E. B., and J. L. Dietz. 2017. "Great Plains." *Encylopaedia Britannica.* https://www.britannica.com/place/Great-Plains

Sauer, J. R., D. K. Niven, J. E. Hines, D. J. Ziolkowski, Jr., K. L. Pardieck, J. E. Fallon, and W. A. Link. 2017. *The North American Breeding Bird Survey, Results and Analysis 1966–2015.* Version 2.07. Laurel, MD: USGS Patuxent Wildlife Research Center.

Smith, L. M. 2003. *Playas of the Great Plains*. Austin: University of Texas Press.

Steiert, J. 1995. *Playas: Jewels of the Plains*. Lubbock: Texas Tech University Press. 134 pp.

US Fish and Wildlife Service (USFWS). 2008. *Birds of Conservation Concern 2008*. Arlington, VA: US Department of the Interior, Fish and Wildlife Service, Division of Migratory Bird Management. 85 pp. https://www.fws.gov/birds/management/managed-species/birds-of-conservation-concern.php

US Geological Survey, Patuxent Wildlife Research Center. 2015. The North American Breeding Bird Survey, Results and Analysis 1966–2013. Version 1.30.2015. https://pubs.er.usgs.gov/publication/70180972

van der Valk, A. G., ed. 1989. *Northern Prairie Wetlands*. Ames: Iowa State University Press.

Whittaker, J. O., Jr. 1980. *National Audubon Society Field Guide to North American Mammals*. Rev. ed. New York: Knopf. 935 pp.

Wilson, D. E., and S. Ruff. 1999. *The Smithsonian Book of North American Mammals*. Washington, DC: Smithsonian Institution Press. 816 pp.

Zevellof, S. I., and F. R. Collett. 1988. *Mammals of the Intermountain West*. Salt Lake City: University of Utah Press. 363 pp.

Multistate Surveys and Guides

Johnsgard, P. A. 1976. "The Grassy Heartland." In *Our Continent: A Natural History of North America*, 234–64. Washington, DC: National Geographic Society. 398 pp.

Johnsgard, P. A. 1986. *Birds of the Rocky Mountains, with Particular Reference to National Parks in the Northern Rocky Mountain Region*. Boulder: Colorado Associated University Press. 504 pp.

Johnsgard, P. A. 2003. *Lewis and Clark on the Great Plains: A Natural History*. Lincoln: University of Nebraska Press. 143 pp.

Johnsgard, P. A. 2011. *Rocky Mountain Birds: Birds and Birding in the Central and Northern Rockies*. University of Nebraska–Lincoln DigitalCommons and Zea Books. 274 pp. http://digitalcommons.unl.edu/zeabook/7. Print edition available from http://www.lulu.com/shop/paul-johnsgard/rocky-mountain-birds/paperback/product-18607006.html

Johnsgard, P. A. 2012. *Wetland Birds of the Central Plains: South Dakota, Nebraska, and Kansas*. University of Nebraska–Lincoln DigitalCommons and Zea Books. 275 pp. http://digitalcommons.unl.edu/zeabook/8/. Print edition available from http://www.lulu.com/shop/paul-johnsgard/wetland-birds-of-the-central-plains-south-dakota-nebraska-and-kansas/paperback/product-18889896.html

Jones, J. O. 1990. *Where the Birds Are: A Guide to All 50 States and Canada*. New York: William Morrow. 400 pp.

Knopf, F. L, and F. B. Samson, eds. 1997. *Ecology and Conservation of Great Plains Vertebrates*. Ecological Studies, vol. 125. New York: Springer.

Lamb, S. 1996. *The Southern Rockies: Colorado and Utah*. The Smithsonian Guides to Natural America. New York: Random House. 304 pp.

Moulton, G. E., ed. 1993–99. *The Journals of the Lewis and Clark Expedition*. 13 vols. Lincoln: University of Nebraska Press.

Pettingill, O. S. 1981. *A Guide to Bird Finding West of the Mississippi*. New York: Oxford University Press. 783 pp.

Riley, L., and W. Riley. 1979. *Guide to the National Wildlife Refuges*. Garden City, NY: Anchor Press/Doubleday. 653 pp.

Schmidt, T. 1995. *The Northern Rockies: Idaho, Montana, Wyoming*. The Smithsonian Guides to Natural America. New York: Random House. 304 pp.

Shepard, L. 1996. *The Northern Plains: Minnesota, North Dakota, and South Dakota*. The Smithsonian Guides to Natural America. New York: Random House. 286 pp.

White, M. 1996. *The South-Central States: Texas, Oklahoma, Arkansas, Louisiana, Mississippi*. The Smithsonian Guides to Natural America. New York: Random House. 284 pp.

White, M. 1999a. *Guide to Birdwatching Sites: Western US*. Washington, DC: National Geographic Society. 224 pp. (Includes states east to ND, SD, KS, OK, and western TX.)

White, M. 1999b. *Guide to Birdwatching Sites: Eastern US*. Washington, DC: National Geographic Society. 320 pp. (Includes states west to MN, IA, MO, and eastern TX.)

Winkler, S. 1997. *The Heartland: Illinois, Iowa, Nebraska*. The Smithsonian Guides to Natural America. New York: Random House. 304 pp.

Grassland and Vegetation

Adelmann, C., and B. L. Schwartz. 2001. *Prairie Directory of North America*. Wilmette, IL: Lawndale Enterprises. 352 pp.

Bachand, R. R. 2001. *The American Prairie: Going, Going, Gone?* Boulder, CO: National Wildlife Federation. 28 pp.

Barkley, T., ed. 1977. *Atlas of the Flora of the Great Plains*. Ames: Iowa State University Press. 600 pp.

Barnard, I. 2014. *Field Guide to the Common Grasses of Oklahoma, Kansas, and Nebraska*. Lawrence: University Press of Kansas. 176 pp. (Includes 70 species.)

Best, K. E., J. Looman, and J. B. Campbell. 1971. *Prairie Grasses*. Pub. No. 1413. Saskatoon, SK: Canada Department of Agriculture.

Bock, C., and J. Bock. 2000. *The View from Bald Hill: Thirty Years in an Arizona Grassland*. Berkeley: University of California Press. 197 pp.

Brown, L. 1985. *Grasslands.* New York: Knopf.

Budd, A. C. 1957. *Wild Plants of the Canada Prairies.* Pub. No. 985. Saskatoon, SK: Canada Department of Agriculture.

Chadde, S. W. 2012. *Wetland Plants of the Northern Great Plains: A Complete Guide to the Wetland and Aquatic Plants of North and South Dakota, Nebraska, Eastern Montana, and Eastern Wyoming.* Bogman Guide. CreateSpace Independent Publishing Platform. 628 pp.

Chadde, S. W. 2017. *Prairie Plants of Illinois: A Field Guide to the Prairie Grasses and Wildflowers of Illinois and the Midwest.* Pathfinder Books. CreateSpace Independent Publishing Platform. 290 pp.

Chadwick, D. H. 1993. "The American Prairie." *National Geographic* 184: 90–119.

Chapman, K. A., A. Fischer, and M. K. Ziegenhagen. 1998. *Valley of Grass: Tallgrass Prairie and Parkland of the Red River Region.* St. Cloud, MN: North Star Press. 122 pp.

Costello, D. F. 1969. *The Prairie World.* New York: Thomas Y. Crowell. 242 pp.

Cushman, R. C., and S. R. Jones. 1988. *The Shortgrass Prairie.* Boulder, CO: Pruett Publishing. 510 pp.

Cushman, R. C., and S. R. Jones. 2004. *The North American Prairie.* Boston: Houghton Mifflin.

Duncan, P. D. 1978. *Tallgrass Prairie: The Inland Sea.* Kansas City, MO: Lowell Press. 113 pp.

Earle, A. S., and J. L. Reveal. 2003. *Lewis and Clark's Green World: The Expedition and Its Plants.* Helena, MT: Far Country Press. 256 pp.

Farney, D. 1980. "The Tallgrass Prairie: Can It Be Saved?" *National Geographic*, January, 1980, 157(1), 37–61.

Freeman, C. C., and E. K. Schofield. 1991. *Roadside Wildflowers of the Southern Great Plains.* Lawrence: University Press of Kansas. 280 pp. (Includes southern Nebraska to the Texas panhandle.)

Great Plains Flora Association. 1977. *Atlas of the Flora of the Great Plains.* Ames: Iowa State University Press. 600 pp.

Great Plains Flora Association. 1986. *Flora of the Great Plains.* Lawrence: University Press of Kansas. 402 pp.

Gruchow, P. 1985. *Journal of a Prairie Year.* Minneapolis: University of Minnesota Press. 144 pp.

Hubbard, D. E. 1989. *Wetland Values in the Prairie Pothole Region of Minnesota and the Dakotas.* Brookings, SD: US Fish and Wildlife Service, Cooperative Research Unit, Biological Report 88 (43).

Johnsgard, P. A. 1976. "The Grassy Heartland." In *Our Continent: A Natural History of North America*, 234–63. Washington, DC: National Geographic Society.

Johnsgard, P. A. 1984. *The Platte: Channels in Time.* Lincoln: University of Nebraska Press. 176 pp. (2nd ed., 2008)

Johnsgard, P. A. 1995. *This Fragile Land: A Natural History of the Nebraska Sandhills.* Lincoln: University of Nebraska Press. 256 pp.

Johnsgard, P. A. 2003. *Faces of the Great Plains: Prairie Wildlife.* Lawrence: University Press of Kansas. 190 pp.

Johnsgard, P. A. 2003. *Great Wildlife of the Great Plains.* Lawrence: University Press of Kansas. 309 pp.

Johnsgard, P. A. 2005. *Prairie Dog Empire: A Saga of the Shortgrass Prairie.* Lincoln: University of Nebraska Press. 142 pp.

Johnsgard, P. A. 2007. *The Niobrara: A River Running Through Time.* Lincoln: University of Nebraska Press. 373 pp.

Johnsgard, P. A. 2008. *A Guide to the Tallgrass Prairies of Eastern Nebraska and Adjacent States.* University of Nebraska–Lincoln DigitalCommons and Zea Books. 156 pp. http://digitalcommons.unl.edu/biosciornithology/39/

Johnsgard, P. A. 2008. *Wind Through the Buffalo Grass: A Lakota Story Cycle.* Lincoln: Plains Chronicles Press. 214 pp.

Johnsgard, P. A. 2009. "Autumn on the Prairie: Nebraska's Grasses." *Nebraska Life*, September–October 2009, 18–21.

Johnsgard, P. A. 2009. "Forbs and Grasses and Cheshire Cats: What Is a Tallgrass Prairie?" *Prairie Fire*, December 2009, 3, 9. http://www.prairiefirenewspaper. com/2009/12/forbs-and-grasses-and-cheshire-cats-what-is-a-tallgrass-prairie

Johnson, R. R., L. T. Haight, M. M. Riffey, and J. M. Simpson. 1980. Brushland/Steppe Bird Populations. In *Workshop Proceedings: Management of Western Forests and Grasslands for Nongame Birds*, edited by Richard M. DeGraaf and Nancy G. Tilghman, 98–112. Ogden, UT: USDA Forest Service General Technical Report INT-86.

Kirkpatrick, Z. 2008. *Wildflowers of the Western Plains.* Lincoln: University of Nebraska Press.

Kirt, R. R. 1995. *Prairie Plants of the Midwest: Identification and Ecology.* Champaign, IL: Stipes Publishing. 137 pp.

Kurz, D. 2004. *Illinois Wildflowers.* Cloudland.net Publishing (online publisher). 256 pp.

Ladd, D. 2005. *Tallgrass Prairie Wildflowers: A Field Guide.* 2nd ed. Guilford, CT: Globe Pequot Press. 263 pp.

Larabee, A., and J. Altman, 2001. *Last Stand of the Tallgrass Prairie.* New York: Michael Friedman Publishing Group. 144 pp.

Madson, J. 1993. *Tallgrass Prairie.* Helena, MT: Falcon Press. 111 pp.

Madson, J. 1995. *Where the Sky Began: Land of the Tallgrass Prairie.* Ames: Iowa State University Press. 340 pp.

Malin, J. 1984. *History and Ecology: Studies of the Grasslands.* Lincoln: University of Nebraska Press. 376 pp.

Manning, R. 1955. *Grassland: The History, Biology, Politics, and Promise of the American Prairie.* New York: Viking. 320 pp.

Moul, F. 2006. *The National Grasslands: A Guide to America's Undiscovered Treasures.* Lincoln: University of Nebraska Press. 155 pp.

Pasture and Range Plants. 1963. Bartlesville, OK: Phillips Petroleum Co. 176 pp. (Includes 70 species of grasses and more than 80 species of forbs.)

Richett, H. W. 1973. *Wildflowers of the United States: The Central Mountains and Plains.* Vol. 6, parts 1–3. New York: New York Botanical Gardens and McGraw Hill.

Risser, P. G., et al. 1981. *The True Prairie Ecosystem.* Stroudsburg, PA: Hutchinson and Ross. 557 pp.

Runkel, S. T., and D. M. Roosa. 2010. *Wildflowers of the Tallgrass Prairie: The Upper Midwest.* 2nd ed. Iowa City: University of Iowa Press. 279 pp.

Samson, F. H., and F. L. Knopf. 1996. *Prairie Conservation: Preserving North America's Most Endangered Ecosystem.* Washington, DC: Island Press. 240 pp.

Savage, C. 2004. *Prairie: A Natural History.* Vancouver, BC: Greystone Books. 320 pp.

Seal, U.S., E. T. Thorne, M. A. Bogan, and S. H. Anderson, eds. 1989. *Conservation Biology and the Black-footed Ferret.* New Haven, CT: Yale University Press. 328 pp.

Shantz, H. L. 1923. "The Natural Vegetation of the Great Plains Region." *Annals of the Association of American Geographers* 13 (2): 81–107.

Shantz, H. L., and R. Zon. 1924. "Natural Vegetation." In *Atlas of American Agriculture.* 28 pp. Washington, DC: US Department of Agriculture.

Shirely, S. 1994. *Restoring the Tallgrass Prairie: An Illustrated Manual for Iowa and the Upper Midwest.* Iowa City: University of Iowa Press. 346 pp.

Smith A. 1996. *Big Bluestem: Journey into the Tall Grass.* Tulsa, OK: Council Oak Books. 304 pp.

Smith, L. M. 2003. *Playas of the Great Plains.* Austin: University of Texas Press. 257 pp.

Steiert, J. 1985. *Playas: Jewels of the Plains.* Lubbock: Texas Tech University Press.

Strickler, D. 1986. *Prairie Wildflowers.* Columbia Falls, MT: Flower Press.

Stubbendieck, J., and S. L. Hatch. 1997. *North American Range Plants. 5th ed.* Lincoln: University of Nebraska Press. 501 pp.

Van Bruggen, T. 1983. *Wildflowers, Grasses, and Other Plants of the Northern Plains and Black Hills.* 3rd ed. Interior, SD: Badlands Natural History Association. 96 pp.

Vance, F. R., J. R. Jowsey, J. S. McLean, and F. A. Switzer. 1999. *Wildflowers of the Northern Great Plains.* 3rd ed. Minneapolis: University of Minnesota Press. 384 pp.

Weaver, J. E. 1964. *North American Prairie.* Lincoln, NE: Johnson Publishing. 357 pp.

Weaver, J. E. 1968. *Prairie Plants and Their Environment.* Lincoln: University of Nebraska Press. 276 pp.

Weaver, J. E., and F. W. Alberson. 1956. *Grasslands of the Great Plains: Their Nature and Use.* Lincoln, NE: Johnson Publishing. 395 pp.

Weeds of the North Central States. 1981. University of Illinois Urbana–Champaign, Agricultural Extension Bulletin 772. 303 pp. (Includes more than 230 species.)

Weniger, D. 1969. *Cacti of the Southwest: Texas, New Mexico, Oklahoma, Arkansas, and Louisiana.* Austin: University of Texas Press. 356 pp.

Williams, D. 2010. *The Tallgrass Prairie Center Guide to Seed and Seedling Identification in the Upper Midwest.* Iowa City: University of Iowa Press. 132 pp.

Williams, D. 2016. *The Prairie in Seed: Identifying Seed-Bearing Prairie Plants in the Upper Midwest.* Iowa City: University of Iowa Press. 115 pp.

Winkler, S. 2004. *Prairie: A North American Guide.* Iowa City: University of Iowa Press. 146 pp.

Wright, H. E., Jr. 1970. "Vegetational History of the Great Plains." In *Pleistocene and Recent Environments of the Central Great Plains,* The University of Kansas Paleontological Contributions, Special Publication 3, edited by Wakefield Dort, Jr., and Knox Jones, Jr., 157–72. Lawrence: University Press of Kansas.

Great Plains Fauna

Mammals

Butts, K. O., and J. C. Lewis. 1982. "The Importance of Prairie Dog Towns to Burrowing Owls in Oklahoma." *Proceedings of the Oklahoma Academy of Science* 62: 46–52.

Chapman, J. A., and G. A. Feldhamer, eds. 1982. *Wild Mammals of North America: Biology, Management, and Economics.* Baltimore: Johns Hopkins University Press. 1,147 pp.

Collenbach, E. 2000. *Bring Back the Buffalo! A Sustainable Future for America's Great Plains.* Berkeley: University of California Press. 303 pp.

Dary, D. A. 1974. *The Buffalo Book: The Saga of an American Symbol.* New York: Avon Books. 374 pp.

Desmond, M. J., J. A. Savidge, and K. M. Eskridge. 2000. "Correlations between Burrowing Owl and Black-tailed Prairie Dog Declines: A 7-Year Analysis." *Journal of Wildlife Management* 64(4): 1067–75.

Doby, J. F. 2006. *The Voice of the Coyote.* 2nd ed. Edison, NJ: Castle Books. 386 pp.

Graves, R. A. 2001. *The Prairie Dog: Sentinel of the Plains.* Lubbock: Texas Tech University Press. 133 pp.

Haines, F. 1995. *The Buffalo.* Norman: University of Oklahoma Press. 244 pp.

Hall, E. R. 1981. *The Mammals of North America.* 2 vols. New York: Wiley. 1,181 pp.

Hanson, H. C. 1997. *The Giant Canada Goose.* Rev. ed. Carbondale: Southern Illinois University Press. 252 pp.

Hoogland, J. L. 1995. *The Black-tailed Prairie Dog: Social Life of a Burrowing Animal.* Chicago: University of Chicago Press. 562 pp.

Hoogland, J. L., ed. 2006. *Conservation of the Black-tailed Prairie Dog: Saving North America's Western Grasslands.* Washington, DC: Island Press. 342 pp.

Laydet, F. 1988. *The Coyote.* Norman: University of Oklahoma Press.

McHugh, T. 1972. *The Time of the Buffalo.* New York: Knopf. 383 pp.

Miller, B., R. P. Reading, and S. Forrest. 1996. *Prairie Night: Black-Footed Ferrets and the Recovery of Endangered Species.* Washington, DC: Smithsonian Institution Press. 254 pp.

Murie, O. J. 1954. *A Field Guide to Animal Tracks.* Boston: Houghton Mifflin. 400 pp.

National Wildlife Federation. 1998. "Petition to List the Black-tailed Prairie Dog under the Endangered Species Act." Washington, DC: National Wildlife Federation.

Putnam, R. 1988. *The Natural History of Deer.* Ithaca, NY: Comstock Press. 191 pp.

Ryden, H. 1975. *God's Dog.* New York: Coward, McCann, and Geoghegan. 288 pp.

Sidle, J. G., M. Ball, T. Byer, J. J. Chynoweth, G. Foli, R. Hodorff, G. Moravek, R. Peterson, and D. N. Svingen. 2001. "Occurrence of Burrowing Owls in Black-tailed Prairie Dog Colonies on Great Plains National Grasslands." *Journal of Raptor Research* 35: 316–21.

Turbak, G. 1995. *Pronghorn: Portrait of the American Antelope.* New York: Cooper Square. 138 pp.

Van Wormer, J. 1969. *World of the American Elk.* Philadelphia: J. B. Lippincott. 159 pp.

Zontek, K. 2007. *Buffalo Nation: American Indian Efforts to Restore the Bison.* Lincoln: University of Nebraska Press. 256 pp.

Birds

Alderfer, J., ed. 2008. *Complete Birds of North America.* Washington, DC: Smithsonian Institution Press. 664 pp.

Allen, D. L., ed. 1956. *Pheasants in North America.* Harrisburg, PA: Stackpole and Washington, DC: Wildlife Management Institute.

Austin, G. R. 1964. *The World of the Red-tailed Hawk.* Philadelphia: Lippincott. 128 pp.

Banko, W. 1960. *The Trumpeter Swan.* North American Fauna No. 63. Washington, DC: US Fish and Wildlife Service. 214 pp.

Bent, A. C. 1919. *Life Histories of North American Diving Birds.* Smithsonian Institution, US National Museum Bulletin 107. 245 pp.

Bent, A. C. 1921. *Life Histories of North American Gulls and Terns.* Smithsonian Institution, US National Museum Bulletin 113. 345 pp.

Bent, A. C. 1922. *Life Histories of North American Petrels and Pelicans and Their Allies.* Smithsonian Institution, US National Museum Bulletin 121. 339 pp.

Bent, A. C. 1923. *Life Histories of North American Wild Fowl*, Part 1, Smithsonian Institution, US National Museum Bulletin 126. 245 pp.

Bent, A. C. 1925. *Life Histories of North American Wild Fowl*, Part 2. Smithsonian Institution, US National Museum Bulletin 130. 276 pp.

Bent, A. C. 1926. *Life Histories of North American Marsh Birds.* Smithsonian Institution, US National Museum Bulletin 135. 490 pp.

Bent, A. C. 1927. *Life Histories of North American Shorebirds*, I. Smithsonian Institution, US National Museum Bulletin 142. 420 pp.

Bent, A. C. 1929. *Life Histories of North American Shorebirds*, II. Smithsonian Institution, US National Museum Bulletin 146. 412 pp.

Bent, A. C. 1932. *Life Histories of North American Gallinaceous Birds.* Smithsonian Institution, US National Museum Bulletin 162. 490 pp.

Bent, A. C. 1937. *Life Histories of North American Birds of Prey*, Part 1. Smithsonian Institution, US National Museum Bulletin 167. 409 pp.

Bent, A. C. 1938. *Life Histories of North American Birds of Prey*, Part 2. Smithsonian Institution, US National Museum Bulletin 170. 428 pp.

Bent, A. C. 1939. *Life Histories of North American Woodpeckers.* Smithsonian Institution, US National Museum Bulletin 174. 322 pp.

Bent, A. C. 1940. *Life Histories of North American Cuckoos, Goatsuckers, Hummingbirds, and Their Allies.* Smithsonian Institution, US National Museum Bulletin 176. 506 pp.

Bent, A. C. 1942. *Life Histories of North American Flycatchers, Larks, Swallows, and Their Allies.* Smithsonian Institution, US National Museum Bulletin 179. 555 pp.

Bent, A. C. 1946. *Life Histories of North American Jays, Crows, and Titmice.* Smithsonian Institution, US National Museum Bulletin 191. 495 pp.

Bent, A. C. 1948. *Life Histories of North American Nuthatches, Wrens, Thrashers, and Their Allies.* Smithsonian Institution, US National Museum Bulletin 195. 475 pp.

Bent, A. C. 1949. *Life Histories of North American Thrushes, Kinglets, and Their Allies.* Smithsonian Institution, US National Museum Bulletin 196. 454 pp.

Bent, A. C. 1950. *Life Histories of North American Wagtails, Shrikes, Vireos, and Their Allies.* Smithsonian Institution, US National Museum Bulletin 197. 411 pp.

Bent, A. C. 1953. *Life Histories of North American Wood Warblers.* Smithsonian Institution, US National Museum Bulletin 203. 734 pp.

Bent, A. C. 1958. *Life Histories of North American Blackbirds, Orioles, Tanagers, and Allies.* Smithsonian Institution, US National Museum Bulletin 211. 549 pp.

Bent, A. C. 1968. *Life Histories of North American Cardinals, Grosbeaks, Buntings, Towhees, Finches, Sparrows, and*

Allies (in three parts). Smithsonian Institution, US National Museum Bulletin 237. 1,889 pp.

Cade, T. J. 1982. *The Falcons of the World.* Ithaca, NY: Cornell University Press. 188 pp.

Desmond, M. J., J. A. Savidge, and K. M. Eskridge. 2000. "Correlations between Burrowing Owl and Black-tailed Prairie Dog Declines: A 7-Year Analysis." *Journal of Wildlife Management* 64(4): 1067–75.

Erskine, A. J. 1972. *Buffleheads.* Canadian Wildlife Service Monograph Series, No. 4. Ottawa, ON: Information Canada.

Green, G. A., and R. G. Anthony. 1989. "Nesting Success and Habitat Relationships of Burrowing Owls in the Columbia Basin, Oregon." *Condor* 91: 347–54.

Griscom, L., and A. Sprunt, Jr., eds. 1957. *The Warblers of North America.* New York: Devin-Adair. 356 pp.

Hancock, J., and H. Elliott. 1978. *The Herons of the World.* New York: Harper & Row. 304 pp.

Haug, E. A, B. A. Millsap, and M. S. Martell. 1993. "Burrowing Owl (*Athene cunicularia*)." In *Birds of North America*, no. 61, edited by A. Poole and F. Gill. Philadelphia: The Academy of Natural Sciences and Washington, DC: American Ornithologists' Union.

Hickey, J. J., ed. 1969. *Peregrine Falcon Populations: Their Biology and Decline.* Madison: University of Wisconsin Press. 446 pp.

James, P. C., and R. H. M. Espie. 1997. "Current Status of the Burrowing Owl in North America: An Agency Survey." In *The Burrowing Owl: Its Biology and Management, Including the Proceedings of the First Burrowing Owl Symposium*, edited by J. L. Lincer and K. Steenhof, 3–5. Research Report no. 9. Boise, ID: Raptor Research Foundation. 177 pp.

Johnsgard, P. A. 1970. "Copulatory Behavior in the American Bittern." *Auk* 97: 868–869.

Johnsgard, P. A. 1973. *Grouse and Quails of North America.* Lincoln: University of Nebraska Press, Lincoln. 553 pp. http://digitalcommons.unl.edu/bioscigrouse/1/

Johnsgard, P. A. 1979. *Birds of the Great Plains: Breeding Species and Their Distribution.* Lincoln: University of Nebraska Press. 538 pp. (Primary coverage is from North Dakota through Oklahoma and the Texas panhandle; parts of adjoining states within the Great Plains are included.)

Johnsgard, P. A. 1986. *Birds of the Rocky Mountains, with Particular Reference to National Parks in the Northern Rocky Mountain Region.* Boulder: Colorado Associated University Press. 504 pp. (Coverage is from northern Colorado to Alberta.)

Johnsgard, P. A. 1988. *The Quails, Partridges, and Francolins of the World.* Oxford, UK: Oxford University Press. 264 pp.

Johnsgard, P. A. 1990. *Hawks, Eagles, and Falcons of North America: Biology and Natural History.* Washington, DC: Smithsonian Institution Press. 403 pp.

Johnsgard, P. A. 1997. *The Hummingbirds of North America.* 2nd ed. Washington, DC: Smithsonian Institution Press. 277 pp.

Johnsgard, P. A. 2002. *Grassland Grouse and Their Conservation.* Washington, DC: Smithsonian Institution Press. 157 pp.

Johnsgard, P. A. 2002. *North American Owls: Biology and Natural History.* 2nd ed. Washington, DC: Smithsonian Institution Press. 298 pp.

Johnsgard, P. A. 2006. "The Howdy Owl and the Prairie Dog." *Birding.* January/February 2006, 40–44. http://publications.aba.org/birding_archive_files/v38n1p40.pdf

Johnsgard, P. A. 2008. *The Platte: Channels in Time.* 2nd ed. Lincoln: University of Nebraska Press. 176 pp.

Johnsgard, P. A. 2009. *A Nebraska Bird-Finding Guide.* University of Nebraska–Lincoln DigitalCommons and Zea Books. 152 pp. http://digitalcommons.unl.edu/biosciornithology/51/. Print edition available from http://www.lulu.com/shop/paul-johnsgard/a-nebraska-bird-finding-guide/paperback/product-21768130.html.

Johnsgard, P. A. 2011. *Rocky Mountain Birds: Birds and Birding in the Central and Northern Rockies.* University of Nebraska–Lincoln DigitalCommons and Zea Books. 274 pp. http://digitalcommons.unl.edu/zeabook/7/. Print edition available from http://www.lulu.com/shop/paul-johnsgard/rocky-mountain-birds/paperback/product-18607006.html. (Coverage is from southern Colorado to Alberta.)

Johnsgard, P. A. 2011. *Sandhill and Whooping Cranes: Ancient Voices over America's Wetlands.* Lincoln: University of Nebraska Press. 155 pp.

Johnsgard, P. A. 2012. *Wetland Birds of the Central Plains: South Dakota, Nebraska, and Kansas.* University of Nebraska–Lincoln DigitalCommons and Zea Books. 275 pp. http://digitalcommons.unl.edu/zeabook/8/. Print edition available from http://www.lulu.com/shop/paul-johnsgard/wetland-birds-of-the-central-plains-south-dakota-nebraska-and-kansas/paperback/product-18889896.html.

Johnsgard, P. A. 2012. *Wings over the Great Plains: Bird Migrations in the Central Flyway.* University of Nebraska–Lincoln and Zea Books. 249 pp. http://digitalcommons.unl.edu/zeabook/13/. Print edition available from http://www.lulu.com/shop/paul-johnsgard/wings-over-the-great-plains-bird-migrations-in-the-central-flyway/paperback/product-20522789.html.

Johnsgard, P. A. 2015. *A Chorus of Cranes: The Cranes of North America and the World.* Boulder: University Press of Colorado. 242 pp.

Johnsgard, P. 2016. "Bittern Surprise." *BirdWatching* 30 (2): 36–39.

Johnsgard, P. A. 2016. *The North American Grouse: Their Biology and Behavior.* University of Nebraska–Lincoln DigitalCommons and Zea Books. 183 pp. https://digitalcommons.unl.edu/zeabook/41/.

Johnsgard, P. A. 2017. *The North American Quails, Partridges, and Pheasants*. University of Nebraska–Lincoln DigitalCommons and Zea Books. 131 pp. http://digitalcommons.unl.edu/zeabook/58/. Print edition available from http://www.lulu.com/shop/paul-johnsgard/the-north-american-quails-partridges-and-pheasants/paperback/product-23364385.html.

Johnson, D. H., ed. Various dates. *Effects of Management Practices on Grassland Birds*. Jamestown, ND: Northern Prairie Wildlife Research Center. https://www.npwrc.usgs.gov/Effects-of-Management-Practices-on-Grassland-Birds-links (Species documented as of 2017 include American bittern, Baird's sparrow, bobolink, Brewer's sparrow, burrowing owl, chestnut-collared longspur, clay-colored sparrow, dickcissel, eastern meadowlark, ferruginous hawk, field sparrow, golden eagle, grasshopper sparrow, greater prairie-chicken, greater sage-grouse, Henslow's sparrow, horned lark, lark bunting, lark sparrow, Le Conte's sparrow, lesser prairie-chicken, loggerhead shrike, long-billed curlew, marbled godwit, McCown's longspur, merlin, mountain plover, Nelson's sparrow, northern harrier, prairie falcon, Savannah sparrow, sedge wren, short-eared owl, Sprague's pipit, Swainson's hawk, upland sandpiper, vesper sparrow, western meadowlark, willet, and Wilson's phalarope.)

Jorgensen, J. G., and M. B. Brown. 2017. "Temporal Migration Shifts in the Aransas–Wood Buffalo Population of Whooping Cranes (*Grus americana*) across North America." *Waterbirds* 40: 195–208.

Kroodsma, R. L. 1970. "North Dakota Species Pairs. I. Hybridization in Buntings, Grosbeaks, and Orioles, II. Species' Recognition Behavior of Territorial Male Rose-breasted and Black-headed Grosbeaks (*Pheucticus*)." PhD diss., North Dakota State University, Fargo.

Ohlendorf, R. R. 1975. *Golden Eagle Country*. New York: Knopf.

Palmer, R. S., ed. 1962. *Handbook of North American Birds, Vol. I. Loons through Flamingos*. New Haven, CT: Yale University Press. 567 pp.

Palmer, R. S., ed. 1976. *Handbook of North American Birds, Vols. 2 & 3. Waterfowl*. New Haven, CT: Yale University Press. 521 and 560 pp.

Palmer, R. S., ed. 1988. *Handbook of North American Birds, Vols. 4 & 5. Diurnal Raptors*. New Haven, CT: Yale University Press. 433 and 465 pp.

Payothong, N. 2017. *Sage Grouse: Icon of the West*. Laguna Beach, CA: Laguna Wilderness Press. 180 pp.

Poulin, R. G. 2003. "Relationships between Burrowing Owls (*Athene cunicularia*), Small Mammals, and Agriculture. PhD diss., University of Saskatchewan, Regina.

Rohwer, S. A. 1971. "Systematics and Evolution of Great Plains Meadowlarks, Genus *Sturnella*." PhD diss., University of Kansas, Lawrence.

Sanderson, G. C., ed. 1977. *Management of Migratory Shore and Upland Game Birds in North America*. Washington, DC: US Department of Interior and International Association of Fish and Wildlife Agencies. (Reprinted 1980, University of Nebraska Press, Lincoln.) 358 pp.

Short, L. L., Jr. 1965. "Hybridization in the Flickers (*Colaptes*) of North America. *Bulletin of the American Museum of Natural History* 129: 309–428.

Short, L. L., Jr. 1983. *Woodpeckers of the World*. Delaware Museum of Natural History, Monograph Series No. 4. 675 pp.

Sibley, C. G., and D. A. West. 1959. "Hybridization in the Rufous-sided Towhees of the Great Plains." *Auk* 76: 326–38.

Sibley, C. G., and L. L. Short, Jr. 1959. "Hybridization in the Buntings (*Passerina*) of the Great Plains." *Auk* 76: 443–63.

Sibley, C. G., and L. L. Short, Jr. 1964. "Hybridization in Orioles of the Great Plains." *Condor* 66: 130–50.

Sidle, J. G., M. Ball, T. Byer, J. J. Chynoweth, G. Foli, R. Hodorff, G. Moravek, R. Peterson, and D. N. Svingen. 2001. "Occurrence of Burrowing Owls in Black-tailed Prairie Dog Colonies on Great Plains National Grasslands. *Journal of Raptor Research* 35: 316–321.

Snow, C. 1972. *American Peregrine Falcon* (Falco peregrinus anatum) *and Arctic Peregrine Falcon* (Falco peregrinus tundrius). BLM Technical Note 167. Habitat Management Series for Endangered Species, Report No. 1. Denver, CO: US Department of Interior, Bureau of Land Management.

Snow, C. 1973a. *Golden Eagle,* Aquila chrysaetos. BLM Technical Note 239. Habitat Management Series for Unique or Endangered Species, Report No. 7. Denver, CO: US Department of Interior, Bureau of Land Management.

Snow, C. 1973b. *Southern Bald Eagle* (Haliaeetus leucocephalus leucocephalus) *and Northern Bald Eagle* (Haliaeetus leucocephalus alascanus). BLM Technical Note 171. Habitat Management Series for Endangered Species, Report No. 5. Denver, CO: US Department of Interior, Bureau of Land Management.

Snow, C. 1974a. *Ferruginous Hawk,* Buteo regalis. BLM Technical Note 255. Habitat Management Series for Unique or Endangered Species, Report No. 13. Denver: CO: US Department of Interior, Bureau of Land Management.

Snow, C. 1974b. *Prairie Falcon*, Falco mexicanus. BLM Technical Note 240. Habitat Management Series for Unique or Endangered Species, Report No. 8. Denver, CO: US Department of Interior, Bureau of Land Management.

Tuck, L. M. 1972. *The Snipes: A Study of the Genus* Capella. Canadian Wildlife Service Monograph Series, No. 5. Ottawa, ON: Canadian Wildlife Service. 428 pp.

Vance, J. M., & N. Paothong. 2012. *Save the Last Dance: A Story of North American Grassland Grouse*. Columbia, MO: Noppadol Paothong Photography. 202 pp.

Other Vertebrate Groups

Behler, J. L., and F. W. King. 1979. *The Audubon Society Field Guide to North American Reptiles and Amphibians*. New York: Knopf. 719 pp.

Conant, R., and J. Collins. 1998. *Reptiles and Amphibians of Eastern and Central North America*. Boston: Houghton Mifflin. 640 pp.

Dodd, C. K. 2001. *North American Box Turtles: A Natural History*. Norman: University of Oklahoma Press. 256 pp.

Page, L. M., and B. M. Burr. 1991. *A Guide to Freshwater Fishes*. Boston: Houghton Mifflin. 432 pp.

Shaw, C. E., and S. Campbell. 1974. *Snakes of the American West*. New York: Knopf. 328 pp.

Smith, H., and R. D. Brodie, Jr. 2001. *Reptiles of North America: A Guide to Field Identification*. New York: St. Martin's Press. 240 pp.

Stebbens, R. C. 2005. *A Field Guide to Western Reptiles and Amphibians*. 2nd ed. Boston: Houghton Mifflin. 533 pp.

Stebbens, R. C., and N. W. Cohen. 1995. *A Natural History of Amphibians*. Princeton, NJ: Princeton University Press. 316 pp.

Tomelleri, J. R., and M. E. Eberle. 1990. *Fishes of the Central United States*. Lawrence: University Press of Kansas. 226 pp.

Invertebrates

Abbott, J. C. 2005. *Dragonflies and Damselflies of Texas and the South-Central United States*. Princeton, NJ: Princeton University Press. 344 pp.

Brock, J. P., and K. Kaufman. 2003. *Kaufman Field Guide to Butterflies of North America*. Boston: Houghton Mifflin. 392 pp.

Borror, D. J., and R. E. White. 1970. *A Field Guide to Insects North of Mexico*. Boston: Houghton Mifflin. 404 pp.

Capinera, J. L., R. D. Scott, and T. J. Walker. 2004. *Field Guide to Grasshoppers, Katydids, and Crickets of the United States*. Ithaca, NY: Cornell University Press. 249 pp.

Dunkle, S. W. 2000. *Dragonflies through Binoculars: A Field Guide to Dragonflies of North America*. New York: Oxford University Press. 266 pp.

Eaton, E. R., and K. Kaufman. 2007. *Kaufman Field Guide to Insects of North America*. Boston: Houghton Mifflin.

Ferris, X. D., and E. M. Brown, 1981. *Butterflies of the Rocky Mountain States*. Norman: University of Oklahoma Press.

Glassberg, J. 1999. *Butterflies through Binoculars, the East: A Field Guide to the Butterflies of Eastern North America*. New York: Oxford University Press. 400 pp.

Glassberg, J. 2001. *Butterflies through Binoculars, the West: A Field Guide to the Butterflies of Western North America*. New York: Oxford University Press. 364 pp.

Howe, W. H. 1975. *The Butterflies of North America*. New York: Doubleday. 633 pp.

Milne, L., and M. Milne. 1989. *Field Guide to North American Insects and Spiders*. New York: Knopf. 992 pp.

Mitchell, R. T., and H. S. Zim. 2001. *Butterflies and Moths*. New York: St. Martin's Press. 160 pp.

Opler, P. A. 1999. *A Field Guide to the Western Butterflies*. Boston: Houghton Mifflin. 560 pp.

Paulson, D. 2009. *Dragonflies and Damselflies of the West*. Princeton, NJ: Princeton University Press. 534 pp.

Pyle, R. M. 1981. *The Audubon Society Field Guide to North American Butterflies*. New York: Chanticleer Press.

Scott, J. A. 1986. *The Butterflies of North America: A Natural History and Field Guide*. Stanford, CA: Stanford University Press. 664 pp.

Williams, P. H., R. W. Thorp, and L. L. Richardson. 2014. *Bumble Bees of North America: An Identification Guide*. Princeton, NJ: Princeton University Press. 208 pp.

Wilson, J., and O. J. Messinger. 2015. *The Bees in Your Backyard: A Guide to North America's Bees*. Princeton, NJ: Princeton University Press. 288 pp.

Other Great Plains References

Allen, D. L. 1967. *The Life of Prairie and Plains*. New York: McGraw Hill. 232 pp.

Dort, W., Jr., and J. K. Jones, eds. 1979. *Pleistocene and Recent Environments in the Central Great Plains*. Lawrence: University of Kansas Department of Geology and University of Kansas Press. 433 pp.

Johnsgard, P. A. 2001. *Prairie Birds: Fragile Splendor in the Great Plains*. Lawrence: University Press of Kansas. 331 pp.

Johnsgard, P. A. 2003. *Faces of the Great Plains: Prairie Wildlife*. Lawrence: University Press of Kansas. 190 pp.

Johnsgard, P. A. 2003. *Great Wildlife of the Great Plains*. Lawrence: University Press of Kansas. 309 pp.

Johnsgard, P. A. 2003. *Lewis and Clark on the Great Plains: A Natural History*. Lincoln: University of Nebraska Press. 143 pp.

Johnsgard, P. A. 2005. *Prairie Dog Empire: A Saga of the Shortgrass Prairie*. Lincoln: University of Nebraska Press. 142 pp.

Johnsgard, P. A. 2008. *Wind Through the Buffalo Grass: A Lakota Story Cycle*. Lincoln, NE: Plains Chronicles. 214 pp.

Johnsgard, P. A. 2015. *At Home and at Large in the Great Plains: Essays and Memories*. University of Nebraska–Lincoln DigitalCommons and Zea Books. 169 pp. http://digitalcommons.unl.edu/zeabook/30/. Print edition available from http://www.lulu.com/shop/paul-johnsgard/at-home-and-at-large-in-the-great-plains-essays-and-memories/paperback/product-22285983.html.

Johnsgard, P. A. 2015. *Global Warming and Population Responses among Great Plains Birds*. University of

Nebraska–Lincoln DigitalCommons and Zea Books. 384 pp. https://digitalcommons.unl.edu/zeabook/26/. Print edition available from http://www.lulu.com/shop/http://www.lulu.com/shop/paul-johnsgard/global-warming-and-population-responses-among-great-plains-birds/paperback/product-22063416.html.

Johnson, S. R., and A. Bouzaher, eds. 1996. *Conservation of Great Plains Ecosystems*. Boston: Kluwer Academic Publishers. 435 pp.

Licht, D. 1997. *Ecology and Economics of the Great Plains*. Lincoln: University of Nebraska Press. 237 pp.

Lynch, T., P. A. Johnsgard, & J. Phillips, eds. 2015. *Natural Treasures of the Great Plains: An Ecological Perspective*. Lincoln, NE: Prairie Chronicles Press. 220 pp.

Moulton, G. E., ed. 1983–2003. *The Journals of the Lewis and Clark Expedition*. 13 vols. Lincoln: University of Nebraska Press.

Vance, J. M., and N. Paothong. 2012. *Save the Last Dance: A Story of North American Grassland Grouse*. Columbia, MO: Noppadol Paothong Photography. 202 pp.

Raventon, E. 2003. *Buffalo Country: A Northern Plains Narrative*. Boulder, CO: Johnson Books. 251 pp.

Shepard, L. 1996. *The Northern Plains: Minnesota, North Dakota, South Dakota*. The Smithsonian Guides to Natural America. New York: Random House. 286 pp.

Trimble, D. E. 2001. *The Geologic Story of the Great Plains*. Medora, ND: Theodore Roosevelt Nature and History Association. Reprinted from the 1980 Geological Survey Bulletin 1493, US Department of the Interior, Washington DC: US Government Printing Office. 54 pp.

White, M. 1996. *The South-Central States: Texas, Oklahoma, Arkansas, Louisiana, Mississippi*. The Smithsonian Guides to Natural America. New York: Random House. 284 pp.

Winkler, S., W. Clay, T. Till, M. Forsberg, and C. Gurche. 1997. *The Heartland: Illinois, Iowa, Kansas, Missouri*. The Smithsonian Guides to Natural America. New York: Random House. 160 pp.

Wishart, D. J., ed. 2004. *Encyclopedia of the Great Plains*. Lincoln: University of Nebraska Press. 940 pp.

Wishart, D. J., ed. 2007. *Encyclopedia of the Great Plains Indians*. Lincoln: University of Nebraska Press. 254 pp.

van der Valk, A. G., ed. 1989. *Northern Prairie Wetlands*. Ames: Iowa State University Press.

Individual State Surveys

Colorado

Andrews, P., and R. Righter. 1992. *Colorado Birds*. Denver, CO: Denver Museum of Natural History. 442 pp.

Armstrong, D. M. 1972. *Distribution of Mammals in Colorado*. Monograph of the Museum of Natural History No. 3. Lawrence: University of Kansas. 415 pp.

Bailey, A. M. and R. J. Niedrach. 1965. *Birds of Colorado*. 2 vols. Denver, CO: Denver Museum of Natural History. 454 pp. and 441 pp.

Bissell, S. 1978. *Colorado Mammal Distribution Latilong Study*. Denver: Colorado Division of Wildlife. 18 pp.

Fitzgerald, J. P., C. A. Meaney, and D. M. Armstrong. 1995. *Mammals of Colorado*. Denver, CO: Denver Museum of Natural History and University Press of Colorado. 467 pp.

Gray, M. T. 1992. *Colorado Wildlife Viewing Guide*. Helena, MT: Falcon Publishing. 128 pp. (110 sites described)

Guennel, G. K. 2004. *Guide to Colorado Wildflowers, Vol. 1. Plains and Foothills*. Rev. ed. Englewood, CO: Westcliffe Publishers. 376 pp.

Harrington, H. D. 1954. *Manual of the Plants of Colorado*. Denver, CO: Sage Books.

Holt, H. R. 1997. *A Birder's Guide to Colorado*. 4th ed. ABA/Lane Birdfinding Guide. Delaware City, DE: American Birding Association.

Johnsgard, P. A. 1986. *Birds of the Rocky Mountains, with Particular Reference to National Parks in the Northern Rocky Mountain Region*. Boulder: Colorado Associated University Press. 504 pp.

Johnsgard, P. A. 2011. *Rocky Mountain Birds: Birds and Birding in the Central and Northern Rockies*. University of Nebraska–Lincoln DigitalCommons and Zea Books. 274 pp. http://digitalcommons.unl.edu/zeabook/7/. Print edition available from http://www.lulu.com/shop/paul-johnsgard/rocky-mountain-birds/paperback/product-18607006.html.

Kingery, H. 2007. *Birding Colorado: Over 180 Premier Birding Sites at 93 Locations*. Guilford, CT: Falcon Guides. 336 pp.

Kingery, H., ed. 1998. *Colorado Breeding Bird Atlas*. Denver: Colorado Division of Wildlife. 636 pp.

Lane, J. A., and H. R. Holt. 1973. A *Birder's Guide to Denver and Eastern Colorado*. Distributed by L&P Photography, Sacramento, CA. 136 pp.

Lechleitner, R. 1969. *Wild Mammals of Colorado: Their Appearance, Habits, Distribution, and Abundance*. Boulder: Pruett Publishing Co. 254 pp.

Mutel, C. E., and J. C. Emerick. 1984. *From Grassland to Glacier: The Natural History of Colorado*. Boulder, CO: Johnson Books. 280 pp.

Shaw, R. B. 2008. *Grasses of Colorado*. Boulder: University Press of Colorado. 647 pp.

Weber, W. 2012. *Colorado Flora, Eastern Slope: A Field Guide to the Vascular Plants*. 4th ed. Boulder: University Press of Colorado. 608 pp.

Williams, F., and H. Chronic. 2014. *Roadside Geology of Colorado*. 3rd ed. Missoula, MT: Mountain Press. 416 pp.

Woodling, J. 1980. *Game Fish of Colorado*. Denver: Colorado Division of Wildlife. 40 pp.

Woodling, J. 1985. *Colorado's Little Fish*. Denver: Colorado Division of Wildlife. 77 pp.

Iowa

Alex, L. 1980. *Exploring Iowa's Past: A Guide to Prehistoric Archeology.* Iowa City: University of Iowa Press.

Anderson, W. 1983. *Geology of Iowa: Over Two Billion Years of Change.* Ames: Iowa State University Press. 268 pp.

Bowles, J. 1975. *Distribution and Biogeography of the Mammals of Iowa.* Lubbock: Texas Tech University Press. 184 pp.

Christiansen, P., and M. Müller. 1999. *An Illustrated Guide to Iowa Prairie Plants.* Iowa City: University of Iowa Press. 237 pp.

Conard, H. S. 1952. "The Vegetation of Iowa." *University of Iowa Studies in Natural History* 19 (4): 1–166.

Cooper, T., ed. 1983. *Iowa's Natural Heritage.* Des Moines: Iowa Natural History Foundation and Cedar Falls: Iowa Academy of Science.

Dinsmore, J. J., L. S. Jackson, B. L. Ehresman, and J. J. Dinsmore. 1995. *Iowa Wildlife Viewing Guide.* Helena, MT: Falcon Press. 95 pp. (77 sites described)

Dinsmore, S. J., T. H. Kent, D. Koenig, P. C. Peterson, and D. M. Roosa. 1984. *Iowa Birds.* Ames: Iowa State University Press. 356 pp.

Eilers, L. J., and D. M. Roosa. 1994. *The Vascular Plants of Iowa: An Annotated Checklist and Natural History.* Iowa City: University of Iowa Press. 319 pp.

Harlan, J. R., E. B. Speaker, and J. Mayhow. 1987. *Iowa Fish and Fishing.* Des Moines: Iowa Department of Natural Resources. 323 pp.

Jackson, L. S., C. A. Thompson, and J. J. Dinsmore. 1996. *The Iowa Breeding Bird Atlas.* Iowa City: University of Iowa Press. 504 pp.

Kurtz, C. 1996. *Iowa's Wild Places.* Iowa City: University of Iowa Press. 248 pp.

Mutel, C. F. 1989. *Fragile Giants: A Natural History of the Loess Hills.* Iowa City: University of Iowa Press. 284 pp.

Pohl, R. W. 1967. "The Grasses of Iowa." *Iowa State Journal of Science* 40: 341–572.

Prior, J. 1991. *Landforms of Iowa.* Iowa City: University of Iowa Press. 168 pp.

Runkel, S. T., and A. Bull. 2010. *Wildflowers of Iowa Woodlands.* 2nd ed. University of Iowa Press. 280 pp.

Runkel, S. T., and D. M. Roosa. 2015. *Wildflowers and Other Plants of Iowa Wetlands.* 2nd ed. Iowa City: University of Iowa Press. 400 pp.

Schlicht, D., J. Downey, and J. Nekola. 2007. *Butterflies of Iowa.* Iowa City: University of Iowa Press. 400 pp.

Shimek, B. 1948. "The Plant Geography of Iowa." *University of Iowa Studies in Natural History* 19 (4): 1–178.

Thompson, C. A., E. A. Bettis, and R. G. Baker. 1992. "Geology of Iowa Fens." *Journal of the Iowa Academy of Science* 99: 53–59.

van der Linden, P., and D. R. Farrar. 2011. *Forest and Shade Trees of Iowa.* Iowa City: University of Iowa Press.

Wolf, R. C. 1991. *Iowa's State Parks; Also Forests, Recreation Areas, and Preserves.* Ames: Iowa State University Press. 234 pp.

Kansas

Barkley T. M. 1983. *Field Guide to the Common Weeds of Kansas.* Lawrence: University Press of Kansas. 176 pp.

Bee, J. W., G. E. Glass, R. S. Hoffmann, and R. R. Patterson. 1981. *Mammals in Kansas.* Museum of Natural History, University of Kansas, Lawrence. 303 pp.

Bowen, D. E. 1976. "Coloniality, Reproductive Success, and Habitat Interactions of Upland Sandpipers, *Bartramia longicauda.*" PhD diss., Kansas State University, Manhattan.

Brosius, L. 2006. *Windows to the Past: A Guidebook to Common Invertebrate Fossils of Kansas.* Educational Series Volume 16. Kansas Geological Survey, University of Kansas. 56 pp.

Buchanan, R., ed. 2010. *Geology of Kansas.* 2nd ed. Lawrence: University Press of Kansas.

Buchanan, R., and J. R. McCauley. 2010. *Roadside Kansas: A Traveler's Guide to Its Geology and Landmarks.* 2nd ed. Lawrence: University Press of Kansas.

Busby, W. H., and J. L. Zimmerman. 2001. *Kansas Breeding Bird Atlas.* Lawrence: University Press of Kansas. 478 pp.

Cable, T. T., S. Sellman, and K. J. Cook. 1996. *Birds of Cimarron National Grassland.* General Technical Report RM-GTR-281. Fort Collins, CO: US Department of Agriculture, Forest Service, Rocky Mountain Forest and Range Experiment Station. 108 pp.

Caldwell, J., and J. T. Collins. 1981. *Turtles in Kansas.* Museum of Natural History, University of Kansas, Lawrence. 67 pp.

Chapman, S. S., J. M. Omernik, J. Freeouf, D. Huggins, J. R. McCauley, C. C. Freeman, G. Steinauer, and R. Angelo. 2001. *Ecoregions of Nebraska and Kansas.* Reston, VA: US Department of Interior, Geological Survey. (Map poster.)

Cockrum, E. L. 1952. *Mammals of Kansas.* Museum of Natural History, University of Kansas, Lawrence. 303 pp.

Collins, J. T. 1982. *Amphibians and Reptiles in Kansas.* Public Education Series No. 5. Museum of Natural History, University of Kansas, Lawrence. 356 pp.

Collins, J. T. 1985. *Natural Kansas.* Lawrence: University Press of Kansas. 226 pp.

Collins, J. T., S. L. Collins, J. Horak, D. Muhern, W. Busby, C. C. Freeman, and G. Wallace. 1995. *An Illustrated Guide to Endangered and Threatened Species in Kansas.* Lawrence: University Press of Kansas.

Collins, J. T., S. L. Collins, T. W. Taggart, and E. D. Hooper. 2010. *Amphibians, Reptiles, and Turtles in Kansas.* Eagle Mountain, UT: Eagle Mountain Publishing. 312 pp.

Collins, J. T. R. (Bob) Gress, G. Weins, and S. L. Collins. 1991. *Kansas Wildlife.* Lawrence: University Press of Kansas.

Cross, F., and J. T. Collins. 1995. *Fishes in Kansas*. Public Education Series No. 3. Museum of Natural History, University of Kansas, Lawrence. 189 pp.

Ely, C. A., M. D. Schwilling, and M. E. Rolfs. 1986. *An Annotated List of the Butterflies of Kansas*. Hays, KS: Fort Hays State University. 224 pp. (Includes 175 species distribution maps.)

Gates, D. E., and L. L. Peters. 1962. *Insects in Kansas*. 2nd ed. Manhattan: Kansas State University Cooperative Extension Division. 307 pp.

Gates, F. C. 1936. *Grasses in Kansas*. Topeka: Kansas State Board of Agriculture. 349 pp.

Gress, R. (Bob), and P. Janzen. 2008. *The Guide to Kansas Birds and Birding Hot Spots*. Lawrence: University Press of Kansas. 368 pp.

Gress, R. (Bob), and G. Potts. 1993. *Watching Kansas Wildlife. A Guide to 101 Sites*. Lawrence: University Press of Kansas. 118 pp.

Haddock, M. J. 2005. *Wildflowers and Grasses of Kansas: A Field Guide*. Lawrence: University Press of Kansas. 374 pp.

Haddock, J. H., C. C. Freeman, and J. Bare. 2015. *Kansas Wildflowers and Weeds*. Lawrence: University Press of Kansas. 526 pp.

Hall, E. R. 1955. *Handbook of the Mammals of Kansas*. Museum of Natural History, University of Kansas, Lawrence. 303 pp.

Johnston, R. F. 1964. *The Breeding Birds of Kansas*. University of Kansas Publications, Museum of Natural History 12 (14): 575–655.

Johnston, R. F. 1965. *A Directory to the Birds of Kansas*. Museum of Natural History and State Biological Survey Miscellaneous Publication No. 41. Lawrence: University of Kansas. 67 pp.

Kansas Fishes Committee. 2014. *Kansas Fishes*. Lawrence: University Press of Kansas. 542 pp.

Küchler, A. W. 1974. "A New Vegetation Map of Kansas." *Ecology* 55(3): 586–604.

Ohlenbusch, P. D. 1976. *Range Grasses of Kansas*. Cooperative Extension Service, Kansas State University, Manhattan. 20 pp.

Owensby, C. 1980. *Kansas Prairie Wildflowers*. Ames: Iowa State University Press. 124 pp.

Reichman, O. J. 1987. *Konza Prairie: A Tallgrass Natural History*. Lawrence: University Press of Kansas. 226 pp.

Robinson, T. S. 1957. *The Ecology of Bobwhites in South-Central Kansas*. Museum of Natural History and State Biological Survey Miscellaneous Publication No. 15. Lawrence: University of Kansas. 84 pp.

Rose, R. (Bob). 2017. "Wetlands." *The Kansas School Naturalist* 62 (1): 1–13.

Salsbury, G. A., and S. C. White. 2000. *Insects in Kansas*. Manhattan: Kansas Department of Agriculture. 523 pp.

Stephens, H. A. 1969. *Trees, Shrubs, and Woody Vines in Kansas*. Lawrence: University Press of Kansas. 256 pp.

Schwilling, M., and C. A. Ely. 1991. Checklist of Kansas Butterflies. Emporia State University, Emporia, KS. *The Kansas School Naturalist* 37(4). 14 pp.

Thompson, M. C., and C. A. Ely. 1980, 1992. *Birds in Kansas*. 2 vols. Museum of Natural History. Public Education Series No. 11 and 12. Lawrence: University of Kansas. 422 and 404 pp.

Thompson, M. C., C. A. Ely, R. (Bob) Gress, C. Otte, S. T. Patti, D. Seibel, and E. A. Young. 2011. *Birds of Kansas*. Lawrence: University Press of Kansas. 528 pp.

Tordoff, H. B. 1956. *Check-list of the Birds of Kansas*. Museum of Natural History Publication 8. Lawrence: University of Kansas. pp. 30–59.

Williams, R. B. 1975. *Ancient Life Found in Kansas Rocks: An Introduction to Common Kansas Fossils*. Educational Series 1. Lawrence: Kansas Geological Survey. 44 pp.

Zimmerman, J. L. 1990. *Cheyenne Bottoms: Wetland in Jeopardy*. Lawrence: University Press of Kansas. 197 pp.

Zimmerman, J. L. 1993. *The Birds of Konza: The Avian Ecology of the Tallgrass Prairie*. Lawrence: University Press of Kansas. 179 pp.

Zimmerman, J. L., and S. T. Patti. 1988. *A Guide to Bird Finding in Kansas and Western Missouri*. Lawrence: University Press of Kansas. 244 pp.

Minnesota

Bosanko, D. 2007. *Fish of Minnesota: A Field Guide*. Cambridge, MN: Adventure Publications. 176 pp.

Breckenridge, W. J. 1944. *Reptiles and Amphibians of Minnesota*. Minneapolis: University of Minnesota Press. 216 pp.

Bray, E. 1980. *Billions of Years in Minnesota: The Geological Story of the State*. St. Paul: Science Museum of Minnesota.

Chadde, S. W. 2012. *Wetland Plants of Minnesota: A Complete Guide to the Wetland and Aquatic Plants of the North Star State*. 2nd ed. Bogman Guide. CreateSpace Independent Publishing Platform. 670 pp.

Chadde, S. W. 2013. *Minnesota Flora: An Illustrated Guide to the Vascular Plants of Minnesota*. CreateSpace Independent Publishing Platform. 788 pp.

Gunderson, H., and J. R. Beer. 1953. *The Mammals of Minnesota*. Minneapolis: University of Minnesota Press. 190 pp.

Hazard, E. B. 1983. *The Mammals of Minnesota*. Minneapolis: University of Minnesota Press. 280 pp.

Henderson, C. L., and A. L. Lambrecht. 1997. *Traveler's Guide to Wildlife in Minnesota*. Minneapolis: Minnesota's Bookstore. 326 pp. (120 sites described)

Janssen, R. B. 1987. *Birds in Minnesota*. Minneapolis: University of Minnesota Press. 367 pp.

Minnesota Department of Natural Resources. 1995. *A Guide to Minnesota's Scientific and Natural Areas*. St. Paul: Minnesota Department of Natural Resources.

Minnesota Natural Heritage Program. 1993. *Minnesota's Native Vegetation: A Key to Natural Communities.* Version 1.5. St. Paul: Minnesota Department of Natural Resources.

Morey, G. B., and H. Dahlberg. 1995. *Geology of Minnesota: A Guide for Teachers.* St. Paul: Minnesota Department of Natural Resources. 34 pp.

Moyle, J. B., and E. W. Moyle. 2001. *Northland Wildflowers: The Comprehensive Guide to the Minnesota Region.* Rev. ed. Minneapolis: University of Minnesota Press. 228 pp.

Nature Conservancy of Minnesota. 2000. *A Guide to the Nature Conservancy's Preserves in Minnesota.* Minneapolis, MN: The Nature Conservancy. https://www.nature.org/minnesotapreserves

Ojakangas, R. W. 2009. *Roadside Geology of Minnesota.* Missoula, MT: Mountain Press. 368 pp.

Ojakangas, R. W., and C. L. Matsch. 1982. *Minnesota's Geology.* Minneapolis: University of Minnesota Press.

Oldfield, B., and J. J. Moriarty. 1994. *Amphibians and Reptiles Native to Minnesota.* Minneapolis: University of Minnesota Press.

Olson, S. T., and W. H. Marshall. 1952. *The Common Loon in Minnesota.* Occasional Papers of the Minnesota Museum of Natural History No. 5. Minneapolis: University of Minnesota Press. 76 pp.

Roberts, T. R. 1932. *The Birds of Minnesota.* 2 vols. Minneapolis: University of Minnesota Press. 891 and 821 pp.

Sansome, C. J. 1983. *Minnesota Underfoot.* Stillwater, MN: Voyageur. (Geology of Minnesota.)

Smith, W. R. 2008. *Trees and Shrubs of Minnesota.* Minneapolis: University of Minnesota Press. 640 pp.

Takiela, S. 1999. *Wildflowers of Minnesota: Field Guide.* Cambridge, MN: Adventure Publications. 423 pp.

Tester, J. R. 1995. *Minnesota's Natural Heritage: An Ecological Perspective.* Minneapolis: University of Minnesota Press. 344 pp.

Wendt, K. M. 1984. *A Guide to Minnesota Prairies.* St. Paul: Minnesota Department of Natural Resources.

Missouri

Chapman, C. H., and E. F. Chapman. 1983. *Indians and Archeology of Missouri.* Columbia: University of Missouri Press. 176 pp.

Denison, E. 2008. *Missouri Wildflowers.* 6th ed. Jefferson City: Missouri Department of Conservation. 280 pp.

Heitzman, J. R., and J. E. Heitzman. 1996. *Butterflies and Moths of Missouri.* Jefferson City: Missouri Department of Conservation. 385 pp.

Jacobs, B. 2001. *Birds in Missouri.* Jefferson City: Missouri Department of Conservation. 375 pp.

Jacobs, B., and J. L. Wilson. 1997. *Missouri Breeding Bird Atlas: 1986–1992.* Jefferson City: Missouri Department of Conservation. 430 pp.

Johnsgard, P. A. 2013. "Squaw Creek National Wildlife Refuge: Gem of the Missouri Valley." *Prairie Fire*, November 2012, pp. 12–13. http://www.prairiefirenewspaper.com/2012/11/squaw-creek-national-wildlife-refuge-gem-of-the-missouri-valley

Johnson, T., 2000. *The Amphibians and Reptiles of Missouri.* Jefferson City: Missouri Department of Conservation. 368 pp.

Kuchera, C. L. 1998. *The Grasses of Missouri.* 2nd ed. Columbia: University of Missouri Press. 320 pp.

Kurz, D. 1997. *Shrubs and Woody Vines of Missouri.* Jefferson City: Missouri Department of Conservation. 389 pp.

Kurz, D. 2003. *Trees of Missouri.* Jefferson City: Missouri Department of Conservation. 399 pp.

Pflieger, W. L. 1975. *The Fishes of Missouri.* Jefferson City: Missouri Department of Conservation. 343 pp.

Robbins, M. B., and D. A. Easterla. 1992. *Birds of Missouri: Their Distribution and Abundance.* Columbia: University of Missouri Press. 399 pp.

Schwartz, C. W. 1945. "The Ecology of the Prairie Chicken in Missouri." *University of Missouri Studies* 20: 1–99.

Schwartz, C. W., and E. R. Schwartz. 2016. *The Wild Mammals of Missouri.* 3rd ed. Columbia: University of Missouri Press and Jefferson City: Missouri Department of Conservation. 396 pp.

Spencer, C. G. 2011. *Roadside Geology of Missouri.* Missoula, MT: Mountain Press. 288 pp.

Stone, M. 2010. *Missouri's Wild Mushrooms.* Jefferson City: Missouri Department of Conservation. 280 pp.

Tekiela, S. 2003. *Trees of Missouri.* Cambridge, MN: Adventure Publications. 264 pp.

Unklesbay, A. G. 1955. *The Common Fossils of Missouri.* Columbia: University of Missouri Press. 98 pp.

Montana

Alt., D. D. 1986. *Roadside Geology of Montana.* Missoula, MT: Mountain Press. 327 pp.

Booth, W. E. 1950. *Flora of Montana.* Pt. I. Bozeman: Montana State University. 232 pp.

Booth, W. E, and J. C. Wright. 1962. *Flora of Montana.* Pt. II (Dicotyledons). Bozeman: Montana State University. 280 pp.

Brown, C. J. D. 1971. *Fishes of Montana.* Bozeman: Montana State University. 207 pp.

Fisher, C., and H. Fisher. 1995. *Montana Wildlife Viewing Guide.* Helena, MT: Falcon Publishing. 111 pp. (109 sites described)

Foresman, K. R. 2012. *Mammals of Montana.* 2nd ed. Missoula, MT: Mountain Press Publishing Company. 440 pp.

Hoffman, R. S., R. D. Fisher, and D. L. Patti. 1968. *A Guide to Montana Mammals: Identification, Habitat, Distribution, and Abundance.* Missoula: University of Montana Printing Services. 133 pp.

Marks, J., P. Hendricks, and D. Casey. 2016. *Birds of Montana*. Arlington, VA: Buteo Books. 672 pp.

McEneaney, T. 1993. *The Birder's Guide to Montana*. Helena, MT: Falcon Press. 327 pp.

Montana Bird Distribution Committee. 2012. *P. D. Skaar's Montana Bird Distribution*. 7th ed. Helena, MT: Montana Audubon. 208 pp.

Robbins, C. 2014. *Birding Trails Montana: 240 Birding Trails for the Avid Birder with GPS Coordinates for All Locations*. A Sandhill Crane Press Guidebook. Belgrade, MT: Wilderness Adventures Press. 508 pp.

Scheiman, D. A. 2005. *Wildflowers of Montana*. Missoula, MT: Mountain Press Publishing Company. 306 pp.

Tekiela, S. 2004. *Birds of Montana Field Guide*. Cambridge, MN: Adventure Publications. 353 pp.

Werner, J. K., ed. 2004. *Amphibians and Reptiles of Montana*. Missoula, MT: Mountain Press Publishing Company. 262 pp.

Nebraska

Barth, R., and N. Ratzlaff. 2004. *Field Guide to Wildflowers: Fontenelle Forest and Neale Woods Nature Centers*. Bellevue, NE: Fontenelle Nature Association. 306 pp.

Barth, R., and N. Ratzlaff. 2007. *Field Guide to Trees, Shrubs, Woody Vines, Grasses, Sedges, and Rushes: Fontenelle Forest and Neale Woods Nature Centers*. Bellevue, NE: Fontenelle Nature Association. 218 pp.

Bleed, A., and C. Flowerday, eds. 1998. *An Atlas of the Sand Hills*. 2nd ed. Resource Atlas No. 5b. Lincoln: Conservation and Survey Division, University of Nebraska–Lincoln. 260 pp.

Brogie, M. A., & M. J. Mossman. 1983. "Spring and Summer Birds of the Niobrara Valley Preserve Area, Nebraska." *Nebraska Bird Review* 51: 44–51.

Brown, C. R., M. B. Brown, P. A. Johnsgard, J. Kren, and W. C. Scharf. 1996. "Birds of the Cedar Point Biological Station Area, Keith and Garden Counties, Nebraska: Seasonal Occurrence and Breeding Data." *Transactions of the Nebraska Academy of Sciences* 29: 91–108.

Brown, C. R., and M. B. Brown. 2001. *Birds of the Cedar Point Biological Station*. Lincoln, NE: Occasional Papers of the Cedar Point Biological Station No. 1. 36 pp.

Brown, M., S. Dinsmore, and J. Jorgensen. 2012. *The Birds of Southwestern Nebraska*. Lincoln: School of Natural Resources, Conservation and Survey Division, University of Nebraska–Lincoln.

Brown, M. B., and P. A. Johnsgard. 2013. *Birds of the Central Platte River Valley and Adjacent Counties*. University of Nebraska–Lincoln DigitalCommons and Zea Books, 182 pp. http://digitalcommons.unl.edu/zeabook/15/. Print edition available from http://www.lulu.com/shop/paul-a-johnsgard-and-mary-bomberger-brown/birds-of-the-central-platte-river-valley-and-adjacent-counties/paperback/product-20723724.html.

Chapman, S. S., J. M. Omernik, J. Freeouf, D. Huggins, J. R. McCauley, C. C. Freeman, G. Steinauer, and R. Angelo. 2001. *Ecoregions of Nebraska and Kansas*. Reston, VA: US Department of Interior, Geological Survey. (Map poster.)

Currier, P. J., G. R. Lingle, and J. G. VanDerwalker. 1985. *Migratory Bird Habitat on the Platte and North Platte Rivers in Nebraska*. Grand Island, NE: Whooping Crane Habitat Maintenance Trust. 177 pp.

Dankert, N., D. Brust, H. Nagel, and S. M. Spomer. 2005. *Butterflies of Nebraska*. Kearney: University of Nebraska at Kearney. http://www.lopers.net/student_org/NebraskaInverts/butterfiles/home.htm (Version 5APR2005)

Dority, B., E. Thompson, S. Kaskie, and L. Tschauner. 2017. *The Economic Impact of the Annual Crane Migration on Central Nebraska*. Kearney: Bureau of Business and Technology, University of Nebraska at Kearney. 22 pp.

Ducey, J. E. 1988. *Nebraska Birds: Breeding Status and Distribution*. Omaha: Simmons-Boardman Books. 148 pp.

Ducey, J. E. 1989. "Birds of the Niobrara River Valley." *Transactions of the Nebraska Academy of Sciences* 17: 37–60.

Faanes, C. E., and G. R. Lingle. 1995. *Breeding Birds of the Platte Valley of Nebraska*. Jamestown, ND: US Geological Survey, Northern Prairie Wildlife Research Center.

Farrar, J. 2004. "Birding Nebraska." *NEBRASKAland Magazine* 82(1): 1–178.

Farrar, J. 2011. *Field Guide to Wildflowers of Nebraska and the Great Plains*. 2nd ed. Iowa City: University of Iowa Press.

Johnsgard, P. A. 1995. *This Fragile Land: A Natural History of the Nebraska Sandhills*. Lincoln: University of Nebraska Press. 256 pp.

Johnsgard, P. A. 2001. "A Century of Ornithology in Nebraska: A Personal View." In *Contributions to the History of North American Ornithology, Vol. II*, edited by W. E. Davis and J. A. Jackson, 329–55. Boston: Nuttall Ornithological Club. http://digitalcommons.unl.edu/biosciornithology/26/

Johnsgard, P. A. 2001. *The Nature of Nebraska: Ecology and Biodiversity*. Lincoln: University of Nebraska Press. 402 pp.

Johnsgard, P. A. 2003. "Great Gathering on the Great Plains." *National Wildlife* 41(3): 20–29. https://digitalcommons.unl.edu/johnsgard/38/

Johnsgard, P. A. 2007. *A Guide to the Natural History of the Central Platte Valley of Nebraska*. University of Nebraska–Lincoln DigitalCommons and Zea Books. 156 pp. https://digitalcommons.unl.edu/biosciornithology/40/.

Johnsgard, P. A. 2007. *The Niobrara: A River Running Through Time*. Lincoln: University of Nebraska Press. 373 pp.

Johnsgard, P. A. 2008. *A Guide to the Tallgrass Prairies of Eastern Nebraska and Adjacent States*. University of Nebraska–Lincoln DigitalCommons and Zea Books. 70 pp. https://digitalcommons.unl.edu/biosciornithology/39/

Johnsgard, P. A. 2009. *A Nebraska Bird-Finding Guide.* University of Nebraska–Lincoln DigitalCommons and Zea Books. 152 pp. https://digitalcommons.unl.edu/biosciornithology/51/. Print edition available from http://www.lulu.com/shop/paul-johnsgard/a-nebraska-bird-finding-guide/paperback/product-21768130.html.

Johnsgard, P. A. 2009. "Nature Notes: The Wings of March." *Prairie Fire*, March 2009, pp. 1, 17, 18, 19. http://prairiefirenewspaper.com/2009/03/nature-notes-wings-of-march

Johnsgard, P. A. 2009. "Nebraska's Eight Great Natural Wonders." *Nebraska Life*, November 2009, pp. 78–84.

Johnsgard, P. A. 2010. "The Drums of April." *Prairie Fire*, April 2010, pp. 12–13. http://www.prairiefirenewspaper.com/2010/04/the-drums-of-april.

Johnsgard, P. A. 2011. *A Nebraska Bird-Finding Guide.* University of Nebraska–Lincoln DigitalCommons and Zea Books. 166 pp. https://digitalcommons.unl.edu/zeabook/5/. Print edition available from http://www.lulu.com/shop/paul-johnsgard/a-nebraska-bird-finding-guide/paperback/product-21768130.html.

Johnsgard, P. A. 2012. *Nebraska's Wetlands: Their Wildlife and Ecology.* Water Survey Paper No. 78. Lincoln: School of Natural Resources, Conservation and Survey Division, University of Nebraska–Lincoln. 202 pp.

Johnsgard, P. A. 2012. "Spring Creek Prairie Audubon Center: An 800-Acre Schoolhouse." *Prairie Fire*, October 2012, pp. 18–20, 22. http://www.prairiefirenewspaper.com/2012/10/spring-creek-prairie-audubon-center-an-800-acre-schoolhouse.

Johnsgard, P. A. 2013. *The Birds of Nebraska.* Rev. ed. University of Nebraska–Lincoln DigitalCommons and Zea Books. 150 pp. https://digitalcommons.unl.edu/zeabook/17/. ition available from http://www.lulu.com/shop/paul-johnsgard/the-birds-of-nebraska-revised-edition-2013/paperback/product-21096798.html.

Johnsgard, P. A. 2014. *Seasons of the Tallgrass Prairie: A Nebraska Year.* Lincoln: University of Nebraska Press. 171 pp.

Johnsgard, P. A. 2014. "Secrets of the Very Long Dead: Ashfall Fossil Beds State Historical Park." *Prairie Fire*, October 2014, pp. 1, 3, 4. http://www.prairiefirenewspaper.com/2014/10/secrets-of-the-very-long-dead-ashfall-fossil-beds-state-historical-park

Johnsgard, P. A. 2014. "The Hutton Niobrara Ranch Audubon Nature Sanctuary." *Prairie Fire*, July 2014, pp. 12–14. http://www.prairiefirenewspaper.com/2014/07/hutton-niobrara-ranch-wildlife-sanctuary

Johnsgard, P. A. 2015. *Birding Nebraska's Central Platte Valley and Rainwater Basin.* University of Nebraska–Lincoln DigitalCommons and Zea Books. 54 pp. https://digitalcommons.unl.edu/zeabook/36/. Print edition available from http://www.lulu.com/shop/http://www.lulu.com/shop/paul-johnsgard/birding-nebraskas-central-platte-valley-and-rainwater-basin/paperback/product-22490704.html.

Johnsgard, P. A. 2015. "Secrets of the Most Sincerely Dead: Agate Fossil Beds National Monument." *Prairie Fire*, November 2015, pp. 15–17. http://www.prairiefirenewspaper.com/2014/11/secrets-of-the-most-sincerely-dead-agate-fossil-beds-national-monument

Jones, J. K. 1964. *Distribution and Taxonomy of Mammals of Nebraska.* University of Kansas Publications, Museum of Natural History 16(1): 1–356.

Jones, S. R. 2000. *The Last Prairie: A Sandhills Journal.* New York: McGraw-Hill. 244 pp.

Jorgensen, J. 2012. *Birds of the Rainwater Basin, Nebraska.* Lincoln: Nebraska Game and Parks Commission.

Kaul, R. 1998. "Plants." In *An Atlas of the Sand Hills*, 2nd ed., Resource Atlas No. 5b, edited by A. Bleed and C. Flowerday, 127–142. Lincoln: School of Natural Resources, Conservation and Survey Division, University of Nebraska–Lincoln.

Kaul, R., D. M. Sutherland, and S. B. Rolfsmeier. 2012. *The Flora of Nebraska.* 2nd ed. Lincoln: School of Natural Resources, University of Nebraska–Lincoln. 966 pp.

Keech, C. F., and R. Bentall. 1971. *Dunes on the Plains: The Sand Hills Region of Nebraska.* Resources Report 4. Lincoln: University of Nebraska, Conservation and Survey Division. 18 pp.

Knue, J. 1992. *Nebraska Wildlife Viewing Guide.* Helena, MT: Falcon Press. 96 pp. (61 sites described)

Krapu, G. L., ed. 1981. *The Platte River Ecology Study: Special Research Report.* Jamestown, ND: US Geological Survey, Northern Prairie Wildlife Research Station. 186 pp. https://digitalcommons.unl.edu/usgsnpwrc/248/

LaGrange, T. G. 2005. *Guide to Nebraska Wetlands and Their Conservation Needs.* 2nd ed. Lincoln: Nebraska Game and Parks Commission. 57 pp. http://outdoornebraska.gov/nebraskawetlands/

Maher, H. D., Jr., G. F. Engelmann, and R. D. Shuster. 2003. *Roadside Geology of Nebraska.* Missoula, MT: Mountain Press.

McCarraher, D. B. 1977. *Nebraska's Sandhills Lakes.* Lincoln: Nebraska Game and Parks Commission. 67 pp.

McMurtry, M. S., R. Craig, and G. Schildmann. 1972. *Nebraska Wetland Survey.* Lincoln: Nebraska Game and Parks Commission. 78 pp.

Mollhoff, W. 2016. *The Second Nebraska Breeding Bird Atlas.* Lincoln: Bulletin of the University of Nebraska State Museum 29: 1–304.

Morris, J., L. Morris, and L. Witt. 1974. *The Fishes of Nebraska.* Lincoln: Nebraska Game and Parks Commission.

Nagel, H. G. 1998. *The Loess Hills Prairies of Central Nebraska.* Kearney: University of Nebraska at Kearney (*Platte Valley Review* 26:2).

Nebraska Department of Agriculture. 1979. *Nebraska Weeds.* Lincoln: Nebraska Department of Agriculture. 247 pp. (216 forbs, 27 grasses, 2 sedges, 2 cacti)

Novacek, J. M. 1989. "The Water and Wetland Resources of the Nebraska Sandhills." In *Northern Prairie Wetlands*, edited by A. G. van der Valk, 340–84. Ames: Iowa State University Press. 400 pp.

Oberholser, H. C., and W. L. McAtee. 1920. *Waterfowl and Their Food Plants in the Sandhill Region of Nebraska.* Bulletin of the US Department of Agriculture No. 794. Washington, DC: US Department of Agriculture. 79 pp.

Panella, M. J. 2010. *Nebraska's At-Risk Wildlife.* Lincoln: Nebraska Game and Parks Commission. 196 pp.

Sharpe, R. S., W. R. Silcock, and J. G. Jorgensen. 2001. *The Birds of Nebraska.* Lincoln: University of Nebraska Press. 513 pp.

Stubbendieck, J., and K. L. Kottas. 2005. *Common Grasses of Nebraska.* Lincoln: University of Nebraska–Lincoln, Institute of Agriculture and Natural Resources, Extension Circular ECO5-170. 121 pp. (180 grasses, 7 sedges)

Stubbendieck, J., and K. Kottas. 2007. *Common Forbs and Shrubs of Nebraska.* Lincoln: University of Nebraska–Lincoln, Institute of Agriculture and Natural Resources, Extension Circular EC-118. 178 pp. (117 forbs, 17 shrubs, 4 cacti)

Voorhies, M. R. 1981. "Ancient Ashfall Creates a Pompeii of Prehistoric Animals, Dwarfing the St. Helens Eruption." *National Geographic* 159(1): 66–75.

New Mexico

Allison, C. D., and N. Ashcroft. N.d. *New Mexico Range Plants.* Cooperative Extension Service Circular 374. Las Cruces: New Mexico State University. 48 pp.

Allred, K. W. 2005. *A Field Guide to the Grasses of New Mexico.* 3rd ed. Las Cruces: New Mexico State University, Agricultural Experiment Station. 388 pp.

Bailey, A. M. 1928. *Birds of New Mexico.* Santa Fe: New Mexico Department of Fish and Game. 807 pp.

Bailey, A. M. 1932. *Mammals of New Mexico.* North American Fauna No. 53. Washington, DC: US Department of Agriculture. 412 pp.

Barnard, C. M., and L. D. Potter. 1984. *New Mexico Grasses: A Vegetative Key.* Albuquerque: University of New Mexico Press. 157 pp.

Carter, J. W. 1997. *Trees and Shrubs of New Mexico.* Silver City, NM: Mimbres Publishing. 546 pp.

Carton, J.-L., ed. 2010. *Raptors of New Mexico.* Albuquerque: University of New Mexico Press. 728 pp.

Chronic, H. 1987. *Roadside Geology of New Mexico.* Missoula, MT: Mountain Press. 255 pp.

Degenhardt, C., W. Painter, and A. H. Price. 1997. *Amphibians and Reptiles of New Mexico.* Albuquerque: University of New Mexico Press. 507 pp.

Dodge, N. N. 1958. *Flowers of the Southwest Deserts.* Globe, AZ: Southwestern Monuments Association. 112 pp.

Findley, J. S., A. H. Harris, D. E. Wilson, and C. Jones. 1975. *Mammals of New Mexico.* Albuquerque: University of New Mexico Press. 360 pp.

Hubbard, J. P. 1978. *Revised Check-List of the Birds of New Mexico.* Publication No. 6. Albuquerque: New Mexico Ornithological Society. 110 pp.

Koster, W. J. 1957. *Guide to the Fishes of New Mexico.* Albuquerque: University of New Mexico Press. 116 pp.

Ligon, J. S. 1961. *New Mexico Birds and Where to Find Them.* Albuquerque: University of New Mexico Press. 360 pp.

MacMahon, J. A. 1985. *Deserts: The Audubon Society Nature Guide.* New York: Knopf.

Martin, W. C., and C. R. Hutchins. 2001. *A Flora of New Mexico.* Oberreifenburg, Germany: Koeltz Scientific Books. 2,512 pp.

McCarter, J. 1994. *New Mexico Wildlife Viewing Guide.* Helena, MT: Falcon Press. (74 sites described)

Olin, G. 1971. *Mammals of the Southwest Mountains and Mesas.* Globe, AZ: Southwestern Monuments Association. 140 pp.

Parmeter, J. E., B. Neville, and D. Emkains. 2002. *New Mexico Bird Finding Guide.* 3rd ed. Albuquerque: New Mexico Ornithological Society.

Patraw, P. 1977. *Flowers of the Southwest Mesas.* Globe, AZ: Southwestern Monuments Association. 112 pp.

Sublette, J., M. D. Hatch, and M. Sublette. 1990. *The Fishes of New Mexico.* Albuquerque: University of New Mexico Press. 393 pp.

Wooten, E. O., and P. C. Standley. 1915. *Flora of New Mexico.* Washington, DC: US Government Printing Office. 794 pp.

North Dakota

Bailey, V. 1926. *A Biological Survey of North Dakota. Physiography and Life Zones. II. The Mammals.* North American Fauna No. 49. Washington, DC: US Government Printing Office. 226 pp.

Bluemle, J. P. 1972. *Geology along North Dakota Interstate Highway 94.* Educational Series, ED-1. Grand Forks: North Dakota Geological Survey.

Hoberg, T., and C. Gause. 1992. *Reptiles and Amphibians of North Dakota.* Bismarck: North Dakota Game and Fish Department. 58 pp.

Johnsgard, P. A. 1953. *Waterfowl of North Dakota.* Fargo: North Dakota Institute for Regional Studies, North Dakota Agricultural College. 16 pp. https://digitalcommons.unl.edu/biosciornithology/42/

Johnson, M. D. 1989. *Feathers from the Prairie.* 2nd ed. Bismarck: North Dakota Game and Fish Department.

Kannowski, P. B. 1989. *Wildflowers of North Dakota.* Grand Forks: University of North Dakota Press.

Knue, J. 1992. *North Dakota Wildlife Viewing Guide.* Helena, MT: Falcon Press. 96 pp. (81 sites described)

Kress, D. 1963. *A List of Publications Pertaining to the Animal Life of North Dakota.* Bibliographic Report No. 1. Fargo: North Dakota Institute for Regional Studies.

Manske, L. L., and W. T. Barker. 1981. *The Prairie Grouse on the Sheyenne National Grasslands, North Dakota*. NDSU Research Report, Fargo, ND. 238 pp.

Nelson, W. T. 1986. *Habitat Type Classification of Grasslands of Cheyenne National Grassland of Southeastern North Dakota*. MS thesis, North Dakota State University, Fargo.

Rich, T. 1992. *Birds of Southwestern North Dakota*. Dickinson, ND: S Department of Interior, Bureau of Land Management, Dickinson, ND.

Royer, R. A. 1988. *Butterflies of North Dakota*. Science Monograph No 1, Minot State Univ., Minot, ND.

Seabloom, R. W., R. Crawford, and M. G. McKenna. 1978. *Vertebrates of Southwest North Dakota: Amphibians, Reptiles, Birds, Mammals*. Grand Forks: Institute for Ecological Studies, University of North Dakota.

Seabloom, R. W., J. Hogansen, and W. Jensen. 2011. *Mammals of North Dakota*. Fargo: North Dakota Institute for Regional Studies. 461 pp.

Stewart, R. E. 1975. *Breeding Birds of North Dakota*. Fargo, ND: Tri-College Center for Regional Studies. 295 pp.

Stevens, O. A. 1950. *Handbook of North Dakota Plants*. Fargo: North Dakota Institute for Regional Studies. 324 pp.

Zimmer, K. 1979. *A Birder's Guide to North Dakota*. Denver, CO: L&P Press. 114 pp.

Oklahoma

Baumgartner, F. M., and A. M. Baumgartner. 1992. *Oklahoma Bird Life*. Norman: University of Oklahoma Press. 433 pp.

Caire, W. 1989. *Mammals of Oklahoma*. Norman: University of Oklahoma Press. 587 pp.

Coffey, C. R., and R. L. Stevens. 2004. *Grasses of Southern Oklahoma and North Texas: A Pictorial Guide*. Ardmore, OK: Samuel Roberts Noble Foundation. 120 pp.

Featherly, H. I. 1946. *Manual of Grasses of Oklahoma*. Oklahoma State University Bulletin 43(21): 1–137.

Folley, P. 2011. *The Guide to Oklahoma Wildflowers*. Iowa City: University of Iowa Press. 312 pp.

Miller, R. J. 2004. *Fishes of Oklahoma*. Norman: University of Oklahoma Press. 496 pp.

Oklahoma Department of Wildlife. 2000. *Oklahoma Watchable Wildlife Viewing Guide*. Lanham, MD: Rowman & Littlefield. 84 pp. (126 sites described)

Reinking, D. A., ed. 2004. *Oklahoma Breeding Bird Atlas*. Norman: University of Oklahoma Press. 532 pp.

Sievert, G., and L. Sievert. 2011. *A Field Guide to Oklahoma's Amphibians and Reptiles*. 3rd ed. Oklahoma City: Oklahoma Department of Wildlife Conservation. 211 pp.

Sutton, G. M. 1967. *Oklahoma Birds*. Norman: University of Oklahoma Press. 674 pp.

Tulsa Audubon Society. 1986. *A Guide to Birding in Oklahoma*. 2nd ed. Tulsa: Tulsa Audubon Society. See online at http://www.tulsaaudubon.org/birding-guide.htm.

Wood, D. S., and G. D. Schnell. 1984. *Distributions of Oklahoma Birds*. Norman: University of Oklahoma Press. 209 pp.

South Dakota

Bailey, R. M., and M. O. Allum. 1962. *Fishes of South Dakota*. Miscellaneous Publications No. 119. University of Michigan Museum of Zoology. 131 pp.

Ballinger, R. E., J. W. Meeker, and M. Thies. 2000. "A Checklist and Distribution Maps of the Amphibians and Reptiles of South Dakota." *Transactions of the Nebraska Academy of Sciences* 26: 29–46. https://digitalcommons.unl.edu/tnas/49/

Bidwell, L. A. 2010. *Mount Rushmore and the Black Hills*. Berkeley, CA: Avalon Travel. 260 pp.

Bryce, S., J. M. Omernik, D. E. Pater, M. Ulmer, J. Schaar, J. Freeouf, R. Johnson, P. Kuck, and S. H. Azevedo. 1998. *Ecoregions of North Dakota and South Dakota*. Reston, VA: US Department of Interior, Geological Survey. (Map poster.)

Colemam, W. S. 2000. *Voices of Wounded Knee*. Lincoln: University of Nebraska Press.

DeSilvestro, R. L. 2005. *Shadows of Wounded Knee*. New York: Walker.

Dorn, R. D. 1977. *Flora of the Black Hills*. Cheyenne, WY: printed by author. 377 pp.

Durrant, M., and M. Harwood. 1988. *The Curious Country: Badlands National Park*. Interior, SD: Badlands Natural History Association.

Fischer, T. D., D. C. Backlund, K. F. Higgins, and D. E. Naugle. 1999. *Field Guide to South Dakota Amphibians*. Agricultural Extension Service Bulletin 733. Brookings: South Dakota State University. 52 pp.

Froiland, S. 1990. *Natural History of the Black Hills and Badlands*. Sioux Falls, SD: Center for Western Studies. 225 pp.

Griffith, T. 1998. *South Dakota*. Compass American Guides. Oakland, CA: Fodor's Travel Publications. 310 pp.

Gries, J. P. 1996. *Roadside Geology of South Dakota*. Missoula, MT: Mountain Press. 358 pp.

Hawk, J. K. 1969. *Badlands: Its Life and Landscape*. Interior, SD: Badlands Natural History Association.

Higgins, K. E., E. D. Stukel, J. M. Goulet, and D. C. Backlund. 2002. *Wild Mammals of South Dakota*. Pierre: South Dakota Department of Game, Fish and Parks. 278 pp.

Jensen, R. E., R. Paul, and J. Carter. 1991. *Eyewitness at Wounded Knee*. Lincoln: University of Nebraska Press.

Johnson, J. R., and G. E. Larson. 1999. *Grassland Plants of South Dakota and the Northern Great Plains*. South Dakota Agricultural Experiment Station Bulletin B 566.

Brookings: South Dakota State University, College of Agriculture and Biological Sciences. 288 pp.

Johnson, R. R., K. F. Higgins, M. L. Kjellsen, and C. R. Elliott. 1997. *Eastern South Dakota Wetlands*. Brookings: South Dakota State University. 28 pp.

Kantrud, H. A., G. L. Krapu, and G. A. Swanson. 1989. *Prairie Basin Wetlands of the Dakotas: A Community Profile*. US Fish and Wildlife Service Biological Report 85(7.28). Washington, DC: US Department of Interior, Fish and Wildlife Service. 111 pp.

Kirtk, R. 1983. *Badlands*. 2nd ed. Interior, SD: Badlands Natural History Association.

Larson, G., and J. Johnson. 2007. *Plants of the Black Hills and Bear Lodge Mountains*. South Dakota Agricultural Experiment Station Bulletin 732. Brookings: South Dakota State University, College of Agriculture and Biological Sciences. 288 pp.

Marrone, G. M. 2002. *Field Guide to Butterflies of South Dakota*. Pierre: South Dakota Department of Game, Fish and Parks. 474 pp.

McGregor, J. H. 1940. *The Wounded Knee Massacre: From the Viewpoint of the Sioux*. Rapid City, SD: Fenske Printing Company.

McLeod, S. J., J. Scott, and K. F. Higgins. 1998. *Waterfowl and Habitat Changes after 40 Years on the Waubay Study Area*. South Dakota Agricultural Experiment Station Bulletin 728. Brookings: South Dakota State University. 40 pp.

Over, W. H. 1932. *The Flora of South Dakota*. Vermillion: University of South Dakota. 161 pp.

Over, W. H., and E. P. Churchill. 1945. *Mammals of South Dakota*. Vermillion: University of South Dakota. 59 pp.

Peterson, R. A. 1995. *The South Dakota Breeding Bird Atlas*. Aberdeen: South Dakota Ornithologists' Union.

Pettingill, O. S., and N. R. Whitney. 1965. *Birds of the Black Hills*. Ithaca, NY: Cornell University Laboratory of Ornithology. 139 pp.

Petsch, B. C., and D. J. McGregor. 1969. *South Dakota's Rock History*. South Dakota Geological Survey Educational Series 3. Vermillion: South Dakota Geological Survey. 39 pp.

Raventon, E. 1994. *Island in the Plains: A Black Hills Natural History*. Boulder, CO: Johnson Books. 272 pp.

Rydberg, P. A. 1896. *Flora of the Black Hills of South Dakota*. Contributions from the US National Herbarium, vol. 3, no. 8. Washington, DC: US Government Printing Office. pp. 463–536.

Tallman, D. A., D. L. Swanson, and J. S. Palmer. 2002. *Birds of South Dakota*. 2nd ed. Aberdeen: South Dakota Ornithologists' Union. 411 pp.

Thilenius, J. F. 1971. *Vascular Plants of the Black Hills of South Dakota and Adjacent Wyoming*. USDA Forest Service Research Paper RM-71. Fort Collins: Rocky Mountain Forest and Range Experiment Station, Forest Service, USDA.

Tomovick, B., and K. Metz. 2000. *South Dakota's Black Hills and Badlands*. Helena, MT: Falcon Publishing. 379 pp.

Turner, R. W. 1974. *Mammals of the Black Hills of South Dakota and Wyoming*. Museum of Natural History Miscellaneous Publication 60. Lawrence: University of Kansas. 178 pp.

Van Bruggen, T. 1985. *The Vascular Plants of South Dakota*. 2nd ed. Ames: Iowa State University Press. 476 pp.

Williams, T. A. 1895. *Native Trees and Shrubs*. South Dakota Agricultural Experiment Station Bulletin 43. Brookings: South Dakota State University. 22 pp.

Texas

Abbott, J. C. 2011. *Damselflies of Texas: A Field Guide*. Austin: University of Texas Press. 292 pp.

Abbott, J. C. 2015. *Dragonflies of Texas: A Field Guide*. Austin: University of Texas Press. 468 pp.

Ajilvsgi, G. 2003. *Wildflowers of Texas*. Fredericksburg, TX: Shearer Publishing. 544 pp.

Ammerman, L. K., C. L. Hice, and D. J. Schmidly. 2011. *Bats of Texas*. Stevensville, TX: Tarlton State University Press. 328 pp.

Bailey, V. 1905. *Biological Survey of Texas*. North American Fauna No. 25. Washington, DC: US Government Printing Office.

Benson, K. L. P., and K. A. Arnold. 2017. *The Texas Breeding Bird Atlas*. College Station and Corpus Christi: Texas A&M University System. https://txtbba.tamu.edu. (July 18, 2017).

Bowers, R., and N. Bowers. 2009a. *Cactus of Texas (Field Guide)*. Cambridge, MN: Adventure Publications. 368 pp.

Bowers, R., and N. Bowers. 2009b. *Wildflowers of Texas (Field Guide)*. Cambridge, MN: Adventure Publications. 432 pp.

Brennen, L. A. 2007. *Texas Quails: Ecology and Management*. College Station: Texas A&M Press. 491 pp.

Cooksey, M., and R. Weeks. 2006. *A Birder's Guide to the Texas Coast*. ABA/Lane Birdfinding Guide. Delaware City, DE: American Birding Association. 344 pp. (more than 200 sites described)

Davis, W. B., and D. J. Schmidly. 1994. *The Mammals of Texas*. Rev. ed. Austin: Texas Parks and Wildlife. 521 pp. Online edition at http://www.nsrl.ttu.edu/tmot1/.

Dixon, J. R., and J. E. Werler. 2000. *Texas Snakes: A Field Guide*. Austin: University of Texas Press. 384 pp.

Finsley, C. 1999. *Field Guide to the Fossils of Texas*. 2nd ed. Boulder, CO: Taylor Trade Publishing. 224 pp.

Flores, D. 2010. *Caprock Canyonlands*. Austin: University of Texas Press. 252 pp.

Gould, F. W. 1975. *The Grasses of Texas*. College Station: Texas A&M University Press. 653 pp.

Gould, F. W. 1978. *Common Texas Grasses*. College Station: Texas A&M University Press. 267 pp.

Graham, G. L. 1992. *Texas Wildlife Viewing Guide*. Helena, MT: Falcon Press. 160 pp. (142 sites described)

Hatch, S. L., and J. Pluhar. 1992. *Texas Range Plants*. College Station: Texas A&M University Press. 344 pp.

Hatch, S. L., K. C. Umphries, and A. J. Ardein. 2016. *Field Guide to Common Texas Grasses*. College Station: Texas A&M University Press. 448 pp. (172 species described)

Hibbitts, T. D., and T. J. Hibbitts. 2015. *Texas Lizards: A Field Guide*. Austin: University of Texas Press. 351 pp.

Holt, H. R. 1992. *A Birder's Guide to the Rio Grande Valley of Texas*. 2nd ed. ABA/Lane Birdfinding Guide. Delaware City, DE: American Birding Association. 189 pp.

Johnsgard, P. A. 2014. "Aransas National Wildlife Refuge: The Whooping Crane's Vulnerable Winter Retreat." *Prairie Fire,* May 2014, pp. 12–13. http://www.prairiefire-newspaper.com/2014/05/aransas-national-wildlife-ref-uge-the-whooping-cranes-vulnerable-winter-retreat

Johnsgard, P. A., and K. Gil-Weir. 2010. "The Whooping Cranes: Survivors against All Odds." *Prairie Fire,* September 2010, pp. 12, 13, 16, 22. http://www.prairiefirenewspaper.com/2010/09/the-whooping-cranes-survivors-against-all-odds

Kutac, E. A. 1998. *Birder's Guide to Texas*. 2nd ed. Houston, TX: Gulf Publishing. 408 pp.

Lane, J. A., and J. L. Tveten. 1984. *A Birder's Guide to the Texas Coast*. Denver, CO: L&P Press. 234 pp.

Lockwood, M. W., and B. E. Small. 2016. *American Birding Association Field Guide to Birds of Texas*. New York: Scott & Nix. 352 pp.

Lockwood, M. W., W. B. McKinney, J. N. Paton, B. R. Zimmer, P. E. Lehman, J. Brumfield, S. Finnegan, M. O'Brien, B. Zimmer, C. Lippincott, and V. Maynard. 2008. *A Birder's Guide to the Rio Grande Valley*. 4th ed. Delaware City, DE: American Birding Association. 336 pp. (230 sites described)

Loflin, B. 2009. *Texas Cacti: A Field Guide*. College Station: Texas A&M University Press. 352 pp.

Matthews, W. H., III. 1960. *Texas Fossils: An Amateur Collector's Handbook*. Austin: University of Texas, Bureau of Economic Geology. 125 pp.

Neck, R. 1996. *A Field Guide to Butterflies of Texas*. Houston, TX: Gulf Publishing. 324 pp.

Neihaus, T. F. 1998. *A Field Guide to Southwestern and Texas Wildflowers*. Boston: Houghton Mifflin. 400 pp.

Oberholser, H. C. 1974. *The Bird Life of Texas*. 2 vols. Austin: University of Texas Press. 1,069 pp.

Peterson, J. J., and B. R. Zimmer. 1998. *Birds of the Trans Pecos*. Austin: University of Texas Press. 216 pp.

Powell, A. M. 2004. *Cacti of the Trans-Pecos and Adjacent Areas*. Lubbock: Texas Tech University Press. 512 pp.

Price, A. H. 2009. *Venomous Snakes of Texas: A Field Guide*. Austin: University of Texas Press. 130 pp.

Pulich, W. M. 1979. *Birds of Tarrant County*. 2nd ed. Fort Worth, TX: Branch-Smith. 188 pp.

Rappole, J. H., and G. W. Blacklock. 1985. *Birds of the Texas Coastal Bend*. College Station: Texas A&M University Press. 352 pp.

Ray, J. D., N. E. McIntyre, M. C. Wallace, A. P. Teaschner, and M. G. Schoenhals. 2016. "Factors Influencing Burrowing Owl Abundance in Prairie Dog Colonies on the Southern High Plains of Texas." *Journal of Raptor Research* 50(2):185–193.

Ritter, J. 2007. *Birding Corpus Christi and the Coastal Bend: More Than 75 Prime Birding Sites*. Helena, MT: Falcon Press. 284 pp.

Robinson, B. C., and J. L. Tveten. 1990. *Birds of Houston*. Houston, TX: Rice University Press. 141 pp.

Schmidly, D. J. 1977. *The Mammals of Trans-Pecos Texas*. College Station: Texas A&M University Press. 225 pp.

Schmidly, D. J. 1983. *Texas Mammals East of the Balcones Fault Zone*. College Station: Texas A&M University Press. 400 pp.

Seyffert, K. A. 2001. *Birds of the Texas Panhandle*. College Station: Texas A&M University Press. 520 pp.

Shaw, R. B. 2012. *Guide to Texas Grasses*. College Station: Texas A&M University Press. 1,080 pp. (670 species described)

Spearling, D. 1994. *Roadside Geology of Texas*. Missoula, MT: Mountain Press. 418 pp.

Tekiela, S. 2009. *Trees of Texas*. Cambridge, MN: Adventure Publications. 374 pp.

Texas Game, Fish and Oyster Commission. 1945. *Principal Game Birds and Mammals of Texas*. Austin: Texas Game, Fish and Oyster Commission. 149 pp.

Tipton, B. 2012. *Texas Amphibians: A Field Guide*. Austin: University of Texas Press. 330 pp.

Truett, J. C., and D. W. Lay. 1984. *Land of Bears and Honey: A Natural History of East Texas*. Austin: University of Texas Press. 198 pp.

Tull, D., and G. Miller. 2003. *Lone Star Field Guide to Wildflowers, Trees, and Shrubs of Texas*. Houston, TX: Gulf Publishing. 344 pp.

Tveten, J. L. 1993. *The Birds of Texas*. Fredericksburg, TX: Shearer Publishing. 384 pp.

Tveten, J. L., and G. L. Tveten. 1996. *Butterflies of Houston and Southeast Texas*. Austin: University of Texas Press. 304 pp.

Tveten, J. L., and G. L. Tveten. 1997. *Wildflowers of Houston and Southeast Texas*. Austin: University of Texas Press. 318 pp.

Wauer, R. H. 1973. *Birds of Big Bend National Park and Vicinity*. Austin: University of Texas Press. 230 pp.

Wauer, R. H. 2004. *Butterflies of the Lower Rio Grande Valley*. Boulder, CO: Big Earth Publishing. 371 pp.

Wauer, R. H., and M. A. Elwonger. 1998. *Birding Texas*. Helena, MT: Falcon Guides. 544 pp. (200 sites described)

Weniger, D. 1984. *Cacti of Texas and Neighboring States: A Field Guide*. Austin: University of Texas Press. 288 pp.

Wyoming

Baxter, G. T., and M. D. Stone. 1992. *Amphibians and Reptiles of Wyoming*. Cheyenne: Wyoming Game and Fish Department.

Baxter, G. T., and M. D. Stone. 1995. *Fishes of Wyoming*. Cheyenne: Wyoming Game and Fish Department. 290 pp.

Beetle, A. A., and M. May. 1971. *Grasses of Wyoming*. Research Journal No. 39. Laramie: Agricultural Experiment Station, University of Wyoming. 151 pp.

Canterbury, J. L., P. A. Johnsgard, and H. Downing. 2013. *Birds and Birding in Wyoming's Bighorn Mountains Region*. University of Nebraska–Lincoln DigitalCommons and Zea Books. 260 pp. http://digitalcommons.unl.edu/zeabook/18/

Clark, T. W., and M. R. Stromberg. 1987. *Mammals in Wyoming*. Lawrence: University of Kansas Museum of Natural History. 314 pp.

Dorn, J. L., and R. D. Dorn. 1990. *Wyoming Birds*. Cheyenne, WY: Mountain West Publishing. 138 pp.

Dorn, R. D. 2001. *Vascular Plants of Wyoming*. 3rd ed. Cheyenne, WY: Mountain West Publishing. 412 pp.

Hallsten, G. P., Q. D. Skinner, and A. A. Beetle. 1999. *Grasses of Wyoming*. 4th ed. Research Journal No. 202. Laramie: Agricultural Experiment Station, University of Wyoming. 432 pp.

Johnsgard, P. A. 1982. *Teton Wildlife: Observations by a Naturalist*. Boulder: Colorado Associated University Press. 128 pp.

Johnsgard, P. A. 2013. *Yellowstone Wildlife: Ecology and Natural History of the Greater Yellowstone Ecosystem*. Boulder: University Press of Colorado. 239 pp.

Knight, D. H., G. P. Jones, W. A. Reiners, and W. H. Romme. 2014. *Mountains and Plains: The Ecology of Wyoming Landscapes*. New Haven, CT: Yale University Press. 352 pp.

Lageson, D. 1988. *Roadside Geology of Wyoming*. Missoula, MT: Mountain Press. 271 pp.

Laun, C. H. 1957. "A Life History Study of the Mountain Plover, *Eupoda montana* Townsend, in the Laramie Plains, Albany County, Wyoming." MS thesis, University of Wyoming, Laramie.

Lewis, D. 2011. *A Field Guide to the Amphibians and Reptiles of Wyoming*, 192 pp. (Updated from *The Wyoming Naturalist,* July 1991. An online version is at http://wyomingnaturalist.com/html/herps/herp_book.html.)

Long, C. A. 1965. *The Mammals of Wyoming*. Lawrence: University of Kansas Publications, Museum of Natural History 14(18): 493–758.

Oakleaf, B., B. Luce, S. Ritter, and A. Cerovski, eds. 1997. *Wyoming Bird and Mammal Atlas*. Lander: Wyoming Game and Fish Department. 188 pp.

Patterson, R. 1952. *The Sage Grouse in Wyoming*. Denver, CO: Sage Books. 341 pp.

Scott, O. 1992. *A Birder's Guide to Wyoming*. Delaware City, DE: American Birding Association. 246 pp.

Skinner, Q. D. 2014. *Field Guide to Wyoming Grasses*. Laramie: Education Resources Publishing, University of Wyoming. 596 pp.

University of Wyoming Agricultural Experiment Station. 1962. *A Flora of Wyoming, Part I*. University of Wyoming Agricultural Experiment Station Bulletin No. 402. 42 pp.

Wyoming Game and Fish Department. 1978. *The Mule Deer in Wyoming*. Wyoming Game and Fish Department Bulletin No. 15. 149 pp.

Wyoming Game and Fish Department. 1996. *Wyoming Wildlife Viewing Guide*. Helena, MT: Falcon Press. 216 pp. (55 sites described)

Wyoming Game and Fish Department. 2004. *Atlas of Birds, Mammals, Amphibians, and Reptiles in Wyoming*. Cheyenne: Wildlife Division, Wyoming Game and Fish Department. 155 pp.

Canada

General Natural History

Banfield, W. F. 1974. *The Mammals of Canada*. Toronto, ON: University of Toronto Press. 438 pp.

Braithwaite, M. 1970. *The Western Plains: The Illustrated Natural History of Canada*. Toronto: Natural Science of Canada. 160 pp.

Fisher C., A. Joynt, and R. Brooks. 2007. *Reptiles and Amphibians of Canada*. Edmonton, AB: Lone Pine Publishing. 208 pp.

Godfrey, W. E. 1986. *The Birds of Canada*. Rev. ed. Ottawa, ON: National Museum of Natural Sciences. 590 pp.

Hickey, C. ed. 2011. *National Geographic Guide to State Parks of the United States and Canadian Provincial Parks*. Washington, DC: National Geographic Society. 480 pp. (Includes 30 provincial parks.)

Layberry, R. 1998. *The Butterflies of Canada*. Toronto, ON: University of Toronto Press. 354 pp.

Looman, J. 1982. *Prairie Grasses Identified and Described by Vegetative Characters*. Publication No. 1413. Agriculture Canada. Ottawa, ON: Canadian Government Publishing Centre. 244 pp.

Looman, J., and K. F. Best. 1987. *Budd's Flora of the Canadian Prairie Provinces*. Rev. ed. Ottawa, ON: Research Branch, Agriculture Canada. 874 pp.

National Geographic Society. 2016. *National Geographic Guide to the National Parks of Canada*. 2nd ed. Washington, DC: National Geographic Society. 384 pp.

Nauton, D. 2014. *The Natural History of Canadian Mammals: Opossums and Carnivores*. Toronto, ON: Canadian Museum of Nature and University of Toronto Press. 190 pp.

Peterson, R. L. 1966. *The Mammals of Eastern Canada*. Toronto, ON: Oxford University Press. 465 pp.

Rand, A. L. 1948. *Mammals of the Eastern Rockies and Western Plains of Canada*. Bulletin of the National Museum of Canada No. 108, Biological Series No. 35. 237 pp.

Scoggan, H. J. 1978. *The Flora of Canada*. Ottawa, ON: National Museum of Canada, Publications in Botany, No. 7. 4 vols.

Scott, W. B., and E. J. Crossman. 1979. *Freshwater Fishes of Canada*. Ottawa, ON: Fisheries Research Board of Canada Bulletin 184. 984 pp.

Vance, F. R., J. R. Jowsey, J. S. McLean, and F. A. Switzer. 1999. *Wildflowers across the Prairies*. Toronto, ON: Greystone Books. 336 pp.

Van Zyll de John, C. G. 1988. *Handbook of Canadian Mammals: Marsupials and Insectivores*. Toronto, ON: National Museums of Canada and Chicago, IL: University of Chicago Press. 482 pp.

Alberta

Acorn, J. 1997. *Butterflies of Alberta*. Edmonton, AB: Lone Pine Publishing. 144 pp.

Butler, J. 1990. *Alberta Wildlife Viewing Guide*. Helena, MT: Falcon Press. 96 pp.

Corns, G. W., J. D. Beckingham, and J. H. Archibald. 2002. *Field Guide to Ecosites of West-Central Alberta*. Special Report 9. Edmonton, AB: Natural Resources Canada, Canadian Forest Service, Northern Forestry Centre. 540 pp.

Godfrey, W. E. 1950. "Birds of the Cypress Hills and Flotten Lake Region, Saskatchewan." *National Museums of Canada Bulletin* 120: 1–96.

Hauff, D. V. 1992. *Alberta's Parks: Our Legacy*. Edmonton: Alberta Parks, Recreation and Wildlife.

Inkpen, W., ed. 1998. *Guide to the Common Native Trees and Shrubs of Alberta*. Edmonton: Alberta Government, Environmental Protection Services, Pollution Control Division, Pesticide Chemicals Branch. 55 pp.

Kondla, N. G. 1978. "The Birds of Dinosaur Provincial Park, Alberta." *Blue Jay* 36: 103–114.

McGillivray, B., and G. P. Semenchuk. 1998. *Federation of Alberta Naturalists Field Guide to Alberta Birds*. Edmonton: Federation of Alberta Naturalists. 350 pp.

Moss, E. H. 2015. *Flora of Alberta*. 2nd ed. Toronto, ON: University of Toronto Press. 687 pp.

Paetz, M. J., and J. S. Nelson. 1970. *The Fishes of Alberta*. Edmonton, AB: The Queens Printer. 281 pp.

Royer, F., and R. Dickinson. 2007. *Plants of Alberta: Trees, Shrubs, Wildflowers, Ferns and Grasses*. Edmonton, AB: Lone Pine Publishing. 528 pp.

Salt, W. R., and J. R. Salt. 1976. *The Birds of Alberta*. Edmonton, AB: Hurtig Publishers. 498 pp. (The species distribution maps include Manitoba and Saskatchewan.)

Semenchuk, G. P. 2007. *The Atlas of Breeding Birds of Alberta: A Second Look*. Edmonton: Federation of Alberta Naturalists. 626 pp.

Sheldon, I., A. Joynt, and M. Sullivan. 2003. *Fish of Alberta*. Edmonton, AB: Lone Pine Publishing. 176 pp.

Smith, H. C. 1993. *Alberta Mammals: An Atlas and Guide*. Edmonton, AB: Provincial Museum of Alberta. 238 pp.

Soper, J. D. 1964. *The Mammals of Alberta*. Edmonton, AB: Hamley Press. 402 pp.

Wilkinson, K. 2010. *Trees and Shrubs of Alberta*. Edmonton, AB: Lone Pine Publishing. 191 pp.

Manitoba

Bezener, A., and K. De Smet. 2000. *Manitoba Birds*. Edmonton, AB: Lone Pine Publishing. 176 pp.

Carey, B., and Manitoba Naturalists Society. 2006. *Finding Birds in Southern Manitoba*. Winnipeg: Manitoba Naturalists Society. 210 pp.

Cooke, F., R. E. Rockwell, and D. E. Lank. 1995. *The Snow Geese of La Pérouse Bay: Natural Selection in the Wild*. Oxford, UK: Oxford University Press.

Cody, W. J. 1988. *Plants of Riding Mountain National Park, Manitoba*. Ottawa, ON: Research Branch, Agriculture Canada. 334 pp.

Friesen, O. C. 2013. *Mammals of Manitoba*. Manitoba Forestry Association. 60 pp. https://www.thinktrees.org/resources/mammals-of-manitoba/

Hochbaum, H. A. 1944. *The Canvasback on a Prairie Marsh*. Harrisburg, PA: Stackpole and Washington, DC: Wildlife Management Institute.

Klassen, P., and W. B. Preston. 1989. *The Butterflies of Manitoba*. Winnipeg: The Manitoba Museum. 296 pp.

Manitoba Avian Research Committee. 2003. *The Birds of Manitoba*. Winnipeg: Manitoba Naturalists Society. 600 pp. (Includes 382 species.)

Oswald, E. T., and F. H. Nokes. 1998. *Field Guide to the Native Trees of Manitoba*. Winnipeg: Canadian Forest Service, Manitoba Natural Resources.

Preston, W. 1982. *The Amphibians and Reptiles of Manitoba*. Winnipeg: Manitoba Museum of Man and Nature. 128 pp.

Scoggans, H. J. 1957. *Flora of Manitoba*. Bulletin No. 140. Ottawa, ON: National Museum of Canada. 619 pp.

Senecal, C. 1999. *Pelicans to Polar Bears: Watching Wildlife in Manitoba*. Clinton, CT: Heartland Publications.

Sowls, L. K. 1955. *Prairie Ducks: A Study of Their Behavior, Ecology, and Management*. Harrisburg, PA: Stackpole and Washington, DC: Wildlife Management Institute.

Soper, J. D. 1961. "The Mammals of Manitoba." *The Canadian Field-Naturalist* 85: 171–219.

Stewart, K., and D. Watkinson. 2003. *Freshwater Fishes of Manitoba*. Winnipeg: University of Manitoba Press. 276 pp.

Stilwell, W. 2006. *Manitoba, Naturally: Scenic Secrets of Manitoba*. Neepawa, MB: William Street Publishing. 96 pp. (about 60 sites described)

Saskatchewan

Anonymous. n.d. *The Cypress Hills (Saskatchewan): A Natural History*. Regina: Saskatchewan Museum of Natural History. 28 pp.

Beck, W. H. 1958. *A Guide to Saskatchewan Mammals*. Saskatchewan Natural History Society Special Publication No. 1. Regina: Saskatchewan Museum of Natural History. 52 pp.

Butala, S. 2002. *Old Man on His Back: Portrait of a Prairie Landscape*. Toronto, ON: Harper Collins Canada. (Butala Ranch and the Nature Conservancy preserve)

Clancy, M., and A. Clancy. 1999. *Discover Saskatchewan: A User's Guide to Regional Parks*. Discover Saskatchewan Series. Regina, SK: Canadian Plains Research Center.

Flora of Saskatchewan Association. 2011–2016. *Flora of Saskatchewan*. Regina, SK. (The association is currently [2017] publishing a Saskatchewan flora series by individual taxonomic units; published segments so far include *Ferns and Fern Allies of Saskatchewan* [June 2011]; *Lilies, Irises, and Orchids of Saskatchewan* [October 2011]; *Sedges* (Carex) *of Saskatchewan* [March 2012]; *Grasses of Saskatchewan* [August 2014]; and *Conifers and Catkin-Bearing Trees and Shrubs of Saskatchewan* [July 2016].)

Richards, J. H., and K. I. Fung. 1969. *Atlas of Saskatchewan*. Saskatoon: University of Saskatchewan.

Runge, W., and D. Henry. 1987. *Wild Furbearers of Saskatchewan*. Regina: Saskatchewan Parks, Recreation and Culture.

Smith, A. R. 1996. *Atlas of Saskatchewan Birds*. Regina: Saskatchewan Natural History Society (Nature Saskatchewan). 456 pp.

Smith, A. R. 2001. *Saskatchewan Birds*. Edmonton: Lone Pine Publishing. 176 pp.

Stegner, W. 1955. Wolf Willow: A History, a Story, and a Memory of the Last Plains Frontier. Lincoln: University of Nebraska Press.

Northern Mexico

Southernmost Great Plains

Cumings, J. 1998. *Northern Mexico Handbook*. Chico, CA: Moon Publications.

Howell, S. N. G., and S. Webb. 1995. *The Birds of Mexico and Northern Central America*. Oxford, UK: Oxford University Press.

Leopold, A. S. 1959. *Wildlife of Mexico: The Game Birds and Mammals*. Berkeley: University of California Press.

Steinhart, P. 1994. *Two Eagles/Dos Aguilas: The Natural World of the United States–Mexican Borderlands*. Berkeley: University of California Press.

Wauer, R. 1992. *A Naturalist's Mexico*. College Station: Texas A&M University Press.

Site Index